Reforma Mexico
and the United States

Reforma Mexico and the United States:

A Search for Alternatives to Annexation, 1854–1861

Donathon C. Olliff

The University of Alabama Press
University, Alabama

Library of Congress Cataloging in Publication Data

Olliff, Donathon C., 1933–
 Reforma Mexico and the United States.

 Bibliography: p.
 Includes index.
 1. Mexico—Economic policy. 2. Mexico—History
—1821–1861. 3. Mexico—Foreign economic relations
—United States. 4. United States—Foreign economic
relations—Mexico. I. Title.
HC135.044   338.972   81-3322
ISBN 0-8173-0070-8   AACR2

Contents

Preface   vii

Introduction   1

1. Attitudinal Setting during the 1850s   10

2. The Revolution of Ayutla
   and the Bases of Liberal Diplomacy, 1853–1856   30

3. Mexican Liberals' Alternative:
   The Montes-Forsyth Treaties, 1855–1857   57

4. Buchanan's Drive for Territorial Expansion, 1857–1858   84

5. Recognition, a Liberal Victory, 1858–1859   111

6. The McLane-Ocampo Treaties: The Last Attempt
   to Compromise Conflicting Goals, 1859–1861   129

Epilogue   153

Notes   156

Bibliography   180

Index   191

Preface

My interest in Reforma Mexico has carried me through a three-step process of study and writing during which I have been inspired and assisted by many people. Although some of their names have now faded from my memory, their numerous acts of kindness are still recalled with gratitude.

In 1966 I completed a master's thesis at Auburn University on John Forsyth's ministership to Mexico during the period 1856–1859. The thesis was done under the direction of a most inspiring and challenging teacher, Oliver Turner Ivey. Professors Lyle N. McAlister and David Bushnell gave me the encouragement and guidance necessary to master the doctoral program in Latin American history at the University of Florida where my dissertation (1974) analyzed Mexico's economic relations with the United States during the Reforma. The present study is a refining and refocusing of the research that went into the two earlier studies. My wife's love and understanding made the darker moments of these years of graduate study and research bearable, and her typing skills have defied my powers of recompense.

The professional competence of the staffs of the following libraries and archives made my research possible and in most cases their friendly concern for my efforts made it a pleasant task: Library of Congress, National Archives, University of Florida Library, Auburn University Library, Nettie Lee Benson Library of the University of Texas, Biblioteca Nacional de México, Biblioteca del Colegio de México, Biblioteca Miguel Lerdo de Tejada, Archivo General de la Nación, Archivo Histórico del Instituto Nacional de Antropología e Historia, and Archivo de la Secretaría de Relaciones Exteriores. A special expression of gratitude goes to Professor Nettie Lee Benson, long-time director of the Latin American Collection at the University of Texas and for whom the collection has recently been named. She not only provided the assistance necessary for the use of the collection but frequently took the time to share her expertise in Mexican history with an itinerant researcher.

The merits of this study can only have been enhanced by the editorial efforts of The University of Alabama Press. I am particularly grateful to Professors Edward Moseley, The University of Alabama, and David C. Bailey, Michigan State University, for the helpful comments they made on the manuscript.

All sources for this study were in either English or Spanish. The only French documents had been translated into Spanish by Lilia Díaz before being published in *Versión francesa de México*. All quotations appearing in this work for which Spanish-language sources are given are my translations. This includes references

to Spanish-language secondary works, printed documentary collections, newspapers, archival materials, and letters exchanged between Spanish-speaking individuals.

Reforma Mexico
and the United States

Introduction

It is axiomatic that history, a contemporary search for meaning in the past, is sometimes as much a product of the historian's fancy as it is of the historical events themselves. This has been particularly true of La Reforma, that period of Mexican history from the onset of the Ayutla Revolution in 1854 to the foreign debt crisis of 1861, which served as a prelude to French intervention the following year. Historians, regardless of their nationality or philosophical bent, have approached this period with concerns and preconceptions that have limited both the extent and validity of their studies. The violence and trauma of the war with the United States, 1846–48, and of the French intervention, 1862–67, tend to divert attention from the Reforma. In the Reforma itself analysts have been preoccupied with political, religious, and military questions. When scholars, particularly those from Mexico, attempt to deal with this period, their tasks are further complicated by two closely related phenomena: the cult of adulation that has grown up around the historical figure of Benito Juárez and the almost irrepressible urge to see the Reforma and its leaders as forerunners of the nationalistic upheaval of early twentieth-century Mexico.

Much of recent Mexican historical writing has conformed to what Charles A. Hale, in *Mexican Liberalism in the Age of Mora, 1821–1853,* refers to as the "law of the centennials," in that it has been the product of a series of public ceremonies sponsored by the government. The government, in turn, is dominated by the Partido Revolucionario Institucional (PRI), the self-proclaimed heir to and guardian of Mexico's twentieth-century revolutionary traditions.[1] Beginning in 1954 with the observance of the centennial of the Ayutla Revolution and carrying through to the *año de Juárez* in 1972, each memorable event of the period of liberal dominance, 1854–76, has been celebrated with ceremonies that have evoked a flood of books and articles. Most of these works merely serve to glorify the events and their liberal participants and to establish or reinforce links between PRI's "nationalistic liberalism" and the heroic liberalism of the nineteenth century.[2] Most of the liberal figures of the period, especially Juárez, have been subjected to panegyrics rather than critical studies.

While such studies have produced much that is valid and worthy of analysis, the picture that emerges remains incomplete and frequently erroneous.[3] One of the most serious gaps in the historiography of the Reforma has been the failure to probe adequately the economic objectives elaborated by Reforma leaders and to assess the role of the United States and its citizens in this aspect of the Reforma.[4] Too often the economic goals have been ignored or equated with those of Mexico's twentieth-century revolutionaries. Not surprisingly, some United States scholars profess to see the period's leaders as primarily concerned with establishing laissez-faire capitalism.[5] Until fairly recently studies of the United States's involvement in the Mexican economy during the nineteenth century have focused on the *porfiriato,* 1876–1911, the obvious assumption being that prior to that era Yankees were too intent on territorial expansion, internal development, and the sectional controversy to give serious attention to Mexican economic opportunities.[6]

To ignore the economic content of the Reforma is to leave out a crucial element of the period. While the Reforma is more noted in historical literature for its political and religious struggles, its leaders often saw these contests in terms of vital economic issues. It is no exaggeration to say that Mexico's leading liberal reformers believed that the key to their entire program was to be found in the resolution of certain economic problems.[7]

Independence served Mexico ill during the decades following the issuance of the Plan of Iguala in 1821. Nowhere was this more apparent by the 1850s than in the economy. Prior to independence its mineral wealth had made Mexico, or New Spain, the "gem of the Spanish crown." A boom in silver mining in the late eighteenth century added further luster to Mexico's exalted economic position.[8] The crown's emphasis on the mining of precious metals, however, produced a structural imbalance in the economy. Agricultural production beyond what was needed for local consumption was given low priority, and as a result much of Mexico's agricultural potential remained unrealized. Closely related to this emphasis on mining was the failure to develop a transportation system that could move agricultural products, or any bulky cargoes, into foreign trade channels. There was no system capable of supporting even significant interregional domestic trade.

Despite its favored position and visible prosperity, the mining industry itself suffered from serious imperfections. Its methods in most areas were technologically antiquated and relatively inefficient. Few improvements had been introduced during almost three centuries of Spanish domination. Among the significant changes that accompanied the mining revival of the eighteenth century, improvements in organization, administration, financing, and governmental policy were more common than were improvements in mining techniques.[9] During the late colonial period Mexico had neither the mining and transportation technology nor the crown support necessary to work her ample supply of base metals, which were increasingly in demand in industrializing Europe.

As long as Mexico remained an insulated part of a paternalistic empire the effects of these shortcomings were muted, but independence unleashed them in virulent form. The wars of independence, 1810–21, not only disrupted or destroyed much of the mining industry but also drove away the Spanish capital and skills that had sustained it.[10] Because little of the loss could be replaced from domestic sources and both internal and external factors impeded the inflow of foreign funds and technology, the recovery was painfully slow. Thrown upon the international market to obtain both the resources necessary to rehabilitate its mining industry and a growing list of manufactured goods, Mexico found itself unable to secure the former in adequate quantities, and with limited mining production and no significant agricultural exports, her acquisition of the latter contributed to a chronic credit crisis in Mexico. The brief period of English speculation in Mexican mining during the 1820s produced financial losses and unpleasant experiences of a sort hardly likely to encourage others to try their hands. Probably the most notable failure was that of a London-based group whose scheme to return the famous Real del Monte near Pachuca to profitable operations saw millions of pounds invested in modernization without a significant return.[11]

Independence, by removing the Spanish crown as a symbol of political legitimacy and social cohesion, opened the door to political and social disorders which further debilitated the Mexican economy. The turbulence that accompanied the quests for power by would-be caudillos consumed vital resources, diverted public attention from more basic problems, and further depressed Mexico's credit status on the international market. Frequent lower-class uprisings and the Yucatán caste war, which broke into the open in the late 1840s, convinced many observers that Mexico was on the verge of social anarchy and cultural suicide. Travelers' accounts of the period are replete with descriptions of abandoned mines, ruined haciendas, and the depressed state of both urban and rural lower classes.[12]

Three decades of political instability, economic stagnation, and social upheaval, culminating in national humiliation and dismemberment at the hands of the United States (1846–48), sent shock waves through the Mexican upper class. The politically conscious elements began to question the ability of their country to survive, and some began to doubt the wisdom of independence. Ideological approaches to politics, which had often been shunted aside by the personalism of *caudillo* politics, now assumed a new currency as the active population coalesced into two groups or parties, liberal and conservative. Each had its own view of the nature, origin, and remedy for the crisis confronting the country.[13]

The most active and successful of the two groups in the immediate postwar period was the conservative, thanks largely to the intellectual vigor and amazing energy of its elder organizer and chief spokesman, Lucas Alamán. As a youthful witness to the lower-class violence of the Hidalgo phase of the independence movement in Guanajuato in 1810, Alamán equated democracy with destructive demagogy. He looked for national redemption to the traditional pillars of colonial life: the church, the aristocracy, the military, and an authoritarian administration. The conservatives saw postindependence troubles as a logical result of the abandonment of Hispanic traditions. Most conservatives, including Alamán after 1846, frankly endorsed the idea of monarchial government for Mexico.[14]

The liberals lacked the ideological unity and philosophical certainty of their opponents. They were also handicapped by the absence of effective leadership during the previous decades. Two early liberal leaders had both failed to solidify effective positions for themselves or for liberal ideas. Lorenzo de Zavala became a traitor in the eyes of his countrymen by siding with the Anglo-Texan rebels, and José María Luis Mora remained in European exile from 1834 until his death in

1850. By default Valentín Gómez Farías became the principal liberal activist during the decades preceding the Reforma. Never an effective practical leader, by the 1850s his age and health had reduced Gómez Farías's position to that of respected elder statesman.[15] Because of these leadership problems and the ideological diversity within liberal ranks, there were numerous and divergent liberal spokesmen in the postwar period.

While it is customary to speak of the liberals as constituting two wings, the *moderados* (moderates) and *puros* (radicals), such a distinction is somewhat misleading. These labels were used by contemporaries to designate ill-defined groupings whose composition varied with the issues and over time. The usefulness of the distinction is further limited by the contemporary practice of extending the *moderado* label on occasion to all those who, regardless of their reasons, failed to respond to the calls to action by the extremists of the moment, whether radical or reactionary. Despite this lack of precision in the contemporary usage of the terms, historians have found them convenient as labels for two factions within liberal ranks, and the terms will be so used in this study.

Mexican liberals, regardless of faction, enjoyed a consensus on the importance of such basic principles as federalism, republicanism, constitutionalism, anticlericalism, individual rights, and the need for economic recovery and general modernization. The distinction between *moderados* and *puros* was based not so much on principles and goals as on emphasis and methods. The *puros* advocated a more active search for solutions to Mexico's problems and were more violently anticlerical than their *moderado* colleagues. For this study, however, perhaps the two most important characteristics of the *puros* were their firm conviction that fundamental economic changes were absolute prerequisites for all liberal reform programs and their willingness to use governmental authority to bring about these changes.

On certain general points, such as the need to bring an end to political anarchy, to realize economic recovery, and to modernize the economy, liberals and conservatives agreed. On Mexico's inability to achieve these goals without external assistance the two parties were again in accord. The patronage of a strong and stable foreign state was generally accepted as essential for national redemption. The conservatives looked to Europe for such a patron, while the liberals found theirs closer at hand, in the United States. It should not be surprising to find that this need for foreign assistance was expressed in terms consonant with contemporary political ideology and thus became a part of the liberal-conservative struggles for power. The conservatives portrayed themselves as seeking the humanitarian and civilizing aid of unselfish European powers, and they spoke of their liberal opponents as traitors whose goal was to deliver Mexico up to her avaricious northern neighbor. Liberals naturally saw the reverse image of this picture. In this context 'protectorate' became a pejorative term. One's political opponents were guilty of seeking a protectorate, while the speaker or writer and his political friends would sacrifice everything to prevent the imposition of such a status on Mexico.

During the 1850s both political groups or parties had opportunities to implement their schemes for rescuing Mexico from the abyss into which it had sunk. The conservatives, benefiting from greater unity and more clearly defined leadership, were the first to grasp the reins of state with determination and purpose. In April 1853 Santa Anna returned from his Colombian exile to head, under Alamán's guidance, what was clearly intended as a caretaker administration until arrangements for European patronage and a stabilizing monarchy could be made. The excesses of Santa Anna after Alamán's death in June 1853 encouraged the liberals to submerge their ideological and personal differences in a united effort to unseat the perennial caudillo. The collapse of Santa Anna's regime in August 1855 ushered in a period of liberal control which, although seriously challenged by the conservatives in the war of the Reforma, 1858–60, and later by the conservatives with French assistance, 1861–67, lasted until it merged with the dictatorship of Porfirio Díaz in the late 1870s.[16] Liberal attempts to remake Mexican life during the period prior to 1861 are known as La Reforma.

Puro efforts during this period to transform the Mexican economy form the central focus of this study. Although Santa Anna's overthrow was a cooperative undertaking by *moderados* and *puros* and the subsequent reform government enjoyed the general support of both factions, the government itself and its reform programs were essentially *puro* creations. *Puros* dominated both the executive and legislative branches, and the philosophy, objectives, and methods of reform were almost exclusively the work of a small group of *puros*.

As we have seen, a principal distinguishing feature of the *puros* was their overriding concern with economic matters. They believed that not only were economic reforms per se vital to national survival and regeneration but that they were also inexorably linked to the political and religious changes sought by most liberals. Just as Benito Juárez, the Oaxacan *puro,* was without question the dominant political figure of the Reforma and received at least the tacit support of most *moderados,* so in the economic realm the Veracruz-born educator and *puro* activist Miguel Lerdo de Tejada was recognized as the chief spokesman. In formulating and executing economic policies Lerdo could count on the active support of Juárez and other leading *puros,* among whom were Melchor Ocampo, an aristocrat from Michoacán; José María Mata, the Jalapa surgeon and principal architect of the 1857 constitution; Francisco Zarco, the youthful editor of the liberal *El Siglo XIX* (Mexico City) from Durango; José Antonio Godoy, editor of the *puro* voice *El Heraldo* (Mexico City); and Matías Romero, Juárez's young protégé from Oaxaca.[17]

Not only did this group of *puro* journalists, politicians, and administrators elaborate, popularize, and attempt to execute an extensive program of economic reform and modernization but they also allocated to the United States a vital role in their activities. The part played by the United States extended far beyond the economic sphere. Many liberals saw the United States as the model for all their reconstructive endeavors. The United States constitution with its federal structure, its guarantee of individual rights, its representative republic, and its limitations on governmental authority struck responsive chords among them. Yankee society with its industriousness, its egalitarian individualism, its religious tolerance, and its ability to attract and assimilate an apparently inexhaustible supply of immigrants was looked upon with awed admiration.

On a more practical level, the liberals, feeling threatened by domestic and European monarchial forces, saw the vigor of their northern neighbor as a natural source of aid in their struggle for survival. While consciously avoiding public reference to a protectorate, the liberals, under *puro* leadership, were busily cultivating a relationship with the United States which would offer them some degree of protection from political enemies, both domestic and foreign. The desired relationship was variously cast in terms of hemispheric brotherhood, republican fraternity, or some form of alliance. The ardor of the liberal drive for close ties with the United States was moderated by the realization that the same Yankee vigor which they so admired was also capable of expressing itself in a policy of aggressive expansion detrimental to Mexican territorial integrity.

In economic terms the liberals rarely found anything to criticize north of the Rio Grande except slavery. Their neighbor's agriculture, industry, commerce, and transportation all offered attractive models for Mexican liberal developmentalists. The *puros* also saw it first and foremost as a source of badly needed capital and technology. In pursuit of developmental resources the *puros* sought to lure United States entrepreneurs to Mexico. They also tried to cover their fiscal needs with loans from both private and public sources in the United States. Initially the quest for such loans was justified primarily as a means by which the government could acquire funds to use as stimulants for economic development, but as the struggle against the conservatives dragged on, the *puros* came increasingly to see the need for loans for noneconomic purposes—to strengthen a liberal regime and to allow it to suppress its opponents and to free itself from dependence upon local speculators and European credit sources. Developmental and fiscal needs were sometimes combined by making the granting of an economic concession dependent upon a loan or by simply selling concessions.

The desire to establish a special relationship with the United States that would provide liberal Mexico with entrepreneurial skills, technological advances, developmental funds, fiscal relief, and protection from the economic and political power of Europe was a consistent feature of *puro* policy throughout the Reforma period. Naturally the manner in which this policy was interpreted and pursued at any given moment reflected the existing conditions in Mexico, Europe, and the United States. The zeal with which *puros* worked for closer ties with the United States was often a good indicator of the degree to which they felt that their ultimate success was threatened by the conservatives and their European sympathizers. As United States domestic politics strengthened those forces desiring territorial expansion at the expense of Mexico, the *puros* would be found intensifying their efforts to divert the acquisitive impulses of Yankees to commercial and economic opportunities.

Although the ends to be served by closer ties with the United States varied with individuals and were affected by constantly changing conditions, what the *puros* sought, first and last, was to give a near monopoly of opportunity to exploit Mexico's economic resources to the United States and its citizens and to insure, if possible, that these opportunities did not go begging. To have the Mexican economy become almost an integral part of the economy of their northern neighbor was, in their minds, the fastest and surest means of bringing about the economic progress and modernization which the *puros* believed to be necessary for national survival and effective reform.

The proper label to apply to this relationship is difficult to determine. United States diplomats, businessmen, and journalists most frequently referred to it as an economic protectorate. Mexican conservatives and their French diplomatic sympathizers, however, normally modified 'protectorate' with such negative adjectives as vile, evil, or treasonous. They professed to see it merely as a transitional stage, as a preparation for annexation. Liberals, including *puros,* usually avoided applying a specific title to the relationship, preferring instead to describe it in terms of the tremendous benefits they believed it would bestow on Mexico.

Probably the most accurate description was contained in a phrase frequently used both by the *puros* and their Yankee supporters in which they expressed their desire to see a relationship between the two countries which would provide "all the fruits of annexation without any of the dangers." Mexicans saw in the special relationship of their country with the United States an opportunity to gain "all the fruits" of capital, technology, entrepreneurial skills, and protection—from both foreign and domestic enemies—that their country would receive if it were annexed. At the same time they would avoid the loss of political sovereignty and the degradation of national honor which annexation would entail.

In the eyes of both official and private United States supporters of the special relationship, the economic potential of Mexico—mineral, agricultural, and commercial—could be put at their country's disposal. A neighbor whose internal political and social disorders were a constant threat to the lives and property of United States citizens both in Mexico and along the common frontier could be converted into a model of stability. The menace to the United States's security posed by the perennial danger of European intervention in Mexico could be removed. Perhaps most important, most if not all the multitude of national impulses that formed a part of manifest destiny[18] could be satisfied as well by a protectorate as by annexation. That a protectorate offered the possibility of lessening rather than exacerbating the already profound sectional crisis in their homeland was equally appealing.

Another advantage of a protectorate over annexation in the eyes of many in the United States was that it avoided introducing into their own political and social organization the "mongrelized races" of Mexico. This appealed particularly to the United States ministers to Reforma Mexico, James Gadsden of South Carolina, John Forsyth of Alabama, and Robert M. McLane of Maryland. All three were from slave states, and Gadsden and Forsyth had specifically expressed abhorrence for Mexico's miscegenated and benighted millions. This volume's subtitle, *A Search for Alternatives to Annexation, 1854–1861,* is recognition of the tenacity with which both parties during the turbulent years of La Reforma sought the benefits of annexation without its dangers.

The *puros* and their moderate liberal colleagues failed to achieve their objective, and the reasons for this failure must be sought primarily in the United States, not Mexico. This is not to argue that the process was unaffected by the vicissitudes of Mexican domestic politics and foreign relations. Rather it is merely recognition of the fact that on two separate occasions, February 1857 and December 1859, *puro*-dominated liberal governments signed and worked vigorously to secure United States ratification of treaties designed to give the United States the power to penetrate and dominate the Mexican economy. On both occasions President Buchanan failed to give the support necessary to insure ratification. Buchanan's inaction stemmed from his apparent inability to understand or to appreciate the value of economic advantages and reflected his longstanding commitment to a policy of territorial expansion.

But the idea of an economic protectorate in Mexico was not without its Yankee advocates. John Forsyth and Robert M. McLane not only signed treaties for this purpose but actively worked for their ratification, sometimes in open opposition to presidential policy. Private United States citizens with economic interests in Mexico also supported such an advantageous economic relationship. Carlos Butterfield was a particularly active and articulate proponent of an economic protectorate over all of Latin America, beginning with Mexico. Their efforts were insufficient, however, to divert their countrymen's attention from the smoldering sectional crisis and, more important, to convince Buchanan that indirect economic control of Mexico was an adequate substitute for or even an essential precondition to the annexation of Mexican territory.

Another factor helping to explain the failure of *puro* economic policy was the mid-nineteenth-century world capital market. Here again the key element was the United States. Just as the *puros* and their Yankee backers misread their ability to interest the United States in treaties providing for closer economic ties, so they also misjudged its position in the world capital market. While modern studies of capital formation make it clear that the United States continued to be a capital-importing country until the end of the century, the *puros* and their United States champions, both official and private, appear to have been unaware of this significant fact. Mexican diplomats constantly sought to direct a steady flow of funds to Mexico by tapping private sources of capital in the United States. The Development Ministry (Fomento) was equally determined to attract this stream of money and skills to economic developmental projects by the judicious use of concessions. Both efforts failed because, as José María Mata, *puro* Mexican minister in Washington, gradually realized in 1860, even funding for low-risk developmental schemes in the United States had to be sought on the London market.

In the following study the attitudes of each country toward the other will be analyzed in terms of their nature, origin, and significance within the context of economic relations between the two countries. Then the relations will be reviewed in detail with emphasis on their economic character. The two sets of treaties will be analyzed for their economic content and special attention will be given to the role of *puro* leadership in formulating these treaties. Attention will also be focused on the persistent efforts by Mexican liberals to obtain loans in the United States, especially during the civil war, 1858–60.

1
Attitudinal Setting during the 1850s

The Plan of Ayutla, proclaimed 1 March 1854, set in motion a chain of events of profound significance for Mexico. The revolutionary standard, raised in Guerrero by the old liberal *cacique* Juan Alvarez, attracted the support of a new generation of Mexican liberals—a generation of politically active individuals with a unique vision of Mexico's past, present, and future.[1] With their support the Ayutla Revolution emerged victorious over the regime of Antonio López de Santa Anna in August 1855. The victorious liberals then embarked upon an ambitious program of reforms (La Reforma) designed to transform Mexico into the country of their dreams. With foreign financial and technological assistance they hoped to create in Mexico a modern and progressive society free of what they saw as the stagnating influence of its colonial heritage. While their plans for the future of Mexico touched upon most facets of Mexican life, economic reforms and material development were recognized by most liberals as the keys to the success of their broader program. Attempts to carry out the liberal reforms provoked a three-year civil war, 1858–60 *(Guerra de la Reforma),* which in turn provided the setting for the French intervention in 1862 and the subsequent ill-fated empire of Maximilian.

The United States played a significant role in each stage and phase of these developments. The sale of territory to the United States by Santa Anna, in December 1853, was a factor in the origin of the Ayutla Revolution; many of the civilian leaders of the revolt had been exiled to the United States by Santa Anna; the revolutionists drew both moral and material support from sources in the United States; and, finally, the United States, both as an international power and as a model for economic, social, and political reforms, formed an inseparable part of the liberal vision of Mexico and its future.

During the first half of the nineteenth century Mexican liberal thought had developed many ties with the United States.[2] Liberals tended to see the United States as a model, particularly for their political institutions.[3] During the years following the war with the United States, significant numbers of Mexican liberals began for the first time to define their ideology in economic terms and to elaborate economic objectives—a trend that would culminate in the excessive emphasis on economic development, which characterized the period of rule by Porfirio Díaz (1876–1911).[4] Despite recent national humiliation at the hands of the United States, Mexico's mid-nineteenth-century liberals continued to draw much of their inspiration from the success of their northern neighbor as it entered the beginning stages of the industrial revolution.

The decade of the Reforma was notable in nineteenth-century Mexico for several reasons. During this period liberals made the first sustained effort to reject the historical past and to move the country toward an idealized utopian future by restructuring institutions and regenerating society. The liberal governments of this decade were controlled for the most part by civilians, a unique occurrence between 1820 and 1910.[5] Prior to the Reforma, generals who had gained prominence during the wars of independence, 1810–21, dominated Mexico. The civil wars of the 1850s and the contest of the 1860s against the French intervention and the Maximilian Empire gave birth to a generation of liberal generals who would dominate Mexico for the next half century. Between these two periods lies the Reforma, a time during which, with rare exceptions, civilians not only occupied responsible positions but determined policy and wielded power.

Except for Juan Alvarez and Ignacio Comonfort, none of the principal liberals had significant military experience prior to the beginning of the Ayutla Revolution. Even Alvarez and Comonfort were not professional soldiers in the traditional sense. To Alvarez, who first fought under Morelos during the war for independence, military rank and responsibility were only facets of a regional strongman or *cacique*. Comonfort's army experience consisted of irregular involvement in the militia since the 1820s.[6] While some future liberal leaders, such as Santos Degollado, Manuel Doblado, and Jesús González Ortega, gained military experience during the fight against Santa Anna, most key figures remained in the background until the end of this phase of the revolution. Missing from the leadership ranks during hostilities were Melchor Ocampo, Benito Juárez, Miguel and Sebastián Lerdo de Tejada, José María Mata, Antonio de la Fuente, and Francisco Zarco. Yet this group, mostly *puros,* would emerge as the key figures in the subsequent liberal governments, dominating even those regimes headed by Alvarez (1855) and Comonfort (1855–58).

This generation could not escape having its outlook colored by Mexico's relations with the United States during the preceding decades. The loss of territory left an indelible scar. The invasion and occupation of the Mexican heartland by the United States in 1847 and 1848 had been even more traumatic.[7] For the first time many of the liberals came into direct contact with the citizens of their aggressive and increasingly powerful northern neighbor. This experience forced the liberals, who had idealized the United States since the days of Joel Poinsett's ministry to Mexico immediately after independence, to reassess their attitudes toward the United States. Most of the older liberals and many of the new generation had been members of the Yorkino masonic lodges promoted by Poinsett.[8]

Such young and extreme liberals, or *puros,* as Manuel Doblado, Melchor Ocampo, Guillermo Prieto, Ponciano Arriaga, and Manuel Siliceo, continued to oppose any peace settlement with the United States even after the fall of Mexico City. Speaking through the liberal newspaper *El Monitor Republicano,* they had recommended in November 1846 that the war be fought by means of guerrilla forces if necessary,[9] and when Mexico's formal defenses collapsed during the autumn of 1847, they took up the cry for continued resistance with irregular forces. The following year most of the *puros* rallied to the Plan of Jarauta, which called for a renewal of hostilities with popular forces. Ocampo, now governor of Michoacán, offered the manpower and resources of his state for such an effort.[10] To illustrate a point made earlier about the mutability of political labels it is worth noting here that while Doblado and Siliceo were consistently numbered among the *puros* during the 1840s, they were equally regular in their adherence to *moderado* positions during the years of the Reforma.

Although the war may have embittered some liberals toward the United States, others came out of the war with a renewed and invigorated admiration for their recent foe. Some young liberals appear to have blamed their conservative compatriots rather than the expansive greed of their northern neighbors for the war and its disastrous consequences. The ease of the conquest convinced many liberals not only that the United States was a worthy political model for Mexico, but also that the enemy's surprising power was based on social and economic institutions worthy of study and imitation.[11]

Some liberals, disillusioned with Mexico's chaotic history since independence, openly cooperated with the conquerors. The most notable example was found in the *ayuntamiento* of Mexico City during the occupation. A group of twenty-one liberals, mostly *puros,* secured election to the *ayuntamiento* with the support of the occupation authorities. The *puros,* led by Miguel Lerdo de Tejada, not only cooperated with their overlords but also used the abnormal situation to launch a program of radical political, social, and economic reforms. While many other individuals, including some conservatives, found reasons to work with the enemy, the cooperative spirit shown collectively by members of the *ayuntamiento* earned them the label of traitors.[12]

Even those directly involved in military action against the invaders did not always come away permanently hostile to them. José María Mata, a young Jalapa surgeon and officer in the *guardia nacional,* was captured during the battle of Cerro Gordo in 1847. When he refused the pledge not to take up arms again, his captors shipped him to New Orleans as a prisoner of war. This involuntary trip had a great impact on the young officer; he returned to Mexico in 1848 as an avid admirer of the political, social, and economic institutions of his recent captors.[13]

While many Mexicans doubtlessly felt rancor toward the United States in the postwar period, this did not prevent the government of José Joaquín de Herrera from maintaining relatively cordial relations with the former enemy. Although disputes arising out of the recent occupation, Indian raids along the frontier, smuggling, inability to define the new boundary, and filibustering raids caused difficulties, the Herrera government was too occupied with the task of re-establishing internal peace to allow these questions to disturb the surface calm of relations. Frightened that the caste war in Yucatán might trigger a general race war, Herrera asked for four or five thousand United States troops to assist the Mexican army in putting down servile revolts and maintaining internal order.[14] Fortunately for Mexico, foreign-policy traditions and domestic politics made it impossible for the United States to accede to this request, for if the Yankees had returned by invitation so soon after having gained access by force, the temptation to remain might have been insurmountable.

A relative calm also reigned in Mexican politics during these years. The Herrera administration, 1848–51, drew from most areas of political opinion in an attempt to establish a coalition government capable of coping with the innumerable political and economic problems of the postwar period. Only the conservatives remained aloof from this effort at national unity.[15]

The postwar calm also reflected a deep disorientation within political circles. Three decades of independence, consisting of what has been called "institutionalized disorder," capped by a rapid and humiliating defeat, required a reevaluation of past actions, present policies, and future objectives.[16] In part this consisted of mutual recriminations as each political faction sought to fix responsibility for the recent disasters on other shoulders.

More important than the recriminations, however, were efforts to analyze the factors that had brought Mexico to its current sad state and to formulate plans for rescue. The newspapers, especially liberal journals of Mexico City such as *El Siglo XIX, El Monitor Republicano,* and *Don Simplicio,* devoted their editorial columns to partisan but searching probes of the country's basic political, economic, and social institutions. The most telling indictment of Mexico's institutional structure, *Consideraciones sobre la situación política y social de la República mexicana en el año 1847,* resulted from the collective efforts of a group of young politicians, moderate and liberal, who took refuge in Querétaro when the Yankees occupied Mexico City in 1847.[17]

Pessimism dominated much of this introspection. From across the political spectrum many agreed that the past thirty years had demonstrated Mexico's inability to govern itself, to establish social harmony, or to attain economic prosperity and progress. The only solution to such a state of affairs appeared to be for Mexico to place itself under the tutelage of a foreign power. Conservatives looked to European powers, while the liberals favored the United States. Under the leadership of Lucas Alamán the conservatives turned increasingly to the idea of a European-style monarchy with sympathetic ties to Spain or France.[18]

Although the friendly protection of the United States was favored by many liberals, few saw such protection as adequate in itself to cure Mexico's basic problems. Having already rejected Mexico's colonial past, the liberals saw in national defeat and humiliation not only proof that the colonial institutions were disintegrating but also the need to rebuild these institutions along modern and progressive lines. To these liberals the protection of their northern neighbor would only help insure that they could capitalize on this opportunity to carry out a massive program of *regeneración.*[19] As defined by Francisco Zarco, regeneration was a dual process, destroying the colonial order with one hand while constructing a new order with the other hand.

Many of the *moderados* and several of the *puros* accepted posts in the Herrera government (1848–51) and in that of Mariano Arista (1851–53) in hope of implementing their projects for regeneration. Melchor Ocampo, Marcos Esparza,

Ponciano Arriaga, and Guillermo Prieto were among the *puros* who held cabinet posts during these five years.[20] Despite their participation little was accomplished. Several factors contributed to this failure. Had the projects and plans been mature (but they were not), the deepening economic crisis and the concomitant fiscal crisis would still not have provided a setting conducive to major reforms. Also such a program required that the liberals at least dominate, if not control, the government. They never acquired such a position in either the Herrera or the Arista governments. Thus they were forced to wait and to let their ideas mature until 1855 and the triumph of the Ayutla Revolution, when they would have the conditions necessary for putting into effect their schemes for regeneration.

Progress was central to the liberal idea of regeneration, particularly economic progress. Even though liberals might disagree on many points, they all recognized the need for a prosperous and modern economy. While a few, notably those led by Melchor Ocampo, might still adhere to the dream of an agrarian democracy as expressed for the previous generation of liberals by Miguel Ramos Arizpe and José María Luis Mora,[21] most saw progress in terms of imitating the developments which they witnessed in the industrializing countries. David A. Brading's assertion that in political terms the liberals felt "progress was synonymous with imitation . . . [and used] the United States for their model,"[22] is equally valid in the economic arena.

While nineteenth-century Mexican liberals have traditionally been seen as preoccupied with essentially political questions—individual liberties, federalism, constitutional democracy, and separation of church and state—their statements during the decade of the 1850s show an equal if not greater concern for economic questions. *El Siglo XIX* and *El Monitor Republicano* devoted generous amounts of editorial space to economic affairs. On 1 March 1854, the same day that liberals proclaimed the Plan of Ayutla in Guerrero state, José A. Godoy established *El Heraldo, Periódico Industrial, Agrícola, Mercantil, de Literatura y Artes,* as a liberal, basically *puro,* voice in Mexico City. Its editorials, mostly written by leading liberals, were devoted almost exclusively to economic questions.

Before joining the Santa Anna government in April 1853, Miguel Lerdo de Tejada informed the president-designate of his ideas for solving Mexico's problems.[23] If, as the facts suggest, Lerdo participated in the Santa Anna government with the approval of the liberal leadership, this expression of views, in which Lerdo implicitly stated the conditions under which he would cooperate with Santa Anna, probably represented a consensus of liberal opinion.[24] While there is no positive evidence to substantiate this supposition, the conditions under which the cooperation originated and subsequent developments support it.

Although the recall of Santa Anna in 1853 was essentially a conservative move, Miguel Lerdo had played a very visible role therein.[25] He was offered and accepted a position on the official delegation sent to escort the *caudillo* home from Colombian exile. Possible motives for this action are numerous and difficult to evaluate. Long-established family friendship has been suggested; the Lerdo de Tejada and Santa Anna families sprang from similar backgrounds and had been neighbors for an extended period in Jalapa, and it was not uncommon for familial ties to outweigh political differences. There is also evidence that Alamán was eager to create the impression that the new government would enjoy the support of all political factions, and the participation of Lerdo, a leading *puro,* on even a ceremonial level would lend credence to this effort. It is also possible that Lerdo, who would later frequently demonstrate his willingness to subordinate political considerations to economic concerns, was acting on his own; he may havé believed that he could trade on his family ties with Santa Anna and on the devotion to Mexican economic development which he shared with Alamán to promote material progress regardless of the political coloration of the new administration. Some have even suggested that the liberals hoped to dominate the new government. This would not have been seriously out of character for the liberals; they had brought Santa Anna to power twice previously, 1833 and 1846.

A more satisfying and probably more realistic explanation for Lerdo's action is a combination of these possibilities. Alamán surely sought the semblance of broad political support for the new regime, and Miguel Lerdo's primary identification with economic and educational matters plus his known familial ties with the returning dictator made him a logical choice. And though it is doubtful that many liberals could seriously still hope as late as 1853 to convert Santa Anna into a bona-fide liberal, they may well have hoped to salvage something from the impending period of conservative dominance. In this case the interest of the liberal party would have coincided with Lerdo's personal dedication to economic development. If Lerdo could secure a responsible position in the new government he might be able to serve a number of useful functions; he could represent the liberal viewpoint in the government, he could try to moderate conservative actions where needed, he could be an inside source of information for liberals, and probably most important, he could promote essential economic growth regardless of the political ideology holding sway in the national palace.

Whatever the motives may have been for all concerned, Miguel Lerdo appears to have participated in the escort delegation, and upon the return of the party to Mexico in April 1853 he presented a letter to Santa Anna spelling out in detail his economic views and, by implication, the conditions under which he would join the administration being formed. A few weeks later Lerdo accepted a subcabinet post, *oficial mayor* of the new Fomento Ministry, a position he still held at the liberal takeover in 1855. After the fall of Santa Anna the liberal press, including *El Heraldo* and *El Siglo XIX,* defended Lerdo for having served the dictatorship and reprinted Lerdo's letter to Santa Anna. Furthermore, Lerdo held key positions in all the liberal governments between 1855 and his death in 1861. Perhaps most significantly, during the bitter 1861 presidential campaign when many of the *puro* leaders opposed Lerdo's candidacy and Ocampo publicly charged him with being a traitor to the cause of reform, no mention was made of Lerdo's having cooperated with Santa Anna.[26]

In the letter Lerdo stated that the recent crisis which had brought Santa Anna back to power resulted from the same factors that had made Mexico's thirty-odd years of independence a continuing series of upheavals. The first factor, and the one emphasized by Lerdo, was economic: "the profound malaise which reigns in our society as a consequence of the errors and vices which plague its economic organization." Such an economy, by suppressing commerce and the enterprising spirit and "obstructing . . . the free development of industry," creates a situation in which the working class *(hombres dedicados al trabajo),* lacking gainful employment, "seek in political revolts that which they cannot gain by other means."[27]

Lerdo warned Santa Anna against accepting the advice of the elite and politically active population as a valid expression of public opinion. Such advice represented only the interests, frequently conflicting, of no more than a few thousand wealthy or upper-class Mexicans. "The true public opinion . . . which is nothing other than the expression of the needs of the great majority of the people, cannot be known without studying what are these needs . . . [and, since] unfortunately in Mexico the majority of the inhabitants neither comprehend nor know how to explain the evils that mar their happiness, it falls to an enlightened and just government to ascertain what they are in order to apply the appropriate remedies."

Having thus defined in rather sweeping terms his view of Mexico's primary problem and his concept of the role of government, Lerdo proceeded to elaborate a program of action for "an enlightened and just government" under Santa Anna. The primary requisite was an understanding that "its mission in society . . . is to promote by all means at its disposal the general welfare of the nation" without ever subordinating itself "to the petty interests which surround it." With this mission firmly in mind the government should undertake, Lerdo asserted, a sweeping reform program in matters mainly social and economic.

Some of the recommendations made by Lerdo would have appealed to most Mexicans regardless of political affiliation—for example, increased immigration and improvements in transportation. Others, such as free trade and secular public education, had a decidedly more partisan appeal. Lerdo's socioeconomic recommendations involved a positive role for government in stimulating immigration, removing restrictions from foreign trade, stimulating industrialization, abolishing monopolies, improving transportation and communication facilities, freeing domestic commerce from restraints, establishing nationwide security for lives and property, and promoting public education free of clerical influence. These items, as amplified by Lerdo and others, formed the nucleus of most liberal thought and action in the social and economic areas for the next decade.

The Lerdo program of economic development struck a responsive chord with Santa Anna and his supporters; Lucas Alamán, conservative in political and social matters, recognized the need for economic innovation. Given Alamán's long-established identification with national economic development programs, dating back to 1830 with his almost single-handed creation of the Banco de Avío, a government investment bank designed to develop national industry, it is quite conceivable that Miguel Lerdo was really speaking to Alamán when he addressed his statement of economic views to Santa Anna. Among its first acts the new administration created a Ministry of Fomento (development) with responsibilities closely paralleling Lerdo's recommendations. Miguel Lerdo was appointed to the number-two position in the new ministry, where he quickly became the principal architect of various schemes to realize his proposals for progress.[28] In view of this and of the importance of Miguel Lerdo and his ideas in the liberal Reforma, his recommendations to Santa Anna warrant detailed analysis and can serve as a springboard for a survey of the maturation of liberal thought during the Reforma years.

The need to stimulate immigration was probably the most widely accepted of Lerdo's recommendations. Even the most stanch conservatives, the monarchists, recognized this need, although they would disagree with liberals on the type of immigrant desired and on his proper role in Mexico. According to Lerdo, European immigrants could serve a dual function: their skills were essential for tapping the great resources of Mexico's vast territory, and by scattering the immigrants among the Mexican people "the education and customs" of the latter could be improved. He subscribed to the popular view that Mexico's lack of industriousness and low level of technological competence could be overcome only by the introduction of foreign colonists.[29] The two liberal newspapers *El Siglo XIX* and *El Monitor Republicano* were particularly active between 1848 and 1853 in promoting colonization as a means of stimulating industriousness and a spirit of association within the Mexican population.

Throughout the early decades of independence the need for immigration had been rationalized on various grounds. Lorenzo de Zavala had seen Yankee and northern European immigration as essential for the growth of democratic political institutions. Most liberals were convinced that it was essential for economic progress and national security. Vacant or sparsely inhabited lands not only represented unexploited resources, a condition synonymous with criminal neglect in the liberal lexicon, but also openly invited colonization by foreign powers and private filibustering interests. Conservatives as well as liberals were convinced by mid-century that Mexico's political survival depended upon filling up these lands. But they differed on the social, intellectual, and religious benefits which immigration would bring.

Emphasis on foreign immigration as essential to the future of Mexico reflected the liberal rejection of both the Spanish and Amerindian heritage.[30] It implied that without the infusion of northern European blood the Indian, Spanish, and mestizo population of Mexico was incapable of acquiring the technological skills, social habits, and philosophical outlook essential for a prosperous modern economy. Among the leading liberal thinkers of the first half of the nineteenth century only Mora seems to have doubted this proposition. He finally rejected it, not necessarily because of the racism involved, but because he feared that northern European colonists would have more affinity for the United States than for Mexico and would make it easier for the United States to expand at Mexico's expense.

By the mid-1850s some of the liberals began to modify their public positions, if not their private beliefs, about colonization. On 15 March 1854, *El Heraldo,* in a long editorial praising the new colonization law enacted by the Santa Anna government, recognized that immigrants were of prime importance for the prosperity of Mexico, but explicitly denied any racial implication. A major impediment to economic prosperity in Mexico was the scarcity of labor, particularly skilled labor. The editorialist probably knew that the normal scarcity of labor was aggravated by the army's recruitment policies under Santa Anna, but he had the good sense not to say so. The French chargé, Alphonse Dano, however, informed Paris that "workers flee to the mountains, preferring the life of privation there over that of submitting to the law of recruitment."[31]

El Heraldo's editorialist, leaving aside the causes of the scarcity, argued that the condition could be remedied by either of two methods: natural population growth and education, or bringing in skilled adult immigrants. The editorialist emphasized the cost and delay involved in the former method as compared to the speed and economy of the latter. He also sought to give colonization a humanitarian basis by stating that it reflected a noble desire to share Mexico's bountiful gifts from Providence with people from less fortunate areas.

While there was thus some retreat from the racism implicit in earlier liberal thought on immigration, there was little evidence at mid-century of support for Mora's fear of non-Catholic northern European immigration. Liberals saw the rise of antiforeignism in the United States during the decades of the 1840s and 1850s, particularly the Know-Nothing movement of the 1850s, as a golden opportunity to divert European immigrants from the United States to Mexico. With this in mind, the liberals sent agents to Europe in 1856 to tap the stream at its source and others to the United States to encourage recent arrivals to move on to Mexico.[32]

A close competitor with colonization for popular support in mid-nineteenth-century Mexico (and a weakness noted by almost every foreign visitor of the period) was the need for improved transportation and communication facilities, particularly railroads. During the decades since independence, Mexico's lack of an adequate transportation network had been advanced frequently as the key factor in the continuing stagnation of her economy. High transportation costs made unprofitable the export of most Mexican products other than precious metals. Ineffective transportation not only added to the cost of imported goods in the interior but constituted an effective barrier to the development of a national market. Without a national market, industry could not develop and agriculture remained tied to restricted local markets. This situation would not change so long as the country's dominant form of transportation remained the pack mule.[33]

By mid-century, liberals were advocating the development of transportation facilities as an economic panacea for Mexico. Lerdo, seeing railroad construction as the greatest stimulant to "the development of agriculture and national industry," called for generous government concessions to companies undertaking such projects.[34] Francisco Zarco, writing in *El Siglo XIX,* claimed that much of the wealth and prosperity of the United States could be attributed to its transportation facilities, particularly railroads, and recommended a policy of concessions patterned on those of the United States. Until adequate railroads could be built, and then as a supplement to railroads, Zarco called for a national system of wagon roads to meet "one of the most imperious needs of the republic."[35] The *puro* organ, *El Heraldo,* not only endorsed the idea that direct economic benefits would flow from railroads but saw their construction and operation as a magnet to draw highly skilled immigrants from Europe.[36] Nor were the *puros* limited to talking about the need for better transportation: in Oaxaca Governor Benito Juárez was involved in building new roads and extending old ones, while in Michoacán Melchor Ocampo pursued a similar program from his gubernatorial post.[37]

Railroad construction was also an area in which the liberals were able to see, and claim credit for, some progress during the Santa Anna dictatorship of the 1850s. With Miguel Lerdo guiding developments from his position as *oficial mayor* of Fomento the government granted a number of significant concessions during the period 1853–55—significant more for their precedent-setting provisions than for the meager construction activity resulting from them. The government contracted for railroads connecting Veracruz with the Pacific Ocean via Mexico City, Mexico City with Santa Anna de Tamaulipas (Tampico),[38] Mexico City with Puebla via the Real del Monte,[39] the lower Rio Grande with Manzanillo, the Upper Rio Grande with Guaymas,[40] and for an urban tramway from Mexico City to Villa Guadalupe.[41] Among the precedents established were provisions designed to encourage and facilitate the work of the concessionaire: exemptions from import and export duties for the purchase of needed material and equipment, free use of public lands, long-term exclusive privilege, exemption of railroad employees from military service, and freedom to raise capital in domestic or foreign markets. Certain interesting limitations were also imposed. The companies and their foreign shareholders were to be considered Mexican and subject to Mexican laws. Several contracts specified that any attempt to claim foreign protection automatically nullified the grant, limits were placed on the amount of profit to be earned, and performance bonds were required of the concessionaires.

Significantly for the future, these pioneer grants also made the government a beneficiary as representative of the Mexican nation. The government would receive preferential rates when using the railroads—sometimes free use, sometimes half fare. Several concessions provided for the government to share in the earnings. The stipulated amount varied from fixed annual payments to a percentage of profits (10–25 percent). Finally the concessions provided that at the end of a prescribed period (fifty to ninety-nine years) the railroads with their equipment would become national property.

The collapse of the Santa Anna regime and the establishment of a liberal government in 1855 only served to arouse further public enthusiasm for railroads. Newspapers launched a campaign praising the work of Miguel Lerdo and the Fomento Ministry under Santa Anna almost immediately. Editorialists expressed confidence that the new enlightened liberal administration would rapidly give Mexico the railroad system it so desperately needed and so justly deserved.[42] The first grant made by the new administration (for a tramline from the Zocalo, or main plaza of Mexico City, to the upper-class residential community of Tacubaya) was made, in part at least, to prove the good faith of the Ayutla Revolution—to prove that it had not been just another political upheaval, "but rather that it represented the beginning of an epoch of progress."[43]

The inauguration of the line from Mexico City to Villa Guadalupe on 4 July 1857 evoked glowing tributes to the transcendent powers of the railroad. Manuel Payno, a liberal politician and one of the original entrepreneurs, soared to rare oratorical heights in the dedication ceremony. He noted that while some people claimed that efforts at material progress did nothing for the moral condition of man,

> it is a sad mistake to think in this manner. There is no material improvement . . . which is not at the same time a moral improvement. Easy, cheap, and rapid communications naturally bring together the great social families called nations. Intercourse and frequent relations with other people make man more sage, more humane, and more tolerant. If vices and defects are transmitted by this eternal law of assimilation, so are the virtues, and above all work, which is the fountain of honesty and morality for the families of the middle class, . . . is developed on a prodigious scale.[44]

Payno made the existence of railroads the sine qua non of progress and modernization. "If in the progress of nations we observe their commerce, their wealth, and their power increasing daily," he noted, "we must reflect that it depends on nothing other than the greater or lesser advance of their means of communication." When Payno attempted to describe what railroads would mean to the future of Mexico his imagination knew no bounds.

> Let us think, and this is the moment to do it, what our beautiful country will be like when it has . . . a communication route of railroads beginning in Veracruz, passing through Mexico City, crossing the states of México, Querétaro, Guanajuato, San Luis, and Jalisco, terminating in one of the Pacific ports. . . . Mexico will be the prime market place of the world and the gold of California, the silks and ivory of China, the products of India, and the thousand manufactures of European industry will necessarily travel by this route, the most secure and most natural of those known between the Atlantic and the Pacific. What value will all our lands and cities have! Such a movement of passengers! Such a powerful impulse to our mining and agriculture! . . . The imagination is humbled and lost in contemplation of the infinite benefits which this work . . . will produce for the world and especially for our country.

Despite the numerous concessions granted and the public enthusiasm attending the completion of the first functioning short line in Mexico, the liberals became increasingly aware that greater exertions would be necessary if Mexico hoped to reap these "infinite benefits" within the foreseeable future. Miguel Lerdo called for the government to make available large subsidies and free land in order to stimulate "the greediness of the speculators for these great and costly undertakings." No subsidy was too great if it resulted in the construction of the necessary railroads. Lerdo, in his plea, equated support of railroads, by both word and act, with patriotism.[45]

As this survey of their thinking during the decade of the 1850s indicates, railroad expansion had become a universal passion among liberals, a passion that was elevated by many to the status of an unquestioned part of a natural law of progress. The characterization of the restored republic (1867–76) as a period in which "widespread faith in the transforming powers of the railroad . . . crystallized in the national ideology" applies equally well to the previous decade. The liberals of the earlier decade were just as firmly convinced that "a country without rails . . . was uncivilized and out of step with the modern march, while a country with rails was a land of progress, democracy, and economic health."[46]

While many liberals, including Miguel Lerdo, have been termed free-trade advocates, no doctrinal unity existed on this question, and views apparently changed over time. Even Miguel Lerdo, who had the reputation as a doctrinaire free-trade *puro,* often moderated his stand. While he endorsed the theory of free trade and saw it as a guarantee of international peace, he also saw the necessity for limiting it in Mexico. The interest of the consumers in low tariffs must be moderated, Lerdo felt, by the revenue needs of the treasury, which was heavily dependent on customshouse receipts, and by the need to protect fledgling industries. Guillermo Prieto and *El Heraldo* shared with Lerdo this pragmatic and realistic approach to tariff rates.[47]

El Heraldo linked low and moderate tariff rates with the solution of the long-standing problem of smuggling and persistently directed public attention to the connection between high tariffs and prohibitions on the one hand, and the flourishing contraband trade on the other. Smuggling, whether across the northern frontier, along deserted coasts, or through the established ports, was a multiple evil. It corrupted government officials, denied funds to the treasury, and drove legitimate trade from the market. Thus, in addition to the doctrinal and practical economic reasons for favoring low tariffs, *El Heraldo* advocated them as the surest cure for ubiquitous clandestine commerce.[48]

Doctrinaire free trade was not without its advocates in the liberal press. L. Pinal, not otherwise identified, addressed a classical plea to *El Heraldo.* Industries unable to produce as cheaply as foreigners deserved no protection, and the welfare of consumers should be the only criterion in determining tariff policy.[49] Zarco's editorials in *El Siglo XIX*[50] and statements by Ignacio Ramírez and José Mata in the constitutional congress[51] suggest a similar free-trade position. But despite their many differences, most liberals, both doctrinaire and pragmatic, agreed that the system of prohibitions and prohibitively high duties had to be replaced with lower and more reasonable rates.

Liberals also found theory and practice irreconcilable in the matter of restrictions on internal trade. Lerdo recommended removal of the two greatest restraints, monopolies and *alcabalas* (special sales taxes).[52] Both practices were deeply ingrained in Mexico's colonial heritage and, although their detrimental effect on domestic commerce was widely proclaimed, their abolition was no easy task.

Tradition, individual self-interest, and the need for government revenues had combined to defeat all previous efforts to abolish these fiscally fecund systems. Thus by mid-century, while most liberals would support the abolition of monopolies and *alcabalas* as a matter of theory, they were also aware of the difficulties involved and of the dangers to public revenues.

The other recommendations made by Miguel Lerdo to Santa Anna reflected the general attachment of liberals to progress. Their writings were filled with exhortations on progress. Many of them saw progress as a scientific law. Prieto held that "political economy . . . has enclosed in its hands the great truths that make for the happiness of mankind; it . . . brings in its throbbing lips the kiss of the fraternity of man; . . . it makes of free trade an evangelist of that universal harmony in which grows the peace of the Universe; it converts credit into the fountain of living waters for the regeneration of humanity."[53] Prieto and other *puros* were more prone than were the *moderados* to see progress as an inevitable product of a mechanistic universe, but a product whose realization could be hastened by intelligent adjustment and tuning of the parts of the mechanism.

Science and technology held a magnetic fascination for mid-century liberals. Most newspaper editors were constantly engaged in the task of disseminating scientific knowledge and technological advances; material improvement committees *(juntas de mejoras materiales)* actively worked toward this goal; fairs were held as a means of popularizing new advances; special concessions were offered to those who would introduce new and more effective machines and techniques of production. Several of the leading liberals were obviously fascinated by the latest marvels of the machine age. Comonfort, Ocampo, and Mata all bought sewing machines while in the United States during the early 1850s, and Ocampo and Mata carried on a lively correspondence for months about the mechanics of operating these machines and on their future role in the Mexican home.[54] Mata's trips abroad were normally marked by his sending home to Ocampo, his father-in-law, and to others, examples of new products and literature on new technology.[55]

Laissez-faire has been deemed a cornerstone of mid-nineteenth-century liberal economic thought,[56] yet we have already seen that most liberals were flexible on this point. While Prieto, Ignacio Ramírez, Lerdo, and Zarco were frequently adamant against government interference in the economy,[57] they could also recognize the need for positive government action in specific situations. The challenge of acquiring adequate railroads best illustrates the ambivalence of liberal attitudes. As early as 1851 Zarco had began using the columns of *El Siglo XIX* to plead the need for subsidies.[58] By 1857 Lerdo, realizing that a laissez-faire approach would not suffice, called for grants of land and money to stimulate construction. He even proposed that the government build and operate a short line as a means of encouraging private efforts.[59] As already noted, the Fomento Ministry under the guiding hand of Miguel Lerdo created precedent-establishing relations between the government and railroad companies. These arrangements, allowing the government to share in profits, to supervise planning and construction, to set maximum profits, and to become eventually the owner of the lines, were hardly consonant with laissez-faire. While some of these precedents were modified or abandoned by later governments, the idea that government must take an active role in stimulating and guiding development in various economic areas was never abandoned.

In matters of free trade and government intervention in the economic realm the leading liberal thinkers clearly assumed both doctrinaire and pragmatic stances.[60] They had read the European economists with care and subscribed to their theories. At the same time most were aware that these theories were inapplicable in contemporary Mexico. In its initial issue *El Heraldo* set forth this position clearly.[61] While praising methods that had achieved success elsewhere, it cautioned against their uncritical application in Mexico. While encouraging its readers to keep abreast of developments elsewhere, particularly in England and the United States, *El Heraldo* felt that the necessary advances in ''industry, agriculture, and commerce'' could only be accomplished by the cooperative efforts of an enlightened, active government and open-minded, practical private interests. Implicit in the presentation of *El Heraldo,* and in the thinking of many liberals, was the belief that while classical ideas of free trade, laissez-faire, and so forth might not be applicable in Mexico at the present or within the immediate future, such a situation would not continue forever. Mexico must find her own path to development, but once that status had been achieved European economic theory would be applicable.

Although the liberal press, particularly *El Heraldo* and *El Siglo XIX,* warned against blind imitation of foreign models, the press itself was unable to resist the temptation. In preaching the necessity of development editors enlightened their readers with examples drawn from the already developed countries. Hardly an issue of the liberal newspapers of the period can be found which does not have some reference to foreign economic advances, those in England, Belgium, and the United States being the most common. Although much of this was intended to keep the public informed on the latest scientific and technological advances, it also placed these countries before the public eye as models.

While the Mexican press appreciated the advanced industrialization of England, the United States was cast most often in the role of a model. The great disparity between conditions in Mexico and England appears to have been fully appreciated. Advances in manufacturing and railroad construction in England were often described in terms of obvious admiration but without any sense that these could be duplicated in Mexico. Yet very similar developments in the United States would frequently be presented in terms suggesting that these were somehow more plausible models for Mexico.

Probably the greatest impact of the United States as an economic model resulted not from any specific development but rather from the impressiveness of its total achievement compared to that of Mexico. The contrast between the dynamic, aggressive, prosperous economy of the United States and the stagnant, decaying economy of Mexico stood out in sharp relief to the development-oriented liberals. Many of them had visited New Orleans, where they had seen at first hand the workings of a more advanced economy. Also the rapid economic growth of Texas after its annexation by the United States was frequently commented on by the liberal press.

The transportation facilities of the United States were most often held up as an appropriate guide for Mexico. As early as 1850 Zarco cited the United States as his model in attacking toll roads and bridges. The following year he again referred to events in the United States to support his claim that generous government concessions for railroad construction were essential for developing an adequate railroad system in Mexico.[62] Despite the inappropriateness of canal transportation for Mexico's mountainous and semiarid terrain, frequent newspaper coverage was devoted to the economies of canal transport in the United States and to its possible application in Mexico.

Inseparable from the liberal admiration of the economic institutions of the United States was the prospect of a protectorate by that country over Mexico. As already noted, sentiment in favor of a foreign protector surfaced as a part of the postdefeat disillusionment. While liberals had ceased to express proprotectorate views publicly by the early 1850s, the reappearance of such expressions during the first days of the Reforma indicates that the idea had not faded from their minds. Reading of liberal literature and an analysis of Mexico's history during the period suggest that most liberals did not favor a protectorate arrangement per se. Only when progressive reform seemed impossible without a protectorate or when the danger of a European protectorate in favor of the conservatives appeared imminent did the liberals openly advocate the establishment of a United States protectorate. Short of that, the liberals sought a closer economic relationship with their northern neighbor that would guarantee the recovery and modernization of the Mexican economy, a relationship to which the title '*economic* protectorate' could be applied accurately. Yet, as we have already seen, for domestic political reasons 'protectorate' was a pejorative term to be used publicly only against one's enemies.

In characterizing liberal thought on the eve of the Reforma one can say that liberalism was dominated by a new generation whose outlook was in many respects more akin to that of later Mexican positivism than to the liberalism of the earlier generation. Stressing the importance of economic development and often giving it priority over political goals was a hallmark of the new liberalism. Infatuated with and extremely optimistic about man's ability to use science and technology to remake his social and economic institutions, many liberals verged on elevating progress-through-science to the level of a mystical religion.

That this emphasis on economic development threatened to overshadow efforts to achieve liberal political goals alarmed some leading liberals. Shortly after the collapse of the Santa Anna government in August 1855, Francisco Zarco warned the readers of *El Siglo XIX* against losing sight of the political goals of the revolution. Without belittling economic development and material progress Zarco asserted that these were unattainable without a stable and orderly political system. Even if one could realize all the desired development goals, Zarco argued, the results would be meaningless without the personal security, liberty, individual guarantees, and national confidence that could be produced only by constitutional democratic government.[63]

The optimistic young liberals had compiled an impressive list of material improvements to be pushed at the earliest opportunity, including roads, railroads, telegraph, river navigation, and port improvement. They had also determined to rid Mexico of chronic ills which they felt had blighted her economic growth—prohibition, protectionism, *alcabalas,* monopolies, smuggling, and the scarcity of capital and technology. On a more positive side they were committed to create a modern prosperous Mexico and to alter the quality of life through public secular education and a liberal immigration policy. Most of them also saw a need for the government's participation in the realization of these objectives.[64]

Foreigners, particularly Yankees, were admired and envied for their successes in the economic realm. Admiration for the United States, the use of its social and economic institutions as models, and a realization that a United States protectorate over Mexico might be necessary and desirable under certain conditions often went hand in hand with fear of the power and expansive policies of the potential protector. A feeling of continental brotherhood was moderated by fear of the treatment Mexico might receive at the hands of an overly powerful brother.

Liberal Mexican concern with the United States was not reciprocated north of the border. In the United States during the years following the war there existed no comparable public interest in Mexico, its development, and relations with it. In contrast to the situation in Mexico, where hardly an issue of the leading newspapers lacked some reference to events and developments in the United States, coverage of Mexican affairs in the press of the United States was infrequent and most notable for its ignorance of the true nature of Mexican developments. The *New York Times* for the period 1851–62 had practically no nonpolitical coverage of Mexico and demonstrated the superficiality of its political treatment by consistently endowing Mexican politicians—including Valentín Gómez Farías and Benito Juárez—with military rank. President Buchanan later displayed the same weakness with his repeated references to "president General Juárez."[65]

The passing of Mexico from public prominence and the cooling of the annexing ardor of the All Mexico movement in the years following the end of the war did not mean that the objectives identified so forcefully during the period of war (1846–48) ceased to have currency.[66] Manifest destiny, reinforced by the vigor and idealism of a growing "Young America" sentiment, had allowed the All Mexico movement to place the need for United States ascendancy over Mexico on grounds that continued to appeal simultaneously to national pride, purse, cupidity, and consciousness. The annexation of Mexico during the war had been justified by the need

to remove a hostile neighbor . . . ; to prevent it becoming a neighbor both hostile and dangerous in European hands; to enable us to command the Pacific and the Gulf of Mexico; . . . to develop . . . the ample resources of Mexico; to redeem the

Mexican people . . . ; to redeem security, civilization, improvement; to keep Cuba
from the hands of . . . the British; to facilitate the entire removal of [the British]
from this continent; to open Mexico, as an extensive market to our manufactures, an
extensive producer of . . . [silver] through which we command the manufactures of
Europe; to prevent monarchy from gaining any additional ground on the American
continent, . . . [and] to facilitate its entire removal.[67]

Although this clearly defined, if somewhat optimistic, statement of goals had
been formulated as rationale for annexation by force, most of the goals continued
to attract public support after the war and to be seen as attainable by peaceful
measures—annexation or even milder methods. Alternatives had been advanced
even during the war, when slavery and sectionalism had aroused spirited opposition to annexation. President Polk had suggested an indefinite military
occupation,[68] while Secretary of State Buchanan had spoken of an ill-defined
protectorate to assist Mexicans in establishing "upon a permanent basis, a Republican Government."[69]

During the following decade policies of both annexation and indirect controls
were advanced as appropriate. Annexation as a political objective survived in
limited and restricted forms. Although the national movement to annex all Mexico
collapsed quickly when the peace terms made by Trist became public in 1848, the
ghost of the idea still walked the land during the following decade.[70] In 1850 the
DeBow's Commercial Review could still foresee a universal political empire ruled
from Washington.[71]

Among extremists on both sides of the slavery question were to be found
advocates of expansion at the expense of Mexico. Some abolitionists, convinced
that slavery could never flourish in Mexico, saw the annexation of Mexico as a
step toward final solution of the sectional problem. Some proslavery groups were
equally sure that the survival of their institution required southward expansion into
Cuba, Mexico, and Central America.

The Democratic administrations of Pierce and Buchanan, with which Reforma
Mexico had to deal, were inclined to pursue a policy of territorial expansion
relative to Mexico. Such a policy was in accord with party traditions; Polk had
established an example to be emulated; and besides, expansion could divert public
attention from the growing sectional rift while holding the party together. Pierce,
responding to the vigor of the Young America movement, promised in his
inaugural message to pursue a policy unhampered "by any timid forebodings of
evil from expansion." Territory acquired by Gadsden in the treaty of 1853, while
not as extensive as Pierce desired, was ample evidence of his lack of "timid
forebodings." Buchanan's inaugural address promised a new wave of expansion,
either "by fair purchase or, as in the case of Texas, by the voluntary determination
of a . . . people to blend their destinies with our own."[72] An embarrassingly full
treasury at the beginning of his term encouraged his strenuous but unsuccessful
efforts to buy Mexican territory.

Despite the continued calls on the more blatantly territorial forms of manifest destiny, most of which were merely partisan politics and focused on Cuba and the Caribbean area rather than on Mexico after 1850,[73] the more significant public interest in Mexico was based largely on economic considerations. Following the acquisition of territories facing on the Pacific Ocean, and particularly after the discovery of gold in California, the matter of transcontinental communications became a national public interest that frequently involved Mexico. Both the northern and southern extremes of the remaining Mexican territory were seen as vital to the transportation needs of the United States. A dubious survey indicating that the best route for a railroad from New Orleans to California lay through the Mexican territory south of the Gila River culminated in the Gadsden Treaty of 1853, Pierce's one successful essay in expansion.[74] Greater public interest, with less positive results, was displayed in securing United States access to and control of the transit route across the Isthmus of Tehuantepec.[75]

The importance of the Tehuantepec route rested not only on its feasibility as a link between the west and east coasts of the United States, but also on the assumption that such a route would facilitate Yankee access to the markets of East Asia. The possibility of a transcontinental railroad within the United States and its advantages for trade with China had been discussed for years, but as a result of knowledge of the western terrain gained during the Mexican War serious doubts arose as to the feasibility of such a route.[76] In view of these doubts, the shorter, cheaper, and more quickly exploitable Tehuantepec route acquired tremendous appeal.

The hope, particularly in the South, that a transit route across Tehuantepec would produce immediate advantages for United States trade in East Asia was of great importance in spurring efforts to secure this route. The southern commercial conventions during the decade of the 1850s held that "commercial expansion was necessary for the South."[77] Several conventions endorsed the idea of a railroad across Tehuantepec as a part of their drive for direct trade and commercial development. Because of its proximity to Gulf ports, southerners favored the Tehuantepec route over all others. New Orleans interests, speaking through *DeBow's Commercial Review,* envisioned a Tehuantepec railroad as an essential element in a broad program to gain for their port a leading position in world trade.

The southern drive for commercial expansion, while clearly a facet of the broader domestic sectional struggle, involved certain basic economic objectives. First in order of importance was a desire to escape commercial, financial, and economic domination by the North. Southern newspapers played on the theme that the South had been reduced to a backward colony of northern economic interests. In addition to freeing itself from northern controls, the South hoped to find foreign markets that it could dominate. The Montgomery Convention in 1858 called for southern commercial expansion into Latin America on the grounds that "the less exploited the field, the greater would be the South's chance of controlling the commercial destiny of that field."[78] James Gadsden, a southern railroad promoter, constantly called for measures to reduce the Gulf of Mexico to a Yankee lake. United States control of Florida, combined with the acquisition of Cuba and the Yucatán, would make the British position in the West Indies untenable and open the area to commercial exploitation from southern Gulf ports.[79]

Desire for an enhanced economic role in Mexico was not limited to the South. A proposal in 1858 for Congress to subsidize a regular steamer service between Mobile, New Orleans, and the Mexican Gulf ports elicited nonsectional support. Declining Yankee trade with Mexico and a corresponding increase in the dominant trade position of the British were seen as both unnatural and undesirable by congressional spokesmen from all areas. Senator Robert Toombs of Georgia and Senator Henry Wilson of Massachusetts agreed that "our India is south of us on this continent." Senator Judah P. Benjamin of Louisiana supported the proposed mail-steamer service as a step designed to create for the United States "a pre-eminent moral power, a commercial power, [and] a power over public opinion" in Mexico, a power the United States must have if it wished to control the political future of Mexico. In the following session the House Post Office Committee called for a network of mail steamers to all Latin American areas. Such a network "with the proper encouragement from the government, would make our people actually, as naturally, almost [Latin America's] sole furnishers, carriers, traders and bankers"[80] Expanded economic activity in Mexico as well as elsewhere in Latin America was seen both as a natural development and as one that would help spread the United States's political influence while bringing about a corresponding weakening of European, particularly British, influence.

During the decade of the Reforma an increasing number of people from the United States went to Mexico and involved themselves in Mexican affairs. Some were driven by no discernible impulse other than a romantic wanderlust; others came as entrepreneurs, speculators, and financiers attracted by the prospects of profit.[81] Some, equipped with only their skills and energy, were looking for a better life. Occasionally there appeared Yankees with skills or capital who saw in their quest for profits an opportunity to accomplish something greater—to assist in regenerating Mexican life and in bringing Mexico into a new and mutually beneficial relationship with the United States. An unprecedented number of filibusterers were also drawn to Mexico during this decade: some answering a vague call of manifest destiny, some motivated apparently only by their desires for glory and profit, others representing that floating population of frontier areas who were always ready for excitement and adventure.

From this survey of conditions at mid-century it becomes clear that attitudes existed in both countries which would give a unique character to relations between Mexico and the United States during the decade of the Reforma. In Mexico a new generation of liberal leaders emerged determined to remake the face of Mexico. They were attracted to the United States by various factors—feelings of hemispheric brotherhood; admiration for the political, social, and economic institutions of their neighbors; attractiveness of Yankee prosperity and technological advances; and a feeling that the brotherly shadow of the United States would protect their reforms from foreign and domestic enemies. Their attraction was moderated by an awe of United States power and a fear of its expansive policies. In the United States this period saw the continuation in moderated form of many of the expansionistic ideas that earlier had given life to manifest destiny and had spawned the All Mexico movement. There was an upsurge of interest in the possibilities for transcontinental transportation in Mexico and an awakening interest, particularly in the South, in the commercial and economic potential of Mexico. The problem of how to exploit for the benefit of the United States the political and economic potential of Mexico without annexation had also received increasing attention.

2
The Revolution of Ayutla and the Bases of Liberal Diplomacy, 1853–1856

Santa Anna's overthrow was the immediate objective of the Ayutla Revolution, which began on 1 March 1854. The general retained power until 8 August 1855, when he abandoned both Mexico City and the political power he had so often held. Despite having the enemy yield without a last decisive battle, the revolutionists dallied for almost two months before organizing a government. Alvarez was chosen interim president on 4 October 1855, and another two months passed before the new government was firmly established in Mexico City.

Although almost two years elapsed after the beginning of the revolution before the liberals had a government capable of conducting normal diplomatic relations, they were not as leisurely in developing external economic ties. From its very beginning the Ayutla Revolution, by both action and ideology, attracted foreign economic attention. By the end of the military phase in August 1855 a pattern of economic policies, attitudes, and relationships had evolved between Mexico and the United States. That pattern would underlie economic and political relations between the two countries until 1861, when civil war in the United States and foreign intervention in Mexico disrupted all meaningful relations.

High tariffs, import prohibitions, and other restraints on internal and external trade were issues which could be exploited for political purposes in Mexico during the 1850s. The desire for greater freedom of trade was a factor in the unrest that resulted in Santa Anna's being returned to power in 1853. Several of the port cities, led by Veracruz, acted on their own to reduce tariff levels and remove import restrictions.[1] Juan Ceballos, interim president after the resignation of Mariano Arista, vainly sought to forestall Santa Anna's recall by acceding to demands for greater freedom of trade. On 29 January 1853, Ceballos decreed a provisional measure lifting prohibitions and sharply reducing the average level of tariffs.[2]

Santa Anna, ignoring the advice of Miguel Lerdo,[3] reversed the trend toward freer trade. Not only did he reestablish prohibitions and high tariff rates, but he also took other steps destined to cause discontent in commercial circles. In addition to making radical and unanticipated changes in customs regulations, Santa Anna created havoc by selling or giving permits to his favorites for the import of merchandise and the export of specie at greatly reduced rates.[4] A navigation act of 24 June 1854 severely penalized foreign vessels bringing to Mexican ports merchandise produced in a third country.[5] The French chargé reported that it took Santa Anna only a year to destroy completely the commercial prosperity of Mexico's port cities. Santa Anna's mismanagement produced such economic distress that when news of Alvarez's pre-Ayutla uprising of 21 January 1854 reached the capital, the French diplomat had no doubt that this was a "true revolution" representing the interests of the port cities and coastal regions. "The reestablishment of the federal system is seen with indifference but the situation in commercial matters has become so intolerable that they will not hesitate to take any measure offering relief."[6]

Since a foreign diplomat found economic discontent so obviously a justification for revolt, the reluctance of the revolutionists to identify it as such is difficult to understand. The Plan of Ayutla relegated economics to the last article and then yoked it in a secondary position to a provision on the future role of the army. After promising that the army would not be destroyed, article 6 pledged the interim government "to protect the freedom of internal and external commerce, issuing as soon as possible tariff schedules to be observed. In the meantime the maritime customhouses will be controlled by that [schedule] published by the Ceballos administration."[7] This rather weak gesture toward free trade was the only nonpolitical item in the plan issued at Ayutla.

On 11 March 1854, the Ayutla plan was restated in amended form by the Plan of Acapulco. The latter, issued by Comonfort and reflecting the commercial interests of that southern port, made two important nonpolitical contributions to the earlier revolutionary statement—a stronger commitment to free trade and a clear endorsement of progress as a revolutionary objective.[8] The provisions concerning commerce were expanded and separated from those dealing with the army. Commerce was now defined as "one of the sources of public wealth and one of the most powerful elements for the advancement of civilized nations." The interim government was committed "immediately to provide [for commerce] all the liberties and privileges which are necessary for its prosperity." To achieve "commercial prosperity" the government was required to establish quickly an appropriate new tariff schedule which could be no less liberal than the Ceballos tariff. Until the new schedule could be established the Ceballos tariff would be observed at both the maritime and frontier customshouses.

The power of the interim president was also amended to give him more authority and to make him responsible for national progress and prosperity. The Ayutla plan had merely provided the interim president with "ample powers to attend to national security and independence and for the other branches of public administration." This provision as amended by Acapulco provided that "the interim president . . . will be immediately invested with ample faculties to reform all branches of public administration, to attend to the security and independence of the nation and to promote whatever is conducive to its prosperity, aggrandizement, and progress." Broad presidential powers were expressly limited only by a requirement to respect the inviolability of individual guarantees.[9]

The hesitancy of Alvarez and his advisors to commit themselves to a program of freer trade is even more difficult to understand in view of the free-trade decrees issued by Alvarez eight days before the appearance of the Plan of Ayutla. At Chilpancingo on 22 February 1854, Alvarez ordered that goods imported through Acapulco or other ports in revolt be assessed according to the provisions of the Ceballos tariff. Goods not covered by the Ceballos tariff would pay a duty of 12½ percent of value. The decree was a war measure designed to finance the uprising, as indicated by a provision giving a 30 percent discount on duties to merchants who would pay immediately for goods to be imported at some future date.[10] Alvarez was apparently prepared to use lower tariffs as a war measure to gain support in port areas but feared to include a strong low-tariff statement in a revolutionary plan designed for a national audience. The influence of Comonfort and the Acapulco commercial interests was apparently sufficient to convert free trade from a reluctantly publicized war measure into a prized element of the revolutionary arsenal.

The Ayutla revolutionists recognized what the French chargé had realized earlier: that economic and commercial discontent under Santa Anna was a great reservoir of potential support which must be exploited to insure the success of the revolt.[11] Convinced that further economic liberalization would be advantageous, Comonfort ordered, on 31 July 1855, that the Alvarez decree of the previous year be observed in the port of Manzanillo. He also prohibited the collection of *alcabalas* and consumption taxes in the areas under his command.

When political ambitions left Mexico without a government for weeks following the fall of Santa Anna, Comonfort seized the initiative by issuing a decree of wide economic impact. From his military headquarters at Guadalajara on 5 September 1855, Comonfort, possibly with an eye on the contest for the presidency, applied a modified version of the Alvarez decree to the enlarged area now under his command. He authorized an additional reduction of 12 percent in the duties on all goods imported through Pacific ports. He also halted the collection of *alcabalas,* consumer taxes, and a group of bothersome taxes on windows, doors, luxury items, and the like. He abolished duties on the internal movement of money and sharply reduced those on the export of money and bullion. All goods other than precious metals could be exported duty free.[12] While many liberals, including the editor of *El Heraldo,* opposed as too drastic Comonfort's actions, which discriminated against Gulf ports and threatened the solvency of the treasury, it is possible that the measures strengthened his position and contributed to his replacing Alvarez as interim president on 8 December 1855.

As the Ayutla revolt developed, a number of leading liberals turned to the United States for assistance and sometimes refuge. Military leaders sought to obtain loans, arms, and recruits in the United States, while a good many liberal politicians were exiled to the United States. Their experiences would figure prominently in Mexican–United States relations during the Reforma.

Shortly after the beginning of the Ayutla revolt the military leadership determined that they needed loans and supplies from abroad. Ignacio Comonfort, recently collector of customs for Acapulco, was commissioned for the task. His popularity with the merchants of Acapulco, foreign and native, recommended him for the mission.[13] With his credentials of authority duly certified by the United States consul at Acapulco, Comonfort departed for San Francisco and New York in search of $500,000 in loans. Besides having authority to borrow money, Comonfort was empowered to determine acceptable terms of repayment, to purchase munitions and supplies, and to hire eighty foreign artillerymen. More significant for this study, Comonfort was directed to encourage foreign ships to call at rebel ports and to promote an increase in the volume of imports there. It should also be noted that since normal international practice limits consular certification to the signatures of officials of recognized governments, this certification of documents signed by a rebel commander, who cited a revolutionary declaration as his source of authority, is an early indication of sympathy for the rebel cause by the certifying consul, Charles L. Denman, if not by his government also.[14]

The steps which Comonfort was authorized to take to guarantee loans were significant for the future economic welfare of Mexico. Customs receipts could be pledged, mortgaged, or sold. Mining grants and contracts to build roads, railroads, and other communications facilities could also be used to guarantee repayment of the loans. In effect, Comonfort had carte blanche to dispose of the resources of the rebel area in his search for immediate financial aid.[15]

Comonfort's trip to the United States in 1854 produced what must have been disappointingly poor results. After finding no acceptable offers in San Francisco in June, Comonfort traveled on to New York where his efforts were seconded by several liberal exiles, including former president Juan Ceballos. Even with the additional assistance the summer passed into fall before meager results began to appear. The liberals had to divert considerable energy to the task of countering the unfavorable stories being spread by Santa Anna's consular and diplomatic agents. In October and November Comonfort negotiated two contracts. The first, 11 October, provided for a loan of $300,000, only $60,000 of which, however, was to be made available immediately in cash. Under the second contract, 7 November, the New York firm of Hitchcock and Company agreed to ship arms valued at $20,400 to Acapulco after a down payment of only $4,500, with the remainder payable on delivery.[16] Comonfort also convinced at least one individual, Carlos Butterfield, to ship military supplies to Mexico on a purely speculative basis.[17]

The circumstances surrounding the negotiation of the $300,000 loan were complicated and suggestive, its provisions complex and expensive. The loan was advanced by a Spaniard, Gregorio de Ajuria, acting as agent for John Temple, a transplanted Massachusetts Yankee who had established himself as a merchant at Los Angeles in Mexican Upper California in 1827. He improved on his status as a leading merchant in the early 1840s, when his marriage into one of the great landed families of the area brought him ownership of a 27,000-acre ranch. Although his wealth was already estimated at $100,000, Temple had enlarged his fortune during the California gold rush by supplying food, livestock, and other items to the booming northern area at inflated prices. While indications are that Temple had acquired extensive Mexican holdings by the 1850s, the nature and location of these are unknown.[18]

Gregorio de Ajuria, the other party in the loan arrangement, was a Spanish citizen whose business ties with Temple date back to at least 1845, when Ajuria, operating out of Mazatlán, had been active in the California coastal trade. The commercial tie between the two men had been augmented by 1859 with a familial bond: at some unspecified date Ajuria had become Temple's son-in-law. If, as indicated by *Diccionario Porrúa,* Ajuria was a millionaire by 1854, it seems likely that his fortune was also a product of the gold rush. By 1854 his Mexican holdings included the Santa Teresa paper factory and the capital daily *El Estandarte Nacional.*[19]

Although *Diccionario Porrúa* indicates that Comonfort and Ajuria had not met prior to the loan negotiation, Anselmo de la Portilla's contemporary account refers to them as old friends, and the known circumstances would suggest that they were not strangers. Since Ajuria and Temple had been involved in the trade between the California coast and the ports of Mazatlán and Acapulco for several decades, it is almost certain that their commercial activities brought them some contacts with the collector of customs at Acapulco, Ignacio Comonfort. Temple and Ajuria were in Mexico City when the Ayutla revolt began in March 1854, and the normal route to and from California would have carried them through both Acapulco and the heart of the rebel leader Alvarez's fiefdom.[20]

The speed and apparent ease with which Temple later secured a lease on the Mexico City mint and Ajuria became an unofficial advisor and confidant of President Comonfort suggests that contacts between the Californians and Comonfort very likely went back much earlier than the October 1854 loan contract. It is reasonable to assume that the future leaders of Ayutla sounded out possible credit sources before initiating hostilities. The negotiations which ended in New York probably began in Acapulco early in the year, were renewed with Comonfort's visit to California in June, and were finally terminated on the east coast only when it became apparent that cheaper credit was not to be found.

Although the contract signed by Ajuria (for Temple) and by Comonfort (for Alvarez and the Ayutla rebels) was silent on the matter of interest, the deal thus struck was expensive for Mexico, in both the short and the long term. It called for Ajuria to deliver $60,000 immediately in cash to Comonfort. The remaining $240,000 would be paid into the national treasury in the form of bonds of the consolidated internal debt of Mexico, and this payment would come only after the rebels had succeeded in establishing a government in Mexico City.[21] Since bonds of the internal debt which were to be accepted as a major part of the loan could be obtained by Temple and Ajuria for a small fraction of their face value, interest charges were not necessary for the creditor to turn a handsome profit. To guarantee repayment of the loan Comonfort pledged one-half of the proceeds of the Acapulco customshouse. While the creditors could withhold four-fifths of the loan until after the rebels had won their struggle, the rebels were not so fortunate; the contract required them to begin repaying the loan immediately.

Having made one attractive deal with the rebels and doubtless with an eye to enhancing his stature in the eyes of Mexico's future rulers, Temple made a second loan on similar terms. At an unspecified time and place Temple lent agents of Ayutla rebel Santos Degollado $105,000, of which $21,000 was in immediate cash and remainder in bonds of the internal debt.[22] The loan to Comonfort was approved by Alvarez soon after Comonfort arrived in Acapulco in early December 1854 with the arms he had secured. On 11 December an order was issued to the administrator of customs at Acapulco to begin making the required payments to Temple's agents.[23] The loan to Degollado was confirmed by the liberal government at Cuernavaca on 19 October 1855, and orders were issed to the customs-houses in Veracruz and Mazatlán to begin payments.[24] Temple's subsequent lease of the Mexico City mint also appears to have been clearly an outgrowth of these loan transactions.

While the rebel military was establishing costly but beneficial contacts north of the border, many of the future civilian leaders were living as political refugees in New Orleans and Texas. By early 1854 Santa Anna's policies had caused a colony of Mexican liberal exiles, including Juárez, Ocampo, Mata, Ponciano Arriaga, former president Ceballos, and Manuel Arrioja, to appear in New Orleans. The exiles formed a *junta revolucionaria* with Ocampo as president and Mata as secretary. The junta, dedicated to the overthrow of Santa Anna, undertook newspaper campaigns and such other activities as their limited financial resources allowed.[25]

After a few months Ocampo decided to transfer the junta closer to the scene of action. He and selected members moved to Brownsville, Texas, where a revolutionary newspaper was established. The revolutionists also tried to replenish their financial resources by selling goods bought in New Orleans.[26] Letters from Mata to Ocampo suggest that some of this commercial activity may have taken the form of smuggling goods into Mexico. Mata, who remained in New Orleans to purchase goods for shipment to Brownsville, was concerned with finding items suitable for the Mexican market. In Brownsville Ocampo sought to make a liberal revolutionist of José María Carvajal, a perennially disaffected Mexican whose raids and smuggling had made him notorious along the Rio Grande for more than a decade. Despite the junta's efforts, no strong backing for a military uprising could be found among Mexican exiles in south Texas or among the military and political figures of the Mexican frontier regions.[27] Its efforts, however, may have contributed to the opposition to Santa Anna which developed in northeast Mexico in the latter stages of the Ayutla Revolution.

Meanwhile Juárez, Mata, and the others who remained in New Orleans had experiences and contacts that were significant for both their personal futures and that of their country. Although Juárez was pressed for funds and, as legend has it, may have been forced to accept menial tasks to earn a livelihood, he seems to have had time to observe and be impressed by the pulsating commercial life of the port city. Mata's biographer indicates that Juárez found the great volume of goods moving along the Mississippi incredible and sought an explanation from Mata. Mata is supposed to have explained that the high level of commercial activity reflected the lack of restraints on domestic and foreign trade.[28] It is doubtful that Mata, Juárez, or any of the other Mexican exiles fully understood the commercial importance of the location of New Orleans in the days before the railroad.

During their many months in New Orleans it was natural for the exiles to form new acquaintances and to feel a special bond with those who showed a sympathetic understanding of their difficult situation. While one can only speculate on the total impact of the relationships thus established, some indications can be inferred from a limited knowledge of Juárez's contacts. Records only reveal that Juárez found three foreigners, two Cubans and a United States citizen of French extraction, helpful and sympathetic to the liberal cause. The two Cuban exiles, Pedro Santacilia and Domingo de Goicuria, owned a livestock business which they used as a cover for dealings in arms and munitions for Cuban insurgents.[29] Both these men were to have numerous and favored business relations with later liberal governments in Mexico.[30] Santacilia married Juárez's daughter and became a lifelong confidant of his father-in-law.[31] The Yankee, Emile La Sere, edited *The Louisiana Courier,* a democratic organ in New Orleans. The friendship between La Sere and Juárez developed quickly into a firm and lasting realtionship.[32] In addition to securing Mexican contracts for the Louisiana Tehuantepec Company, La Sere later served Juárez as advisor and fund raiser.

While the lines along which informal relations and private contacts were developing between Mexican liberals and the United States would have a significant impact on later formal relations between the two countries, the policies pursued by the Santa Anna government were such as to drive the liberals and their northern neighbors closer together. Santa Anna's attempts to secure European assistance demonstrated to many that only the cooperative efforts of Mexican liberals and their Anglo-American friends could prevent the conservatives from delivering the country over to monarchial Europe. The increasingly belligerent United States policy toward Mexico, partly reflecting the pressures of domestic Yankee politics and partly a response to Santa Anna's overtures to European powers, served to convince many conservatives that Mexico would soon disappear in a Yankee embrace. In this complicated picture the voluntary transfer of territory by the Gadsden Treaty had a multifaceted impact: it weakened conservative support of Santa Anna, swelled the ranks of those determined to overthrow him, thoroughly frightened Mexican conservatives, aroused European suspicions, and seemed, in some perverted way, to have strengthened rather than weakened the liberals' attachments to the United States.

That relations between the United States and the Santa Anna regime were laced with hostility should not be surprising. The anti-Yankee attitudes of Lucas Alamán and the conservatives who had backed Santa Anna's return were sufficiently strong to have prevented any cordiality toward the United States even if Santa

Anna had wanted to be polite. The restored dictator needed little encouragement, however, to express his disdain for the Yankees. Upon his arrival at Veracruz he commented on the pain and humiliation he had felt when he was forced to abandon the country while it was occupied by the enemy army. If the United States should again threaten the independence of Mexico, Santa Anna declared, it would provide him with a welcomed opportunity to wipe this blot from the record. He followed this with an order dismissing all army officers who had voluntarily surrendered to the United States during the war and subsequent occupation. Among his first acts after formally assuming the presidential sash of office was a decree designed to stop the introduction of gold coinage from California. His appointment of Juan N. Almonte as minister to Washington was not designed to allay fears concerning his attitude, since Almonte had held this same position during the crisis leading up to the war with the United States.

While he was forming his government, Santa Anna and his politically astute foreign minister, Lucas Alamán, began making overtures to European powers for support against the United States. On 25 April 1853, five days after the formal establishment of the Santa Anna government in Mexico City, Alamán requested French aid and protection so that Mexico could develop into an effective counterweight to the expansive power of the United States. Before Mexico could fill such a role, he stressed, it would have to rebuild its institutions and ''regenerate'' its society, but the United States would not remain idle meanwhile. Only the benevolent aid and protection of France could protect Mexico from her neighbor's greed during this period. If left unchecked, he asserted, the United States would soon annex everything north of Panama and close this region to European political and economic influences. ''The general [Santa Anna] and I are convinced that if the emperor wishes he can guarantee our independence and contribute to the development of our power which can be converted into a counterweight to the power of the United States. There would then be an American equilibrium similar to that of Europe.'' Alamán was confident Napoleon III could secure British and Spanish cooperation in such a project.

The French minister, André Levasseur, reacted favorably and agreed to submit the proposal to Paris. Seeing in the Mexican attitude an opportunity for favorable action on French claims, Levasseur, without committing France to anything, indicated that his country had been thinking along the same lines and would welcome Mexico's recovery as means of blocking United States expansion. France, he assured Alamán, was fully alive to the need for a balance of power on the American continent.

Levasseur also reported that a few days later Santa Anna approached the Prussian minister, Baron von Richthofen, with a request that Prussia make available its officers to train the Mexican army. He assured von Richthofen that France was leading the European maritime powers in a policy to protect Mexico and that, while a French military training contingent would arouse fears in Washington, such a mission from Prussia, which had no navy, would arouse no fears and would be positively welcomed by France, Britain, and Spain. This tactless approach did not elicit a warm response, but Santa Anna, insensitive to von Richthofen's coolness, persisted with a new request for a complete Prussian military unit of five or six thousand men. To this proposition von Richthofen expressed his frank opposition but agreed to submit it to Berlin.[33]

Not satisfied with working through the European ministers in Mexico, Santa Anna directed the Mexican ministers in Paris, London, and Madrid to seek aid in containing the expansionistic drives of the United States. The ministers were instructed to emphasize the danger posed to monarchical institutions and to European economic interests. If these views were favorably received by the host governments, the ministers were authorized to propose treaties of alliance directed against the United States.[34]

The responses to Santa Anna's search for European allies were not encouraging. The British chose to ignore the request, while the French became apprehensive that Santa Anna might misinterpret French expressions of sympathy. The French minister warned against any thought of a war against the United States. France would be happy to see Mexico with an army capable of repelling a Yankee attack, he noted, and was ready to assist Mexico in securing the Latin Catholic immigrants necessary to develop Mexican resources, "but not even for an instant is it possible to suppose that the government of His Imperial Majesty will break its friendly relations with the United States and lose, even momentarily, the immense markets which that country offers to French commerce in order to aid you in a war which you might have provoked."[35] French interests in promoting a monarchical Latin Catholic resurgence in Mexico were obviously less important than profitable trade relations with the United States.

Only Spain responded in an encouraging manner to the Mexican proposals. Angel Calderón de la Barca, Spain's first minister to independent Mexico and now Spanish foreign minister, expressed more than a casual sympathy for Mexico's plight. Since the United States also threatened Spanish Cuba, Calderón raised the possibility of secret steps for Spain and Mexico to affect a common defense. Santa Anna responded with a proposal for a mutual defense alliance. But Spain, fearful that such an arrangement might become known and serve as a pretext for an American move against Cuba, refused to give serious consideration to the Mexican proposal.[36]

France, unencumbered by exposed possessions, could afford a more active interest in Mexico's relations with the United States. Refusal to be drawn into a war against the United States did not mean that France was willing to allow Anglo-American influence to flow southward unimpeded. French ministers sought to use their influence with responsible Mexican conservatives and within the sizeable French and Spanish commercial communities as a means of checking Yankee advances. France was particularly concerned for the security of Mexico's northern frontier in the face of filibustering activities from the United States and sought in vain to encourage colonization of the area by Frenchman as a a barrier to the Yankees. The filibustering activities of William Walker in Baja California during 1853–54 were watched anxiously by French consuls and diplomats in Mexico and the United States and reported in detail to Paris.

Until they became convinced that he was actually promoting United States interests, French diplomats encouraged the efforts of the French adventurer Count Gaston Raousset de Boulbon to colonize Sonora with Frenchmen from San Francisco. His capture along with some two hundred Frenchmen by Mexican forces at Guaymas in July 1854 proved highly embarrassing to the French image as Mexico's protector. Frustrated in their indirect and peaceful efforts to convert Mexico into a barrier against Yankee expansion, French diplomats began to elaborate during Santa Anna's regime a rationale for the French intervention which was to be realized during the following decade.[37] Despatches from the French legation in Mexico setting forth the need for intervention became increasingly frequent and insistent after the Raousset fiasco and after the arrival of Jean Alexis de Gabriac as minister in December 1854.

French fears of United States designs on Mexico were not unfounded. Pierce had warmly endorsed a policy of expansion in his inaugural address of March 1853.[38] In an attempt to heal sectional schisms within his party and country, Pierce proposed a vigorous policy of both territorial and commercial expansion.[39] Although this pronouncement aroused fears in the minds of Mexicans, Pierce was actually referring to Cuba rather than Mexico. As for Mexico, Pierce probably envisioned nothing more frightful than commercial expansion as a part of a broader program directed at Latin America and East Asia.[40]

But events did not allow the new administration leisure in which to determine its Mexican policy. A strong sense of political indebtedness to the southern wing of the Democratic party and to its representative in the cabinet, Jefferson Davis, resulted in the appointment of James Gadsden of South Carolina as minister to Mexico. Gadsden's longstanding interest in transcontinental railroads and his advocacy of economic independence and commercial expansion for the South blended well with the foreign-policy plans of the president, while his opposition to the All Mexico movement during the war appeared to augur well for the territorial integrity of Mexico. That conclusion would be a misreading of the signs, however, for Gadsden's aversion was to the bestowing of United States citizenship on the mixed races of Mexico rather than to the acquisition of land. Since the Treaty of Guadalupe Hidalgo, Gadsden had advocated separating the Spanish and Anglo-Saxon races by a natural boundary in the mountain ranges south of the Rio Grande.

The determination of policy toward Mexico was affected by the importunings of various individuals and groups with special interests. Those interested in a southern transcontinental railroad professed to believe that the boundary as specified by the Treaty of Guadalupe Hidalgo left the best route in Mexican hands. These interests, coupled with disagreement within the joint commission charged with marking the boundary, had led to suspension of the effort to run the boundary from the Rio Grande to the Colorado River. United States policy on the Tehuantepec transit question was also becoming more complicated. Since P. A. Hargous of

New York had secured the Garay grant in 1849, the policy had been to protect it. A. G. Sloo's acquisition, on 5 February 1853, of a new grant covering the same route made necessary a reassessment of United States policy.[41]

How insistently advocates of manifest destiny pressed the White House to include territorial goals in its Mexican policy cannot be ascertained. Both the Cass and Buchanan elements within the party advocated acquisition of Mexican territory, and obviously if Pierce hoped to heal party rifts these elements had to receive a sympathetic hearing.[42] Doubtless there were also many personal ties which demanded presidential attention. For example, Jane McManus (Storms) Cazneau, who had decided views on Mexico and friends in high places, came to Washington at this time. Cazneau, who wrote for the leading expansionistic journals under the pen name of Cora Montgomery, had been a colonizer and land speculator in Texas during the 1830s and a leading crusader for the annexation of Texas. While on a secret mission to Mexico City for the State Department in 1847 she met and became friends with the future president, Brigadier General Franklin Pierce. In 1853 Jane and her husband, William L. Cazneau, moved to Washington, where her friendship with the new president and her speculatory interest in Mexico and Santo Domingo could be profitably combined.[43]

To complicate further Pierce's task, a crisis along the unmarked border between New Mexico and Chihuahua threatened to erupt into armed conflict. The crisis point was the Mesilla valley north of El Paso, where faulty language in the Treaty of Guadalupe Hidalgo left the ultimate disposition of the area uncertain. As settlers from the United States moved into the area, officials of both Chihuahua and New Mexico claimed it and threatened to seize control of it by force. The United States lessened tensions somewhat by removing New Mexico's belligerent territorial governor and suggesting that neither side try to exercise legal jurisdiction over the disputed region while diplomatic efforts were made to resolve its status.[44]

With the border crisis in mind and under the pressures noted above, instructions were formulated for Gadsden's mission in July 1853. Hoping to resolve a number of questions with a single stroke, Gadsden was directed to negotiate an adjustment of boundaries. Land could thus be acquired for railroad interests; the problems preventing the running of a boundary could be sidestepped; the question of the Mesilla valley could be settled favorably; claims against Mexico could be settled; and a territorial acquisition, even though it was not Cuba, would be popular in expansionist circles. Without specifying the amount of territory desired or the price to be paid, Secretary of State William L. Marcy instructed Gadsden to present the proposal as motivated only by Washington's desire to acquire control over the most suitable route for a transcontinental railroad.[45]

So concerned was Washington with a favorable conclusion of the boundary question that commercial and economic matters were secondary in Gadsden's instructions. The Tehuantepec transit question, which had been a source of diplomatic activity since 1848, was shelved. Washington no longer found it a simple task to pose as protector of private United States interests now that two of its citizens held conflicting grants. Authorization to adjust and promote commercial relations between the two countries appeared in the instructions almost as an afterthought.

Gadsden arrived in Mexico City in mid-August 1853 and within less than five months had signed a treaty which satisfied at least the minimum objectives of his mission. Once Santa Anna indicated a willingness to consider a new boundary treaty, Washington responded with detailed instructions to guide the negotiations. "Ample land south of the Gila River to facilitate the construction of a transcontinental railroad" now became the minimum demand. This minimum area, along with a release from claims for damages under article 11 of the Treaty of Guadalupe Hidalgo (which made the United States responsible for preventing Indian raids across the frontier) and abrogation of that article, was worth $15 million. More generous cessions of land were assessed accordingly until a cession providing for the most satisfactory and most natural boundary was valued at $50 million. The most natural boundary was defined in such a way as to give the United States all of Baja California, most of Coahuila and Nuevo Leon; about half of Tamaulipas, Chihuahua, and Sonora; and a small portion of Durango. Great stress was also placed on securing control of a port on the Gulf of California.[46]

The instructions as drawn up in Washington cautioned Gadsden to avoid complicating the negotiations with any matters other than the boundary, mutual claims settlement, and the release of the United States from the obligation to restrain Indian raids. Yet these instructions as delivered to him orally in Mexico City had been altered by the courier, Christopher L. Ward, to require a settlement of the Tehuantepec railroad question in a method favorable to the Hargous interests. Either knowingly or unwittingly a Hargous agent had been selected to carry unwritten instructions to Mexico, and he used this opportunity to further the interest of his principal.[47]

Gadsden, who had doubts about the veracity of the instruction as conveyed to him by Ward, reluctantly added the Tehuantepec grant to the list of items upon which he must secure Mexican agreement. Not content with relying on Santa Anna's greed and the desperate fiscal plight of the Mexican government, Gadsden used a number of techniques to insure the success of his proposals. Sympathetic appreciation of Mexico's problems and reasoned statements of the advantages of natural frontiers based on mountain barriers were coupled with only slightly veiled threats about the operation of the natural laws of manifest destiny.[48]

If Gadsden's heavy-handed essays in diplomacy were not enough to confirm the Mexicans' belief that their sovereignty was seriously threatened by the United States, the filibustering expedition of William Walker in Baja California dispelled any doubts. Walker, with the apparent connivance of local, state, and federal officials, fitted out an armed expedition in San Francisco and sailed to La Paz, Baja California, where he decreed the establishment of a sovereign republic of Baja California, to which Sonora was later added. The Mexican Foreign Ministry made the reasonable assumption that Walker's was an official expedition designed to give substance to Gadsden's threats.[49]

Gadsden was furious when he learned of Walker's expedition, believing that such enterprises, by arousing popular support for the Mexican government, would make his task more difficult. He called for efforts by United States consular and naval agents to prevent them.[50] Pierce agreed with Gadsden's assessment and on 18 January 1854, unaware that negotiations in Mexico were already complete, issued a proclamation exhorting his fellow citizens not to take part in filibustering and ordering procedures to prevent the departure of such expeditions.[51]

If he had felt strong enough Santa Anna might, as Gadsden feared, have refused to continue the negotiations for a new boundary treaty in the face of Walker's invasion. Instead, Santa Anna made three unsuccessful moves to strengthen his hand against the United States. He renewed his proposal for a comprehensive alliance with Spain[52] and simultaneously authorized his agents in Europe to contract for mercenary troops.[53] His third move was to inform the British minister to Mexico, Percy W. Doyle, that the United States was threatening war if Mexico did not agree immediately to sell half her territory. This was pictured as a preliminary step to total annexation, which would severely damage British commercial interests.

A strongly worded British statement of support for Mexico would probably have given pause to Gadsden, but none was forthcoming. Doyle, in reporting the request to London, said that he had tried to discourage Santa Anna, whose sincerity he doubted. Instead Doyle advised Santa Anna to avoid conflict with the United States and to put his government on firm ground financially.[54]

Santa Anna later characterized his treaty with the United States as a successful defense of Mexican territory, claiming that by selling a small section of useless territory he had prevented the United States from forcefully seizing the whole northern tier of states and territories.[55] While not discounting the difficulties of Santa Anna's position, it must be noted that he capitulated quickly to the pressures and that Gadsden was equally brisk in retreating to his minimal demands. On 29 November Gadsden formally presented his maximum territorial demand; on 3 December he agreed to limit the negotiations to only enough territory to facilitate the construction of the transcontinental railroad.[56] The Mexican foreign minister suggested the specific boundary line included in the treaty.[57]

The treaty, signed 30 December 1853, contained provisions of interest to the United States other than the change in boundaries. It released the United States from the obligations and responsibilities imposed by article 11 of the Treaty of Guadalupe Hidalgo. A claims commission was provided for and the United States agreed to assume all claims by its citizens against Mexico, including any made on behalf of the Hargous grant, "whose lawful existence Mexico does not recognize." The United States acquired the right of uninterrupted navigation of the Colorado River and the Gulf of California. For these favors the United States agreed to pay $20 million, $5 million of which would be retained to satisfy its claimants. The United States agreed to recognize land titles held by Mexicans in the ceded territory and to cooperate in suppressing filibustering expeditions.

Pierce was opposed to the provisions of the treaty providing compensation for the holders of the Hargous grant but decided to submit it to the Senate nevertheless. The treaty occasioned a battle of sectional and special interests in the Senate that lasted more than two months and produced a treaty little resembling that signed by Gadsden. The debate revealed numerous divisions within the Senate as each group suggested changes to benefit its interest. The result was the mutilation and apparent death of the treaty. Only after the Southern Commercial Convention meeting in Charleston had elicited strong southern and western support for the treaty was it revived and forced through the Senate on 25 April 1854. Opposition votes came mostly from northern antislavery and anti-Democratic senators.[58]

The Senate version of the treaty, the one finally ratified, was more limited than had been the one negotiated in Mexico. The amount of territory was reduced to the absolute minimum deemed essential for the railroad, and the payment was reduced from $20 million to $10 million. The claims settlement was eliminated, as was the agreement to act against filibustering. Finally, provisions were inserted specifically recognizing Sloo's Tehuantepec grant, confirming the rights of the United States and its citizens to use the transit route, and giving the United States power to intervene to protect the route.[59]

While few if any of the parties involved, either Mexican or Yankee, were satisfied with the Senate version, all reluctantly accepted it. Only Pierce's fear that delay in achieving a boundary settlement might result in war induced him to accept the changes. Gadsden returned to Mexico City hoping the altered agreement would be rejected by Santa Anna. Santa Anna and his foreign minister, Manuel Díez de Bonilla, were dissatisfied with the failure to settle claims and described the provision allowing the United States to provide protection for Tehuantepec transit route as a "surrender of nationality."[60] But Santa Anna's need for money, more pressing now in the face of the spreading Ayutla Revolution, was sufficiently strong to overcome any doubts. The ratifications were exchanged in Washington on 30 June 1854.

During the months between the signing and the ratification of the treaty, France and Great Britain reversed their earlier attitudes. When Santa Anna had appealed for aid against probable United States aggression during his first months in office, the French minister to Mexico, Alphonse Dano, had responded in sympathetic but noncommittal terms, while the British minister could only advise him to put his finances in order and avoid war. During the intervening months the French minister had become convinced that nothing could be gained by supporting Santa Anna and his monarchial schemes, while the British minister saw the Senate's version of the treaty as a threat to British interests.[61]

The activities of the Frenchman Count Raousset de Boulbon during early 1854 helped to change Dano's position. Dano learned that the nobleman was organizing Frenchmen in California to seize Sonora and was convinced that the result would be annexation by the United States. Aware that many residents of northwestern Mexico, including numerous Frenchmen, favored annexation, he welcomed the provision of the original treaty for the mutual suppression of filibustering. In an attempt to undermine Raousset's project, letters from Dano and from the French foreign minister warning French citizens against filibustering were published in the newspapers of San Francisco and various Mexican cities. When these efforts to halt Raousset's activities failed, Dano found himself in the embarrassing position of supporting the sale of territory in the hope that this would prevent his fellow countrymen from delivering even larger chunks of Mexico to the United States. Diplomatically handcuffed by his efforts to limit the damage to French interests resulting from Raousset's filibustering, Dano could only hope that the money from the treaty would strengthen Santa Anna against the Ayutla rebels.[62]

The British minister, on the other hand, encouraged Santa Anna to reject the altered treaty without committing Britain to assist Mexico in any way. The changes which most disturbed him were those recognizing the Sloo grant and giving the United States power to intervene in the isthmian region. When he urged resistance to such provisions, Santa Anna agreed to reject the altered treaty if Doyle would allow Mexico to suspend payments to British creditors and would urge the same policy on France and Spain. Santa Anna had gone to the heart of the matter and had called Doyle's hand. He had to have money and the only other readily available source was the customs receipts assigned to pay Mexico's foreign debts.[63]

While the relationship of the Gadsden Treaty to Mexican revolutionary activity is obvious, its impact is difficult to assess. Opposition to Santa Anna and efforts to organize resistance among political and commercial circles predated Gadsden's arrival in Mexico. By the time the negotiations had reached a serious stage even the French minister realized that the forces gathering around Alvarez in Guerrero constituted a major challenge to Santa Anna. Santa Anna's decision, on 17 December 1853, to invest himself with unlimited powers for an indefinite period served to galvanize the opposition. He precipitated matters by attempting to send a loyal regiment to Acapulco. This move provoked a clash with Alvarez forces on 21 January 1854, apparently before the rebels had learned of the treaty signed with the United States.[64]

Once the agreement became known it became an additional item in the rebels' arsenal of charges against Santa Anna. When news of the treaty reached New Orleans the liberal exiles there protested and condemned Santa Anna for having entered into it.[65] In the preamble to the Plan of Ayutla, issued on 1 March while the fate of the treaty in the United States was still uncertain, Santa Anna was denounced on many counts, including his failure to safeguard the integrity of the nation.[66] The sale of territory, which Santa Anna rationalized as essential for the funds necessary to put down the expected liberal revolt, doubtless weakened his public image, strengthened the resolve of the rebels, and turned many of the responsible conservatives against him.

After the exchange of ratifications on 30 June 1854, Gadsden's relations with the Santa Anna government deteriorated rapidly. Problems left unresolved by the treaty fed the ill will already existing on both sides. Gadsden saw the rescue of Mexico from Catholicism and European monarchial influence as his essential task. To prevent Santa Anna's close ties with European powers from being converted into a protectorate, Gadsden recommended naval or military actions to insure a liberal victory. The $3 million still due Mexico under the recent treaty must be denied to Santa Anna at all cost, Gadsden felt, since he would only use it to reinforce his absolutist regime.[67]

Gadsden assumed such an arrogant and hostile attitude in pushing his country-men's claims that on 2 October 1854, Díez de Bonilla directed the Mexican minister in Washington to request his recall.[68] This request resulted in a situation with few parallels in the annals of diplomatic history. Gadsden, informed by Washington of the request, addressed an insulting note to the Mexican foreign minister suspending relations until the request had been withdrawn and suitable apologies made. To the dismay of Díez de Bonilla, Washington refused to recall Gadsden, and much to the disgust of Gadsden, Díez de Bonilla refused to recognize the suspension of relations and continued to address notes to "Señor Gadsden" at the United States legation. Two subsequent requests for Gadsden's recall were also unproductive.[69]

Though Gadsden remained at his post, his effectiveness as a diplomatic agent had been destroyed. His communications both with Mexican officials and with Washington increasingly assumed an argumentative tone and a rambling, some-times incoherent character. In what appear as paranoiac rantings, Gadsden por-trayed himself as being hounded and persecuted by the countless forces of evil.[70] But while fighting his quixotic battles with evil he followed a course of action friendly to the Ayutla rebels. As their strength waxed, he became vocal in praise of them and in demands that the United States actively support them. According to the British minister in Mexico, Gadsden did not limit his proliberal stance to recommendations to Washington but converted the United States legation into an intelligence center for the rebels and maintained close ties with insurgent elements throughout Mexico.[71]

The failure of the Santa Anna government to expel the troublesome Gadsden is understandable, if not justifiable: the government's position was precarious. Washington's refusal to recall him, however, is neither justifiable nor readily understandable. Leaving Gadsden at his post may have been seen as a means of expressing official disapproval of the Santa Anna regime, yet one is hesitant to credit Secretary of State William L. Marcy with such a blunt and heavy-handed policy. The real reason may have been, as Marcy himself hinted later to a liberal Mexican minister, that Gadsden had too many politically powerful friends to be easily dismissed.[72]

Despite the anomalies of Gadsden's position, there were developments of commercial interest during the closing months of the Santa Anna administration. Although little attention was devoted to the deteriorating commercial situation by the legation, the United States consul in Veracruz was not reticent in bringing the situation to the attention of Washington. When asked in 1854 to supply Washing-ton with a copy of the existing Mexican tariff, John T. Pickett responded that such a document would be useless since new laws affecting the operation of customs-houses were being issued almost daily and special rates and exemptions were being granted or sold with equal frequency to friends of the government.[73]

The commercial situation had worsened steadily since Santa Anna's return in April 1853. First, the low Ceballos tarriff issued in January 1853 had been replaced by a new schedule with prohibitively high duties on most imports. Then a decree of 30 January 1854 placed a 50 percent duty on imported goods when their origin was different from the flag of the vessel on which they were imported. This decree also sought to spur the creation of a Mexican merchant fleet by imposing onerous port and tonnage duties on foreign-flag vessels. Such provisions were a hard blow to the reexport trade of the United States. The French also found the measure "a terrible blow to all commercial interests."[74]

The cumulative effect of high tariffs, high and numerous taxes, special privileges, and arbitrary practices in enforcing revenue measures was disastrous for United States commerce. Pickett reported that all foreign trade was declining in Veracruz, especially that of his country. The only exception was trade coming in from New Orleans, which had increased recently owing to the establishment of a biweekly line of mail steamers. Franklin Chase, United States consul in Tampico, reported a similar depression in commercial circles. Even the Mexican press offered carefully worded criticism of foreign-trade measures which had ruinous consequences for internal trade and prosperity.[75] United States citizens with commercial interests in Mexico also voiced their unhappiness with Santa Anna's commercial policy in letters to the Department of State.[76] Newspapers in the United States called for steps to safeguard national commercial interests, and southern commercial conventions of 1854 and 1855 recommended a new commercial treaty with Mexico to protect and promote United States export trade.[77]

Despite the need for action and the increasing willingness of the Santa Anna government to make any arrangements which might strengthen its position, Gadsden made no serious effort to negotiate on commercial matters. Instead, he appears to have determined that his best course would be to press for the speedy fall of Santa Anna and reserve all serious negotiation for the more amenable liberal government to follow. He used the Crimean War as a vehicle to pressure Mexico. Expressing sympathy for Russia, he suggested an alliance with Mexico against the allied powers, and when this was rejected, he indicated that if the war should reach America the United States would immediately occupy Mexico's frontier regions.[78] He badgered Mexico with demands for settlement of claims and for new cessions of territory. When Mexico protested Walker's filibustering in Baja California, Gadsden responded that in a democracy such expeditions were often true reflections of public opinion which would eventually determine policy. The only solution, Gadsden hinted, was to sell the territory while Mexico still held legal title to it.[79]

Gadsden's attitude and the increasingly frequent filibustering expeditions convinced European representatives in Mexico that the United States was embarking on a major drive for expansion. While the British and Spanish ministers expressed concern that these activities would damage their interests, the French minister recommended more positive action. The Anglo-French alliance, "so powerful in the Old World" must be extended to halt the expansion of the United States. De

Gabriac, the new French minister, feared that the United States might, as Gadsden had threatened, join Russia in an aggressive alliance. The French consul at Mazatlán believed that through filibusterers the United States government was seeking to gain possession of the wheat-producing regions of Mexico, knowing that without these an independent existence for Mexico would be impossible. Stressing the importance of trade with Mexico to France's internal economy, he called for action to prevent Mexican commerce from falling into hands of the Yankees, "the modern pirates of the New World."[80]

Mexico used French fears of losing profitable trade relations to reinforce its pleas for aid. Díez de Bonilla stressed that the United States's insatiable drive for control of land and natural resources would not stop until it controlled all the continent north of Panama. Then, Díez de Bonilla warned, the United States would dominate the entire hemisphere, would control all the isthmian trade routes with Asia, and could deny Europe access to the markets of America. The United States could then easily foment socialist and anarchistic movements in Europe. Díez de Bonilla saw an analogy to the Eastern Question: Mexico was the Ottoman Empire of the Western Hemisphere, the United States its Russia, and only France could insure the balance of power in the West as in the East.[81]

The French were convinced, however, that their interests could not be served by supporting Santa Anna's continuation in power. Almost without exception, de Gabriac's despatches, from March to August 1855, included statements on the hopelessness of the situation under Santa Anna. Nevertheless, he was fully alive to the potential threat posed by the United States, and in a despatch of 6 July 1855 he recognized the United States as another Russia, although still relatively weak, which must be prevented from further extending its power.

> Today twelve to fourteen thousand Frenchmen live in Mexico and our general commerce increases annually. . . . Once in the power of the Yankees, the profits from the mines of this vast territory will serve to finance production of those factories whose numbers increase as if by magic in the United States. On taking Cuba, its [the United States's] only view is to close the Gulf of Mexico and convert it into a new Black Sea. Then she can cause revolutions in Europe by merely raising or lowering tariffs.[82]

Abandoned by the European powers and simultaneously facing bankruptcy and defeat by the rebels, Santa Anna threw himself at Gadsden's feet. In July 1855 Díez de Bonilla informed Gadsden that all requests for his recall were being withdrawn and Mexico was prepared to negotiate on any question desired by the United States minister, including the sale of territory. But, having weakened Santa Anna's position, Gadsden had no desire to strengthen it now by placing money in his hands. While he allowed Díez de Bonilla to continue to present proposals for the sale of territory until the eve of Santa Anna's decision to flee abroad on 9 August 1855, Gadsden informed Washington that under no circumstances would he agree to such a proposal.[83] In fact, de Gabriac reported in July that Gadsden had withdrawn from all relations with Santa Anna, leaving his secretary and nephew to answer correspondence from the Foreign Ministry.[84]

With the collapse of the Santa Anna government conservative and military elements attempted to forestall a complete liberal victory by endorsing the Plan of Ayutla and installing their own candidate, the conservative general Martín Carrera, as president.[85] As the European powers hastened to recognize the government of Carrera, Gadsden rejected in an insulting fashion an invitation to join the diplomatic corps in this act.[86] Instead, he sat back and enjoyed the fruits of his months of hostility toward Santa Anna. The liberal press gave prominence to accounts of how he had broken relations with Santa Anna and had refused to recognize Carrera.[87] Meanwhile rumors spread, unchecked by Gadsden, that while maintaining nominal relations with Santa Anna, he had served as intermediary to get $200,000 of official United States funds into the hands of the rebels.

The French minister was certain that Gadsden was actively working as an ally of the *puros* to insure the presidency for Juan Alvarez. He reported on 5 September 1855 that irrefutable evidence proved the full complicity of the United States legation in efforts to prevent any compromise in the selection of an interim president. He charged that John S. Cripps, secretary of the legation, was acting as recruiting agent for the liberals among Carrera's troops in Mexico City. Soldiers so subverted appeared at night at a house rented by the legation, where they surrendered their arms to a *puro* general and in return were given ten pesos furnished by Gadsden. The arms secured in this manner, and others purchased by Gadsden through an agent, were turned over to forces loyal to Alvarez.[88] Although no official United States or Mexican documents were found to substantiate the French diplomat's charges, Valentín Gómez Farías, the *puro* elder statesman, seemed to confirm the use of official United States funds to support the Ayutla rebels in a letter to Alvarez.[89] The failure of the Mexican newspapers to take note of de Gabriac's charges or to publish his documentary proof could indicate that they believed the charges were groundless and the proof fabricated. Their inaction could equally well signify, and this seems more likely, that they knew the charges were valid and the proof authentic, and were merely trying to avoid embarrassing the victorious rebels.

Gadsden continued to follow an independent course after the revolutionary conclave in Cuernavaca elected Alvarez as provisional president on 4 October 1855. Upon the establishment of the new government, the diplomatic corps called a meeting to seek a common policy on recognition of a government not located in the traditional capital. Gadsden's response to this maneuver was an ill-tempered and nearly incoherent note to the dean of the diplomatic corps in which he made it clear that he would not cooperate with the diplomatic corps and gave as a reason the traditional United States policy of avoiding entangling alliances. The French minister could not decide if the insulting tone of Gadsden's note had been intentional or merely the result of the author's well-known practice of being inebriated by midafternoon each day.[90]

After refusing to cooperate with the diplomatic corps, and without informing them of his intentions, Gadsden departed immediately for Cuernavaca, where on 10 October 1855 he became the first foreign diplomat to recognize the Alvarez government. By this course of action he apparently sought to create the best possible impression in the eyes of Mexico's new rulers while making it more difficult for European members of the diplomatic corps to use recognition to extract commitments from the new government. At the ceremony Gadsden delivered an address so filled with sympathy for Mexico that it embarrassed even the liberal press. He reassured his hosts that the recent filibustering incursions were the natural consequences of Santa Anna's hostile policy toward the United States and of his inability to control the frontier region.[91]

The process of creating a liberal government in the wake of Santa Anna's collapse was complicated not only by counterrevolutionary plots and personal rivalries and ideological schisms among the victorious liberals, but also by reports of an attempt to establish a protectorate over Mexico. The idea of a benevolent protectorate over Mexico had been in the air for years; the foreign ministers in Mexico, including Gadsden, had routinely included in their despatches discussions of the feasibility and desirability of such an arrangement. Since the beginning of the Ayutla Revolution there had been constant rumors of one or another power preparing to establish such a protectorate.[92]

A public crisis erupted on the question when the Mexico City press, led by the French-language *Trait d'Union* on 19 September 1855, published two treaties which it claimed had either already been signed or would soon be signed by the liberals and Gadsden. The treaties, as given by *Trait d'Union,* were in the form of defensive and offensive alliances and provided for the United States to support a Mexican government established by mutual agreement, to renounce all designs on Mexican territory, to guarantee Mexico's territorial integrity against all threats, to prevent United States citizens from immigrating to Mexico, to lend Mexico $30 million secured by the hypothecation of church property in Mexico (with or without the consent of the clergy), and to establish in Mexico a loan bank *(banco de avío)* with a fund of $100 million to be used for projects to develop mining, agriculture, and transportation. A final provision of the treaties would give the United States control over Mexican commercial policy—Mexican tariff rates would be established by mutual agreement, the United States could determine the amount of protection required for Mexican industries, and all internal customs and monopolies would be prohibited.

Despite the obvious attractiveness for the liberals of the program of security and development as outlined in the treaties, they were denounced immediately by the liberal press, by the liberal leadership, and by Gadsden as the work of counterrevolutionary enemies. "It is better to perish, to have our fields destroyed and our cities leveled than to suffer such a humiliation," editorialized *El Heraldo.*[93] Alvarez, acting also in the name of Comonfort, vehemently denied that there were any liberals who would consider such a scheme.[94] Miguel Lerdo, who had been mentioned prominently as a supporter of the protectorate plan, labeled as "vile calumniators" those who would attribute such desires to him. Gadsden, in a letter to *El Monitor Republicano,* expressed sympathy for the methods and objectives of the rebels but denied that he had ever discussed the possibility of a protectorate with any of their leaders. The only suggestions he had received for a protectorate, Gadsden asserted, came from prominent conservatives associated with the previous regime.[95]

The private reactions of the liberals to the rumored treaties did not always match their public denials. The initial reaction of Valentín Gómez Farías was one of cautious interest. Several days before the treaties appeared in the press, Gómez Farías informed Alvarez that such a proposal had been received. In forwarding the proposition Gómez Farías carefully weighed its pros and cons. While he was clearly alert to the dangers of a trap, he was intrigued by the benefits of such a relationship. Aware that some liberals would see the proposal as aimed merely at absorption of Mexico, Gómez Farías stressed that the territorial integrity and political sovereignty of Mexico appeared to be guaranteed by the proposal. He could not disguise his pleasure at the prospects of a development bank, of modern transportation facilities, and of thousands of European immigrants which the proposal promised. His private assessment of the idea suggests that Gómez Farías believed, or was aware, that Alvarez and other liberals were actively pursuing a policy to secure a protected status and feared premature publicity would hinder their efforts.[96]

Alvarez's public response to the proposed treaties, as we have seen, was immediate, indignant, and completely negative. In the portion of a letter obviously intended for publication, Alvarez assumed an insulting tone in rebuking Gómez Farías for having ever doubted the total opposition of all responsible liberals to any protectorate scheme. The proposal was, he charged, nothing more than a conservative attempt to discredit the Ayutla Revolution and its leaders. In a more private portion of the letter, Alvarez apologized, indicating that the vehement language was necessary to dispel any doubts from the public mind.[97] It is not clear whether Alvarez's concern reflected his opposition to a protectorate or a fear that public knowledge of his involvement in such a project would undermine public confidence and rob the liberals of victory.

The origin of the protectorate proposition negates the liberals' charge that the proposal was merely groundless rumors spread by conservatives to discredit liberal leadership. Manuel Robles Pezuela, who returned to Veracruz in early September from exile in New York, where he had served as an agent for the Ayutla rebels, brought with him a protectorate proposal very similar to that published a few weeks later. According to Robles, he had been contacted in New York by unnamed but high officials proposing that the United States assist in overthrowing Santa Anna by making a loan of $500,000 to the rebels and by seizing Veracruz. Once a new liberal government was established an offensive and defensive alliance would be formed on the basis of the following United States commitments: to respect Mexico's territorial integrity; to suppress and punish all filibustering efforts; to provide funds necessary to maintain the Mexican government until its finances could be reorganized; to protect the Mexican government from all enemies, foreign or domestic; and to respect property rights in Mexico, particularly those of the clergy. While it would not be surprising for United States officials to be so poorly informed that they would try to entice Mexican liberals with a promise of protection for clerical property, the inclusion of such a proposal was more likely the work of Robles Pezuela. An opportunist, he abandoned the liberal banner when the *puros* later gained control of the government, and still later he tried to place himself at the head of a conservative government. As the only compensation for its assistance, the United States would require Mexico to admit the European immigrants whose presence in the United States threatened to provoke civil strife. This project, modified to give the United States broader powers over the Mexican government and to include two features dear to the hearts of liberals, a development bank and a move against church property, appears to have been the basis for the proposed treaties published later.

While definite conclusions about the involvement of the United States government or its officials in the protectorate scheme cannot be drawn, some interesting speculations can be made. Had Gadsden served to channel Yankee funds to the liberals as believed by the French minister and by Gómez Farías? If he did perform such a function, what was source of the funds? Were they from secret official accounts or from private parties? In either case the money could have been in the form of a down payment for a protectorate. Gadsden approached several liberal leaders in late August and early September in an attempt to find one who would be amenable to direction from Washington. He was prepared to assist such an individual in securing the Mexican presidency.[98] These contacts may have resulted from Gadsden's propensity to take steps that were both unorthodox and unauthorized, or they may merely represent his aversion to orthodox procedures.

The conduct of John Pickett, United States consul at Veracruz, during the spring and summer of 1855 raises the probability that he was also involved in some secret and perhaps extraofficial project. On 4 March he informed Washington that he was returning to the United States for "a brief period" of leave but would not be visiting Washington. On 7 July, however, he was in Washington, where he borrowed from State Department files the extensive consular report on his country's commercial interests in Veracruz that he had submitted in March 1854. He then traveled to New York, where he discussed Mexican affairs with "important" but unnamed individuals before returning to Veracruz in early August.[99] Since Pickett had secured the consular post so as to be of service to the Sloo interests in Tehuantepec,[100] one is led to suspect that among the people he consulted in New York was the rebel agent Robles Pezuela.

Regardless of whether the proposed treaties had really represented an official United States offer, for several weeks the idea contained in them had been real in the minds of key figures in Mexico City. The liberals were fascinated by the promise of protection and assistance for development; Gadsden had seen in the treaties an opportunity to check European threats to the United States's natural right to hegemony over Mexico; the French minister de Gabriac considered the treaties a move inimical to French interests.

Alexis de Gabriac saw in everything that happened after the fall of Santa Anna sure signs of the Yankee hand assisted by a sympathetic attitude on the part of the British. The lowering of tariffs was thought more advantageous for British commercial interests than for those of France. He charged that the reduction would endanger the French debt by reducing the customs receipts, which were assigned to service it, ignoring the fact that the much larger British debts were also serviced from the same source. The motivating force behind the tariff reductions, in his view, was a desire to force Mexico to turn to the United States for credit, which would only be made available in return for territory. The proposed treaties were proof that disaster awaited European interests in Mexico; under the umbrella of a protectorate Mexico would refuse to pay its European creditors, and the United States would refuse to allow European powers to use coercive measures against Mexico.[101] De Gabriac thus foresaw a perverted version of the Roosevelt corollary.

Gadsden had assumed a proliberal stance during the revolution, hoping that once the liberals were in power they would be receptive to United States influences, political and economic. He spoke confidently of "democratizing" Mexico through his influence on Alvarez. Even without a formal protectorate democratization would counter efforts to bring about "Europeanization of Mexico."[102] In apparent confirmation of Gadsden's assessment of his future influence, he was for several weeks the darling of the liberal press and liberal politicians displayed a gratifying desire for his advice. Alvarez filled his cabinet with men who were admirers of the United States—Juárez, Ocampo, Prieto, and Comonfort.[103] Comonfort publicly stated that their recent success was heavily dependent on "economic, ideological, and political assistance from the United States." This statement and Santa Anna's parting manifesto blaming the United States for his downfall only served to reinforce the view that Yankee aid had been essential to the liberal victory.[104]

The honeymoon between Gadsden and the new liberal government did not last long, despite its auspicious beginning. The first sour note arose over the $3 million withheld from the amount due under the Gadsden Treaty until the new boundaries had been formally established. Santa Anna had made several attempts to secure these funds directly and finally in desperation had sold drafts on these funds to speculators at considerable discount.[105] Upon assuming the presidency Alvarez asserted that Santa Anna's drafts were invalid and demanded that, since the United States had already occupied the land in question in violation of the treaty, the $3 million should be immediately paid directly to Mexico.[106] Although Gadsden initially supported the Mexican demand, by December 1855 he requested that the funds be withheld indefinitely from both the speculators and the government. This course, he argued, would provide him with a lever to force the new government to take a more responsive attitude toward his country's demands.

The dispute over the $3 million convinced Gadsden that the liberal government could be influenced only by intimidation or bribery.[107] When Comonfort replaced Alvarez as acting president, 8 December 1855, Gadsden's relations cooled even more with his hosts. Comonfort, a *moderado,* was less inclined to subordinate his ambitions to the dictates of the Yankee minister. Within a few months Gadsden was denouncing Comonfort in terms comparable to those used earlier against Santa Anna—Comonfort was a usurper, a dictator, a traitor to the goals of Ayutla, and a man whose services were available to the highest bidder.[108]

Gadsden's task of maintaining amicable relations was complicated by renewed filibustering during 1855–56. The most difficult to handle was the expedition led by Jean Napoleon Zerman, another French exile. Zerman, purporting to be an agent of Alvarez and the Ayutla Revolution, sailed from San Francisco in October 1855, apparently unaware of Santa Anna's fall. Zerman and his entire party were captured at La Paz, Baja California. In this case Gadsden had denounced the filibusterers to Santa Anna as international outlaws on 5 July 1855, apparently in the belief that they were serving French interests. In November both Gadsden and de Gabriac warned Alvarez that Zerman was leading a piratical raid.[109] Soon after the captives reached Mexico City in March 1856, however, Gadsden attempted to secure their release as United States citizens who had been misled by Mexican agents.[110]

Gadsden's animosity toward Comonfort was reciprocated, and on 3 May 1856 Manuel Robles Pezuela, now the Mexican minister in Washington, requested Gadsden's recall. The request made the same complaints which Santa Anna had lodged the previous year: Gadsden's hostile attitude toward Mexican officials, his insistence upon maintaining relations with *caciques* who refused to recognize the central government, and his frequent indiscreet public statements. Marcy referred to the delicacy of removing so powerful a political figure as Gadsden and requested Robles to put his reasons in a formal note to be presented to Pierce. Robles correctly surmised that no final decision would be made until after the Democratic convention, scheduled to meet in Cincinnati in early June.[111] On 30 June Gadsden was informed that he would be relieved as soon as a successor could be chosen.[112]

Gadsden remained at his post until October 1856, and while his relations with his host government were strained, there were economic developments of interest. Of prime importance for Mexico and for speculators and entrepreneurs from the United States was the decision to retain the Development Ministry (Fomento) and to honor most of the contracts made since its creation in April 1853. Although the immediate reaction of the liberals to the fall of Santa Anna had been to destroy every vestige of the late dictatorship, a successful campaign was conducted in the newspapers to save Fomento and to defend its *oficial mayor,* Miguel Lerdo, for having served under Santa Anna.[113] The ministry was saved and, although Congress reviewed closely all Fomento activity, most of the measures for material improvements were confirmed—including several railroad concessions held by Yankees.[114]

In fact, private United States interests in development projects appeared to have suffered little during the revolution or at the hands of the victorious liberals later. Hostilities in the vicinity of Mexico City were so limited that work on the telegraph lines being built to Cuernavaca and Guadalajara by William G. Stewart continued on schedule, as did the railroad to Villa Guadalupe, in which numerous Yankee interests were involved. Work on the railroad had progressed so far that on 22 July 1855, only weeks before the fall of Santa Anna, Gadsden had joined the *caudillo* in dedicating a completed portion of the road.[115]

Once in power the liberals quickly removed Santa Anna's harsh measures toward foreign economic interests. New measures to stimulate the economy and to encourage foreign participation were adopted. Restrictions which discouraged both the foreign immigrant and entrepreneur were lifted. In addition to confirming most of the previous administration's developmental contracts, new contracts for railroads, gas lighting, river navigation, and the like were let. Where formerly most of such contracts were given to individuals representing British capital, now preference seemed to be given to projects involving Yankee capital.

With considerable encouragement from Washington, Gadsden made a token effort to promote United States commercial interests. He suggested a frontier reciprocity agreement similar to that signed in 1854 for the Canadian frontier. He also unsuccessfully tried to open the Mexican market to tobacco from the United States. Various efforts to interest Mexico in a new commercial treaty to replace the one signed in 1831 were also unfruitful.[116] Gadsden's lackadaisical pursuit of his objectives was probably more responsible for his failures than any resistance on the part of the Mexicans.

In the effort to negotiate a postal treaty Gadsden's efforts almost succeeded despite his apparent lack of zeal. Progress here resulted from the activity of a United States citizen, Carlos Butterfield, one of the more interesting Yankees involved in Reforma Mexico and among its most consistent and supportive foreign friends during the next decade. His Mexican connections were of long standing. Butterfield, a native of upstate New York and a military academy graduate, had served for four years as an engineer with the Spanish army in Cuba before coming to Mexico in the mid-1840s, where he was commissioned as colonel and served as an aide to Santa Anna. Released from Mexican service during the war with his homeland, Butterfield was appointed *alcalde* of Veracruz by the invading force. After the war he remained in Mexico, where he resumed his military career, accepted several diplomatic and financial assignments for subsequent administrations, served as advisor and courier for United States ministers, and acquired a partnership interest in an import-export firm. Although he appears never to have sought to benefit from it, he had also acquired Mexican citizenship by a law of 30 January 1854 which bestowed Mexican nationality on all foreigners holding commissions in the Mexican army. By the time he began supplying arms to the Ayutla rebels in late 1854, Butterfield was well established and respected in both the liberal and conservative camps.[117]

After their victory over Santa Anna, Butterfield used his connections within the liberal camp to promote a project for a mail-steamer service between the Gulf ports of Mexico and the United States. His project called for a binational line of steamers providing weekly service between Veracruz and New Orleans with stops at the lesser ports of both countries. The line would be subsidized by both governments and its position would be guaranteed in a postal treaty. Using his influence both in the United States legation and in Mexican governmental circles, Butterfield pushed his object to the verge of success. The project had already cleared Fomento, Treasury, Post Office, and Foreign Affairs when the death of Luis de la Rosa, the foreign minister, prevented the signing of the necessary treaty. The new foreign minister, Juan Antonio de la Fuente, refused to sign the treaty or to renew negotiations with Gadsden, whose successor had already been named.[118]

Gadsden closed out his ministership with an action which caused a sensation in Mexico. On 8 September 1856 a ceremony was held honoring the memory of those Mexicans killed in the Battle of Molino del Rey during the war with the United States. Gadsden attended the ceremony in an apparent effort to demonstrate the friendship of the United States for the Mexican people. Had the gesture been made a year earlier when the liberals, fresh from their victory over Santa Anna, were still appreciative of the minister's efforts to aid them, it might have produced positive results; now it appeared only as a tactless attempt to appeal to the Mexican people over the head of their government.[119]

The arrival of John Forsyth as Gadsden's successor in October 1856 marked the end of Gadsden's three-year ministry to Mexico. Little of economic importance had been accomplished on the diplomatic front during this period, despite the announcement of a vigorous policy of commercial expansion in Washington and a receptiveness in Mexico after August 1855 toward closer economic ties with the United States. Much of responsibility for this failure rests with Gadsden. Despite his long association with the southern commercial conventions and his espousal of economic independence and commercial expansion for the South, Gadsden lacked both an understanding of and an interest in economic and commercial objectives. He saw his role in Mexico largely in political terms—to thwart the sinister plans of European powers to deny the United States its rightful sphere of influence. His concern with political ascendancy made it impossible for him to maintain harmonious relations with the liberals, who were basically pro–United States. Gadsden apparently expected to be treated as a proconsul, while the liberals were, for good historical reasons, very sensitive to undue Yankee political influence. His effectiveness was also hampered by a marked disdain for Mexicans, which was repeatedly voiced in his despatches to Washington and which was probably very visible to Mexicans.[120]

In contrast to the diplomatic failures, private United States citizens were active and successful in cultivating valuable contacts within the liberal camp. The liberals themselves believed that their victory over Santa Anna had been aided by the United States. They had introduced a number of measures of immediate or potential economic interest to the United States and its citizens: lower tariffs, removal of restrictive measures, general encouragement of foreign participation in the Mexican economy, and measures to force the sale of clerical property. Among the liberals there existed a reservoir of goodwill toward the United States and a desire for closer nonpolitical ties. This potentially profitable situation was not exploited by the United States because of Gadsden's limitations as a diplomat and Washington's concern with other issues, both foreign and domestic, which were deemed to be of greater significance.

3
Mexican Liberals' Alternative:
The Montes-Forsyth Treaties, 1855–1857

Despite the adverse public reaction in 1855 to the protectorate idea, sentiment for such an arrangement continued to grow among Mexican liberals. This trend resulted from a number of problems that blocked their dreams of utopia. The radical reforms had not produced the anticipated results, internal peace and order had not been achieved, and reform measures provoked new rebellions that kept the government on the verge of financial collapse. Mexico's financial distress also produced difficulties with her European creditors. Creditor countries, particularly France and Spain, opposed the reform programs and felt increasingly inclined to intervene in Mexico on behalf both of their citizens and of conservative political elements with whose views they sympathized. In this setting Mexican liberals and their Yankee friends sought to save Mexico, keep the reform program alive, and promote the United States's economic and political interests by making Mexico an economic protectorate of its northern neighbor. This growing willingness to see Yankee economic ascendancy spread over their country cut across *puro-moderado* factional lines. Extreme *puros,* such as Miguel Lerdo and José Mata, who placed economic development above all else, looked upon the United States as model and patron without reference to the course of events; the less extreme *puros* and *moderados* found themselves facing the alternative of economic tutelage or economic chaos and social and political collapse.

The liberal victory over Santa Anna in August 1855 failed to produce internal peace. There was no decisive military defeat of the conservative forces; their leader had merely abandoned them. While the leaderless conservatives faltered badly, losing control of the government, their social and economic power was not seriously weakened. In an attempt to forestall a complete liberal victory and to prevent Juan Alvarez and the lower-class elements he represented from assuming national power, conservatives, aided by numerous *moderados,* created what they hoped would be a transitional government in Mexico City in the weeks following Santa Anna's fall. Selecting the governor of the valley of Mexico, conservative general Martín Carrera, as interim president, they sought to negotiate a settlement with the Ayutla rebels which would exclude the more radical elements from power.[1] Liberal rejection of this conservative attempt to coopt themselves into the ranks of the rebels prevented any compromise.

The failure either to defeat or to reach a compromise with the conservatives seriously endangered the success of the liberal reform program. Each new measure became the occasion for conservative *pronunciamientos* against the government. Ley Juárez (Juárez Law) of November 1855, restricting military and ecclesiastical *fueros,* and Ley Lerdo (Lerdo Law) of June 1856, divesting the church of its property, produced several such rebellions. Puebla became the center of a series of church-military-conservative uprisings against the liberal government.

Continuing dissension within revolutionary ranks further complicated matters. In addition to the clash of ambitions among the various revolutionary chieftains, the groups who supported the revolution often disagreed on objectives and methods. The *puros* dominated the early phases, electing Alvarez as interim president and filling most of the cabinet posts. Comonfort's replacement of Alvarez in December 1855 was a partial victory for more moderate elements. Yet the reformers continued to dominate the government through most of 1856 and were able to direct developments in the constitutional congress which opened in February 1856.[2]

Foreign affairs offered the liberals little encouragement. Relations with Europe's big three, Great Britain, France, and Spain, were particularly troubled by the new government's inability to protect the lives and property of their subjects and to meet its obligations to the holders of Mexico's foreign debt. For these tasks internal peace and a solvent treasury, two conditions lacking in Mexico, were essential.

Relations with Great Britain were the most important. Not only was Britain the superpower of the era, but its subjects dominated Mexico's foreign trade and held most of the external debt. Yet the British were also the easiest with which to deal since their objectives were more economic than political. Britain supplied about half of Mexico's imports and accounted for as much as 90 percent of its exports. British subjects also held from two-thirds to three-fourths of Mexico's foreign indebtedness.[3] Freedom and protection for merchants and regular payments to bondholders were the major British concerns. Since the interests of merchants and bondholders often clashed—merchants profited from low tariffs while the bondholders, whose payments were frequently tied directly to customs revenues, benefited from high tariffs—British diplomats tended to pursue a cautious policy in Mexico.

British diplomats did not hesitate, however, to defend British interests when these were clearly jeopardized. They made vigorous protests when conservative revolts in Puebla threatened either to cut the flow of goods from Veracruz or to force the importers to pay double duties, first to the liberals in Veracruz and then to the conservative rebels in Puebla.[4] The expulsion by the liberal governor of Jalisco in early 1856 of Eustaquio Barron, a long-established British merchant, banker, consul at Tepic, and notorious smuggler, on the charge of promoting a revolt against state authorities caused a suspension of relations and almost led to hostilities before Mexico apologized and agreed to pay an indemnity.[5]

Mexican relations with Spain were troubled by longstanding hostilities and outbreaks of popular anti-Spanish sentiment. The failure of Mexico to fulfill the terms of a claims convention caused threats of blockade and invasion from Cuba.

A series of attacks on individual Spaniards and their property resulted and led to further deterioration of relations. At San Dimas in Durango independence celebrations on 16 September 1856 led to the sacking and burning of property belonging to Spanish citizens. When Spanish threats of coercive action over the claims question increased, masked gangs raided two Spanish-owned haciendas in Morelos on 18 and 19 December and killed all Spaniards present. These and other acts of violence were seen by Spanish and French diplomats as a systematic effort directed by General Juan Alvarez, with government backing, to drive all Spaniards from Mexico. Spain responded by breaking relations and renewing threats of military action.[6]

No such deep-seated problems intruded on the surface calm of Mexican-French relations, a calm which was underscored by the comic confrontation between the pompous French minister, Viscount Jean Alexis de Gabriac, and Francisco Zarco, editor of the prestigious *El Siglo XIX* and a *puro* member of Congress. When de Gabriac refused to preside over the efforts of the local French benevolent society in behalf of flood victims in France and sent what was considered a niggardly contribution, a group of Frenchmen treated their minister to a charivari. Zarco gave this serenade of ridicule prominent and detailed coverage in his paper. De Gabriac protested to the Foreign Ministry that he, the French flag, and the French nation had been insulted by Zarco's action. The government asked Congress to investigate the charges against Zarco, which it did in a session serving only to give greater notoriety to the embarassing incident. After amusing itself with details of bad relations between the French community and its minister, Congress agreed unanimously, to the accompaniment of applause from Frenchmen in the galleries, that there was no case against Zarco.[7] Finding his attempt to embarass the government had backfired, de Gabriac dropped the matter, apparently without ever having informed Paris of these grave "insults."

The de Gabriac–Zarco incident did not, however, reflect the true state of Franco-Mexican relations. After failing to get Comonfort to establish a strong military government with French backing, de Gabriac decided that even the moderate liberals were pursuing policies favorable to United States expansion. He retained close ties with conservative and monarchial elements and forwarded to Paris petitions for a monarchy guaranteed by Europe. By October 1856, the French legation and Mexican conservatives had drawn up plans for French military action to establish a monarchy in Mexico as a "barrier against the United States."

The next month, de Gabriac, who had counted on Anglo-French cooperation in blocking the southward expansion of the United States, was shocked to learn that his British counterpart did not share his assessment of the dangers it posed for European trade. William Garrow Lettson, the British chargé, felt that Yankee expansion could only produce "a new and powerful stimulant to commerce." De Gabriac credited such views to British fear of antagonizing their chief supplier of cotton. He undertook a campaign to educate his diplomatic colleague about the evils of Yankee expansion.[8]

At the heart of Mexico's difficulties with European powers was the government's precarious fiscal condition. The victorious liberals inherited a government with debts estimated at $120 million and an annual income of only $10 million.[9] The major source of government funds was customs revenues, but 70–90 percent of these were committed to servicing Mexico's debt. New loans at ruinous rates were the only means of financing the daily costs of government. Mexico was trapped in a vicious circle in which the debt-ridden government's inability to protect foreign lives and property by suppressing political turmoil and brigandage drove away all but the most unscrupulous sources of credit while providing grounds for new foreign claims. In this chronic fiscal crisis the treasury portfolio was accepted only reluctantly by experienced politicians and abandoned at the earliest opportunity.

The attempt to expel Eustaquio Barron illustrates the difficulties Mexico faced. Barron was widely known as a speculator who preyed on hapless Mexican governments. While the liberals publicly justified banishment by citing his involvement in fomenting revolts, Santos Degollado, who as governor of Jalisco had ordered the expulsion on 8 January 1856, defended the decision before Congress by pointing out that Barron had defrauded the government of untold revenues by using his official position as British consul at Tepic to cover extensive smuggling operations. The deputies' consideration of the question, however, was dominated by the realities of Mexico's debtor status.[10]

The one power from which the liberals expected sympathy, understanding, and assistance during this trying period was the United States, but it was too occupied with domestic problems and other international questions to give more than passing attention to Mexican affairs. Gadsden, whose recall had been requested four times, whose despatches suggested a paranoid complex, and who was conducting a personal and political feud with both the president and the secretary of state, was inexplicably allowed to remain at his post for months. That most of his despatches went unanswered suggests that during the first half of 1856 Washington attached little significance to Gadsden or to Mexican affairs.

Despite international problems and domestic difficulties, progress was made toward the realization of liberal reforms during 1856. The constitutional congress mandated by the Plan of Ayutla began meeting in February and served as a forum for liberal economic ideas and as a barometer of the deputies' admiration for the United States. Issues ranging from religious toleration to the origin and nature of private property provoked statements of economic and developmental ideas varying from moderate to radical, and almost all such questions elicited favorable comment on conditions in "the model republic" to the north. Consideration of a proposal for religious tolerance produced a discussion of the relationship between religion and immigration in the United States. To the *puros,* religious toleration would attract foreign immigrants while simultaneously reducing the preponderant influence of the clergy. Questions of governmental powers, individual liberties, and property rights were all submitted to similar analyses of their effects on economic development and to comparisons with conditions in the United States.

While there was no direct discussion on the floor of the congress of a protectorate status for Mexico, the persistent references to the United States by Mata and other *puros* led to some interesting exchanges. When 4 July 1856 was set as the day on which to begin consideration of the proposed constitution, the conservative press charged that this reflected liberal admiration for and subservience to the United States. *Puros* retorted that while the coincidence of dates was purely accidental, they hoped it would augur well for Mexico's future. On another occasion, when *puro* opposition to a requirement for foreigners to register with the Foreign Ministry and to carry identity documents led to statements about the absence of such requirements in the United States, deputy Juan de Dios Arias demanded a halt to the constant comparisons with the "classical republic." He suggested that for Mexico to try to imitate the United States would be like a skinny man trying to wear a fat man's clothes; the pants would be too large and the hat would fall down over the eyes.[11]

The constitutional provisions adopted by the congress did not always reflect the radical rhetoric of the *puros,* although there were some notable gains. Article 124 abolished *alcabalas* effective 1 June 1858. Article 28 prohibited all monopolies, except those for the coinage of money, for post offices, and for limited patent privileges. Article 11, guaranteeing freedom of travel for both Mexicans and foreigners and abolishing *cartas de seguridad* (identity documents) was attractive to immigrants and entrepreneurs. Article 30, bestowing citizenship on foreigners acquiring real property in Mexico, was approved unanimously without debate. Article 33 guaranteed foreigners all the rights of man as defined in the constitution.

Provisions designed to attract the foreigner, both as entrepreneur and as immigrant, were counterbalanced by others allowing the government to expel pernicious foreigners, making them subject to Mexican laws, and denying them any special status before Mexican courts. The constitution also gave Mexican citizens preference in government appointments, employment, and contracts. The discussion of restrictions on foreigners, and of such topics as the power to levy tariffs, abolition of monopolies, and religious toleration, took the form of analyses of how foreigners could assist in stimulating economic development without infringing on national economic independence or reducing Mexicans to the status of mere laborers in their own economy.[12]

Fear of dictatorship caused the constitution writers to restrict the role of the president. Missing from his powers were the sweeping provisions of the Plan of Acapulco for "promoting whatever was conducive to its [Mexico's] prosperity, aggrandizement, and progress." Nor were such powers specifically given to Congress by the new charter. Despite this lapse, discussions in the constitutional congress made clear the confidence of the liberal leadership that national progress and development would be an objective of the government under the federalist constitution.[13]

Despite congressional suspicions of a strong executive and the *puros'* open antagonism toward the *moderado* Comonfort,[14] the provisional government made considerable progress toward economic reform during 1856. The most radical measure was the Ley Lerdo, issued 25 June and approved by Congress three days later, forcing ecclesiastical and civil corporations to divest themselves of all real property not directly related to their functions. Its author, treasury minister Miguel Lerdo, saw this decree as a multipurpose measure. In a circular explaining the new law, Lerdo directed attention to two aspects under which it should be considered:

> first, as a resolution which will cause to disappear one of the economic errors which has contributed most to maintaining amongst us the stagnation of property and to impeding the development of those arts and industries dependent upon it [property]; second, as an indispensable measure to remove the principal obstacle which has until now been present for the establishment of a uniform and scientifically arranged revenue system [by] mobilizing real property which is a natural base for any good system of taxes.[15]

The forced sale of church property was expected to stimulate the economy and with the end of mortmain a new basis for taxation would be possible—taxes on sales of real property. Lerdo also hoped that a special tax on forced sales would provide an immediate windfall for the treasury, that the law would create a new class of small-property owners who would be strong supporters of reform, that by encouraging new enterprises work could be provided for the unemployed masses of the cities, and that the church's ability to mislead the working class would be weakened.[16]

Ley Lerdo fell short of expectations. The lower classes, for and from whom the *puros* expected much, failed to respond adequately as a result of lack of funds, lack of understanding, and fear of the clergy. Foreigners and the "few thousand" wealthy Mexicans, about whom Lerdo had earlier warned Santa Anna, were quick, however, to acquire church property.[17] Many Yankees made purchases. For example, during the period from October to December, Carlos Butterfield, along with several Mexican partners, purchased twenty-nine pieces of property in the Federal District for $174,328. Gabor Naphegyi, a Hungarian refugee who was treated by the Mexican press as a Yankee, purchased a significant amount of church property in Puebla.[18]

Less radical but equally significant was the decision to retain the Fomento Ministry, a governmental agency whose function the *puros* increasingly saw as attracting and supervising the application of foreign capital and technology to the country's economic problems. A newspaper campaign prevented executive repeal of Santa Anna's 1853 decree establishing Fomento. Under Alvarez, Miguel Lerdo was recognized as the acting head of Fomento, and on 12 December 1855 Comonfort appointed Manuel Siliceo as *fomento* minister. Congress indirectly recognized the office as permanent when it included a special commission for Fomento among the commissions created to investigate and review each ministry's activities under Santa Anna. The commission made its study and reported favorably to Congress without questioning the validity of the decree creating the ministry.[19]

The liberals enacted a new general tariff on 31 January 1856 to replace earlier temporary measures. The number of items on the prohibited list was reduced sharply, and the average tariff rate was set at a reasonable 30 percent. To attract United States commercial interests new ports of entry were created along the Rio Grande, on the Gulf of California in Sonora, and in the Tehuantepec Isthmus. Santa Anna's harsh navigation law was repealed on 11 January 1856 by an act subsidizing Mexican-flag vessels without penalizing foreign vessels importing goods from a third country.[20] The United States consul in Veracruz found the new measures so favorable to his countrymen's interests that he expected their early repeal.

Immigration and foreign participation in the Mexican economy were also encouraged. Santa Anna's decree outlawing the use of foreign currency gave way to specific recognition of foreign coins as legal tender.[21] The liberal press successfully campaigned against the requirement for foreigners to register with the Foreign Ministry and to carry registration documents *(cartas de seguridad)*.[22] Laws restricting the property rights of foreigners were replaced on 1 February 1856 by a Fomento decree giving foreigners almost the same real property rights as Mexican citizens. It also allowed the acquisition of real property to serve to naturalize the foreign purchaser.[23] These measures, endorsed by the liberal press as important steps in attracting foreign immigrants and investment,[24] also served as models for constitutional provisions.

During 1856 the number of foreigners, particularly those from the United States, seeking Fomento contracts and other investments opportunities in Mexico increased notably. Among the most active was the Hungarian Gabor Naphegyi, whose sojourn of several years in New York allowed him to pass as a Yankee in Mexico although he had failed to take the steps necessary to acquire citizenship.[25] In addition to buying church property under Ley Lerdo, Naphegyi built gaslighting systems. He provided Veracruz with gas lighting during Santa Anna's administration and in June 1856 became a partner in a faltering firm holding a contract for gas lighting in Mexico City. At the same time, and in conjunction with a trip to the United States to secure financing and equipment for a new gas-generating plant, Naphegyi was appointed special Fomento agent to secure examples of new instruments and machines for possible use in Mexico. Concurrently he was to serve as Mexico's colonization agent in the United States and Canada, with authority to appoint subagents for the major port cities.[26]

Interest in railroad concessions revived during this period. In August 1856 Albert C. Ramsey, whose Mexican ties dated back to the recent war, in which he had held the rank of colonel, acquired a Fomento contract for a railroad from Antón Lizardo, just south of Veracruz, to Acapulco with branches to Puebla and Mexico City.[27] A few days later George L. Hammeken contracted to build a tramway from Mexico City's main plaza to the nearby community of Tacubaya, where many of the upper class maintained country estates. Hammeken, identified as from New Orleans, had been in Mexico for several years as a Rothschild agent and was married to the daughter of General José A. Mejía, an old liberal federalist.[28] Only on Hammeken's contract was work begun and a transport system completed; Ramsey's was apparently secured only for speculative purposes. Estevan Zenteno and José Dionisio González secured a grant on 15 May 1856 for a railroad from Matamoros to Monterrey. Although the recipients of this grant were apparently Mexican citizens, the grant allowed them to organize their company in New Orleans, which was done on 19 May 1856.[29]

To gain expertise and public support for economic reforms, the government created a series of special commissions to advise on specific areas. Prominent figures were appointed to commissions for mining, agriculture, tariffs, colonization, and railroads. The railroad commission, *junta directiva de caminos de hierro,* was the most prestigious and permanent of these bodies; its three-man panel was charged with speeding up work on routes already under construction and promoting the start of others. The junta was given special responsibilities for the railroad from Veracruz to Mexico City. As the government's agent, it could use funds produced by a special additional tariff of 20 percent, known as the material-improvements tariff, to insure a return of 6 percent on money invested in building and operating the route. For money thus expended the junta received stock in the company. The junta could also use the material-improvement funds to finance surveys of various other routes.[30]

Liberal enthusiasm, reform measures, and the letting of contracts by Fomento proved inadequate to change materially the general picture in Mexico. Liberal enthusiasm could neither unite the country nor fill its coffers. In many cases persons securing Fomento contracts made no effort to carry out their terms, but sought instead to sell their privileges for a quick profit. Tariff reductions resulted in a loss of governmental revenues at the same time that radical reforms were provoking new conservative revolts. The revolts could be put down only at the cost of ruinous new loans or defaults on old obligations which, in turn, increased the threat of European intervention. The liberals' inability to bring order to the country was of crucial importance; not only did it waste resources and increase the foreign threat but it also severely hampered the task of economic development. The developmental commissions and Fomento concessions used for this purpose by the Reforma liberals were almost identical to the techniques employed successfully by the Díaz regime during the last quarter of the century; the most visible difference was the greater stability and order of the later period.

The activities of John Temple and Gregorio de Ajuria illustrate the difficulties facing Mexico and how foreigners took advantage of the situation. As noted in chapter 2, Ajuria and Temple already had business interests in Mexico before making a loan to the Ayutla rebels in 1854. Comonfort later labeled this loan as essential to the success of the revolution. The loan was secured and partially repaid by assignments of customs revenues from the ports of Acapulco and Mazatlán.[31] To suppress the conservative uprising at Puebla in the winter of 1856 the treasury again turned to Ajuria and associates for a loan of $300,000.[32] In June the government's indebtedness ot Ajuria and Temple was canceled and a new loan of $500,000 was secured in return for a ten-year lease on the Mexico City mint. This generous settlement allowed the new leaseholders to collect and retain most of the duties chargeable on gold and silver mined in the central and southern regions of Mexico.[33] A few months later Comonfort terminated publication of the official newspaper and gave the government's business to *El Estandarte Nacional,* owned by Ajuria.[34]

There were also developments in the United States during 1856 of significance for Mexico. At the Democratic convention meeting in Cincinnati in June an unsuccessful effort to renominate Pierce was led by John Forsyth, head of the Alabama delegation, owner and editor of the *Mobile Register,* and son of John Forsyth the elder, who had served as governor of Georgia and as secretary of state under Andrew Jackson and Martin Van Buren.[35] The younger Forsyth had been valedictorian of his Princeton class in 1832, and in 1834 he was admitted to the bar in Augusta, Georgia. After serving a term as federal attorney for the southern district of Alabama he returned to Columbus, Georgia, where for the next twelve years he combined the roles of lawyer, planter, and newspaper editor. After military service in Mexico he settled in Mobile, where he first tried his hand in the lumber business before turning his attention to journalism and politics, pursuits which he continued until his death in 1879. Already recommended by twenty-five members of Congress for diplomatic or consular posts, the forty-four-year-old Forsyth's service in the renomination battle gave him first call on available patronage positions. The demands for Gadsden's removal made the Mexican ministership available, and Forsyth's knowledge of Spanish and his service during the Mexican War recommended him for that post.[36] Forsyth was formally notified of his appointment as minister to Mexico on 21 July 1856.[37]

As a lame-duck president, Pierce had apparently decided to improve relations with Mexico. Manuel Robles Pezuela, the Mexican minister in Washington, reported that Pierce had attempted to find the most capable and acceptable individual for the minister's post. Senator Judah P. Benjamin of Louisiana had been considered, but his close ties with groups interested in the Tehuantepec transits made him unacceptable to both Pierce and Mexico. Pierce assured Robles that Forsyth would be the best diplomat that the United States had ever sent to Mexico and that he would work to achieve ''friendly and cordial relations.'' Under the circumstances Robles thought that Pierce was sincere and that the appointment was the best that could be expected.[38]

The written instructions issued to Forsyth were in accord with Pierce's expressed desire for better relations. Forsyth's principal task was to counter ''the impression that the United States have sinister views toward Mexico'' and to emphasize ''the friendly regards and fair purposes of the United States.'' His specific objectives were to encourage favorable reductions in Mexican tariffs, to promote friendly commercial relations, to seek a settlement to the long-standing claims question, to negotiate a postal treaty if this proved possible, and to evidence a continuing interest in the completion of a transit route across Tehuantepec.[39]

Forsyth may have received oral instructions that went beyond those furnished in writing. In the archives of the Mexican Foreign Ministry there is an extract in

English of instructions from Marcy to Forsyth authorizing the negotiation of a frontier reciprocity treaty along the lines of that signed with Great Britain for the United States–Canadian frontier in 1854.[40] There are three possible explanations for this document. It could have been furnished to Robles in Washington by Marcy. Forsyth may have given it to the ministry to support his oral instructions. Or perhaps Forsyth forwarded the extract to the Foreign Ministry to back his efforts to negotiate a frontier reciprocity treaty for which, in fact, he had no authority.

The last possibility is the most likely explanation. When Forsyth in February 1857 forwarded to Washington a series of treaties including a frontier reciprocity agreement, the administration appeared not to have anticipated that any treaties would be negotiated. Also in the despatch forwarding the treaties, and in several others, Forsyth admitted that he had exceeded his authority, without indicating to which of the several treaties this admission applied.[41]

This explanation is strengthened by earlier expressions of Forsyth's views. As an active politician and newspaper editor, Forsyth had studied the economic aspects of sectional differences. He saw economic activity as divisible into two categories—productive and distributive. Production was the source of wealth; distribution, of power. The agriculture of the South and West was the real source of national wealth. But the South and West were economic colonies of the North through its control of commerce and manufacturing. Commerce and manufacturing were parasitic forms of activity which converted the natural wealth of agriculture into economic and political power. A region or country could reap the full benefits of its economy only when it could control both the productive and distributive phases.[42] For this reason Forsyth advocated commercial independence for the South.

What Forsyth saw in Mexico reinforced his views. Shortly after his arrival he became acquainted with Miguel Lerdo's statistical study of Mexico's foreign trade. Here he saw that the British dominated the Mexican economy just as the North did that of the South. Approximately half of Mexico's imports were supplied by the British, while almost all Mexican exports went to the British. By controlling commerce the British were able to enjoy most of the benefits of Mexico's legendary wealth.[43]

Within a few weeks of his arrival in Mexico, Forsyth was discussing the wealth of Mexico in hyperbolic terms. Ways must be found, he felt, for the United States to control these great riches. He noted that his country's commerce with Mexico had suffered greatly during the past decade and that United States influence in Mexico would not increase until methods were found to protect and promote United States commercial activities.[44] To increase Yankee commercial power and decrease that of the British became Forsyth's goal.

Forsyth doubtless found fellow countrymen in Mexico who encouraged his push for economic expansion. Traveling on the same ship with him from New Orleans was Edward Lee Plumb, a young mining promoter from California. Plumb had been to Mexico several times during the past few years and had established contacts in both liberal and conservative circles. On 15 November 1854, Plumb, in partnership with Santa Anna's son-in-law, had secured an exclusive Fomento grant to exploit iron and coal deposits over a large area of Guerrero and Michoacán. He had also become interested in railroad development through his contacts with Gadsden. In October 1856, Plumb, having found in the United States financial backing for his mining grant, was returning to Mexico to secure an extension of time on his grant and to arrange a more extensive survey of Mexican mining prospects.[45]

When he arrived in Mexico City Forsyth found Carlos Butterfield anxious to reopen negotiations for the postal treaty upon which a mail-steamer service would depend. Butterfield probably used the same arguments with Forsyth that he would use later with the United States Congress when he argued persuasively that a subsidy for his steamship line was a small price to pay for the economic benefits such a line would bring. Regular steamer service was the first step in diverting Mexico's foreign trade from British to Yankee hands. As Mexican commerce shifted toward the United States, Butterfield foresaw such an flow of capital and technology from the United States that Mexico would soon become the Yankee counterpart of Britain's India.[46]

Forsyth's interest in expanding United States commercial interests in Mexico was heightened and a sense of urgency added by the situation he found in Mexico. Like his predecessor, Forsyth quickly decided that Comonfort was not a true liberal but only a weak moderate who was playing into the hands of Britain and France. He concluded that his country's interests could best be promoted through the true liberals and *puros*. "A leading feature of their plan is to encourage American emigration, to develop the great natural resources of this superb country, build railroads, etc." These favorable views reflected a conviction in the minds of many liberals that "without the intervention, aid, or guarantee of the United States, . . . a stable Government can never be secured to this people."

After discussions with liberal leaders and observation of conditions, Forsyth quickly elaborated a new protectorate project, or perhaps he only revived the one which his predecessor and the liberals had denounced so strongly in 1855. Regardless of its origin, Forsyth lost no time in pushing it; he presented his credentials 23 October and on 8 November he forwarded an elaborate protectorate scheme to Washington as his own creation.[47] While there is no sure means of determining how this scheme was developed, the Mexican historian José Fuentes Mares unhesitantly attributes Forsyth's plan to Miguel Lerdo.[48] Although it is doubtful that even an extreme *puro* such as Lerdo would have publicly advocated an economic protectorate by that name, the ideas contained in Forsyth's proposal were goals dear to Lerdo and other *puros*. Faced with *puro* desires and his own perception of economic forces, it is conceivable that Forsyth merely applied to the relationship what he considered to be the appropriate term, 'protectorate'. After all, he had labeled the South an economic colony of the North and this relationship would not have appeared very different to him. It is equally possible, however, that Miguel Lerdo or other *puros* used the expression '*economic* protectorate' in private discussions with Forsyth. During the Reforma liberals generally displayed little sensitivity on questions of economic nationalism. Their sensitivity was political; a protectorate that infringed on national sovereignty, political independence, or territorial integrity was an anathema, while foreign economic penetration and domination seems to have been accepted by most liberals and almost all *puros* as the necessary and appropriate means of promoting material development and appears to have been actively courted and welcomed by many.

While these attempts at attribution are clearly speculative, there are some items of evidence which lend credence to Miguel Lerdo as the source of the idea and point to the acceptance by puros of the term 'economic protectorate' at least in private discussions. Lerdo and Forsyth, who were approximately the same age, quickly became close friends. Forsyth praised Lerdo above all others in his reports to Washington, he actively assisted in a move to have Lerdo wrest the presidential office from Comonfort in late 1856, and for much of 1858 Lerdo enjoyed protective asylum in the United States legation. Newspaper reports, congressional discussions, and private correspondence clearly indicate that most liberals were firmly convinced that Mexico's survival was inexorably tied to material development and that for both practical and ideological reasons the resources for this development could come only from the United States. Finally, it should be noted that Matías Romero, who in his singleminded dedication to material progress would be the Miguel Lerdo of the next generation, chided a New York audience in 1864 for their failure to respond during the previous decade to the economic advantages pressed upon them by Mexico—advantages which, while safeguarding Mexican independence and sovereignty, would have been the economic equivalent of annexation.[49]

The heart of Forsyth's proposal was an alliance between the liberal Mexican government and the United States. The United States should provide loans to enable the liberals to stabilize their government and, with United States cooperation, to crush the church-conservative opposition. As Forsyth saw it, the church and the army were the most powerful institutions in Mexico, and for a government to survive it must control one of these sources of power. Loans would allow the liberals to purchase the allegiance of the army; and with the army behind it, the government could destroy the political and economic power of the church. To insure full liberal control of the army, Forsyth recommended that several thousand of his fellow countrymen be carefully selected to serve in its officer ranks.

Not only would loans allow the liberals to put down the *pronunciamientos* in favor of *religión y fueros,* but they would make less likely a successful alliance between European powers and Mexican conservatives. Again, like his predecessor, Forsyth saw the large Mexican debt held by British, French, and Spanish interests as a threat to the survival of an independent and liberal Mexico. The inability of the fiscally distressed liberal government to service these debts created the danger of European intervention—an intervention actively courted by the conservatives. A loan from the United States to liquidate this debt would forestall both intervention and alliance.

To justify this expenditure of United States diplomatic power and financial resources, Forsyth pointed both to economic benefits and the political desirability of ''Americanizing'' Mexico. Merchants, ship captains, and other commercial interests of the United States had suffered ''a series of atrocious wrongs and outrages'' because of ''the deep rooted prejudice and jealousy of Americans'' in the minds of many local and state officials. Justice and his country's prestige demanded that the claims growing out of these abuses be satisfied and future abuses avoided. But traditional diplomatic means of settlement, Forsyth argued, were useless in this case. The central government could not, or would not, accept responsibility for damages caused by state and local officials. The alternatives were to so intimidate local officials by naval forces stationed along the coasts that United States interests would be protected, or to pursue a friendly and pacific policy through a protectorate as a means of removing the popular prejudice against his fellow countrymen.

Forsyth foresaw the potential for using the liberal-*puro* predilection for the United States as a vehicle to gain full control over Mexico's economy and her fabulous natural resources, and like most of his contemporaries, Forsyth accepted without question the view that Mexico possessed agricultural and mineral resources of inestimable value. With popular prejudices removed and friendly liberals in power, settlers, capitalists, and technicians from the United States would sweep across Mexico building railroads, opening mines, operating prosperous farms and ranches, handling the commercial transactions, and supplying the manufacturing needs. If the favorable moment were acted upon, Forsyth inquired, ''should we not enjoy all the fruits of annexation [without] its responsibilities and evils? Could we not secure for our countrymen the enjoyment of the rich resources of the Mexican country, without the danger of introducing, into our social and political system the ignorant masses of the Mexican People?''[50]

While Forsyth could not expect a response from Washington to his recommendation in less than six or eight weeks, he conducted himself as if he already had unlimited authority. He established close contacts with *puro* leaders, especially with Miguel Lerdo, who was minister of the treasury and, after 14 November, acting foreign minister.[51] In what may have been an effort to impress the new minister, Lerdo undertook to guide Plumb's applications for a time extension on his mining grant and for surveying permits through the appropriate Mexican offices in less than a week.[52] Lerdo and Forsyth discussed relations between their countries, apparently including the possibility of a protectorate. Forsyth became aware of and encouraged *puro* efforts to have Lerdo replace Comonfort as president. Lerdo also kept Forsyth fully informed of the difficulties encountered in raising funds to operate the government and to suppress a series of conservative revolts.[53]

Apparently Forsyth and Lerdo discussed matters in terms of what might be possible once Lerdo assumed the presidency. As this became less likely, they decided to use Lerdo's position as acting foreign minister to get the protectorate question introduced before the cabinet. To disguise their prior understanding on the matter, and perhaps that of several other members of the cabinet, a long-standing case involving the protection of United States citizens was used as the vehicle for formal presentation of the proposal. The specific case was that of the Zerman filibustering expedition of 1855. Zerman, an adventurer of French origin, demanded protection as a United States citizen, a status to which most of the members of his expedition were clearly entitled. Despite Gadsden's efforts the case still languished in the courts when Forsyth assumed his duties as minister.[54]

Forsyth and Lerdo set forth their respective positions on the Zerman case in an exchange of notes before arranging for a conference at the National Palace.[55] The meeting took place on 16 December and after preliminaries, in which each side set forth again its formal position on Zerman, the conferees quickly moved to an analysis of the difficulties facing the Mexican government. Forsyth's demands that the Zerman prisoners be furnished with adequate money to cover their needs for food, clothing, and shelter gave Lerdo the opportunity to inform the minister of the desperate plight of the Mexican treasury. The treasury was bankrupt, while reactionary rebels and ambitious generals were challenging the government on every side. According to Forsyth's report, "the present government he [Lerdo] was convinced was the best, was the most liberal in principle she [Mexico] had ever had, but he was equally persuaded that the Govt. could not sustain itself against the disorganizing elements now unhappily rife, throughout the country, without the pecuniary aid of some friendly power. For that aid he could only look to the United States, as the natural ally of his country." Lerdo also stressed the importance of the British debt as a threat to Mexican survival. This obligation, which produced a continuing threat of British intervention, "could be got rid of by Mexico unaided, but only in a manner that might involve consequences, *threatening the national integrity*."[56]

Forsyth reported that Lerdo proposed a loan as a means of rescuing Mexico from her difficulties. The pending postal treaty, settlement of all other outstanding problems, and the loan could be handled simultaneously. The amount required by Mexico would be insignificant for the United States but would produce inestimable advantages for both countries. With the money Mexico could achieve financial solvency, suppress the revolts, and remove the British threat by paying off the debt. Action, Lerdo emphasized, must be soon, for Mexican cabinets and governments changed quickly and this opportunity might be lost forever.

At the conference Lerdo did not clearly specify what would be the benefits to the United States of this course of action, but Forsyth was not at a loss in explaining these to Washington. The alliance and loan would give United States interests an almost exclusive privilege to exploit the vast resources of Mexico; they would be the first steps in the process of "Americanizing" Mexico, of securing all the advantages of annexation without any of the risks and dangers. "The moment seems to be propitious [Forsyth wrote] to take advantage of the financial strait in which Mexico finds herself, to close up all of the business of the Legation with her Government & to accomplish some objects of great interest to the U. States. . . .

It is not easy to perceive how a few millions can be disbursed from our plethoric Treasury with superior results & profit & advantage.''[57]

The moment did indeed seem propitious. The outlook for the liberal government and its reform program were bleak in December 1856. Pronouncements against the government became more and more frequent. The British and French ministers were responding positively to feelers from conservatives promising shortly to drive the liberals from power. The British minister's hostility toward the Comonfort administration gave substance to press accounts that a British fleet would arrive soon at Veracruz. Apparently spontaneous attacks on Spanish subjects and their property in various parts of Mexico seemed to presage war with that power.[58] In the face of these problems the government was paralyzed by two internal struggles—between the president and Congress and between the moderates and the *puros*.

Miguel Lerdo added to the confusion by precipitating a cabinet crisis. He was the favorite of most *puros* to replace Comonfort and had been maneuvering for months to drive Comonfort from power. Lerdo, whose primary cabinet responsibility rested with the treasury, presented the proposed United States loan and alliance to the cabinet as the only measure which would allow Mexico to be saved by reorganizing the treasury on a firm basis. When the proposition that a United States protectorate was only means of saving the liberal government had been suggested to the cabinet by Lerdo early in November, Comonfort had indicated he would rather join the rebels than accept such a proposal. Now Lerdo announced that he would leave the cabinet unless his plans were accepted.[59]

The resulting cabinet crisis lasted over two weeks. The liberal press began immediately to line up behind one or the other of the principals in the dispute—Comonfort and Lerdo. The *puros* rallied to Lerdo's support and aroused public opinion in his behalf, predicting that the collapse of the liberal government and a conservative takeover were certain to result from Lerdo's resignation. Conferences between Comonfort and Lerdo encouraged belief that a compromise was in the making. Lerdo did not want a compromise, however, since his objective was to force the resignation of Comonfort. Forsyth believed Comonfort lacked the courage to accept either Lerdo's proposal or his resignation, but Comonfort displayed unexpected courage and accepted Lerdo's resignation on 3 January 1857.

Lerdo's failure to unseat Comonfort forced Forsyth to halt his preparation of protectorate treaties, but it did not materially lessen his conviction of ultimate success. He remained in contact with Lerdo and other sympathetic liberals, confident that "hard necessities" would soon force Comonfort either to restore Lerdo to the cabinet or to continue the negotiations through someone else. The Zerman case now served to signal the government's attitude on the protectorate project. During the cabinet crisis the duties of foreign minister were exercised by the *oficial mayor* of the ministry, and Forsyth encountered a very inflexible attitude on the Zerman case. The new minister, Ezequiel Montes, who was a political opponent of Lerdo, also adopted a rigid attitude about Zerman.[60]

Forsyth's assessment of the effect of "hard necessities" appeared correct, however, for on 8 January Montes confidentially informed him of the government's desire to resolve in a friendly and generous manner all issues pending between the two countries. Montes indicated his willingness to discuss any proposal that might help them "arrive at a total arrangement." Although Forsyth may have believed that conditions were forcing the government to consider his scheme, a study of the Mexican Foreign Ministry's archives on these negotiations reflects a very different picture. The voluminous file covering earlier negotiations with Gadsden contains ample evidence that the Foreign Ministry was anxious for closer relations with the United States, for more regular communications guaranteed by a postal treaty, for financial and moral support, and for closer economic and commercial ties.[61] If this was the case, then the delays encountered by Gadsden and Forsyth likely were products of good negotiating technique—the enhancement of bargaining power by appearing to be opposed to the proposals at hand. If so, Lerdo may have been a victim of his own cleverness. Comonfort's display of opposition to Lerdo's proposals may have merely been a clever maneuver to force a challenger out of the cabinet.

At any rate, Montes's guarded indication of a readiness to negotiate opened the door to a series of conversations, and within two weeks Montes and Forsyth were exchanging drafts of loan and postal treaties. The project now differed from the Lerdo proposal only in failing to include an overt alliance. By 2 February Forsyth assumed that everything was settled and that only the formality of signing remained. Unexpected Mexican resistance developed, however, causing Forsyth to fear that the negotiations were being scrapped. But it was only a last bid for more favorable terms. On 10 February 1857, after some significant adjustments had been made, an interdependent set of five agreements was signed and forwarded to Washington for approval.[62]

The agreements consisted of three treaties and two conventions. The key document, entitled "Treaty of Loan and Anticipation of Duties," provided for a loan of $15 million. Of this sum $7 million was to be retained by the United States, $3 million for claims of its citizens and $4 million for the English convention debt, which the United States would now assume. The remaining $8 million was to be made available to Mexico immediately upon ratification of the treaty. The $7 million retained for claims and convention debt would constitute a conventional loan bearing 4 percent interest. Repayment, to begin after three years, would be covered by an assignment of 13 percent of all Mexico's import duties. The remaining $8 million with 4 percent interest was to be repaid by 20 percent rebates of duties on all imports and exports, except European cotton fabrics, made directly to or from United States ports in either United States or Mexican vessels. When these rebates equaled the amount of the loan plus interest the loan would be considered liquidated and the rebates would be discontinued.

In its final form the postal treaty contained a statement of purpose which included the "stimulation of mutual commerce." A mixed-flag line would provide weekly service between Veracruz and New Orleans with intermediate stops in both countries. Half the flags and half the crews were to be Mexican, and each country would provide an annual subsidy of $120,000. In addition to setting up procedures for the free flow of mail, the treaty guaranteed half fares for official Mexican use and required the contractor to support two Mexican apprentice machinists on each of his vessels. Over the objections of Butterfield, who was the presumed contractor under the treaty, and Forsyth the steamers were forbidden to engage in Mexican coastal shipping.

The frontier reciprocity and claims agreements involved major mutual compromises. The list of items permitted to cross the land frontier in either direction was less extensive than Forsyth desired, but he was pleased with the inclusion of foodstuffs and machinery for mining and agriculture. The four-year life of the treaty was less than Forsyth wanted and more than Mexico preferred. A listing of goods duty free only when exported from Mexico was a concession to Mexico, while a promise to negotiate in the near future for a more extensive free list allowed Forsyth to hope for eventual complete free trade along the frontier. He was also encouraged by a Mexican commitment to renew or renegotiate the commercial treaty of 1831. The claims convention created a claims commission authorized to accept all claims regardless of origin and then provided that if the United States denied the validity of Indian depredation claims the matter would be submitted to the French emperor for arbitration.

The general convention was the least difficult to negotiate. It recognized the other four specific agreements as forming "a single indivisible whole in such a manner that the rejection of one, involves the rejection of the whole." This unorthodox arrangement was accepted because each party apparently feared that without such a provision its favorite agreements would be rejected by the other.

The most desirable aspects of the agreements from the Mexican point of view were the loan and the regular steamer service to United States ports. In a proposal advanced on 22 January Mexico had sought to combine the loan and claims provisions. Under this proposal, Mexican claims against the United States were estimated at $12 million. To this sum was added a loan of $10 million. Out of the total $22 million due Mexico, $7.5 million would be withheld by the United States, $3 million to satisfy its claims against Mexico and the remaining $4.5 million to cover Mexico's English convention debt, which would now be assumed by the United States. Of the remaining $13 million Mexico would receive $4.5 million immediately upon ratification of treaties and the remaining $8.5 million would follow in monthly installments of $500,000.[63]

To encourage the United States to advance the loan the Mexicans devised a novel method of repayment. The loan of $10 million with interest at 5 percent would be repaid by a reduction or rebate of 15 percent in the duties charged at maritime ports on all imported Yankee goods and on third-country products imported from United States ports in Yankee bottoms. The rebate would continue until it equaled the amount of the loan plus interest. This would give United States shipping and commerce an advantage and when combined with the provision for paying off the English convention debt would mark a sharp decline in the degree to which Mexico was subject to British influence. Doubtless the *puro* developmentalists envisioned the growth of United States commerce as a forerunner of a flood of Yankee capital and technology.

Forsyth had countered the Mexican proposal by recommending an increase in the interest rate from 5 to 6 percent and, while suggesting that the loan amount be increased to at least $13 million, he felt that at least half the loan must be repaid by conventional means. He proposed that repayment be guaranteed by a mortgage on 20 percent of all Mexican customs revenues. He also sought to extend the rebate procedure for the remainder of the loan to all his country's commerce—all imports and exports in United States bottoms regardless of nationality or port of origin of the goods. He also sought to increase the rebate to 20–25 percent.

Mexico agreed to increase the amount of the loan but not its cost. The rebates should be held at 15 percent, but Mexico proposed to extend them not only to all goods imported or exported in United States bottoms, but to Mexican vessels engaged in Mexican commerce with the United States. In the view of the broad sweep of Yankee interests to be served the Mexicans called for a reduction in the interest rate to 4 percent. The final version of the treaty was essentially a compromising of these proposals. The title given this agreement, "Treaty of Loan and Anticipation of Duties," also constituted a compromise. Forsyth originally labeled it a "loan and commerce treaty" but Montes suggested changes to avoid "an embarrassing misinterpretation."[64]

At the heart of the postal treaty was a matter that had been the subject of complaint in Mexico for years, the lack of regular steamer service to the ports of its northern neighbor. In 1853 the United States Post Office began paying $69,000 annually for a packet service from New Orleans to Veracruz. In addition to mail the packet brought freight, chiefly raw cotton, from New Orleans and provided passenger service in both directions.[65] The packet service proved to be undependable, suspending service occasionally for months, and was criticized in the Mexican press for failing to serve Mexico's maritime needs. Early in 1856 a proposal by Francisco Reibaud, a Mexican naval officer, to establish a service using surplus Mexican war steamers received warm support from the liberal press. The line could employ surplus Mexican naval officers, train young Mexicans as machinists, and grant special fares for immigrants.

Butterfield may have been influenced by press reaction to Reibaud's proposal, for in the spring of 1856 he began negotiating on a proposal containing many of the same features. By May his proposal, combined with a postal treaty, had been approved by the Treasury and forwarded to Foreign Affairs. In July the press in Mexico and New Orleans learned of the negotiations and endorsed the project.[66] By August the negotiations were completed and the treaties were ready for signature, but the death of the Mexican foreign minister and news of Gadsden's impending replacement caused action to be suspended.[67] In September, as rumors spread that the existing bimonthly service would be discontinued as unprofitable, the press demanded that the government protect and subsidize it.[68] When Forsyth opened negotiations in January 1857, Mexico submitted for his consideration a modified version of agreement drawn up for Gadsden's signature.[69]

The Mexican proposal called for each government to subsidize a steamer line providing weekly service to United States and Mexican ports on the Gulf with $75,000 annually. Half the ships would be under Mexican flag, half under that of the United States. Half of each crew would be Mexican, and all ships and crews were to be treated as nationals in both countries. Advantageous rates were to be established for the Mexican government. In apparently contradictory articles it first specified that all steamers used by the line be suitable for fitting out as warships and then that the service not be interrupted during war, even war between the signatory countries.

From Forsyth's perspective the most attractive features of the treaties were the commercial advantages in the loan repayment scheme and the frontier reciprocity agreement. The reciprocity proposal, as originally submitted by Forsyth on 24 January, allowed free movement across the common land frontier of a list of goods produced in either country. This appears to have been Forsyth's pet project, for he concentrated most of his attention on it, attempting to make the list as comprehensive as possible and to secure a treaty of indefinite duration.

After each side had presented proposals on 21 and 24 January, negotiation proceeded rapidly to agreement on 10 February, but not without differences and occasional threats of collapse as each side sought to maximize its advantages. Minor difficulties troubled the progress of negotiations—whether the subsidized mail steamers would be allowed to engage in Mexican coastal trade, whether its subsidy ought to be larger, what would be the specific wording of the loan treaty, whether Mexico should receive an advance on the loan before the treaties were ratified, whether all the treaties ought to be made interdependent—without seriously endangering the success of the overall project.

Differences on two key issues, however, threatened to prevent the signing of any agreements. Mexico insisted that any claims settlement must recognize the United States's responsibility for damages resulting from Indian raids across the frontier since 1848. Forsyth found such responsibility distasteful. On the other hand, Mexico found Forsyth's insistence on a broadly defined agreement for reciprocal free trade along the frontier equally difficult to accept. Realizing that the frontier's ties with the Mexican core region were tenuous and sympathy for annexation by the United States widespread, Mexico was reluctant to sanction close economic ties across the frontier. These points were discussed at a conference of the negotiators and Comonfort on 1 February. The conference appeared to produce compromises on the issues and Forsyth confidently began preparing treaties to be signed on 3 February. He even drafted a covering despatch for them before he discovered there had not been a meeting of minds at the conference.

An additional week was required to resolve the differences. Mexico still refused to give up the Indian damage claims or to remove all barriers to trade across the northern frontier, while Forsyth refused to sign treaties which specifically made the United States responsible for Indian damages or did not give substance to frontier reciprocity. The Mexico City press, which had carried rumors of the negotiations, apparently failed to get word of the last-minute hitch and announced in approbatory terms that the treaties had been signed and dispatched to Washington on 3 February. This may have been an attempt to pressure Forsyth, since the press version of the treaties conformed to the Mexican position. Within a few days, however, the error was acknowledged and the differences were reported in a manner favorable to Mexico.[70] The issues were finally resolved by two compromise provisions, one which avoided fixing responsibility for the Indian depredations but allowed for the claims growing out of these to be settled and another promising that Mexico would agree to add a significant number of items to the free list for frontier trade after a study of frontier commerce had been completed.[71]

Despite the compromises, Forsyth enthusiastically supported the treaties, especially those covering loan, reciprocity, and postal questions. He justified them on both economic and political grounds. His country's share of Mexico's foreign trade would increase from some $4.5 million annually to over $40 million. The rebate on Mexican imports would, Forsyth asserted, "have the effect of more than doubling our commerce with Mexico, of turning the bulk of the European trade with this country, through the U.S., and in bottoms of the U.S., and in enabling our manufacturers of cotton fabrics at least to compete with those of G. Britain, for a period of several years to come, instead of being, as now, absolutely excluded from the Mexican markets."[72]

Forsyth sought to show that the treaties would serve the economic interests of various groups in the United States. Shipping would obviously benefit from the rebates, while the southern desire for direct commerce would be served by the steamer service. Merchants engaged in reexport trade would gain from both agreements. Eastern manufacturers, commerce houses, and financiers would profit from the increased trade. Reciprocity would serve southern and western interests. The greater volume of trade would produce a marked increase in United States customs revenue.

The treaties were also justifiable in political terms. Forsyth felt that British domination of Mexican foreign trade and control of her foreign debt gave Britain a dominant voice in Mexican political councils. Paying off the debt and diverting the trade into United States channels would undermine this influence. At a later date Forsyth, in opposition to Buchanan's policy of territorial expansion, argued that the treaties would have served "to sustain Mexico and keep her from falling to pieces, perhaps into the hands of Foreign Powers, until such time as we were ready to 'Americanize' her." Given the proximity of the United States to Mexico and the political and economic ties which would result from the treaties, Forsyth believed that Mexico would become increasingly "Americanized" and in the future would voluntarily seek union. The United States could then decide whether to grant the boon of annexation or to retain the existing advantageous relationship.[73]

The Mexican reaction to the treaties as evidenced in the press was quick and positive. In late 1856 when Forsyth's conversations with Lerdo had led to public speculation about a Yankee protectorate, *El Heraldo,* whose editor, José Godoy, was a Lerdo partisan, charged that the conservatives were creating rumors to discredit the liberal government. When the press learned of the negotiations between Montes and Forsyth, *El Heraldo* and the other liberal newspapers avoided mentioning the possibility of a protectorate.[74]

Despite efforts at secrecy, journalists obtained fairly accurate knowledge of the final treaties within a few days, and even though they were similar to the protectorate scheme of 1855, the liberal press warmly supported them. While recognizing that Yankee commerce would benefit from the treaties, editors lauded the government for having obtained a loan without staining the nation's honor or endangering its territorial integrity. They saw the loan as essential for the survival of the reform program. Since the claims convention eliminated the one problem that had marred relations with the United States, the press hoped soon to see closer political and economic ties between the countries. Without being explicit the liberal editorialists suggested that the loan would make Mexico strong internally and that Yankee friendship could protect her from European threats.[75]

The press was so convinced of the unusual mutual benefits provided by the treaties that ratification was taken for granted. When the first rumors began to appear in Mexico that the United States would not ratify the treaties, these were denounced as conservative efforts to dishearten the government and to spread panic among the populace. When the rumors were confirmed, the reaction was one of disbelief. One correspondent found it impossible ''to believe that the American government rejected so stupidly the great advantages she could have gained.''[76]

Leading liberals, both in and out of the government, had been encouraged by the signing of the treaties. The French minister reported that the liberals expected these treaties to rescue them from disaster and resolve all their difficulties.[77] The cabinet and leading editors had endorsed them without reservation. Benito Juárez, who was serving as governor of Oaxaca, on being informed of the agreements, responded with a hope for speedy ratification so that the necessary aid would not be delayed.[78] On 3 March, in an official manifesto to the nation reporting on and justifying the government's action in all areas, the treaties were reported, individually analyzed, and justified. The manifesto declared:

> If the referenced convention and treaties are ratified, the government will have the satisfaction of having consummated an agreement, which without ceding a foot [*palmo*] of national territory, without consenting to anything indecorous or humiliating for the country, and, finally, without prejudicing in the least our agriculture and industry, will give the Republic the great advantages of relieving it of two large and pressing debts [United States claims and English convention], of improving the situation along the frontier, of giving new impulse and development to foreign commerce, of facilitating communications with foreign countries, and of putting into the government hands considerable resources which will serve, not only to rescue it from the critical and painful position in which it has found itself for so long, but also to put it in position to form a well conceived treasury plan.[79]

The government's commitment to the treaties was reflected in the steps it took to insure their early ratification. Carlos Butterfield, who had a clear interest in them, was commissioned to accompany the treaties to Washington with special instructions for the Mexican legation. The Mexican naval steamer *Guerrero* was ordered to transport Butterfield and the treaties from Veracruz to New Orleans and to remain there awaiting word of ratification. Butterfield was also authorized to work for the ratification of the treaties, coordinating his efforts with those of the Mexican minister, Manuel Robles Pezuela. Robles was authorized to give final signature to Butterfield's steamship contract once ratification had occurred.[80]

Robles needed no encouragement to support the treaties; he had long been convinced of the importance of a settlement with the United States. Pierce, in his last annual message to Congress, had made the numerous unsettled claims the basis for his comments on relations with Mexico.[81] This statement plus the election of Buchanan, who was identified with a policy of territorial expansion, had provoked a rash of newspaper articles advocating that force be used to collect claims. Editorials proposing that the United States seize Mexico's frontier states as security for the claims frightened Robles. He proposed that steps be taken to settle all points of friction before Buchanan took office. He endorsed a project advanced in a New York newspaper for a Yankee firm to manage Mexican finances and economy under contract.

The treaties and special instructions, delivered by Butterfield on 24 February,[82] reassured Robles that his government was alert to the dangers. He was informed that the treaties would remove all dangers and "demonstrate forever Mexico's willingness to attend the demands of American citizens." Their importance sprang not only from the settlement with the United States but also from their weakening of the British position. The loan would provide money to stabilize the government and to finance an effective reform policy. By developing closer commercial ties with the United States, the treaties would demonstrate that Mexico's economic survival did not depend on Europe. Europeans would now see that more equitable and friendly policies were necessary to protect their commercial and political interests.

Robles was given unlimited authority to marshal forces in support of ratification. English bondholders, Yankee merchants, banking firms, persons interested in Butterfield's steamship venture or in the Tehuantepec transit route, and even individuals with private claims against Mexico were to be utilized. The importance of favorable newspaper coverage for the treaties was stressed. To carry out these activities the Foreign Ministry authorized Robles to make unlimited expenditures. Fearful that Washington might make changes in the treaties, Mexico later directed Robles to accept any changes which did not infringe on Mexican sovereignty or seriously reduce the loan.[83]

Elements in the United States favorable to the treaties seemed impressive. While the negotiations were still going on in Mexico, Plumb and Butterfield had been busy lining up support in the United States.[84] The *New York Herald* carried accounts of the negotiations and frankly endorsed the treaties as a means of converting Mexico into a protectorate.[85] Robles reported that the only open opposition came from the groups involved in the Tehuantepec grants, who feared that a claims settlement would damage their position. He hoped to win them over.

When the treaties arrived Robles began daily meetings with Marcy urging immediate submission of the treaties to the Senate. Robles found Marcy friendly toward the agreements but unwilling to submit them. Robles's efforts to make a special plea to Pierce and to deliver a personal letter from Comonfort were unsuccessful. Unable to reach the president, Robles concentrated his efforts on Marcy, to no avail. Marcy informed Robles that the loan treaty and provisions for subsidizing a steamship line might be unconstitutional and that there would be opposition to arbitrating the Indian claims. He also pointed to the impending end of Pierce's term of office as the major obstacle.[86]

Marcy waited until 3 March, one day before a new administration would come into office, to inform Forsyth that Pierce had some mild objections to the treaties, especially the novel loan treaty, and had decided to leave the matter pending for his successor.[87] Robles believed the treaties would have been approved by the Senate given enough time. Marcy indicated that relations were so strained between Buchanan and Pierce that for Pierce to submit the treaties would insure that Buchanan would make an effort to defeat them. Thus, Marcy felt, the best policy was to express objections to the treaties but leave them available for Buchanan to submit. After the inauguration, Pierce claimed that only the shortness of time had prevented him from submitting the treaties and that the prospects for approval had been good. Pierce explained that he had avoided Robles during his last days in office not because of opposition to the treaties but rather to prevent the delivery of the letter from Comonfort, maintaining that presidents could not receive confidential communications from other governments. Robles accepted this lame excuse.[88]

Despite the efforts of Robles and Butterfield, Buchanan's inauguration sealed the fate of the treaties. Buchanan and his secretary of state, Lewis Cass, rejected the treaties and directed Forsyth to inform the Mexican government of this decision.[89] Robles felt it was fortunate that the new administration agreed to leave Forsyth at his post rather than replace him with someone more acceptable to Buchanan.[90] The administration later explained its position on the treaties:

> In the four treaties which you negotiated last winter, and which were all dependent upon each other, provision was made for a generous loan of money to Mexico, without any other equivalent than was to be found in certain commercial arrangements of which, in this way, the United States were to become practically the purchasers. If these arrangements had been far more valuable than they really were, it would still have been a dangerous departure from our established policy to have given for them a pecuniary equivalent. A treaty of commerce . . . should rest upon the basis of reciprocity . . . [otherwise] the nations of the earth should go about bidding against each other for the monopoly of commerce . . . and the longest purse would buy the richest market. Such a doctrine . . . can meet no favor in a republic like ours—whose interests demand the most liberal competition and the freest trade.[91]

No commercial advantage warranted the expenditure of money in the eyes of Buchanan; only land could justify such an outlay.

Despite their cavalier treatment in Washington, the treaties had for a moment aroused passionate hopes and fears in Mexico. While Mexican liberals had seen the treaties as the key to a bright future, British and French ministers in Mexico had found in them grave threats to their nations' interests. The British minister and the local representative of the English bondholders feared that the result would be the loss of security for English investments in Mexico. Mexico's English creditors felt that all its revenues were already mortgaged to cover existing obligations and urged the Foreign Office to prevent any agreement affecting these securities. The loan agreement, they felt, would dilute responsibility for Mexican indebtedness by dividing it between Mexico and the United States.[92]

The French minister was more upset with less apparent reason. Already convinced that the ultimate objective of the United States was to destroy world civilization by replacing stable monarchies with anarchic and demagogic republics, de Gabriac saw every Yankee move as an attack on France, guardian of world order. He was equally certain that most liberals were willing tools of United States policy.[93] The only method, short of war, to prevent the United States from gaining monopoly power over the commerce of the Western Hemisphere was to assist Mexican conservatives establish a strong European-oriented monarchy. With French support such a government would be able to resist pressure from the United States, protect Central and South America, and open new fields for European commerce.[94]

Forsyth's arrival in October with a policy of moderation and understanding only increased French apprehension. De Gabriac was sure that Yankee flattery would undermine whatever *puro* resistance remained to United States expansion. The United States, using an alliance as bait, would encourage Mexico to become involved in a war with England or Spain, a war sure to terminate in Yankee acquisition of Cuba and Mexico. Rumors of Lerdo's desire for a protectorate confirmed de Gabriac's fears, and he saw Lerdo's assuming charge of the Foreign Ministry as a prelude to the disappearance of independent Mexico.[95]

News of the impending signature of treaties caused de Gabriac to warn again of the economic dangers of the United States' policy of expansion.

> The absorption of Mexico by the United States [he wrote] will . . . [necessarily result in the loss of both] the Mexican market for manufactured products from France and England . . . [and that] of the United States for these same products. The reason is very simple and natural: from the moment of absorption, the production of precious metals in Mexico will increase fivefold at least . . . since presently nine of every ten mines are abandoned for lack of capital, labor, security, and roads. With the aid of a differential tariff against Europe in this new territory, the industry of the United States, which will receive as pay the precious metals of Mexico, will increase [while] the rapid increase of population [in Mexico] will provide a sure outlet for all the new products, formerly a monopoly of Europe. . . . Mexico will never succeed in creating an industry capable of competing with the United States and will send [to the

United States] her iron, copper, wood, sugar, coffee, indigo, tallow, hemp, skins, oils, even silks. . . . These . . . will return to Mexico in the form of finished products. Thus to allow the United States to realize its plans with respect to Mexico is to expose oneself to a grave risk. Europe would lose, in one stroke, two important markets and the [resulting] commercial crisis . . . will be more complete and more profound. Nothing will be able to destroy this giant, more frightening for the power of its material position than for purely political interests.[96]

The loan treaty, de Gabriac maintained, was the death blow to the commercial strength and political influence of France and Great Britain in Mexico. Mexico had sold herself for $8 million. The United States was now the hemispheric banker, a position that would allow for foreclosure at its leisure.[97]

Mexico was aware of British and French opposition to the treaties. Mexican ministers in London and Paris were instructed to counter this opposition. The French objections were considered less serious. In Paris the minister was to stress that the treaties would not damage French trade since Yankee and French exports were noncompetitive. In London the position was that the Montes-Forsyth Treaties did not violate the treaty rights of any other power and that the loan would benefit Mexico's English creditors. A rather stiff attitude was in order: how and where Mexico secured loans and how she repaid these were of no concern to Great Britain. The custom rebates were merely an assignment of customs revenues to the United States, to which London could not object since such assignments existed to pay off English creditors. What the United States chose to do with this assignment was of no concern to Mexico or Great Britain. In the circumstances British economic interest in Mexico could best be served by a British policy of justice and friendship.[98]

How the British and French governments might have reacted to the ratification is an interesting point of speculation, but if their reaction had been consistent with their attitude toward the signing of the treaties then there would have been no European challenge to a United States economic protectorate in Mexico. London warned both the bondholders' association and the British legation in Mexico that Mexican debts did not mortgage her sovereignty and that Britain would not interfere in the affairs of the United States—refunding of the Mexican customs assignment was an internal Yankee question. This provoked the bondholders' representative to observe that perhaps his clients should begin looking to the United States for their security since Mexico was rapidly falling under her control.[99]

After months of dire warnings about the future of Mexico, the French reaction in both Paris and Mexico City to the treaties seemed to be one of resignation. De Gabriac's efforts to rally the large French community in Mexico produced what were, for him, sobering results. He found Frenchmen unmoved at the prospects of having to secure most of their imports from the United States. He reported that many were pleased since Yankee goods were of better quality and would now be cheaper than similar French products.[100] It is interesting to note in this regard that, according to the United States consul at Veracruz, Frenchmen were dominant in the wholesale trade, buying from importers and selling to retailers.[101] French merchants apparently had a better eye for a bargain than they did for the grand civilizing mission of their homeland. Needless to say, the rejection of the treaties by both Pierce and Buchanan left de Gabriac pleased but puzzled.[102]

The rejection of the treaties may have saved Mexico, as de Gabriac believed, from becoming a subservient part of an expanding United States economy. The combination of factors at this point was favorable to such an expansion. In Mexico the liberal government pursued a policy of moving closer to the United States. Private Yankee investors, speculators, and entrepreneurs received generous treatment. Tariff measures, definition of foreign rights, and efforts to encourage immigration were all framed with United States interests in mind. Continuing conservative revolts and financial distress threatened the survival of both the reform program and the government. Internal difficulties served as a pretext for menacing actions by European powers.

Under these conditions, Yankee money and power would have been welcomed by the liberals. Money was necessary to crush the revolts, to establish a stable government, and to finance major economic development. While the Comonfort government was obviously attracted to the loan treaty by the money it made available, equally important was the fact that it interposed United States power, political and economic, between Mexico and Europe. By increasing Yankee economic involvement in Mexico and creating a corresponding desire to preserve Mexican political independence from European threats, the treaties would give Mexico an alternative to economic dependence on Europe.

These attitudes in Mexico coincided with favorable conditions in the United States. The Pierce administration was openly dedicated to a policy of commercial expansion. Various elements, particularly in the South, were beginning to express an interest in commercial expansion into Latin America. Both the ministers to liberal Mexico, Gadsden and Forsyth, were involved in southern efforts at commercial expansion and both expressed opposition to territorial expansion into Mexico on racial grounds. Forsyth's view of the proper economic relationship between the two countries would be labeled economic imperialism today.

These circumstances resulted in the elaboration and signature of treaties which, without mentioning 'protectorate', would, in fact, have reduced Mexico to an economic appendage of the United States. The nature of this relationship seems to have been recognized and accepted by Great Britain, whose favorable trade relations with the United States prevented any excessive alarm over the prospects of an expanded realm for Yankee influence. France appeared to exaggerate the negative economic impact of the treaties on French interest but was unwilling to act alone. The French reaction, while expressed most forcefully in economic terms, appeared to have been motivated more by noneconomic factors. France saw and feared the economic consequences of the expansion of United States power because of its presumed effect on the future of monarchy, Latin civilization, and the Second Empire's position of world leadership.

The failure of the treaties was related to the change of administrations in

Washington. With ample time the Pierce administration doubtless would have attempted to secure ratification of at least a modified version of the agreements. With only eight days remaining to it when the accords reached Washington, the old administration could do little. The incoming Buchanan administration gave scant attention to the treaties; they represented an initiative of the previous administration and made no direct contribution to the Buchanan policy of territorial expansion. Economic imperialism was still an idea whose time had not come, at least not in Washington.

4
Buchanan's Drive for Territorial Expansion, 1857–1858

The failure of the Montes-Forsyth Treaties marked a turning point in United States policy toward Mexico, while in Mexico their rejection coincided with increased difficulties for the Reforma. Buchanan not only rejected the idea of commercial expansion but was insensitive to the idea that aid, moral or financial, to Mexico was in the best interest of the United States. Instead he embarked upon a clear and persistent policy designed to despoil Mexico once again of land. Rather than aid Mexico through her difficulties, Buchanan wished to use these to force a cession of territory. Forsyth, who had already demonstrated his opposition to territorial expansion, reluctantly attempted to execute this policy.

The prospects of Comonfort's government had appeared bright in the opening months of 1857 only to deteriorate as the year wore on.[1] During the previous year, Comonfort successfully confronted two persistent challenges and the ever-present threat of bankruptcy. Radical reform measures, the most notable being the Juárez and Lerdo laws, and the consideration of these plus other radical measures by the constitutional congress, which began meeting in February 1856, provoked a series of revolts which the government could ill afford the energy and resources required to suppress. Meanwhile within the government a struggle raged between the supporters of Comonfort—*moderados,* centrists, and some opportunists without regard to political coloration—and the activist liberals led by the *puros.* This struggle was fought in both the cabinet and Congress. The new year brought a series of encouraging victories for Comonfort: he survived the cabinet crisis provoked by Lerdo in December; the persistently troubled northeast seemed secure with the submission of Santiago Vidaurri, Monterrey's opportunistic and ambitious *cacique;* the new constitution, formally completed on 5 February, was at heart a moderate document which avoided most of the extreme measures desired by the *puros;* and the treaties of 10 February promised critical aid, both monetary and symbolic.

The rejection of the Montes-Forsyth Treaties in Washington was merely an early and visible portent of things to come. Each step in the implementation of the new charter, which despite its relatively mild character was not accepted by conservative-church elements as a viable compromise, was accompanied by progressively more serious challenges to governmental authority. Its formal adoption by Congress on 5 February, its promulgation 12 February, its official publication 11 March, and its full implementation 16 September were all occasions for plots, intrigues, maneuvers, and open resistance. The government's inability, in the face of this rising tide of public disorder, to protect foreign lives and property and to satisfy the foreign creditors brought renewed threats of foreign intervention. In the face of these problems and despite the harsh territorial expansion policy adopted in Washington, the Comonfort government sought to draw closer to the United States.

In its quest for closer relations with the United States, Mexico encountered a cold and covetous neighbor who demanded territorial dismemberment as the price for its aid. The United States minister actively encouraged the suspension of the Mexican constitution, a step which, when taken by Comonfort in December 1858, triggered a fiery civil war. When presented with a choice between a liberal and a conservative government, Forsyth recognized the conservative one, believing it would be the more likely to agree to territorial cession. When, despite threats of United States military occupation of the frontier regions, the conservative regime refused to cede territory, Forsyth used the power of his position, including his influence over Yankee economic interests, to force the government into a position where, he believed, it could only sell territory or collapse. The failure of this policy led to a partial break in diplomatic relations between the countries.

While Washington's decision to reject the proffered key to Mexico's considerable storehouse of economic wealth in favor of a crude demand for territory may appear incredibly shortsighted, it was in harmony with the prevailing manifest-destiny views and reflected Buchanan's past political experience, his views of his country's domestic crisis and the role that foreign policy could play in that crisis, and the circumstances surrounding his nomination and election to the presidency. The highlight of Buchanan's public career had been his tenure as secretary of state under Polk, 1845–49. Beginning the war with Mexico as a reluctant expansionist, Buchanan sensed the mood of the people and became increasingly enthusiastic for large slices of Mexican territory. Having discovered an issue with national appeal, Buchanan pursued it with determination. In his unsuccessful bids for the Democratic nomination in 1848 and 1852, he sought to still agitation on the slavery question by uniting the party behind a program of expansion. Pierce's endorsement of territorial expansion in his inaugural address reflected Buchanan's influence. As Pierce's minister to the Court of St. James, Buchanan negotiated for the British withdrawal from Central America in accordance with the United States interpretation of the Clayton-Bulwer Treaty and with expansionist views that Central America constituted an area predestined for Yankee expansion. While in London, Buchanan made public in the Ostend Manifesto his long-established views on the purchase of Cuba.

Sectionalism, exacerbated by the violence and threat of violence resulting from the Kansas-Nebraska Act of 1854, made party unity and preservation of the union, rather than expansion, key issues in 1856. Buchanan's nomination probably owed more to his having been absent from the country for the past three years and thus untainted by the sectional struggle than it did to any endorsement of his expansionistic views or appreciation of his leadership abilities. The party platform adopted at Cincinnati focused mainly on solving the sectional issue while including secondary planks looking to a vigorous policy in Latin America to promote the Monroe Doctrine, commercial expansion, control of isthmian transits, and ascendancy in the Gulf, a plank which could be interpreted as a call for the acquisition of Cuba. But Buchanan, out of touch with affairs at home and supremely confident of his own leadership, focused his campaign biography on his expansionistic views. The role of the "Sage of Wheatland" in the Mexican cession was highlighted, as was his continuing interest in the acquisition of Cuba.[2]

Buchanan's nomination and subsequent election were heavily indebted to southern support. Judah P. Benjamin and John Slidell, Louisiana senators, helped manage his nomination and did yeoman duty in marshaling the southern vote, both traditional Democrat and former Whig, for the Democratic slate. Both played key roles in organizing the new administration and establishing its policies. The result was a Mexican policy designed to realize their dreams of converting New Orleans into a great commercial emporium. Central to their dreams were plans for constructing railroads across the Tehuantepec Isthmus and across northern Mexico to the Gulf of California. Such a policy was attractive to Benjamin, who had a financial interest in and served as attorney for the Louisiana Tehuantepec Company, and conformed to Buchanan's desire to emulate his illustrious Democratic predecessors. If vigorously pursued, it was believed, such a policy could serve to divert attention from sectionalism and slavery.[3]

Buchanan set the stage for his Mexican policy by asserting in his inaugural that "no nation will have a right to interfere or to complain if . . . by fair purchase . . . we shall still further extend our possessions." Only by "fair purchase" or voluntary association, as in the case of Texas, could expansion be accomplished with "justice and honor." In condemning William Walker's Nicaraguan expedition specifically and filibusterers generally, Buchanan noted in 1858:

> It is beyond question the destiny of our race to spread themselves over the continent of North America, and this at no distant day should events be permitted to take their natural course. The tide of emigrants will flow to the south, and nothing can eventually arrest its progress. If permitted to go there peacefully, Central America will soon contain an American population which will confer blessings and benefits as well upon the natives as their respective Governments.[4]

Buchanan, who would handle most of the duties of the secretary of state himself, appointed another old expansionist, General Lewis Cass, to head the Department of State. Buchanan exercised direct control of foreign affairs through John Appleton, a close and trusted friend, who served as chief clerk under Cass. In matters of patronage, Buchanan adopted the general rule that Pierce appointees against whom there was no negative information should be allowed to retain their posts until the terms of their appointment expired or until they had held the posts for four years.[5] This policy, coupled with pressure from the Mexican legation and from Forsyth's friends, resulted in his retention despite the obvious conflict between his views, as reflected in the February treaties, and the territorial expansion policy being adopted by the president.

Buchanan outlined the terms of his Mexican policy in two instructions to Forsyth on 17 July 1857.[6] Forsyth was to secure a treaty reaffirming the United States's transit rights in Tehuantepec and to negotiate an adjustment of boundaries and a settlement of mutual claims. He was to purchase Baja California, Sonora, and that portion of Chihuahua north of the thirtieth parallel. For this transfer of territory $12 million was to be offered, with the maximum price set at $15 million. All claims against the United States must be dropped, while all noncontractual claims against Mexico were to be assumed by the United States and $2 million of the purchase price retained to satisfy them.

Buchanan's policy of territorial expansion represented a frank endorsement of the cruder forms of manifest destiny, as indicated by the arguments furnished for Forsyth's use. Remoteness, sparseness of population, and the hostility of local Indians were to be emphasized. That the region was sparsely inhabited would demonstrate the area's lack of value to Mexico. The inevitability of United States acquisition was to be made clear. Suggestions that Mexico should sell the area while she still had some actual control over it, as well as a legal title, were clear threats of future seizure. The threat to use force was also to be made in connection with the claims settlement. Only by the sale of territory could Mexico hope to satisfy the great number of United States claims—claims which "appeal very strongly . . . [for] intervention to enforce them."

Forsyth was also instructed to expand the terms of the Gadsden Treaty to give the United States a clear and perpetual right to use any and all means of communication which might be opened across Tehuantepec. The United States should also be allowed to protect all such routes in any case where Mexico might be unable or unwilling to provide adequate security. Mexico should be required to open free ports on both the Gulf and Pacific sides of the isthmus. No reciprocal compensation was to be offered Mexico for agreements on Tehuantepec.

For immediate political dividends, the Tehuantepec transits were considered more important than the territorial question. Conflicting claims over the right to construct the transisthmian railroad had been put aside for the moment and all the former competitors brought together in one organization. P. A. Hargous, who had purchased the Garay concession in 1849, A. G. Sloo, who had secured a new grant in 1853, and F. P. Falconnet, a British banker whose loan of $600,000 to Sloo in 1853 to secure the grant had never been repaid and whose foreclosure and subsequent sale of the grant to Hargous had not been recognized by Mexico or by Sloo, were all cooperating with a group of New Orleans investors, led by Emile La Sere and Judah P. Benjamin. These groups had organized the Louisiana Tehuantepec Company with La Sere as president and Benjamin as attorney. Benjamin's position as attorney for and stockholder in the new company encouraged him to use his influence with Buchanan to best advantage.[7]

The frail nature of the unity of interests represented in the recent merger also caused Buchanan and Benjamin to give first priority to the transit question. Both Sloo and Falconnet were distrustful of the new company and were taking steps outside the company to safeguard their interests. Each of them sent personal agents to Mexico City and Sloo later challenged the legality of the company's organization in court. Only an immediate success in Mexico could hold this weak coalition together long enough to realize either political or financial profit from the venture. Forsyth was assured that the desired transit agreement "will be productive of great and enduring benefits to your country and entitle your name to be enrolled in the list of her most distinguished Diplomatists."

The instructions on Tehuantepec marked a considerable gain for Benjamin. Assurance of the United States's protection for the transit route would greatly enhance the company's ability to raise money by public subscription. Benjamin's position was further strengthened when he was commissioned to deliver the new instructions to Forsyth. Benjamin and La Sere were coming to Mexico to negotiate a contract for the new company. Forsyth was instructed to endorse their efforts and to aid them wherever advisable. He was also authorized to use their services in his diplomatic negotiations.[8]

Forsyth, who had already shown a propensity to assume responsibility and to try new experiments in diplomacy, did not accept his instructions complacently. When informed that his treaties had been rejected, he concluded that the rejection applied to the treaties but not the policy behind them and so informed the Mexican government. He immediately embarked upon a campaign to convince the new administration of the wisdom of his policy.[9] He informed the Mexicans that the principal problem had been the Senate's lack of time to consider the treaties before adjournment. He assured them that he would shortly receive instructions to negotiate on terms differing very little from those in the February treaties.[10]

Even before the arrival of new instructions, rumors that Buchanan desired to purchase territory caused Forsyth to warn against such a policy and to renew his pleas for a sympathetic and generous policy toward Mexico and its reform program.[11] The arrival of the instructions in August provoked Forsyth to use sharp words with Washington. He charged that anyone who had read his despatches over the last several months would know that a policy to purchase territory was unwise and impossible. The Comonfort government, Forsyth stated, was pledged by the organic act of May 1856 and by its manifesto to the nation of 4 March 1857 to refrain from any alienation of territory.

Forsyth also believed the mere public mention that a Mexican government was considering the sale of national domain would insure its immediate overthrow. Much of the hostility to Santa Anna, he noted, sprang from his sale of territory in the 1853 treaty. If a government were willing to ignore the legal restrictions and to brave popular indignation in order to raise money through the sale of territory, it would demand a much higher price than he was authorized to tender. Noting that in 1853 Gadsden had offered $30 million for a slightly smaller version of the territory now desired, Forsyth characterized the $12 million now being offered as a "paltry" sum which fell far short of the "exaggerated estimate which the Government and Nation place upon the value of their National Domains."

Forsyth adopted the attitude that he had been insulted by the new instructions.

> If the Department had had confidence in my capacity to make correct observations, . . . it was in possession of the fact, admitting of no qualification or doubt . . . that the success of the negotiation confided to me, was hopeless from the beginning. I must have greatly misused the ten months period of my residence here, not to have been able to discover this at a glance.

Forsyth's opposition to the purchase of territory was equaled by his reaction to the terms under which he was to negotiate a new and expanded Tehuantepec transit agreement. In the case of the purchase of land, he endorsed the ultimate goal but disagreed on the best method of realizing it. In the matter of the transit agreement, however, Forsyth was convinced that Buchanan, by acting on the faulty advice of Senator Benjamin, was verging on unethical practice. In his eyes, the instructions on transit rights smacked of official backing for one group of speculators— Benjamin, Hargous, and associates—to the detriment of another group—A. G. Sloo and associates. Worse, it even suggested that national interests had been subordinated to the private concerns of Benjamin and his friends.

Forsyth also believed that he was again being directed to negotiate on impossible terms. He was to negotiate a transit treaty containing more liberal provisions than the Gadsden Treaty, yet no money payment was to be offered for these concessions. Forsyth had already sounded out the Mexican cabinet on this question and had found its members "fully alive . . . to the immense value of the Isthmus." Any attempt to improve on the United States position without appropriate compensation would surely fail. "Mexico remembers that ten years ago [when Buchanan was secretary of state] . . . the U.S. offered fifteen million for the right of way across the Isthmus." Mexico should not now be expected to give away this asset, Forsyth argued, especially when several Mexican citizens were able and willing to purchase the transit rights without endangering Mexican sovereignty.[12]

Forsyth's attitude on the transit question was complicated by his relations with Benjamin. They had led opposing camps in the Cincinnati convention and their relations in Mexico were to be permeated with suspicion and mistrust. Forsyth believed that Benjamin had been instrumental in turning Buchanan against the February treaties; Benjamin suspected that Forsyth's true sympathies lay with the Sloo interests, whose agent, Pierre Soulé, was already in Mexico City to work against Benjamin.

Unable to bury his personal dislike of Benjamin and feeling that Buchanan's transit policy represented political favoritism and that any attempt to purchase territory was unwise, Forsyth settled on a course of action apparently designed to insure the failure of all negotiations. He immediately discussed with Sebastián Lerdo de Tejada, *moderado* brother of the *puro* Miguel Lerdo and now foreign minister, the terms of the two treaties he had been directed to negotiate indicating that the proposals would not be presented formally until Mexico had had an opportunity to make a contract with one of the contending groups. Lerdo found the territorial proposal unacceptable and would negotiate on the transit question only if the proposal were changed so as not to violate Mexican sovereignty. Mexico would not consider any proposal that allowed United States troops to use or to protect the transit route.[13]

Because his instructions specified that any contract signed by Benjamin and La Sere must conform to the terms which he was instructed to write into a treaty, Forsyth assumed that Sebastián Lerdo's objections to these terms insured that no contract would be let. Forsyth then fulfilled the letter of his instructions to aid Benjamin and La Sere by introducing them to Comonfort and stating in their presence that their project had the approval of his government. Beyond this initial courtesy, Forsyth carefully avoided giving any semblance of official sponsorship to their private negotiations. To prove his neutrality Forsyth also introduced Soulé, the Sloo agent, to Comonfort.

In assuming that no agreement could be reached between the Benjamin party and the government, Forsyth had erred seriously. Rumors that a contract would be signed spread quickly and created grave doubts in Forsyth's mind. Was Benjamin agreeing to terms that would endanger the isthmian treaty rights of the United States? Benjamin's repeated public boast of having secret powers from Washington would lend extra weight in Mexican eyes to any contract he might make. Hoping to prevent an agreement or, failing that, to set the United States's position clearly before the Mexican government, Forsyth formally presented a copy of the draft transit treaty and instructions he had received to Comonfort. He emphasized that the United States would only recognize a contract which conformed to these and which preserved all its rights under article 8 of the Gadsden Treaty.

Forsyth pushed for an official Mexican reaction to the proposal for expanded transit privileges. The results were as he had anticipated: Comonfort declined to consider the matter and the foreign minister respectfully refused to deal with any proposal that infringed on national sovereignty. Regarding Forsyth's effort to insure that contract negotiations with Benjamin and La Sere conformed to the policy contained in his instructions, he was informed that this was not a diplomatic matter, that the negotiators were being treated as private parties and any agreement with them would have to be in Mexico's interest.

Still believing that economic and commercial domination were superior to territorial expansion, Forsyth decided to secure an unequivocal Mexican rejection of the proposed boundary change. He raised the question with Comonfort and received the expected negative response. "Each President has his system," Comonfort said, "that of Don Antonio [López de Santa Anna] was to sell his country; mine is to preserve it." When he presented the draft boundary treaty to the foreign minister the rejection was polite but firm. "The Govt. of the Republic," wrote the foreign minister, "considers inadmissible any plan based upon the cession of any portion of the national territory."[14]

Forsyth's effort was in vain, for the Mexican government was fully aware of his breach with Benjamin and was exploiting it. Knowing that Benjamin refused to confide in the United States minister, the Mexican negotiators fed this distrust in order to drive a better bargain. At a crucial point in the negotiations, they informed Benjamin that Forsyth had withdrawn his endorsement. At another time, Benjamin was told that Forsyth had warned Mexico against making any contract, for the United States would consider this as a *casus belli*.[15]

Pressed by the Mexicans to agree quickly or lose all chance of reaching an agreement and feeling that he had been betrayed by Forsyth, Benjamin panicked and accepted a contract on Mexico's terms. The contract fell far short of the policy outlined in Forsyth's instructions. The Louisiana Tehuantepec Company was made completely subservient to the Mexican government by a requirement to submit to the supervisory power of the Fomento Ministry and to pay Mexico fixed sums for everything transported across the isthmus. The government would also receive 15 percent of the company's net profits. The company was required to construct and turn over to Mexican control lighthouses, docks, jetties, and other navigational improvements. More serious for the United States, the contract provided for the annulment of the Sloo grant,[16] an action which undermined its position under article 8 of the Gadsden Treaty. Its privileges under the Gadsden Treaty were further weakened in that United States military forces could only be transported across Tehuantepec with the express permission of Mexico. Finally, the Falconnet debt, now totaling more than $1 million, was to be paid by the Louisiana Tehuantepec Company rather than by the Mexican government as stipulated in Forsyth's instructions.[17]

The Tehuantepec contract negotiations had become inseparably involved in diplomatic relations. Forsyth had intended to take no action on his instructions until after his protests and pleas had been considered in Washington, but Benjamin's actions had forced him to do otherwise. While his diplomatic efforts had done little to ease his fears, they had created hope in a new direction, for Comonfort appeared anxious for a transit agreement which would not infringe on national sovereignty. He had suggested that generous grants could be made to United States citizens for the construction of railroads from the Rio Grande to the Gulf of California. To assist in financing their construction, Comonfort suggested that the grants carry cessions of alternate leagues of land on each side of the right of way.

Forsyth thought he saw in this attitude an opportunity to resurrect his protectorate scheme in modified form. Realizing the degree to which Buchanan was committed to territorial expansion, Forsyth now argued that this must be accomplished indirectly. He proposed a new set of agreements, unembarrassed by territorial cessions, for special commercial advantages similar to those in the February treaties, a postal treaty for regular steamer service, an expanded frontier reciprocity agreement, and a treaty covering railroad concessions and transit rights in Tehuantepec and on Mexico's northern frontier. With large land grants along the railroad routes in Yankee hands, Forsyth argued, the area would soon be "Americanized." He now maintained that the ultimate objective of his February treaties had been to Americanize Mexico preparatory to annexation.

When Forsyth learned the full details of the contract signed by Benjamin and La Sere, he felt that the United States was in danger of losing all its privileges under the Gadsden Treaty. Washington's position had been that the Sloo grant was valid and only required agreement among the claimants and between them and the Mexican government to implement it. The strength of this position lay in the inviolability of contracts. If the United States allowed a new contract to be made on the basis of the unilateral annulment of the Sloo contract, how could Mexico be prevented from annulling the new contract at some future date? Would Mexico not try to use the contract restrictions on the transit of United States troops to free itself from obligations imposed by the Gadsden Treaty?

Forsyth attempted to salvage what he could from the wreckage. He requested an interview with Comonfort in the hope of making a treaty to safeguard his country's interests in Tehuantepec. But Comonfort, who by adroit handling of the private negotiations with Benjamin had secured for his country the most favorable position it had held in the transit question since the first concession in 1842, was not willing to endanger his gains by reopening negotiations. Comonfort was conveniently too ill to receive the minister; Forsyth labeled it a ''diplomatic illness.''

Approaches to the foreign minister were no more productive. Sebastián Lerdo indicated his willingness to negotiate, but the perpetual right of way, the right to pass military forces, and the unilateral right of the United States to protect the transit route were specifically ruled out. Since Forsyth could negotiate on no other terms and since the position adopted by the foreign minister coincided with the terms of the recent contract, Forsyth dropped the matter, convinced that Mexico now maintained that United States rights in Tehuantepec were defined not by the Gadsden Treaty but by the provisions of the contract with the Louisiana Tehuantepec Company.

The most immediate and direct result of the imbroglio left in the wake of the collapse of Buchanan's Mexican policy was an acrimonious episode in which Forsyth and Benjamin both sought to escape responsibility. With charge, counter-charge, and name calling, each side appealed to Buchanan for support. In a diary kept by Benjamin, and turned over to Buchanan, the charges against Forsyth were summed up as follows: ''We have not the slightest hesitation in saying that Mr. Forsyth's treacherous conduct towards us has cost the Company the whole of the Falconnet debt . . . and a loss of fifteen years addition to the terms of the concession, the value of which we will not undertake to estimate.''

Forsyth answered, charge for charge, and countered by recounting Benjamin's grandiose actions—his attempts to speak in the name of Buchanan, his belittling of Secretary Cass, and his hunger for the spotlight. Forsyth asserted that Benjamin had attempted to exceed his authority and had been outmaneuvered and outwitted by the Mexicans. He emphasized that both his position and instructions had dictated that his first responsibility should be to national interests, not the private business interests of Senator Benjamin. This, Forsyth felt, was the crux of the matter. The charges against him were being made ''not for failing in . . . [his]

public duty . . . but rather because he had not permitted [himself] to be the pliant tool of the clique of Tehuantepec speculators who for ten years past have constantly kept this Legation in hot water—a clique that has vaunted its ownership of more than one American Minister.'' Forsyth closed his defense with an offer to resign if the administration did not have confidence in him.[18]

Forsyth's bid for a vote of confidence went unanswered. The best Washington ever did, in a communication which could only be considered a reprimand, was to regret that mutual distrust and jealousy had prevented the agent and the friend of the president from working together on a matter of such importance. ''The public interests may have suffered from an unfortunate misunderstanding'' was the sad verdict of Washington.[19]

A second result of the failure of Buchanan's policy was a renewal of Forsyth's efforts to induce Washington to adopt his dream of a protectorate as its policy. He continued to revise and refine the key points of his February treaties and to point to the varied interests which would be served. He argued that his policy would ultimately lead to a situation where partial or total annexation of Mexico could be accomplished by mutual consent. In the meantime, the incalculable economic benefits generated by a protectorate would lessen domestic sectional strife. North, South, and West would be brought together in the pursuit of economic profit. Each segment of the economy—merchants, bankers, investors, farmers, shippers, manufacturers—would gain.

He noted that there were far fewer of his fellow countrymen in Mexico than Frenchmen, Spaniards, Germans, or Englishmen. No Yankee owned an import firm in Mexico City. The scarcity of Yankees made the Mexican government less responsive to their interests and contributed to their mistreatment. His plans would bring an influx of people from the United States who would strengthen the government and cause an increase in Mexican respect for their lives, property, and other interests. Forsyth summoned all his considerable journalistic skills in an effort to convince Buchanan that this was the ideal plan under the circumstances.[20]

Forsyth's planning and pleading were all in vain. A vast gap existed between his views and those of Buchanan—a gap made obvious by the response given to his request for new authority. In an instruction notable for its bluntness, Forsyth was informed that Buchanan would never agree to a loan or a payment of any kind to obtain transit rights, railroad rights of way, or a commercial treaty—the implication being that money would only be paid for land. A United States pledge to defend the isthmian transit route was more than ample compensation for transit rights and privileges since, as Buchanan saw it, private interests would never construct a railroad across Tehuantepec if only Mexican protection was offered. Regarding the purchase of railroad rights of way, Buchanan felt that ''the importance of a railroad across her Northern territory, ought to induce [Mexico] to adopt the most liberal measures in order to secure the necessary protection and capital. . . . It is hardly to be expected that the United States will pay . . . for the privilege of conferring on that country this great and important benefit.''

Forsyth's halfhearted handling of the president's initial instructions, coupled with his attempts to revive the protectorate scheme, aroused Buchanan's ire and brought a strongly worded censure. Forsyth was reminded that he was only an agent charged with carrying out presidential orders—not with determining policy. The manner in which Forsyth had presented the president's proposals was interpreted as a violation of the spirit, if not the letter, of his instruction. Buchanan, speaking through the secretary of state, charged that Forsyth, convinced of the superiority of his own plans, had presented the president's proposals in such an informal and listless manner as to insure their rejection. "If the negotiation confided to you was 'hopeless from the beginning' as you declare it to have been, you had the consolation of knowing that you were not responsible for it." If Forsyth had honestly tried to execute the president's policy and had failed, "no blame for the indignity could possibly have rested on him." The implication was clear: Forsyth had not faithfully tried to execute presidential policy, so the blame rested squarely with him.

Thus chastized for not having loyally pursued Buchanan's expansionist policy, Forsyth was left at his post and informed that the instructions of 17 July 1857 would continue to be a statement of the Mexican policy of the United States. The policy, "having been adopted deliberately," was "not likely to be changed." Buchanan would be pleased if Forsyth concurred, but whether he did or not, it was his duty to do all possible to gain its realization.[21] Forsyth's retention by Buchanan, given the obvious conflict in views, is inexplicable.

The impasse created by the collapse of Buchanan's Mexican policy in the fall of 1857 was soon relieved by events in Mexico. After having argued for a year that Mexico would never agree to sell territory, Forsyth now learned informally that Comonfort was willing to negotiate for the sale of territory.[22] This change in attitude reflected the steady deterioration of the position of the liberal government since the promulgation of the new constitution the previous February. Elections had been held for a new Congress scheduled to meet simultaneously with the coming into force of the new constitution on 16 September. Most of the *puros* had been excluded from this Congress by a combination of changes in electoral laws requiring delegates to be residents of the districts from which they were elected and manipulation of the election process by Comonfort and his supporters. But the Congress did little to strengthen Comonfort's position even though it was much more amenable to executive direction than the constituent assembly had been. The constitution, with its elevation of the Juárez and Lerdo laws to constitutional precepts and its failure to protect the exclusive position of the church, was still an insurmountable barrier for most conservatives, and the new Congress's subservience to Comonfort alienated most *puros* and many other liberals. The prospect of Comonfort's converting his position from substitute provisional president to constitutional chief executive on 1 December only served to intensify the opposition, especially that of the church, and to increase the frequency and fervor of revolts. Comonfort, assailed from all sides and heading a bankrupt government, doubted the wisdom of the more radical features of the constitution and of the weak executive provided for in that document.[23] This conjunction of events convinced him to seek assistance at the expense of national honor and territory.

Forsyth now hoped to convert disaster into victory and to redeem his reputation as a diplomat, but only if Comonfort could remain in power long enough to effect the transfer of territory. He was not very sanguine about Comonfort's ability to retain his position. Neither the liberals nor the conservatives trusted or fully supported Comonfort, yet neither had made a concentrated effort to oust him for fear of losing control of the presidency to the opposition. If Comonfort were replaced by a strong leader of either party, Forsyth felt, the purchase of territory would become more difficult. Benito Juárez, whose position as chief justice of the Supreme Court made him ex officio vice-president and placed him first in line for the presidency should Comonfort be forced out, was a *puro* of considerable talent and character who would oppose the sale of territory as a matter of principle. A strong conservative government would be even worse: it would be pro-European and hostile to the United States.[24]

Forsyth, believing that the purchase of territory depended upon Comonfort's remaining in office, undertook to bolster the president's shaky position. He supported an effort to float a loan of $6 million among the local bankers. Although the government proposed to sell $6 million in bonds for only $2.5 million, the local financiers, doubtful of its ability to remain in power, refused the loan. To build public confidence, Forsyth spread stories that he had full authority from Washington to extend financial aid to Mexico on the basis of a treaty for commercial privileges, transits, or territory. He also persuaded Gabor Naphegyi to indicate that his New York bankers were prepared to cover the first repayment installment on the loan if assistance by treaty had not been completed by then.[25] Despite the favorable terms and Forsyth's efforts, the bankers remained unconvinced and the loan failed.

Forsyth also turned to Washington for assistance in capitalizing on Comonfort's new attitude. The natural wealth of the regions to be purchased convinced Forsyth that "they would be a cheap bargain at almost any money price." To secure such riches by forcing a "hard bargain" on a "feeble and embarrassed neighboring nation" would damage "American national character." To safeguard the priceless "national character" and at the same time to insure "the success of so important an object," Forsyth requested that he "be empowered at the critical moment to offer an irresistible temptation" to Comonfort and the Congress in the form of "a price that would in some degree satisfy the expectations of the [Mexican] public mind."[26]

Comonfort, keenly aware of Washington's fears of European influence in Mexico, sought to enhance his bargaining position. He had his agent and friend, Gregorio de Ajuria, approach the French minister with accounts of the desperate plight of the government.[27] Rumors circulated that Spain was aiding Santa Anna to subvert the junior officers in the Mexican army. Comonfort casually informed Forsyth of a plan, reportedly approved by France and Great Britain, for Spain to furnish "25,000 Spanish troops, & the necessary supplies of money to establish himself firmly in power, & to become the head of whatever form of Government he chose." The object of the scheme was candidly reported to be European domination of Mexico as the first step toward restoring Spanish control over all Spanish America and protecting "Cuba against the designs of the United States." Comonfort's actions had the desired effect; Forsyth reported that "Mexican institutions are crumbling to pieces, and interposition to gather up the wreck . . . is as certain as it is indispensable. . . . Shall that interposition be American or European?"

Despite his success in arousing the concern and support of the United States minister, financial succor was not forthcoming and Comonfort's position became less tenable. Prior to assuming office under the constitution, Comonfort sought conservative support for his governing without the constitution. Only after this effort failed did he agree to become constitutional president.[28] He did not, however, cease to seek an understanding with the conservatives. If the liberals and their Yankee friends were unable or unwilling to furnish the necessary monetary support, possibly the conservatives would. He held discussions with conservatives aimed at a government of reform which "would not openly clash with conservative principles or the religious habits and beliefs of the people." He also discussed with the French minister the possibility of monetary aid in the event he suspended constitutional government.[29]

The result of these considerations and maneuvers was a coup d'état on 17 December in which the constitution was suspended, Congress dismissed, and Juárez, the ex officio vice-president, arrested. A carefully rehearsed *pronunciamiento* at Tacubaya by the conservative general Félix Zuloaga in favor of a dictatorship under Comonfort followed immediately. The conspiracy, however, had misjudged the attachment of local governments to the constitution. Since state and municipal officials who had taken oaths to support the constitution had done so in the face of certain excommunication and many of them had already been cast out of the church for acquiring ecclesiastical property under Ley Lerdo, they probably felt that they had little else to lose and much to gain by maintaining the liberal charter. Almost without exception the local levels of government began declaring in favor of the constitution. Even his conservative support proved largely illusory. As his position deteriorated Comonfort first requested $1 million in aid from the French minister and then $600,000 from Forsyth. The French minister refused; Forsyth indicated his willingness, but it would take months to secure the money.[30]

When it became obvious that Comonfort's effort to establish a coalition dictatorship was doomed to failure, his last major supporter deserted him. On 9 January 1858, Zuloaga abandoned Comonfort and pronounced anew on 11 January for a purely conservative regime without Comonfort. With the defection of Zuloaga the civil war, which for months had simmered in the countryside, became general and the fighting moved into Mexico City. Soon three contending armies were in the city—liberal, conservative, and the small force still loyal to Comonfort. On 11 January Comonfort sought to rejoin the liberals. Juárez was released, Comonfort recognized him as constitutional president, and his escape to Guanajuato was arranged. These steps gave Comonfort no relief, and on 21 January he abandoned the National Palace and escaped to Veracruz, where preparations had been made for his flight into exile.[31]

During the last weeks of his presidency, Comonfort received the assistance not only of Forsyth, but also of a number of private United States residents. The most active was Gregorio de Ajuria, who, although he may not have been a citizen, claimed United States residence and was involved in the Mexican business ventures of his Yankee partner, John Temple. In addition to being Temple's agent in the operation of the Mexico City mint, Ajuria owned the newspaper used by Comonfort as an official organ and had made several profitable loans to the government. As Comonfort's position worsened Ajuria became his messenger— to the French minister, possibly to Forsyth, to Doblado in Guanajuato, and he may have escorted Juárez to safety on 11 January. Ajuria had made standby emergency travel arrangements for Comonfort and himself, although he apparently did not depart on the same ship from Veracruz as Comonfort. Carlos Butterfield was also in Mexico City during this period trying again to negotiate a mail-steamer contract and to collect an old claim. What Butterfield may have done is not clear—he was noted for his ability to obtain arms—but he was later referred to as having given great aid to the liberal cause at this time. Jean Napoleon Zerman and his filibustering companions probably gave the most direct aid. Charges against them were dropped and they took up arms for Comonfort during the last days before his flight. Zerman accompanied Comonfort to Veracruz and embarked on the same ship for New Orleans.[32]

Forsyth viewed the events of December and January as a lesson for him in Mexican politics and in the appropriate diplomatic techniques to be employed in such situations. Fiscal insolvency had driven the Comonfort government to consider the sale of territory. Only the lack of ready cash had prevented Forsyth from concluding a deal giving the United States the desired territories. Asserting that similar situations would arise again and again in the future, he appealed to Washington to put at least $500,000 at his disposal "to be applied as part payment immediately upon the signing of a treaty of cession." With ready cash, Forsyth believed, he could entice a future government to sell territory by being able to place in its hands immediately an amount of money sufficient to sustain it in power.[33]

With the collapse of Comonfort two focal points of power emerged, each claiming an exclusive right to govern. Juárez, released from confinement and recognized as president by Comonfort on 11 January, formed his liberal government at Guanajuato on the 19th.[34] In Mexico City Comonfort held out until the 21st, thus delaying the creation of a conservative government under Zuloaga until 23 January.[35] Hence in late January 1858 Forsyth faced the task of choosing a government to recognize.

Forsyth apparently felt that he must make an early choice. He could have referred the question to Washington, or he could simply have waited a few weeks to see if the situation would clarify before acting. But, on 27 January, only four days after it was established, Forsyth recognized the Zuloaga government. The lengths to which Forsyth went in justifying his action indicate that he had serious misgivings as to its justice. Ignoring information reported earlier, he sought to create the impression that he had had no choice. He argued that Juárez's legal rights had been destroyed by his failure to oppose the coup of 17 December, conveniently ignoring the fact that one of the first acts of the coup had been to arrest Juárez to prevent his opposition. Again ignoring Juárez's imprisonment, Forsyth asserted that he had waited in vain for the liberal government to contact him since 17 December, and then inexplicably calculated this wait as forty-seven days.[36]

The facts in the case were somewhat different from the picture presented by Forsyth. The release of Juárez, his escape to Guanajuato, and the establishment there of a constitutional government were fully reported in the Mexico City press.[37] Forsyth doubtless realized that he soon would be officially informed of the existence of the liberal government and asked to extend diplomatic recognition to it. His decision to recognize Zuloaga's government had much to recommend it. Zuloaga held Mexico City, the traditional capital; he appeared the strongest since he had the support of both the army and church; and Forsyth apparently decided that the conservatives would be more likely to sell territory than would Juárez and the *puros*. In view of the stern reprimand recently received relative to his failure to pursue vigorously his instructions on the purchase of territory, Forsyth was extremely sensitive to any indication that such a proposal might be entertained.

If Forsyth's haste in recognizing Zuloaga was motivated by a desire to avoid an open decision on the relative merits of the two claimants, he barely acted in time. On 29 January, two days after recognizing Zuloaga, Forsyth received an official communication from Melchor Ocampo, Juárez's foreign minister.[38] But the die had already been cast; Forsyth could only express his sympathy for the views of the liberals and attempt to justify his failure to recognize their government. He argued that by established diplomatic practice, the holder of Mexico City had always been given de facto recognition. He repeated the same arguments he had made to Washington. Forsyth's note to Ocampo was a valiant effort to turn the tables—to make the liberals responsible for his recognition of Zuloaga and to make him appear the aggrieved party.[39]

The liberal government considered United States recognition vital and had gone to great lengths to obtain it. Ocampo's official note was accompanied by a personal letter in which Forsyth was assured that all matters pending between the two countries could be resolved in an amicable manner.[40] Benito Gómez Farías, son of the late liberal leader Valentín Gómez Farías and now undersecretary in the liberal Foreign Ministry, wrote assuring Forsyth that a generous and friendly policy would be pursued toward the United States.[41] Manuel Doblado wrote as governor of Guanajuato and second in command of constitutional forces pleading with Forsyth not to recognize the reactionary regime. Doblado informed Forsyth that if he wished to move his residence to Querétaro or Guanajuato while the constitutional army reduced the rebels in Mexico City, Doblado could assure him of security and respect.[42] Even after learning that Forsyth had recognized Zuloaga, the liberals continued to press him for several weeks, warning him that no agreement made with the conservatives would be honored by the liberals after the conservatives had been defeated.[43]

Forsyth's decision to recognize Zuloaga has continued to be the source of controversy. Although no displeasure was expressed at the time by Washington, Buchanan later sharply criticized the "indecent haste" shown by Forsyth. The United States historian, Stuart A. MacCorkle, accepted Forsyth's claim that established diplomatic practice dictated recognition of whoever controlled Mexico City.[44] This rationale ignores Gadsden's recognition of the Alvarez government at Cuernavaca in 1855. It also ignores the fact that in 1848 the Treaty of Guadalupe Hidalgo was made with a government located in Querétaro. The Mexican historian José Fuentes Mares charged that Forsyth lied about the dates on which he received official notice of the establishment of the constitutional government—that he had received this notice before granting recognition to Zuloaga on the 27th. Fuentes Mares concluded that Forsyth lied to cover his deliberate choice of the Zuloaga government as the most likely to accede to demands for territory.[45]

Fuentes Mares's assessment, although somewhat exaggerated, comes very near the truth. Forsyth was certainly aware of the existence of the Juárez government and made a conscious decision to favor Zuloaga with recognition. This action was doubtless influenced by Forsyth's assessment of the conservatives' attitude toward a boundary change: three days after recognition he could report that he had already sounded out the new government and found few indications of strong hostility to the sale of territory. But this could not have been the only factor considered in making his decision. He probably felt that the liberals had little chance of success even with his recognition and that subsequent relations with the victorious conservatives would be made more difficult. He may also have realized that if the liberals had any success they would be able to control the coastal areas and the customhouses, leaving the conservatives in the core region hard pressed for funds and thus more open to offers to purchase territory.

But the evidence does not fully support Fuentes Mares's charge of fabrication. He asserts that Forsyth's statement "I have been forced to make a choice of evils" is proof that he had received Ocampo's note before 27 January. The statement read in context does not support this contention. A complete reading of the 30 January despatch strongly suggests that Forsyth's "choice of evils" was between the known qualities of the Zuloaga government and the unknown qualities of that of Juárez. Rather than proving outright fabrication, the evidence only convicts Forsyth of being aware of the existence of the liberal government and of acting with haste to preclude having his position complicated by official confirmation of his knowledge.

That the liberals should have felt that they had been betrayed by Forsyth was not surprising. Having already been deceived by Comonfort and well aware that their conservative enemies had the sympathetic understanding of the major European powers, the liberals had assumed they could count on the support of their "natural ally." United States recognition was important not only for the prestige it would lend but also because it would facilitate the raising of loans and buying of arms in the United States, tasks essential to a liberal victory. On 10 February, Ocampo ordered Robles Pezuela, Comonfort's minister to Washington, to work to reverse Forsyth's recognition of Zuloaga. Robles took the position, however, that he would represent whichever regime his hosts chosé to recognize and thus he became an agent for Zuloaga.[46]

The liberals then entrusted the task of representing the constitutional cause in Washington to a proven *puro,* José María Mata, the son-in-law of Ocampo. In early March, as the Juárez government fled westward in search of a haven, Ocampo ordered Mata to proceed to the United States in search of recognition, official aid, and private loans. In the United States, Mata soon realized that Buchanan would not seriously consider countermanding Forsyth's action until the prospects for a liberal victory became brighter and that loans, both private and official, depended on recognition.

When Mata arrived in Washington in late April he found sentiment so favorable to Zuloaga that he did not present himself in an official capacity. Unofficially Buchanan expressed sympathy for the liberal cause but raised numerous objections to recognition. Already aware of the position taken by Forsyth, Buchanan maintained that recognition of the liberals would be a radical and unjustifiable departure from the traditional policy of de facto recognition for whichever force held Mexico City. Mata's argument that the liberals constituted the de jure government did not impress Buchanan. To Mata's amazement, Buchanan demanded an English translation of the Mexican constitution in order to determine if a regime which did not control the capital city could be considered de jure. Convinced that Buchanan was stalling, Mata decided to concentrate his efforts on public relations and private loans.

With all possibility of an official loan closed off, Mata traveled to New York in a vain search for private funds. He found the money circles of New York generous with sympathy but cautious with credit. Three times he had loans apparently arranged only to see bad news from Mexico frighten off the creditors. After spending a month in New York, Mata decided that official recognition must precede even private loans and he returned to Washington to concentrate on reversing official policy. If this failed, Mata was determined to return to Mexico to take an active part in the civil war.[47]

Upon his return to Washington, Mata used Jane Cazneau, the expansionist who had been so influential during the Pierce administration, to further his efforts. With rather frequent and easy access to Buchanan, she was a valuable asset to Mata both as an editor and opener of doors. Probably trading on a claimed distant kinship with the president, she now arranged for a conference between the two men.[48] Since the suggestions contained in her letter to Buchanan setting up the interview conform closely to Mata's views at the moment, the letter is worth quoting extensively.

> Mr. Mata of Mexico, whom I named the other day as the minister of President Juárez, is now here awaiting an interview. He has I believe full powers to raise funds by any means short of alienating territory.
>
> It has been suggested that a free transit at Tehuantepec, with all but free ports at the termini, might be worth a million of dollars, . . . and that another million expended under the joint supervision of the two republics in improving these free harbors would open that splendid country to the right class of settlers.
>
> If any other nation is willing to pay for similar concessions, there need be no objection for neither money nor navies can buy the power of *proximity*.
>
> Another million will secure the like advantages of way on the northern frontier, with neutral territory down to 28° N.L. under conditions amounting to a sale.
>
> Two millions will give us two free highways to the Pacific and put Juárez in the city of Mexico. Once there he is pledged to a policy that saves Cuba.
>
> Intimate and sincere friends who have studied the position and probabilities of Mexican affairs assure me of facts and intentions that may, if acted upon in season, produce the most important changes outside of Mexico. . . .
>
> The points I have now stated will be confirmed by Mr. Mata and the Juárez government.[49]

A number of interesting though speculative inferences can be drawn from the letter. Obviously neither Buchanan nor Mata had fully confided in the writer, since she was unaware of their having met in April. While there is no proof that Mexico was prepared to make the suggested deals in return for money and recognition, Mata was now very pessimistic and most anxious for some arrangement. He doubted that the liberals could win without foreign assistance, but he was convinced that the Mexican nation and nationality would survive only if liberal cause were victorious. The deals suggested in the letter were remarkably similar to components of Forsyth's economic-protectorate scheme which had received warm Mexican support. The greatest departure from the Forsyth project was the vague allusion to saving Cuba, doubtless an appeal to Buchanan's well-known desire to acquire that island. It is quite conceivable that the letter was drafted with Mata's concurrence. Such a view is supported by glowing endorsements Mata subsequently gave the Cazneaus' applications for land grants in the Yucatán and for transit routes in the frontier area.[50]

Although Mata never related the details of the interview, he was heartened by it. He reported that Buchanan previously had not fully understood the Mexican situation. Buchanan recommended that a true account of the situation be published to enlighten the public as a first step toward a reversal of official policy. With this encouragement, Mata returned to New York, where, with the aid of Jane Cazneau, the *Herald* (New York) published two articles which suggested that the people of the United States had no reasonable claim on Mexico that the liberal government would not be willing to satisfy.[51]

The favorable public reaction to the *Herald* articles and telegraphic news that

Forsyth had suspended relations with the government in Mexico City seemed to promise an early reversal of United States policy. In a conference on 1 July, Mata reported that Buchanan showed still greater interest in the liberal government, which, after having been formed in Guanajuato in January, had barely eluded capture by the conservatives until it had finally found refuge in Veracruz. He asked for information on the conditions of the Tehuantepec transits and harbors. When Buchanan learned that Mata planned to return to Mexico to participate in the military phase of the civil war, he requested him to remain in Washington and promised to recall Forsyth, implying that recognition would follow shortly. With his hopes thus revived Mata decided to remain and work for early recognition.[52]

The gradual improvement in Mata's prospects in Washington reflected the deterioration of Forsyth's position in Mexico City. When Forsyth opened relations with the Zuloaga regime he had been sanguine of realizing Buchanan's policy of territorial expansion. To improve his bargaining position, he again requested that the authorized price be increased. But, remembering the recent reprimand he had received for questioning the wisdom of decisions made in Washington, Forsyth hastened to add that regardless of the adequacy of the price he would urge Mexico to accept it. He noted that while the intrinsic value of the territory might be more than the amount he was authorized to offer, the value of the territory to Mexico would diminish as manifest destiny ran its prescribed course.

Forsyth foresaw developments that would force the conservatives to sell territory, regardless of the inclinations of Zuloaga and his cabinet. "The new Govt. is wholly dependent upon the Church for support," he reported, "all the Coasts & Customs Houses being in the hands of the 'coalition' [Juárez forces]." The church had to support Zuloaga, for it knew that a victory for Juárez meant the nationalization of its property. The church was thus caught "between two fires; in danger, first of being ruined at a blow from the *Puros,* and equally sure of being ruined by degrees by its friends, the present Govt." Forsyth believed that he could turn the church's dilemma to advantage. Working behind the scenes, he sowed "in the minds of several of the leading friends & advisers of the Clergy" the idea that church property could be saved only if Zuloaga secured funds by the sale of territory. Having planted the seed in early February, Forsyth could only wait to see what would germinate.

By early March Forsyth could report that the seed had fallen on fertile ground. The archbishop of Mexico and bishop of Michoacán had been won over to the extent that they were pressuring Zuloaga and the cabinet in favor of a judicious sale of territory. But something more was necessary before action could be taken. Forsyth was convinced that the government felt too weak to risk the popular reaction to such an act, "for while the Govt. admits that this measure should and *must* be adopted, it lacks the courage to do it." Forsyth believed a decided military victory over the liberals was a necessary precondition for the successful conclusion of his task.[53] He apparently did not realize that a "decided military success" might be counterproductive—that it might so improve conservative prospects as to make them feel that a radical step to raise money was unnecessary.

The desired conservative victory was achieved at Celaya in early March. By the middle of the month, Forsyth reported that Zuloaga stood poised "between the flush of success and the incipiency of new revolutionary movements" and should now have the courage to conclude a sale. Rumors of the impending return of Santa Anna were welcomed by Forsyth. It would stimulate Zuloaga to act quickly, for everyone knew that Santa Anna would not hesitate to make a sale.

A private note from Zuloaga to Forsyth was the signal for Forsyth to present a formal proposal to the foreign minister, Luis Cuevas, on 22 March. The heart of the proposal was a "natural boundary" to follow the Rio Grande to 30° north latitude, westward along that parallel to the easternmost branch of Río Yaqui, and down this river to its mouth on the Gulf of California. This would give the United States all of Baja California, most of Sonora, and the northern third of Chihuahua. Forsyth also proposed the settlement of all claims and a perpetual right of way across Tehuantepec. Not entirely abandoning his own ideas, Forsyth proposed the inclusion of postal and reciprocity treaties similar to those negotiated with Comonfort the previous year.

To support his proposals Forsyth used manifest-destiny arguments. The territory was worthless to Mexico, but when developed by his countrymen it would become a powerful generator stimulating economic growth in adjacent Mexican lands. United States control and development would drive hostile Indians away from Mexico's borders. The argument stressed most, however, was that if Mexico did not sell now she would eventually lose the subject region through the operation of the inflexible laws of Providence. If the United States were selfish she would just wait until "God's natural law" delivered these territories to her instead of offering a fair price for them. The Tehuantepec proposal was presented as merely an amplification and clarification of rights already held under article 8 of the Gadsden Treaty. These changes were designed to provide the security necessary to entice investors to risk the capital required to open a railroad.[54]

Forsyth's dreams of success were destined to remain just dreams. In a note dated 5 April the conservative government firmly but politely rejected the proposals. "The president of the republic is thoroughly convinced," wrote Cuevas, "that a change of boundary is neither conducive to its true interest, nor its good name, whatever advantages it might realize as just compensation." Cuevas also refused to negotiate on Tehuantepec transits and pronounced it dangerous to treat the claims question. He even suggested that "serious difficulties" might be encountered in any attempt to negotiate postal and reciprocity treaties.[55]

Forsyth found Zuloaga's refusal inexplicable and decided on more aggressive tactics. He assumed the role of the aggrieved and insulted party, warning that the failure of Mexico to accept its responsibility for injuries suffered by its citizens gave the United States "the right to take redress in it's [*sic*] own hands."[56] Conservative resistance led Forsyth to adopt dual objectives: to force the acceptance of his proposals and to encourage the formation of a new government which would be more amenable.

To pressure the existing government, Forsyth directed a series of increasingly hostile notes to Cuevas. To Washington he pictured the existing government as hopeless.

> I was taught to expect that it embraced in its personnel some men of higher moral stamp than those I had been used to dealing with under Comonfort. Mr. Cuevas was particularly signaled out as . . . the man who holds his mind & his honor above price, and himself impervious to every sinister influence. From such a minister I hoped for candor & fair dealing. But these expectations have proved to be dreams. The men of the present Cabinet, like their predecessors, are Mexicans all. Zuloaga is a cypher without knowledge, dignity or courage. Mr. Cuevas is a Jesuit and a shuffler, & the rest of the Ministry . . . are the merest blanks.

Forsyth declared that normal diplomatic techniques were useless in Mexico. The United States must choose between the only two viable policy alternatives—the use of force or the establishment of protectorate.

The use of threats as diplomatic tools was ineffective, Forsyth felt, because Mexicans knew these were only bluffs which would not be backed by force. Because the United States was unwilling to use force against Mexico "our relations . . . have been left to take their own course, & . . . Mexico has been allowed to do just as she pleased in respect to our Govt., our people and our commerce, & she had been pleased to do as badly as it is possible to imagine." If the United States wished to pursue a strong policy it must be ready to use force.

> You want Sonora? The American blood spilled near its line would justify you in seizing it by way of reprisal the moment Mexico refuses to atone for it. You want other Territory? Send me power to make an ultimate demand for the settlement of the several millions Mexico owes our people . . . & a fleet to back the demand & you will enable me to force a treaty of Cession for a money consideration. . . . You want Tehuantepec transits? Say to Mexico "Nature has placed the shortest highway between the two oceans so necessary to the commerce of the world in your keeping— you will not open it yourself, nor allow others to open it to the wants of mankind— you cannot be allowed to play the dog in the manger. . . . Give us what we ask in return for the manifest benefits we propose to confer upon you for it, *or we will take it*."

Forsyth's use of such strong language was not designed to pressure his government to adopt a more bellicose policy, but rather was intended to frighten it into seeing that the other alternative, a protectorate, was the only realistic policy. He reported that leading liberals believed that Mata's mission to Washington was to negotiate for such an arrangement. He warned against this, however, for Juárez "has the heart, it is said, but not the head" for the job. Forsyth had two more attractive candidates in mind to head such a government, Miguel Lerdo and General Luis Osollo, the chief officer of the conservative army. Both these men were described as "pro-American," honest, and free of subservience to the church. Both doubted the ability of the Mexican army to maintain order and both were convinced that outside help was essential. Forsyth was busy encouraging

Osollo and Lerdo to cooperate in overthrowing Zuloaga. The coup, if it succeeded, would be followed by a request for United States protection.[57]

Despite having been severely reprimanded for pursuing his own policy in Mexico, Forsyth was determined to present Washington with a protectorate as a *fait accompli*. He would drive the Zuloaga government to the wall, forcing it either to sell territory or collapse. Either case would create conditions favorable for Lerdo and Osollo to seize power in Mexico City, and once in power they would give the United States a dominant voice in Mexican affairs. For his vehicle to pressure Zuloaga, Forsyth chose a special tax decreed on 15 May 1858. The decree levied a 1 percent tax on all real or personal property valued in excess of five thousand dollars. Forsyth claimed that the tax constituted a forced loan from which United States citizens were exempt. If he could prevent them from paying the tax, then other foreigners would refuse to pay, and if foreigners refused then most Mexicans would also refuse. This would force Zuloaga into a corner where he must choose between a sale of territory and bankruptcy. Either alternative was likely to prove fatal to the conservative regime.[58]

As Forsyth had expected, the government declared foreigners subject to the new tax law on the same terms as Mexican citizens, and United States citizens turned to Forsyth and their consul, John Black, for advice and protection. The situation seemed perfect for Forsyth's plans. He wrote a letter to Consul Black labeling the special tax a violation of international law and of the treaty rights of United States citizens. Forsyth advised them not to pay the tax unless force was used to collect it. Not content with simply reaching those fellow countrymen who actively sought advice, Forsyth had his letter to Consul Black published in the local English and Spanish press.[59]

Forsyth's attempt to secure agreement among the diplomatic corps to oppose the tax measure failed. Only the new British minister, L. C. Otway, was sympathetic, requesting that the law not be applied to English subjects until he could refer the matter to the Foreign Office. The French minister openly urged compliance. As a result of Forsyth's activities the press began carrying articles critical of the tax, of the government for ordering it, and of the French minister for defending it. Under Forsyth's influence French merchants drew up a petition critical of their minister's stand.[60]

The next step in Forsyth's attack was to make the tax a diplomatic issue by directing a note of protest to the Foreign Ministry against its application to citizens of the United States. In this note, dated 22 May, Forsyth argued that the tax measure, viewed in all its aspects, did not "come at all within the purview of the theory or laws of taxation." On the contrary, it was "a simple & naked forced loan." He maintained that "any citizen of the U.S. who complies with its requisitions, makes himself, in a certain sense, a party to the political dissensions of the country." Forsyth advanced two distinct legal grounds for holding that the tax could not be imposed upon his compatriots. First, under international law, he asserted, the property of foreigners could only be subjected to "lawful, customary taxation." This tax, he maintained, was neither lawful nor customary. Secondly, since the tax was in reality a forced loan, United States citizens were exempted by treaty provisions; an 1826 treaty between Mexico and Great Britain had exempted British subjects from forced loans and the most-favored-nation clause of the 1831 commercial treaty with the United States extended this exemption to its citizens. Forsyth also had this arrogantly phrased note published in the local press. Forsyth assured Washington that his actions had made him spokesman for all foreigners in Mexico and had made the idea of a United States protectorate almost universally popular.

If Forsyth believed that his display of arrogance would reduce the Zuloaga government to a state of frightened paralysis, he was mistaken. In a calm and reasonable manner which seemed impervious to Forsyth's pressure campaign, Cuevas responded, labeling Forsyth's conduct as "offensive to the sovereignty of the nation." He refused to even consider Forsyth's arguments since, as he rightly foresaw, to do so would make all Mexican tax measures subject to the approval of the United States legation. The decree, Forsyth was informed, would be "punctually & exactly executed." Cuevas could not "believe for a single instant that the . . . [United States government] will ever agree that this class of measure shall be made to depend upon the consent of a foreign govt." The Zuloaga administration was not reacting as Forsyth had confidently expected. It was skillfully avoiding the trap so carefully prepared for it.

Forsyth had not planned his confrontation, however, without preparing follow-up stages. He now brought a major gun to bear in a thinly veiled reference to the probability that his government would use force to protect its citizens and their property from "whatever coercive measures" might be taken by Mexico. The present dilemma could have been avoided, he hinted broadly, if serious attention had been given to his March proposals for a boundary change. But all was not lost; Mexico could still agree to the sale, after which he would assist in redrafting the tax measure so as to remove all objections.[61] Throughout May Forsyth, as a part of his concerted campaign, assumed an increasingly hostile tone in his communications with the government.[62]

For a time Forsyth's second-stage attack seemed to be working. On 1 June, Cuevas informed the legation that the execution of the tax decree had been temporarily postponed as a result of Forsyth's protests. He appealed for Forsyth's cooperation in making United States citizens realize their responsibility to abide by the laws of Mexico. Shortly thereafter Zuloaga sent word privately that with the failure of the tax measure he had no recourse but the sale of territory. A conference was arranged with Zuloaga in which Forsyth thought a firm agreement was reached for Cuevas to be removed if he continued his opposition. Forsyth, however, refused to initiate the new negotiations as requested by Zuloaga.[63]

Forsyth did not realize that in refusing to take the initiative in presenting a proposal for a boundary change he avoided a trap set for him. He based his refusal on a fear that he would again be deceived as in March and made to appear ridiculous. He also wanted Mexico to take the initiative to avoid later charges that force had been exerted to secure a treaty of cession. He did not know that Cuevas already saw through the carefully planned diplomatic maneuvers and was willing to risk a break in relations. Nor was he aware that his recall had already been requested.[64] In view of these developments, Zuloaga's private and informal request that Forsyth resubmit his proposals was probably designed to force Forsyth to reveal officially his true objective so that the subsequent break in relations could be premised on that ground. This supposition is reinforced by subsequent events; after Forsyth's refusal to assume the initiative, he was informally notified that the cabinet had convinced Zuloaga to make another effort to enforce the tax decree before resorting to more radical measures.

When Forsyth learned that his recall had been requested, he sought to justify fully his actions to Washington and to secure official backing. He felt that the tax question represented an ideal issue upon which the United States could and should force a general settlement of all outstanding questions with Mexico. He again emphasized that all foreign merchants and businessmen looked to him for leadership. He requested an early endorsement of his actions. If his position were strongly backed by Washington, no Mexican government could refuse to make an acceptable settlement and hope to survive.[65] Washington's reaction to the tax question came too late to aid Forsyth in his confrontation with the conservatives and would have been of no assistance had it been timely. Cass first agreed that the tax was a forced loan in disguise, but changed his mind after consulting with the attorney general. Nevertheless, Cass concluded that the tax was "unjust and unfriendly" if imposed on foreigners.[66]

Although Forsyth had lost the preliminary phases of his battle, he was confident that he would win the final showdown. He continued to believe that the Zuloaga government lacked both the courage and stability necessary to enforce the decree against United States citizens. The actual test case was that of Salomon Migel, a naturalized citizen of Russian origin who operated a jewelry firm in Mexico City and was involved in the pearl fisheries of La Paz, Baja California. Migel reportedly did 500,000 dollars' worth of business annually and employed over a hundred workers. When Migel, acting upon Forsyth's advice, refused to pay the $730 assessed against him, his property was seized. On 17 June the Foreign Ministry ordered him to be expelled via Tampico no later than 19 June. Since practically all the foreigners were refusing to pay, the expulsion order for Migel would be the test; if it were executed foreign resistance to the tax would collapse. If not carried out, however, the government would have lost and the foreigners would continue to defy the government.[67]

In fighting the order banishing Migel, Forsyth followed his established practice of trying to make the matter an issue between the two governments rather than one between the Mexican government and a private citizen of the United States. Since "Mr. Migel and such other American Citizens as may fall under its displeasure," Forsyth informed the conservative regime, "was counselled and advised by . . . their lawful protector in Mexico," their minister should be held responsible, not the private parties. Any expulsion order would have to be directed at the minister and could only be done "at the peril of Mexico's responsibility to the Sovereignty of the United States."

The purposely hostile and insulting tone of the note was designed to frighten Cuevas into submission, but it failed. Cuevas would have given Forsyth his passports, but the cabinet wanted Forsyth to initiate the break. Cuevas gave in to his colleagues and responded to Forsyth with a harsh but memorable lecture on international law and diplomatic practices. He reviewed in scathing terms Forsyth's conduct from the beginning of the controversy but directed the sharpest attacks at his attempt to assume official responsibility for Migel's acts. Cuevas asserted that he had

> never heard that a foreign minister had the power to tell the subjects of his nation not to obey the laws of the country in which they live. It would appear that H. E. Mr. Forsyth believes the contrary & that he wishes to convert his official representation as minister of the U.S. into a government opposed to another government; forgetting that . . . he can only shield his countrymen through the protection accorded by the laws of the land, by the good advice he may give them, and by cultivating frank & friendly relations which shall be advantageous to all.

Terming Forsyth's conduct as unjustifiable, Cuevas concluded that Migel's punishment was appropriate and the banishment order would be executed.

Forsyth had gambled and lost; Migel was expelled as ordered. Having pushed to bring about a confrontation in which the government would be left without acceptable alternatives, Forsyth now found himself facing a similar dilemma. He could not, after having publicized his challenge to the Foreign Ministry, now accept defeat and continue to maintain relations with his victorious adversaries. Once the expulsion of Migel took place, failure to break relations would only open him to public ridicule. On 21 June Forsyth accepted the inevitable and informed the Foreign Ministry that relations were broken until new instructions could be received. In a final desperate effort to reverse their respective positions, Forsyth informed the government of the break in an extremely long note in which he sought to create the impression that war would be the inevitable result of recent developments. Cuevas refused to be baited by Forsyth's abusive note and merely acknowledged its receipt.

News that this confrontation was pending contributed to Buchanan's more sympathetic treatment of Mata in early June and a telegraphic notice of the break of relations prompted Buchanan to request on 1 July that Mata cancel his plans to return to Mexico. Both Mata and Forsyth hoped this presaged a radical change in Buchanan's policy. Mata hoped that recognition would be extended to Juárez quickly and without too many demands on Mexican resources. Recognition, if not purchased at too high a price, would aid Mata in raising loans from private sources in the United States. Forsyth hoped that his decision to break relations would be endorsed by Washington and that he would be authorized to recognize Juárez. He also hoped that Buchanan would now abandon the policy of territorial expansion as unfeasible, if not undesirable, and would adopt a policy looking to the establishment of economic dominance in Mexico.

Both Mata and Forsyth overestimated the rapidity with which Buchanan would act and the degree to which he would alter his objectives. How Forsyth could have expected to be allowed to remain as minister to the Veracruz government is a mystery. His breaking relations provided Washington with an excellent opportunity to remove an individual who had opposed Buchanan politically and had consistently argued the superiority of his views over those of the president. Cass gave lukewarm approval to the break and ordered Forsyth to return to the United States, withdrawing the mission.[68]

But Buchanan was not yet ready to commit himself to the Veracruz regime. Routine relations were maintained with Robles, the conservative minister in Washington, and Forsyth's actions were repudiated when Cass requested that Migel be allowed to return to Mexico since he had acted on faulty advice.[69] Forsyth delayed his departure for several months during which he continued to support liberal plots in the Mexican capital, allowed the legation to be used as a haven for Lerdo and other liberals, and allowed the liberals to bury on legation grounds forty-six bars of silver made from objects taken from the cathedral of Morelia by General Epitacio Huerta.[70]

Mata fared little better in Washington. Encouraging words from Buchanan hardly compensated for the failure to suspend relations with the representative from Mexico City. Mata's pleas for action were met with vague promises and frustrating delays. Despairing of speeding action in Washington, Mata turned again to New York in search of loans. He now had authority to secure two million dollars in loans and to offer generous security and profit in return. While his credentials allowed him to mortgage church property and customs receipts to secure the loans and to offer interest up to 12 percent, he was authorized to alter his credentials in any way that might produce success. La Sere, Zerman, and Butterfield were pressed into service as loan agents with disappointing results.

The position of the Veracruz government had deteriorated despite its control of the seaports and customshouses. The civil war paralyzed commercial activity; with import facilities controlled by the liberals and the consumer markets in conservative hands, trade slowly ground to a halt. With the decay of commerce and decline in customs revenues, control of the ports lost much of its advantage. To sustain his hard-pressed government, Mata offered potential creditors greater enticements—church property of twice the value of the loan could be given as security, creditors could establish a committee to manage the mortgaged property, Mexican property taxes could be mortgaged to cover the loans, only a fraction of the loan needed to be made available to the liberal government prior to its capture of Mexico City, generous discounts on the loan would be acceptable, and so on. Even these concessions did not produce adequate results. How far Mata may have gone to entice creditors is not clear, but he did reject one offer—the sale of $2 million in Mexican bonds for only $500,000.[71]

The long delay in the appearance of new policy initiatives was occasioned not by any need to recast policy objectives, as hoped by Mata and Forsyth, but rather by Buchanan's cautious efforts to adjust his strategy so as to achieve maximum advantage. Buchanan saw the failure of his policy as resulting from the opposition and subsequent half-hearted efforts of Forsyth. He appears never to have questioned the wisdom of his rejection of the Montes-Forsyth treaties nor to have realized that the policy upon which they were based would have drawn Mexico inexorably into the economic and political orbit of the United States.

Buchanan's inflexible policy of territorial expansion denied official funds to Mexico except on humiliating terms and probably discouraged private sources from making loans. Despite the obvious desire of the liberals to draw closer to their northern neighbors, the general public sympathy in the United States for the ideology of the liberals, and a fear that Mexico would fall under European domination, the Buchanan policy had no place for understanding and supporting the liberal cause. Instead, Buchanan sought to increase the fiscal embarrassment of Mexico as a means of acquiring territory. Increasing fiscal difficulties, to which United States policy contributed, were a significant factor in Comonfort's suspension of constitutional government. This in turn, triggered a civil war which Forsyth, under proddings from Washington, attempted to capitalize upon to purchase territory.

Forsyth's continuing efforts to secure a government anxious for his country's protection and to gain a favored position in the Mexican economy for its interests were undertaken without the knowledge or approval of Buchanan. All commercial interests in Mexico suffered as a result of the civil war. The interests of private United States citizens were used as a tool to bring pressure to bear on the conservative government. That government responded by punishing an individual Yankee businessman as a means of asserting its independence. The result was that almost two years after its beginning the Buchanan administration was no nearer to realizing its policy objectives and Mexico had suffered considerably in the process.

5
Recognition, a Liberal Victory, 1858–1859

By the time Forsyth broke relations with the Zuloaga government in June 1858, Mexico was caught up in a bitter, destructive civil war. The conservatives controlled Mexico City and most of the central highlands, the core region of Mexico; the liberals with their government based in Veracruz controlled the coastal regions and the northern frontier. The conservatives enjoyed several initial advantages: their compact interior position made their supply and communication tasks simpler than those of the peripherally based liberals; they held the allegiance of most of the regular army while the liberals had to build an army from civilian elements; controlling the traditional capital city allowed them to inherit the widespread recognition held by the Comonfort government while the liberals went unrecognized; France led the European powers in encouraging and supporting the conservatives; the almost universal support of the church hierarchy placed the prestige, leadership, and wealth of that powerful institution at their disposal; and finally, they probably received greater popular support than did the liberals—the lower classes motivated by a deeply ingrained respect for authority and an unshakable reverence for the church, the upper class seeking protection for property, position, and privilege.

The Buchanan administration used the opportunity presented by Forsyth's suspension of relations to make a cautious reassessment of how best to achieve its objectives in Mexico. Demands for action were growing steadily in both Congress and the press. Unsettled claims, border raids, and injuries to United States citizens and their property resulting from the civil war kept the Mexican situation in the public eye. Buchanan reluctantly realized that a direct purchase might not be the easiest method of achieving his goal. Instead, he suggested the establishment of a miliary protectorate over the frontier regions of Mexico. When Congress refused to grant the authority for military occupation he turned his attention to Mexico's liberal government. Knowing that the liberals saw United States recognition as the essential precondition for obtaining desperately needed financial resources, Buchanan, using the possibility of military protectorate as a threat, opened discussions with the Juárez government in hopes of securing territory in return for recognition.

The financial distress of the Juárez administration was such that, while it was not willing to sell territory, it would accede to almost any other demand to secure recognition. Aware of Buchanan's determination to acquire Baja California, Sonora, and other frontier regions, the Veracruz government encouraged him to believe that boundary changes would follow recognition. The liberals believed that recognition by the United States would give them access to financial resources which would allow them to terminate the civil war while resisting Yankee demands for territory. This policy was risky; conditions could force them to sell territory. Such a risk was acceptable because of their desperate need for credit and because they felt that recognition would cast a protective shadow over the Veracruz government, decreasing the likelihood of European intervention. The policy also reflected the liberal belief that recognition would be followed by closer economic ties with the United States which would assist in the task of reforming and modernizing the Mexican economy. United States recognition, which would end the diplomatic isolation of the liberal government, was thus seen by the liberals not only as essential for a successful prosecution of the civil war but as vital to the reform program.

The reform program, so carefully elaborated during the previous years, had to be temporarily laid aside as the liberals fought for survival during 1858. The government established by Juárez at Guanajuato in January 1858 was so hard pressed for several months that avoiding capture was its principal concern. Forsyth observed that had he recognized Juárez, "I would have become an itinerant representative in quest of the Govt. of my recognition." Failing to understand the reasons behind their peregrinations, Forsyth condemned the conduct of Juárez and his cabinet as indecisive and imbecilic. He confidently predicted after the liberal defeat at Celaya in March that "the constitution of 1857 has sunk never to rise again."[1]

What Forsyth failed to understand was that the liberal regime was seeking to escape from western Mexico to the liberal stronghold at Veracruz. On 11 April 1858, Juárez and his cabinet began a slow and circuitous trip from Manzanillo to Veracruz, via Acapulco, Panama, Havana, and New Orleans. This trip, made aboard Yankee steamers, brought Juárez to Veracruz on 4 May.[2] Only after reaching this haven could Juárez and his colleagues really concentrate on the problems of civil war and diplomatic relations.

The foreign policy adopted by the liberals, as we have seen, was directed toward the United States and toward the achievement of two primary objectives—recognition and credit. Mata had gone to Washington to secure these objectives and when neither was forthcoming, friendly Yankees were commissioned to assist him. La Sere and Zerman were authorized to raise loans and to create propaganda favorable to the liberal cause. Butterfield was similarly commissioned, but his greatest contributions came indirectly from his efforts to promote congressional support for his Gulf mail steamship line.

Butterfield needed official United States support for the steamship line which he had contracted with Comonfort to operate between United States and Mexican ports. To support his request for an indirect subsidy in the form of a $200,000 mail contract, Butterfield presented the appropriate congressional committees with petitions from merchants in Mexico and other material designed to show that the United States economy would reap great benefits from the steamship operation. He argued that Mexican commerce would be more valuable than the possession of

Cuba. Mexico, he argued, produced everything which was being imported from Cuba, plus precious metals. Mexican agriculture production, heretofore limited to domestic consumption, would expand rapidly under the stimulant of a steamship line and Yankee entrepreneurship. He estimated that Mexico could export $40 million worth of sugar and $30 million of coffee each year. The export of tobacco, indigo, cochineal, vanilla, and cocoa could also be increased. Not only could Mexico replace Cuba as a source of supply but its much larger population offered a greater potential market for United States goods. Using arguments similar to those employed by Forsyth to support an economic protectorate, Butterfield argued that the United States should replace Great Britain as the dominant economic force in Mexico. He portrayed his country's domination of Mexico as only the first step toward establishing its economic control over all Latin America.

Butterfield found strong support for both his steamer proposal and for United States economic penetration of Mexico. In the Senate the subsidy proposal received intersectional support. Senators from Texas, Louisiana, Alabama, Minnesota, Vermont, and Massachusetts spoke in favor of the mail subsidy. The senators seemed most impressed by the potential of the steamer line to promote their country's commercial interests in Mexico and the Caribbean. Different versions of the subsidy measure were approved in each house, but the project died when the two houses failed to reach a compromise.[3]

William L. Cazneau and his wife Jane Cazneau also performed valuable public relations chores for the liberal cause. The general (the military title was apparently an honorific one bestowed by the Texas Republic) and his wife were well known and influential in Washington's political circles; Jane Cazneau, as noted earlier, had relatively ready access to Buchanan. The Cazneaus, already experienced in speculative ventures in Spanish America, doubtless saw the Mexican situation as offering numerous opportunities for the speculator with good political connections. By interceding with Buchanan on Mata's behalf and using Jane's journalistic talents to gain favorable publicity for the liberal cause, the Cazneaus created Mexican obligations for future use.[4]

The combined efforts of Mata and his Yankee friends, however, did little to change the basic stance of the Buchanan administration. Despite growing evidence of sympathy in Congress and the press for the liberal cause and for the pursuit of economic goals, Buchanan was not prepared to abandon his drive for territory and for control of the transisthmian transit routes. He continued to see these objectives as achievable by either of two methods, by purchase or by settlement of large numbers of United States citizens in the subject areas. Such settlers in a transit zone would facilitate, if not insure, United States control of that area, while in areas which the United States wished to annex a large Yankee population could result in annexation by the will of the inhabitants, as had happened in Texas.

In his public addresses Buchanan constantly linked these two objectives with their alternative methods of achievement. In his inaugural he had referred to the right of his country to expand "by fair purchase or . . . by the voluntary determination of a brave, kindred, and independent people to blend their destinies with our own." After the panic of 1857 had seriously depleted the treasury, Buchanan placed greater emphasis on "peaceful emigration" as a means of securing control over communications routes in the isthmian area. To protect United States treaty rights in Central America and Mexico and to create conditions which would encourage Yankee settlers, Buchanan requested special congressional authority to use land and sea forces of the United States in the area. In the first annual message in December 1857 and a special message on 7 January 1858, Buchanan condemned filibustering as counterproductive to national policy, which was to facilitate "our race to spread themselves over the continent of North America . . . as a means to open and . . . protect every transit route across the Isthmus." The Walker expedition to Nicaragua was condemned for having adversely affected United States influence in Central America.[5]

The chaos accompanying the fall of Comonfort combined with the presidential ambitions of Senator Sam Houston of Texas served to focus attention again on the question of a protectorate in Mexico. On 16 February 1858, Houston, with an eye on the 1860 presidential elections, introduced a resolution calling for an inquiry into the feasibility of establishing a protectorate over Mexico and Central America as a means of stabilizing and democratizing the area. Although no action was taken on this resolution, it presaged a new spate of press demands for official intervention or increased filibuster activity.[6] In April Houston reintroduced his resolution amended to refer only to Mexico.

Houston's project sought to divert attention from sectionalism and secession. He linked his protectorate proposal to the successful Canadian reciprocity agreement. Reciprocity had secured the northern frontier and, it was hoped, set the Canadian provinces on the road to eventual voluntary annexation. Mexico, however, was an "international outlaw" whose people were incapable of self-government and unsuited for annexation. Nevertheless, the Southwest deserved a secure frontier. To protect its inhabitants from the anarchy endemic in Mexico, to prevent filibustering activities, and to forestall a dangerous European intervention, the United States had "no alternative . . . but to arrange plans immediately for ruling her [Mexico] wisely, and, as far as possible, gently." Feeling that Houston's primary objective was to secure national attention preparatory to launching a drive for the presidency, the Senate printed his speech and tabled his resolution.[7]

Although Houston failed to gain favorable Senate action on his resolution, he continued publicly to advocate a protectorate. He solicited and received a favorable reaction from the English bondholders association to the project. In the Senate he hinted at independent Texas action if the national government did not act. In Texas, where he was candidate for governor, Houston gave his project a decidedly more sectional coloring. A temporary protectorate would allow for suppression of Indian raids, the recovery of fugitive slaves, and the spread of slavery into the central valley of Mexico. After a period of Americanization under the protectorate additional slave states would be ready for voluntary annexation.[8]

While Houston failed to secure any of his goals, he may have contributed to Buchanan's decision to request congressional approval for a military protectorate over the frontier provinces of Mexico. In the December 1858 state of the union message Buchanan analyzed the problems existing in relations with Mexico. He reviewed in misleading detail Forsyth's dealings with the conservative government, particularly Forsyth's failure to secure satisfaction for claims, estimated at $10 million. He described the disastrous effects of the civil war upon United States citizens and their property and the illegal measures taken by both parties to extort money from the foreign community. His harshest words, however, were reserved for the conservatives, against whom, he charged, "abundant cause now undoubtedly exists for a resort to hostilities." Only if the "constitutional party" should prevail did Buchanan see hope of avoiding war.

Interpreting the commander in chief's powers in a very restricted way, Buchanan pictured himself as helpless unless given specific authority by Congress. He repeated the request made the previous year for authorization to use land and naval forces to protect national interests in the Nicaraguan transit, adding Panama and Tehuantepec to this request. In the case of Mexico his plea for permission to use military force was cast in more urgent terms. If the constitutionalists lost the civil war, he warned, the only avenue open to satisfy United States claims would be to seize Mexican territory of equivalent value. But until the civil conflict was resolved, Buchanan was not prepared for such extreme action. In the meantime, to protect the Southwest from the ruinous effects of lawlessness and uncontrolled Indians along the frontier, Buchanan asked for authority to establish a temporary military protectorate over the northern portions of Sonora and Chihuahua.[9]

The proposal for a military protectorate was an ingenious approach to achieving Buchanan's Mexican objectives. While Buchanan referred to the many complaints about raids by Indians and lawless elements along the frontier to justify his request for special powers, these raids were occurring mainly along the lower Rio Grande opposite Tamaulipas and Coahuila, not in the uninhabited regions adjacent to Sonora and Chihuahua. It was hardly coincidental that the areas Buchanan wished to occupy were those which Forsyth had been instructed to purchase. Military occupation of these regions would enhance Buchanan's bargaining position regardless of which side emerged victorious in Mexico. If hostilities became necessary, the string of forts he proposed to erect in the occupied regions would become invaluable staging areas for an invasion of Mexico. Finally his verbal assurances that the governments of Sonora and Chihuahua would welcome the occupation as a means of bringing order and security to the region suggest that he foresaw annexation by the "will of the people."

Buchanan's espousal of a military protectorate following so hard on Houston's related demand spurred considerable public support for the scheme. The Foreign Ministry in Mexico City compiled a large file of articles from the United States press favorable to the project, many suggesting that the British would cooperate in such a project since it offered protection to their bondholders and an enlarged market for their manufactures.[10] Congress, deeply engrossed in the question of

Kansas and slavery and fearful that a protectorate would actually serve the sectional interests of the South and West, refused to give serious consideration to Buchanan's proposal.

Despite the failure of Congress to endorse the military protectorate proposal, Buchanan was moving toward breaking the impasse in Mexican–United States relations. For months while he studied the situation, he had used the need to confer with Forsyth before determining a new course of action to excuse his inactivity. Forsyth's dilatory return from Mexico had allowed for months of welcomed inactivity, during which Mata and Robles, representing the competing Mexican factions, bade for favor. Pressures on Buchanan to take action favorable to the liberal cause had been mounting. New York bankers, interested in loans to the liberals, were insisting that recognition precede their loans. Also propaganda activities in favor of closer commercial ties rather than territorial expansion were endangering Buchanan's position.[11]

Forsyth's return to Washington in December 1858 not only removed Buchanan's excuse for inaction but raised difficult problems which had to be settled. Forsyth expected to return to Mexico as minister. Before leaving his post he had written demanding that as a matter of justice serious consideration be given to his proposals for a Mexican policy based on economic and commercial considerations. Charging that his personal honor and ''reputation as a public man'' were at stake, Forsyth asked to be sent back for a limited period and allowed to resign his mission voluntarily under favorable circumstances. To avoid seriously weakening his control of the party Buchanan had to handle this problem carefully. Apparently he decided upon a policy of indirection and delay. In meeting with Forsyth, Buchanan was vague and noncommittal. In the state of the union address, mild praise for Forsyth's handling of the Mexican mission was coupled with a clear denial that the tax measure over which Forsyth had broken relations constituted a forced loan. No further contacts were allowed with Forsyth, who was left to fume in limbo. When in frustration Forsyth resigned his post, effective 2 March 1859, Buchanan had accomplished his objective without having taken an overt action for which he could be held politically responsible.[12]

While terminating his troubled relations with Forsyth, Buchanan was probing to ascertain which faction would pay the highest price for recognition. Butterfield, who had close ties with the liberals and whose contract was valueless unless they emerged victorious, was invited to submit his views.[13] Even Forsyth was utilized to explore with Mata just how far the liberals were willing to go in seeking recognition. Mata, realizing the nature of the contact, sought to create the impression, free of any specific commitment, that the liberals were ready to meet every demand. On 21 December the cabinet considered without decision the question of recognizing a government in Mexico; the following day Forsyth again called on Mata to explore possible steps to achieve recognition of the liberals; and on 23 December Cass granted Mata a long interview and invited him to dinner. Cass indicated that the cabinet was still undecided but leaning in favor of liberals. While Mata was thus being encouraged, Buchanan informed an unidentified friend of the

Veracruz government that recognition would not be granted until Robles returned from Mexico City with new offers from the conservatives relative to Chihuahua and Sonora.[14]

This story of Robles's impending return, for which Mata could find no source, raises interesting questions. At the time that Buchanan was confidently predicting his imminent return to Washington, Robles was in the midst of an unsuccessful attempt to seize control of the conservative government in Mexico City.[15] Since Robles was the same individual who, on behalf of unidentified high United States officials, had brought a proposal for a Yankee protectorate to Mexico in 1855, a strong presumption is raised that he was again acting in concert with responsible United States officials. That Buchanan was this official is indicated by his having kept another special agent ready to travel to Mexico City to close a land purchase deal until 20 January 1859.[16] If this were the case, and circumstantial evidence suggests it was, then Robles may have attempted to improve upon his understanding with Buchanan by staging a coup while in Mexico rather than just serving as an intermediary.

Despite Buchanan's efforts to keep his options open, events were driving him toward recognizing the Juárez government. During the previous September the United States merchants of Veracruz and Tampico had petitioned Washington to station naval vessels off Mexico's Gulf ports to protect their lives and property.[17] The subsequent visit of the *Saratoga* produced a good reaction from the public and from the liberal government. Following hard on the visit of the *Saratoga* came news of Buchanan's annual message, which Veracruz officials elected to see in the best possible light. No threat was seen in Buchanan's harsh words. Instead, they chose to emphasize Buchanan's declaration that the United States would extend its protection to Mexico before it would allow Spain to reestablish her dominance in the area. If the liberals had to choose between a Yankee and a European protectorate, there was no doubt which would be more popular.[18]

Liberal interest in a United States protectorate was enhanced by fear that conservatives were in the process of acquiring French aid, a fear strengthened by the French minister's self-proclaimed influence over the Zuloaga government. Forsyth had never tired of sounding the alarm that the conservative leaders were mere tools of the evil Frenchman "M. de Gabriac."[19] Zuloaga had approached de Gabriac in August requesting that France take the lead in establishing an understanding with Spain and Great Britain which would assure the conservatives of credit, French mercenaries, and a French general "who would discipline us, beginning with me." Using the same arguments which Alamán and Santa Anna had advanced five years earlier, Zuloaga insisted that it was in the interest of Europe to build up Mexico as a counterweight and barrier to United States power. The liberals and Anglophobe Yankees were apparently unaware that London saw the annexation of Mexico by the United States as a plus for British interests because it would stimulate British trade, and France would not act without British support.

Despite efforts to secure European protection, the conservative regime had not shut the door completely to an understanding with the United States. Through Robles steps were taken to retain a semblance of diplomatic interchange with the United States and to prevent aid to the liberals. Although Zuloaga claimed that his attempt to secure credit and arms from the United States was designed only to mislead Washington as to the true intentions of the conservatives,[20] it is unlikely that a generous offer of Yankee money would have been refused. If it were a stratagem intended to deceive Buchanan, it worked. He continued to hold open his options, hoping until the last moment that the conservatives would make a better offer than the liberals.

To ascertain more clearly just how far each Mexican group would go to secure recognition by the United States, and possibly to learn what had happened to Robles and any proposals that may have been pending with him, Buchanan appointed a special agent to go to Mexico. On 27 December 1858 William M. Churchwell, a little-known individual from Tennessee, was commissioned to make an evaluation of the contending factions in Mexico. Although national sympathies were said to be with the liberals, Churchwell was directed to determine the strength of both Juárez and Zuloaga and to recommend which should be recognized.[21] This mission appears to have been a last effort to secure a higher bid for United States recognition.

Churchwell's Mexican tour had a whirlwind character. He arrived in Veracruz on 19 January 1859, departed for the interior on the 21st, visited Jalapa, Perote, Mexico City, Orizaba, and Córdova before returning to Veracruz on 7 February.[22] This trip into conservative territory before any extended discussions with the liberals was doubtless designed to raise doubts in liberal minds as to the United States policy and thus increase their willingness to make concessions. The trip certainly upset R. B. J. Twyman, the United States consul at Veracruz. He submitted a strong plea to Washington for immediate recognition of the liberal regime. Using arguments that echoed Forsyth's earlier efforts, Twyman advised a liberal and generous policy toward the Veracruz government.[23] The character of this despatch differed so radically from others submitted by the alcoholic Twyman[24] and its contents were so attuned to the ideas of the liberals that one must wonder if he had more than a copyclerk assisting him.

Twyman's despatch, regardless of the extent to which it may have represented the ideas of its putative author, constituted an eleventh-hour appeal for Buchanan to abandon his policy of territorial expansion and to deal with the Veracruz government on a reasonable basis. Recognition and the exchange of ministers would give Juárez a ''moral force'' sufficient to insure a complete liberal victory within sixty days. Washington was reassured of the pro-Yankee sentiments of all the prominent liberals. The ideas on the proper relationship between Mexico and her powerful neighbor and the language in which they were expressed were so uncharacteristic of Consul Twyman that extensive passages warrant full reproduction.

> The liberal party are struggling to maintain a Constitution and Government as nearly assimilated to those of the United States, as the condition of Mexico and her people

will permit. . . . The leaders . . . believe that our Government and people sympa-
thise with them in this struggle. When that party is again triumphant . . . the United
States can readily negotiate a most advantageous treaty with it; and if that treaty and
an alliance were entered into, offensive and defensive, not only as to foes from
abroad, but revolutionists and traitors from within, it would give permanent peace to
Mexico and stability to her institutions. Such an alliance would constitute a firm
foundation upon which the Democracy of Mexico, under the advisement and
influence of the United States, could go on to build up a Democratic Republican
Government, which would stand side by side with that of the United States, and each
would give to the other an additional strength that could never be shaken.

This course of policy would throw open the doors of Mexico to immigration, and
the Anglo-Saxon race feeling secure in their lives, liberty and property, would pour
in upon the productive soil and the rich mines of Mexico, and with their capital, their
industry, their energy and their skills in mechanics, arts and the sciences, would soon
open a new and magnificent world, in this beautiful country. . . . This policy would
give to the United States a controlling influence, not only over the commerce and
trade of Mexico, but over her political institutions—and, in twenty years, the two
Republics would stand together, as one nation and one people.[25]

Few Mexican liberals, regardless of how intoxicated they may have been with
the possibilities of development, ever painted a more vibrant picture of Mexico's
future. The sentiments appear to be purely Mexican. Few Americans were sufficiently free of nationalistic and racist feelings as to wish to see Mexico and the
United States standing side by side as equals, "as one nation, and one people."
Certainly Buchanan and most of his compatriots wished to profit, either economically or territorially, from Mexico's weaknesses rather than build her into an
equal. Twyman, who had enough political influence to land the consulship of
Veracruz, must have known that Buchanan had never shown any interest in
securing commercial and economic advantages.

In contrast to his report of a month earlier, in which he had recounted a generally
warm liberal response to Buchanan's state of the union message, Twyman now
found that the message had caused great consternation among leading liberals.
Nothing was more likely to unite the warring factions in Mexico and to drive them
into the arms of the French and Spanish, he warned, than a United States attempt
to occupy Sonora, Chihuahua, or other frontier areas. He stressed the determination of the liberals to resist all demands for territorial cessions. To add weight to
the plea Twyman, or those helping him, included a statement that all intelligent
Yankees in Veracruz concurred in his recommendations, including Captain
Turner of the war sloop *Saratoga* now in port.

Churchwell gave no explanation of the conversations he may have had with the
conservative leaders during his sojourn in the interior. Upon his return to Veracruz
he informed his superiors that he had visited the camps of both parties and was
ready to recommend the recognition of the Juárez government. Generals Miguel
Miramón, the new conservative hope, and Zuloaga were dismissed as usurpers
while Juárez was president by virtue of the constitution. In view of this, Churchwell argued, there existed "no valid reason" why Juárez should not be recognized

in Veracruz "just as though he were at the city of Mexico." He stressed the widespread support he had encountered for the liberal cause. He was particularly impressed by the willingness of the liberal soldiers to remain in arms despite lack of food, supplies, and pay. After numerous defeats, the liberals were still able to raise large armies of willing volunteers. "Although it may be an experiment," he asserted, "we have no alternative left but the immediate recognition of the Juárez Government."[26]

The recommendation for recognition did not mean that the liberals agreed to all United States demands. In fact, Churchwell was convinced that the acquisition of territory would be very difficult. "If we shall satisfy them that we are not inclined to despoil them of their territory," the liberals will "adopt us as their virtual Protector." The liberals were making the same presentation to Churchwell that had been so effective with Forsyth but so ineffective when made to Buchanan by Mata. The rich soils and valuable mineral resources of Mexico were being offered for Yankee exploitation. The liberals were also willing to grant perpetual transit rights across northern Mexico from Texas to the Gulf of California and to combine these with vast tracts of lands to assist United States companies to build railroads along these routes.

Churchwell was favorably impressed with the liberal idea of a dominant position for the United States in the Mexican economy. After several interviews with Juárez and the cabinet Churchwell was convinced that "the maintenance of the Liberalists in power is an object worthy of the ardent moral cooperation of our Government. . . . A new phase in Mexican nationality is now a positive necessity, and that phase, if we are not utterly deaf to the dictates of common sense, must be our own creation. . . . The present condition of affairs in Mexico affords the best and it may be, the last opportunity which will ever be presented to the United States" to establish its undisputed dominance over Mexico. He noted that the brilliant young conservative general, Miguel Miramón, whose recent elevation to the presidency in Mexico City had been the principal result of Robles Pezuela's unsuccessful bid for power in December 1858, was planning a new siege of Veracruz.[27]

Churchwell, in seeking to cast the liberals in the best possible light, helped to create in Washington an expectation for a radical improvement in the military fortunes of the Veracruz government. Although liberal victories on the battlefield had been few, he accepted uncritically their boasts that definitive liberal triumphs were only weeks away. For example, he reported, in the awed tones of the credulous, that the liberals were actually enticing Miramón to strike at Veracruz so that their armies from the west could fall upon an undefended Mexico City during his absence. If this happened, he reported, the liberal support, which was growing every day, would become so great that the liberals would no longer need to make major sacrifices to secure United States recognition. "The occasion is one which should be improved without the intermission of a single hour of unnecessary delay."[28]

Churchwell appears to have fallen under the influence of the *puros* Lerdo and Ocampo, for his subsequent communications were filled with glowing references to these two, to their roles in the Reforma, and to their "pro-American" sentiments. He described Ocampo and Lerdo as intellectuals who dominated the cabinet and who had drawn up a liberal program of action which included a definite break between church and state and the nationalization of church property. Lerdo was described as the most practical of the *puros* and "All-American" in his political views. "We should look up to him as the man most reliable in his preferences for us; open, bold and always ready to approach a question and to assume a responsibility."[29]

A comment on Miguel Lerdo by Churchwell has led some scholars to challenge the veracity of all his statements. In his letter of 22 February to Buchanan, Churchwell referred to Lerdo parenthetically as being in the cabinet "by the suggestion of your Agent," which Fuentes Mares erroneously translates into Spanish as *"quien se encuentra en el Gabinete a sugestión mía."* Since Lerdo became minister of hacienda on 2 January, over two weeks before Churchwell's arrival in Veracruz, the referenced statement is obviously false if he was claiming credit for Lerdo's being in the cabinet. Assuming that this is what he meant, scholars have tended to discount most of his reports as fabrications designed to exaggerate his own importance and to please his superiors in Washington.[30] While there are some inaccuracies and exaggerations in Churchwell's reports (he underestimated Juárez's age by some eight years and accepted the liberal claim that the church property was worth at least $300 million), the general tone and content of his reports accurately reflect the sentiments of a man who sympathized with the liberal dreams of development under United States protection but who realized that this did not conform to the expansionist desires of his superiors.

Another possible interpretation of the statement in question not only removes doubts as to its veracity but throws additional light on the entire Churchwell mission. When Churchwell wrote, "by the suggestion of your Agent," he was referring not to himself but to Forsyth. Lerdo had remained in Mexico City during most of the previous year and had spent much of his time conspiring from within the safety of the United States legation. It is probable that Lerdo came out to Veracruz with the Forsyth party in late October. Forsyth refused an official escort, securing instead his own private armed party, and the conservatives later protested that he had forcibly removed from the area of conservative control criminals and others for whom arrest orders had been issued.[31] Forsyth, who hoped to return as minister to the liberal government, spent several days in Veracruz, where he conferred with members of the cabinet and where he may have promoted the entry of his old friend and recent house guest into the cabinet. In Washington Forsyth assured Mata that he was working "from several directions" to promote recognition. Forsyth probably contacted Churchwell, possibly even briefed him on Mexico for the Department of State. While the above suppositions are unsupported by documentary evidence, they conform to the known facts and help explain not only the reference to Lerdo's presence in the cabinet but the speed with which Churchwell made contact with Lerdo and became an advocate of the protectorate scheme which Forsyth and Lerdo had promoted for so long.

Despite his sympathy for the liberals and his endorsement of their proposals, which in fact constituted an invitation to establish a protectorate, Churchwell did not forget his president's interest in territory. His insistence on this point produced a protocol agreed to by Ocampo and Lerdo which held out the promise of territory. The protocol identified nine points as the basis for future negotiations. These included a statement that in view of Baja California's isolation Mexico was willing to negotiate for its transfer to the United States. The remaining points involved a pledge to concede rights of way from Guaymas and Mazatlán to El Paso and the lower Río Grande, a perpetual right of way in Tehuantepec, a stipulation that a portion of any money received by Mexico should be used to extinguish Mexico's British indebtedness, the appointment of commissioners to settle claims, and provisions for closer and less restricted commercial relations. Except for the agreement to discuss a cession of territory the points were not materially different from those contained in the Montes-Forsyth Treaties of 1857. Three additional articles were included as desired by the United States but not agreed to by Mexico: free entry into Mexico of all goods intended only for transit, a treaty specifying the means to be used in protecting and defending transit routes, and a transit privilege from the Gulf of California northward into Arizona.[32]

In his letter to Buchanan of 22 February, Churchwell concentrated on the liberals' need for aid, their worthiness to receive it, and the benefits which his countrymen would enjoy as a result. He included reports on Mexican economic conditions, commercial prospects, and the resource potential of Sonora and Chihuahua when opened by Yankee railroads. He also provided extracts of the liberal reform program. He stressed that a desire to liquidate the heavy debts of Mexico figured into the plans to nationalize church property. The British convention debt was particularly noted as having a detrimental effect on Mexico. A large percentage of Mexican customs revenues were committed to service this debt. This assignment denied Mexico adequate funds for governmental expenses and allowed the British to intervene in Mexican tariff matters. Churchwell saw the paying off the British debt from the compensation received from the United States as an essential step in the creation of an effective but indirect protectorate.[33]

While the liberals in Veracruz worked to insure that Churchwell's report would be favorable, Mata was busy in the United States with measures to force Buchanan's hand. Hoping to take advantage of newspaper predictions of an impending change in policy, he hurried to New York in search of credit soon after Churchwell departed for Mexico. If he could secure a large private loan, he believed that Buchanan would be forced to abandon his dilatory tactics and recognize Juárez without extorting preconditions. When such a loan again proved to be unattainable, Mata renewed his advice that the liberals must make whatever sacrifice might be necessary to secure recognition and credit, even if it involved selling Baja California (for which he suggested a price of $20 million). He also hoped that the transits across northern Mexico, in which the Yankees were showing increasing interest, would bring a good price. Although Mata's letter arrived too late to influence the liberals in their dealings with Churchwell, his views were already well known to his colleagues in Veracruz. In July of the previous year, Mata had written that treaties must be arranged with the United States which would bring money to the liberals and would force the Washington to assume some responsibility for guaranteeing Mexican sovereignty. He hoped that the United States would purchase transit rights in the north under conditions which would require them to protect that area from filibusters.[34] In November he had returned to Veracruz for consultations and had presented his views in person.

The liberals were doing quite well in Veracruz without benefit of Mata's advice. They had been forced to include a territorial concession in the protocol, but to counterbalance this they had converted Buchanan's special agent into a firm advocate of an economic protectorate. Juárez was so pleased with Churchwell and his sympathetic attitude that he directed Mata to secure his appointment as minister. Mata's efforts were unsuccessful; but he reported that Buchanan's appointment of Robert M. McLane of Maryland appeared to be an equally acceptable choice. Mata noted, in a private letter to Ocampo, that McLane was an intimate friend of Juárez's old New Orleans friend Emile La Sere.[35] The liberals were not slow to find any connections which might give them additional leverage.

Events were forcing Buchanan to act. Had Congress responded favorably to his request for a temporary military protectorate over Sonora and Chihuahua, he would have been able to increase the price for action; but the Senate rejected the request in February by a vote of thirty-one to twenty-five. To counter this defeat, he made a special plea to Congress for authority to use the naval forces to protect United States citizens and property in Mexican ports.[36] Whatever he had hoped to gain from Robles's return to Mexico was obviously lost. In January the British and French fleets staged a joint demonstration off Veracruz demanding debt settlement; it appeared to be suspiciously well coordinated with the impending conservative attack. If the conservatives should win with the aid of European powers there would remain no hope of achieving his Mexican objectives. On the other hand, if, as Churchwell and Mata assured him, the liberals were preparing to fall on Miramón's rear in a successful operation to end the civil war, the liberals would be in a stronger position to bargain for recognition. Mata reported that Buchanan was all "irresolution and fear."[37] The resignation of Forsyth had removed the last excuse for inaction.

Despite having been disappointed so many times on securing speedy recognition, even Mata now believed that recognition would come automatically. The official report would arrive from Churchwell, the cabinet would consider the question, and he would be invited to present his credentials to the president. But Mata was to be disappointed again. After the cabinet had agreed on recognition, Buchanan found a means to delay the act. McLane was instructed first to determine if a de facto government worthy of recognition existed in Mexico and then authorized to recognize it at his discretion.[38] The entire question was reopened and responsibility for action shifted to a subordinate. Mata, who had made preparations for the long-awaited ceremony, fumed at the new delay. He charged that Buchanan was so anxious to secure every possible advantage and to avoid responsibility if anything went wrong that news of Miramón's appearance outside Veracruz with a large army had frightened him into this unusual maneuver. Mata helped prepare McLane with letters of introduction to the liberals in Veracruz, the conservative government's chargé in Washington was informed that relations were being broken, and McLane departed for Veracruz to ascertain if any government worthy of recognition existed in Mexico.[39]

Fearing that Miramón might be able to capture Veracruz, Buchanan had issued unusual orders to McLane. Not only was he authorized to recognize either government or neither, but he was also permitted to keep the legation aboard the naval vessel *Savannah* anchored at Sacrificios for as long as he deemed it advisable. As for his specific objectives, McLane was referred to the instructions given Forsyth in July 1857. Despite the talk of a protectorate, Buchanan's goals had not changed; the purchase of Baja California, Sonora, and Chihuahua and a strong position in the Tehuantepec transits continued to be the official objectives. If the cession of Baja California and transit rights in northern Mexico and Tehuantepec proved to be the only attainable items, McLane was empowered to offer $10 million.

When McLane arrived at Veracruz on 1 April 1859 he not only found the liberal government still in existence but angered that recognition had not already been granted to Mata in Washington. The conservative siege had been lifted, and the liberals were now prepared to consider the conditions for recognition to be still an open question. Ocampo took the position that since Mata had not been recognized any understandings reached with Churchwell were no longer operative. McLane began a campaign to force the liberal government to recognize the Churchwell protocol as binding. Ocampo asserted that a commitment to sell Baja California was inadmissible, that several other points were objectionable, and that the United States was unfairly attempting to put a price tag on its recognition. McLane denied the latter charge, claiming that he was only making proposals his predecessor had already presented.

During a hectic week of negotiation a compromise basis for recognition was settled upon. McLane summarized the points of the Churchwell protocol in a note to Ocampo and required its acceptance prior to recognition. Ocampo replied that "Churchwell correctly informed the president . . . by assuring him: 1st that there exists in Mexico a government in possession of the political right to adjust in an honorable and satisfactory manner the questions which were pending when relations were suspended. . . , [and] 2nd, That said government is disposed to exercise its political rights . . . with a loyal and friendly spirit." The statement carefully avoided any mention of specific commitments and only obligated Mexico to settle points in "an honorable and satisfactory manner." While the Churchwell protocol had not been entirely scrapped, its terms could no longer be held as indisputable obligations. McLane was afraid to wait any longer; the liberals had successfully withstood the attack of Miramón and were now confidently claiming that their western armies were descending upon an undefended Mexico City. Fearful that a liberal victory would deny him any bargaining power, McLane hastened to grant formal recognition on 6 April 1859.

McLane felt that recognition of the Veracruz government under conditions differing from those envisioned in the Churchwell protocol required a full explanation to Washington. He cited four reasons to support his decision: the liberals controlled the Tehuantepec area "in which American citizens have consolidated a large commercial and political interest" and which was vital to United States mail shipments to the West Coast; all the states bordering on the United States recognized the authority of Juárez; United States interests, private and public, in the transit route from Arizona to the Gulf of California were being endangered by the refusal of the Sonora government to recognize the power of the central government over public lands; and finally, United States commercial interests in Mexico must be protected at a time when British and French fleets were off Veracruz to enforce compliance with commercial concessions granted their subjects by earlier Mexican governments. These factors, coupled with the prospects of an early termination of the civil war, made it imperative, McLane felt, that he act with dispatch.[40]

Three of the four specific grounds cited by McLane for recognition involved protection and promotion of economic interests, and two of these involved protection of concessions held by persons close to Buchanan. The "large commercial and political interest" in the Tehuantepec transit route referred to the contract secured from Comonfort by Buchanan's powerful friend Judah P. Benjamin. The value of this concession had been enhanced the previous October by a mail contract from the United States Post Office and by a timely, 28 March 1859, modification of its 1857 contract by the Veracruz government.[41]

The Sonora transit route involved a more recently acquired Yankee interest. On 3 February 1859, William L. Cazneau, husband of the influential editorialist Jane McManus Cazneau, whose proliberal writings and assistance in gaining access to Buchanan had been of such service to Mata, applied for a concession to build a wagon road from the frontier to the Gulf of California. Mata recommended the project on its merits as a means of developing and retaining control of the frontier region and on the basis of the great service which Jane Cazneau had rendered to the liberal cause. The concession, granted (perhaps not coincidentally) on the day McLane arrived at Veracruz, contained generous terms, including free right of way through public land and twenty square leagues of land in alternating blocks along the route.[42] McLane believed that a controversy between the central government and Sonoran authorities over control of public lands endangered the success of the Cazneau grant.

While McLane felt compelled to justify to Washington the bases upon which he had extended recognition, Juárez felt compelled to reassure liberal supporters that these bases contained nothing detrimental to national honor and territorial integrity. In a circular issued to liberal governors on the day McLane presented his credentials, 6 April, United States recognition was portrayed as opening "a new era in relations between two people'' who shared a common interest in their mutual prosperity and who, by standing together, could defeat the monarchist conspiracy to control the world. The two countries were embarking upon a policy which would bring all the democratic peoples of the world together, would make the Christian ideal of universal brotherhood a reality, and would disprove the Hobbesian belief that war was the natural state of man. Finally, in embarking on this new policy, the liberal government claimed to be in agreement with "the economists who think that a rich and powerful neighbor is worth more, and secures more advantages, than a desert laid waste by poverty and extermination."[43]

United States recognition and the liberals' partisan method of announcing this development provoked a biting protest from the conservative Foreign Ministry in Mexico City. Forsyth's suspension of relations was attributed to conservative refusal to sell territory and the subsequent recognition of liberals could only mean that liberals were willing to sell territory. McLane felt that the stinging conservative protest must be answered, and in so doing he weakened his bargaining position. In responding to the conservative charges, McLane made himself and his government partisans of the liberal cause and effectively nullified any possibility of using the threat of withdrawing recognition as a means of pressuring the liberals. By implication he committed the United States to respect Mexican sovereignty and territorial integrity. This impression was strengthened when Ocampo attached McLane's statement to another circular to liberal governors in which any intention of selling territory was denied.[44]

The reestablishment of diplomatic relations marked the beginning of a new phase in the struggle, with the United States seeking to gain the maximum advantage and Mexico trying to give up as little as possible. To Juárez, half the battle must have appeared won when recognition was secured without crippling commitments. Mata had assured Juárez and Ocampo that lack of recognition was the major obstacle to realization of the most immediate goal, the acquisition of credit. Over the previous year Mata had constantly stressed the relationship between recognition and credit: bankers refused to lend large sums until recognition had been obtained, while without credit the liberal government could not achieve the stability required for recognition. Now that this vicious circle had been broken the gates should be opened to private credit. Many liberals felt that the United States could not now resist Mexican requests for an alliance, government-to-government credit, and those closer relations which would assure Mexico of continuing stimulants to her economic development.

The Mexican liberals had expected United States recognition to produce immediate tangible benefits in the form of money. Mata's original instructions issued in March 1858 had directed him to negotiate a loan of $25 million with the United States government as soon as recognition had been obtained. The loan could be secured by a mortgage on church property and must not be connected with any claims settlement or any existing Mexican debt. Mexico would immediately receive $3 million and the remaining $22 million would come in monthly installments of $1 million each.[45] While there is no evidence that this authority was ever withdrawn, Mexican expectations had become more limited with the passage of time. By April 1859, the liberals no longer were confident of official loans, but assumed that recognition would remove the barrier to sizeable private loans which could suffice until treaty arrangements could be made for generous official payment for commercial privileges and transit rights. On 7 April Mata and La Sere were jointly authorized to appoint Mexican financial agents in New York and New Orleans to handle the expected loans.[46]

The lack of harmony between the objectives of the two parties was obvious. Whatever sympathy the public might have for the liberals' political ideas, reform programs, and development projects had not caused Buchanan to change his goals. Acquisition of Mexico's northern area and unrestricted control of the Tehuantepec Isthmus continued to be the key objectives. Transit rights across northern Mexico with large land grants to United States railroad companies, first offered by Comonfort in September 1857, had aroused little official interest in Washington. Buchanan was willing to pay for transit rights only if they were combined with a cession of territory, at least Baja California.

Buchanan's messages to Congress and the instructions issued to McLane make it clear that his ideas of establishing his country's influence over Mexico were cast in political terms. He saw British and French activities and their influence over the conservative regime as threats to the future expansion of the United States and to the Monroe Doctrine. While the popularity in Congress of Butterfield's ideas of a commercial manifest destiny and public demands for protection and expansion of commercial operations in Mexico had made him more responsive to Mexican offers of commercial advantage, Buchanan did not see commercial expansion as a method of blocking European designs on Mexico nor of securing the desired United States influence there. Buchanan still held the view that money payments could be made to acquire land but not economic privileges.

Fourteen months after Forsyth had chosen Zuloaga over Juárez and a year after he had announced that the 1857 constitution had sunk forever, Juárez and the government based on that constitution had won a partial but significant victory. Since its creation the liberal government had made United States recognition and credit its principal diplomatic objectives. Buchanan, blinded by the desire for territorial expansion, had attempted to deny Mexico either of its goals until a transfer of territory had been assured. In the ensuing diplomatic battle of wits, Washington was defeated by the liberals in the field where its power, that of recognition, was undisputed; the Veracruz government, through skillful public relations work, astute diplomatic maneuvering, and patience, had gained United States recognition without alienating national territory.

By delaying recognition, Buchanan made the task of securing credit more difficult for the liberals, but in his zeal to extract the last ounce of advantage from recognition he became a victim of his own deviousness. By attempting to exploit developments in Mexico's civil war he committed himself to forces beyond his control and created a situation in which Mexican liberals could on occasion manipulate or color war news to their benefit. By giving McLane final responsibility to decide the question of recognition, Buchanan provided the Veracruz government with an opportunity to stampede the United States minister into granting recognition quickly and cheaply for fear that any delay would further diminish its value. The Mexican liberals, for whom the civil war thus far had been an almost unbroken string of reverses, had demonstrated a diplomatic ability which compensated in some degree for their lack of military prowess.

6
The McLane-Ocampo Treaties:
The Last Attempt to Compromise
Conflicting Goals, 1859–1861

During 1859 and 1860, as the Mexican civil war continued its course of destruction, Mexican and Yankee diplomatic agents pursued their respective and conflicting goals. Liberal leaders in Veracruz hoped that diplomatic recognition would be the first of a series of successful moves. In their vision of the future of liberal Mexico, United States friendship and assistance occupied a vital position. Yankee money, technology, immigrants, leadership, and protection remained the goals of their relations with the United States.

United States goals did not remain as firmly set as did those of Mexico. Having used its trump card, recognition, without securing territory, Washington encountered increasing Mexican resistance to a boundary change. Buchanan gradually realized that by making a transfer of territory the sine qua non of negotiations, he jeopardized all his Mexican objectives. Without abandoning territorial expansion as the ultimate goal, he decided to compromise, to achieve his goals in stages. After securing the United States position in Tehuantepec and placating liberal sensibilities by purchasing transit rights and commercial privileges in northern Mexico and extending the protective shadow of the United States over their government, he hoped that Mexican resistance to his major objective would diminish.

From McLane's recognition of the constitutional government on 6 April 1859 until the signing of the McLane-Ocampo Treaty on 14 December of that year, the parties waged a continuous diplomatic contest over a formula to harmonize their discordant views. The struggle took place mainly in Veracruz; in Washington Mata was isolated from the stream of diplomatic activity and devoted most of his energies to securing loans and arms on the private market, either directly or through the agency of Yankee friends. Both sides attempted to use unfolding events and nondiplomatic factors to bolster their positions.

Ocampo saw as his immediate task, once recognition had been secured, preventing the Yankees from exacting too high a price for this recognition. Mata, whose pessimistic views of the liberal future made him willing to accept any demand, was informed on 22 April that all negotiations would be conducted in Veracruz.[1] Ocampo and Lerdo had committed their government to "negotiate affirmatively" on the question of the cession of Baja California, but they now wished to avoid this step if at all possible. To accomplish this Ocampo evolved a three-part strategy which became clear by June: concentrate on the question of transits, separate transits from the cession of territory, and introduce an alliance proposal into the negotiations.

As a basis for negotiation, McLane submitted the draft boundary and transit treaties furnished to Forsyth by Washington in July 1857. This demand for Sonora and much of Chihuahua in addition to Baja California far exceeded the reasonable expectations of Washington, if not Buchanan's desires. If McLane's later statement, that he had felt more could be gained "from intimate commercial relations than from the acquisition of territory,"[2] can be accepted, then he may have presented these extreme demands to give the liberals an opportunity to reject territorial cession without violating their apparent pledge to Churchwell.

Although key early despatches from McLane are missing from the files of the National Archives, summaries of these communications found elsewhere indicate that as he and Ocampo probed each other's position the new minister quickly apprised Washington that prospects for a boundary change were dim.[3] The price authorized for territory and transits, $10 million, was embarrassingly low in view of Mexican expectations. While McLane felt that Juárez would agree to the sale of Baja California, he warned that the Mexican Congress would probably reject such a treaty. He was unaware, or chose to keep Washington unaware, of the fact that the Veracruz government considered itself as operating under an extraordinary mandate which gave the executive branch full legislative powers and made congressional approval of treaties constitutionally unnecessary.[4]

Rather than openly reject the proposition for the sale of territory, the liberals preferred to separate this question from that of transits and other matters.[5] Buchanan correctly saw the attempt to separate the negotiations as a maneuver to allow for Mexican acceptance of the transit agreement and rejection of that on limits. Only after McLane had convinced Buchanan that no agreement was possible without separate treaties did Washington reluctantly agree to two treaties.[6]

On the matter of transits, difficulty quickly arose over the power of the United States to protect the Tehuantepec route. Buchanan desired a provision allowing the United States to determine when the conditions required its military protection and to extend this protection without the prior consent of Mexico. This had been a key feature of the instructions to Forsyth.

The Mexicans, responding in detail for the first time to this proposal, refused to accept this broadly defined power of intervention. While most liberals were willing to accept United States protection and many *puros* actively sought it, this was neither the place nor the kind of protection they had in mind. They were fully as sensitive as their conservative opponents to United States infringements of Mexico's political sovereignty and territorial integrity, and a unilateral right to protect the transit route smacked too much of a loss of political control, of a preliminary step to annexation. Besides, Tehuantepec neither was nor was likely to be the scene of the kinds of dangers for which the liberals sought protection.

They desired protection in the form of immediate aid in crushing the conservative government, of a continuing commitment that would make future conservative challenges less likely, and of a friendly big brother whose presence would effectively neutralize European threats. The terms of such protection must be defined by treaty in such a fashion as not to injure the national honor, they must be largely obligatory for the United States, and Mexico must retain as much discretionary authority as possible. To further complicate the negotiation, Mexico sought to nullify the right of the United States to transport troops and supplies across the isthmus, a right which Washington thought to have secured in article 8 of the Gadsden Treaty.[7]

Buchanan endeavored to break the impasse created by the Mexican intransigence on the questions of combining transits and limits in the same treaty and of allowing for unilateral intervention by opening negotiations in Washington. Playing upon Mata's pessimistic view of the liberal position in the civil war, he pressed for agreement on his demands. Mata, whose authority to negotiate had already been withdrawn, could only recommend a compromise to Veracruz. His compromise could not have been pleasing to Buchanan, for it hedged the right to act unilaterally in Tehuantepec with so many restrictions as to make it meaningless and camouflaged the sale of Baja California as a loan arrangement in which Mexico would have six years in which to pay off the loan and save Baja California. Privately, however, Mata urged Veracruz to find some quick means of securing official United States funds since his efforts to secure private loans were still disappointing.[8]

In order to divert United States attention from Tehuantepec and Baja California, Ocampo pressed for agreement in two other areas, northern transits and a broadly based alliance. The latter proposal was advanced by Ocampo on 22 April in an attempt to take advantage of McLane's heated reaction to the "massacre of Tacubaya." The liberal plan to lure Miramón away from Mexico City and fall on the capital in his absence had miscarried; the liberal army under Santos Degollado was destroyed by a conservative force led by Leonardo Márquez in a battle at Tacubaya on 10 and 11 April. This crushing defeat coming hard on the heels of American recognition made the positions of both McLane and the Veracruz government more difficult. McLane's discomfort increased when he learned that, in what had become a customary postbattle execution of prisoners, Márquez had ordered the execution of civilian doctors found treating the liberal wounded. At least one Yankee was among the medical party.

The combination of adverse developments led McLane to address a heated note to Ocampo demanding that the liberal government take effective steps immediately to protect the lives and interests of United States citizens. Failure of the liberals to provide prompt satisfaction, McLane said, would force the United States to act on its own to protect its interests and to punish those guilty of damaging those interests. To avoid responsibility for a situation it could not control and to remove the danger of a unilateral American intervention, the Juárez cabinet decided upon the alliance invitation. An alliance to protect democratic representative government in each country would allow the constitutional government to request the United States's assistance against antidemocratic forces.[9]

Although the alliance proposal may have originated as a diversionary tactic, it became a persistent element in the Mexican negotiating stance. As subsequently elaborated, the proposal contained most of the features of earlier protectorate plans. It would have committed the United States to guarantee Mexico's territorial integrity and the liberals' control of power. The latter feature originated with Ocampo, the former with Miguel Lerdo. As the unbridgeable gap between the United States and Mexican positions on the discretionary power for the United States to protect the Tehuantepec transit became evident, the alliance was put forward as a possible compromise. Within the context of the alliance Mexico was willing to give the United States broad discretionary power to intervene in Tehuantepec and elsewhere to maintain order and representative government.

The most formal presentation of the alliance project, made in June, would have committed each country to aid the other against both internal and foreign enemies in a relationship described as the first step in the creation of a hemispheric defense for democratic principles.[10] Despite the terminology relative to mutual obligations, the alliance would have made the United States responsible for assisting the Juárez government in suppressing the challenge to domestic order posed by the "antidemocratic" government of Miramón. The United States would also be obligated to protect "democratic Mexico" from the dangers of European intervention. It was a protectorate scheme thinly disguised. It would give Mexico the protective shadow of the United States, which most liberals felt was necessary for their regeneration of Mexican society.

Whether McLane, Cass, and Buchanan understood the ideological implications of the alliance is not clear. The immediate and persistent reaction was that such an alliance was unthinkable because it would violate the United States's traditional policy of "no entangling alliances." Washington feared that the liberals were attempting to shift to the United States the responsibility for defeating the conservative forces. Mexico might also use such an alliance to involve the United States in an endless series of wars with European powers. None of these were acceptable risks, and the proposal was consistently rejected without any evidence that consideration was given to the desirability of establishing a client-patron relationship.[11]

No consideration appears to have been given to the fact that the alliance would convert the Monroe Doctrine from a unilateral declaration of intent into a bilateral obligation, as obliquely hinted at from time to time by Ocampo, that it would be the first step toward making the doctrine a multilateral commitment sustained by all the "democratic constitutional republics" of the hemisphere. McLane's counterproposal, that after a satisfactory arrangement of all other points, including the cession of Baja California, the United States would be willing to make an agreement which would allow her to assist Mexico in maintaining domestic order,[12] may have been made to protect the unilateral nature of the Monroe Doctrine. It is more likely, however, that McLane merely sought the cession of

Baja California and that any subsequent agreement would not have obligated the United States to take any significant action.

Frontier questions upon which there was little disagreement between the negotiators were also considered. Two distinct questions were involved, reciprocal free trade and transit rights. Mexico was anxious to negotiate on these matters because it believed that the United States would pay at least $5 million for these concessions and because these privileges, being popular with Yankees, would improve Mexico's image in the United States. They could also be made without infringing upon Mexican sovereignty or territorial integrity.[13]

The negotiators quickly decided to increase trade and communication across the frontier by acting under the terms of article 32 of the amity and commerce treaty of 1831. Both Ocampo and McLane claimed to have suggested this move. The article, designed to facilitate trade between Missouri and New Mexico, provided that arrangements for exchange of trade caravans on a regular basis, for determining their routes, and for their military protection could be made by executive agreement. On 25 April McLane and Ocampo signed such an agreement, appointing a joint military survey team to determine the best routes to connect Guaymas with Tucson and Mazatlán with Brazos Santiago in Texas. The surveyors were also to identify the points along the routes at which military garrisons should be located to provide escorts for trade caravans. While each country would control the garrisons within its territory, the agreement allowed escorts of either country to accompany a caravan over the entire route, or the escorts could be changed at a convenient point. Both negotiators considered this agreement essential for later treaties covering transit rights, railroad construction, reciprocal free trade, and free transit privileges for the United States in this region.[14]

The pains taken by McLane to justify this agreement to Washington suggests that northern transits, although included in his instructions, were considered valueless by Washington. He was aware that Mexico expected to be compensated generously for these concessions. He stressed the value of the Guaymas-Tucson road in reducing the cost of freight to Arizona—the per-ton cost from San Francisco would be reduced from $350 to $95 and that from New York from $425 to $125. This would promote the rapid settlement and development of Arizona. More significantly, McLane suggested, this road would result in the Americanization of Sonora, "perhaps even before Arizona has enough inhabitants to warrant its admission to the Union." McLane was obviously trying, as Forsyth had done earlier, to suggest to Buchanan that slow and indirect acquisition through the extension of United States economic and cultural influences was just as effective as purchase and more acceptable to the Mexicans.

By June it became obvious that agreement would not be achieved soon in the negotiations at Veracruz despite general harmony in several areas. There was accord on transit rights in Tehuantepec as well as across the northern frontier. Realizing that proximity would make it nearly impossible for Mexico to resist United States action to protect the northern transit routes and doubtless preferring that this irresistible intervention at least be defined by treaty, Mexico indicated her willingness to accept Yankee military protection of northern transits—this, by saddling the United States with major responsibility for suppressing nomadic Indian raids on both sides of the frontier, would also go far toward removing a major source of domestic embarrassment and an international friction for Mexico. Reciprocal free trade was welcomed as a means of rescuing the generally liberal-dominated frontier region from what was recognized as one of Mexico's worst cases of economic stagnation and hardship. Major disagreements were limited to two topics, the cession of Baja California and the conditions under which the United States could protect the Tehuantepec transit route.

McLane believed that it was bad diplomacy to insist on territorial cession at this point, and he advanced a number of arguments against continuing efforts to secure Baja California. Liberals were opposed to a cession in principle; it would weaken liberal support in the frontier states, heretofore a liberal stronghold; and the validity of a title based on an agreement made with one side in a civil war would be insecure in international law.[15] McLane was saying, for Buchanan's benefit, that the sale of territory might cause the collapse of the liberal regime despite the money received as compensation. If this happened, the victorious conservatives would doubtless refuse to recognize the validity of the sale, forcing the United States either to forfeit the purchase price or to fight a war to establish its title.

On the question of United States protection of the Tehuantepec transit, Mexico would grant this privilege and even make it obligatory, but only when that protection was requested by Mexico. The United States did not wish to be obligated but rather to have discretionary power. Mexico rejected this as an infringement upon national sovereignty.

An interesting but soluble minor disagreement involved a desire by the United States to have the company operating the transit facilities limited by treaty to an annual 15 percent profit.[16] As the potential principal user of this route such a restriction seemed reasonable to the United States, and its inclusion in a treaty could be used by Buchanan to counter charges that the treaty was overly favorable to the financial interests of his political friend Benjamin. Mexico, sharing in the profits of the Louisiana Tehuantepec Company, found any restriction unreasonable. Ocampo further argued that such a restriction would adversely affect both domestic and foreign investment in the company.[17]

The liberals' continuing failure to gain financial resources by treaty matched Mata's attempts to secure them from private sources. Mata had been so busy with loan negotiations in New York that Butterfield had to be sent to locate and escort him to the White House for the formal presentation of his credentials on 29 April.[18] Anyone who held a profitable concession from the liberal government was called on for assistance. Many, like Butterfield, realized that their grants were worthless if the conservatives won and needed little encouragement to exert themselves in behalf of the Veracruz government. Even Churchwell was enlisted as a special loan agent after his return from Veracruz.

Despite the number and motivation of Mata's agents, loans were small, infrequent, and expensive. An attempt to arrange a loan through a brother-in-law of

McLane failed. The otherwise unidentified brother-in-law was probably Colonel Joseph E. Johnston, husband of McLane's sister, who had accompanied McLane to Veracruz and had been named as the United States surveyor in the executive agreement of 25 April 1859. A small loan was obtained through Lapegre, president of the Louisiana state bank and a relative of La Sere. Butterfield was able to secure arms on credit, but other efforts, including an elaborate $500,000 loan for $1.2 million in 6 percent bonds promoted by Churchwell and an attempt by Pierre Soulé to secure $2.4 million in return for $8 million in twenty-year Mexican bonds, either failed or produced meagre results. The outbreak of war between Austria and France and the danger that this war would become generalized made credit even more scarce. News of liberal reverses also shattered on occasion the creditor confidence Mata had so carefully nurtured. The failure of the Hargous Company of New York in April 1859 was taken as a bad omen. The bankruptcy of Hargous, a principal figure in the Louisiana Tehuantepec Company, cast doubt on the ability of the company to survive. If the transit company failed to survive despite its favored position then Mexico's credit standing would be further depressed.[19]

The failure of the liberals to raise adequate money on either front was obvious by early summer of 1859. Recognition had not brought the bonanza of credit so confidently expected. Military reverses, increasingly menacing attitudes by the French, British, and Spanish diplomats, and ominous visits by European fleets demanded that some source of money be found immediately. For some, including Mata, there appeared no alternative but the sale of Baja California.

But Miguel Lerdo, the strongest cabinet opponent of a sale, was ready to try one more maneuver before surrendering to Buchanan's demands. Ever since the establishment of the Juárez government the desirability of a radical reform program, including nationalization of church property, had been discussed and planned. Now seemed a good time for such a program. After his defeat at Tacubaya Degollado demanded nationalization as a war measure. Lerdo pressed for nationalization as an escape from the financial impasse. Liberal Mexico had been unable to raise loans because it could offer no acceptable collateral. Nationalization would mean little in direct resources since most of the property involved lay in areas controlled by the conservative forces. But the liberals hoped that titles to this nationalized property could be used to secure either public or private loans in the United States.[20]

Under Lerdo's prodding the Juárez cabinet issued a reform manifesto on 7 July 1859. Although signed by all the members of the cabinet and the president, the manifesto was obviously the work of Lerdo, who held the portfolios of Hacienda and Fomento. The thirty-page manifesto was an expanded and refined version of Lerdo's 1853 letter to Santa Anna. Attraction of foreign laborers, technicians, entrepreneurs, capital, and technology was given high priority. Domestic and foreign trade, which were magnets for these, should be facilitated and protected by measures ranging from lowering or abolishing taxes and duties to railroad construction and port improvements. The impending nationalization of church property was justified as a means of encouraging colonization and paying off the foreign debts which endangered Mexican sovereignty.

The last third of the manifesto, devoted to Fomento activities, promised to create an economic utopia. Progress was the key to the future, and only with the cooperation of foreigners could Mexico secure this key. Mining must be stimulated by abolishing all taxes and reserving for the government only one-twelfth of the profits, and generous railroad grants would attract domestic and foreign investors. Great attention was given to colonization, "without doubt one of the first needs of the Republic upon which depends not only its progress and the development of its wealth, but also the preservation of its nationality." The manifesto proposed to stimulate colonization not by attractive offers and promotional schemes as in the past but by attacking the barriers to immigration— religious intolerance, lack of employment opportunities, and lack of security. Separation of church and state accompanied by religious freedom would remove the first barrier, a development program financed by foreign investors and by the funds derived from church property would provide ample employment, and an honest and effective system of courts and police would solve the problem of insecurity.[21]

Lerdo's plan to use the nationalized church property as security for loans to finance the prosecution of the civil war was implied in the manifesto. The nationalization decree, issued on 12 July, was designed to put the title to almost all ecclesiastical property into the hands of the state. Any private party having an interest in property under Ley Lerdo of 1856 must publicly declare and establish his claim within thirty days. At the end of thirty days all unclaimed church property would revert irrevocably to the state.[22] There was little likelihood that persons living in areas controlled by the conservatives would risk the vengeance of church and state by attempting to establish their claims. Armed with a copy of the decree and with lists of nationalized property Lerdo departed immediately for the United States in search of life-sustaining credit.

Lerdo's mission was doomed from the beginning; there were too many powerful forces in opposition. Not only would he have to cope with the verities of a strange and immature capital market, but also with the efforts of both his own and the United States governments to insure his failure. McLane alerted Washington to the purpose of Lerdo's trip and warned that if Lerdo succeeded in securing loans all hope of acquiring Baja California would disappear. If he failed, however, McLane felt that his support for a sale could be obtained.[23] There is no evidence to indicate what, if anything, Buchanan did in response to this warning, but it is inconceivable that he failed to act upon such a clear threat to his desire to be a successful expansionist president.

On the other hand, the actions taken by the Veracruz government to prevent Lerdo from securing loans were clear, if its motives were not. In the absence of Lerdo, Ocampo served as acting head of Hacienda along with his Foreign Ministry position. On 27 July he issued a clarifying order providing that the thirty-day limit specified in the original decree did not apply to property located in regions controlled by the conservatives.[24] When news of this change reached New York, Lerdo's lists of church property became worthless as security for loans.

While Ocampo claimed that the order of 27 July and subsequent changes, which left little of the 12 July measure intact, were necessitated by a desire to do justice to those who in good faith had previously invested in church property, this was a weak rationalization. Why was this point not brought up in the cabinet when Lerdo had justified the thirty-day limit as a means of forcing people with an existing interest in church property to come out publicly in support of the liberal government or face the permanent loss of their investment? Other factors were obviously at play in the situation. Relations between Ocampo and Lerdo had been strained for years as a result of personality clashes and of the unwillingness of either to subordinate his views to those of the other. Also Ocampo's son-in-law, Mata, had indicated in April that he would consider any trip by Lerdo to raise loans in the United States as indicating a lack of confidence in his abilities. Finally, it should be noted that Lerdo's success in negotiating loans would not only endanger Buchanan's pet project, the purchase of Baja California, but also the prospects for a Mexican-American alliance, Ocampo's pet project. Thus Ocampo's concern for those who had already invested in church property may have been sharpened by his personal dislike for Lerdo, his desire to protect his son-in-law, and his plans to secure an alliance with the United States.

The failure of Lerdo's loan mission produced a new crisis. Lerdo requested authority to negotiate a treaty in Washington but was refused. In the meantime, Mata had become convinced that the United States Treasury was the only accessible source of money. Money could not be raised from private sources in the United States or Europe for any venture in Mexico, he warned Ocampo. The inability of Mexico to provide adequate guarantees of security to projects and property made all investors reluctant. Internal order was an essential precondition for the inflow of private capital. Until the civil war could be terminated, Mata argued, the only significant source of credit for Mexico was a treaty with the United States.[25]

The crisis in the search for credit was accompanied by a break in the negotiations in Veracruz. After weeks of arguing with Ocampo and pleading with Washington for more flexible instructions, McLane became dispirited. He asked permission to negotiate a treaty without reference to Baja California and to increase the amount to be paid for transit rights and commercial privileges nearer to the $5 million price placed on them by the Mexican negotiators. Reluctantly Washington agreed to separate territorial and transit matters into two treaties and to pay $4 million for transit rights with the proviso that $2 million be withheld to satisfy the claims of its citizens.[26] It is interesting to note how far the amount of claims, estimated at $10 million by Buchanan in his latest state of the union address, had been scaled down.

Despite the modification of his instructions, McLane was still unable to secure an acceptable settlement. Ocampo resigned from the cabinet on 15 August and was replaced by Antonio de la Fuente.[27] De la Fuente was even less tractable than Ocampo had been. He adhered to the position of his predecessor on all key points and added the additional obstacle of demanding that in any treaty the money must be paid immediately without waiting for ratification. McLane found this completely unrealistic and felt that it was merely a delaying tactic. Disheartened by the impasse and fearful of the fever season then gripping Veracruz, McLane decided to return to Washington for vacation and consultations. He now believed that a military alliance was necessary to sustain the liberal regime.[28]

The continuing civil war and the debility of the Veracruz government were damaging private United States interests in Mexico. The liberals had recognized as valid the many concessions made to Yankees by the Comonfort government. Some of these, such as Temple's mint, Naphegyi's gas works, Hammeken's Tacubaya tramway, and Stewart's telegraph lines, were located in areas controlled by conservatives and subject to retaliatory action. Temple's position deteriorated steadily from the time of the establishment of the Zuloaga government in January 1858 and became critical after Churchwell's visit in February 1859. In August 1859 he suspended operation of the mint and appealed to McLane and Juárez for protection. The withdrawal of exequaturs from United States consuls in conservative areas left Yankees in these areas without an official spokesman. The British minister, Otway, compounded the problem by refusing Consul John Black's request that United States interests be protected by the British legation.[29]

Outside the conservative areas United States nationals had the sympathy of the liberal government and functioning consuls to help protect their interests. But frequently these were of little actual value. Local commanders, motivated by avarice or by the necessities of war, did not hesitate to seize Yankee property. The Veracruz government was often unable to prevent such actions or to give immediate compensation. Merchants in Veracruz and Tampico requested the presence of United States naval vessels as a means of protecting their interests.[30] Although the Yankee naval presence was increased, McLane was warned that without special congressional authority the president could not order these ships to use force in the protection of United States citizens and interests.[31]

Beyond the specific acts which resulted in damage, the civil war was detrimental to United States interests in other ways. Commerce between the coastal regions and the interior was paralyzed by the war. Even those holding concessions in areas only lightly touched or unaffected by the civil war found it difficult to operate. Many state officials were sufficiently autonomous to ignore orders and commitments of both national governments. Concessionaires soon realized the truth in Mata's observation that investors were unwilling to risk their capital in Mexico while the civil war continued. The most prestigious Yankee group, the Louisiana Tehuantepec Company, sent Benjamin to London during the summer in a vain effort to raise $2 million in capital. Recent grants made to Cazneau for agricultural development on Cozumel and for a frontier road, Mata's arrangements for German settlers,[32] and liberal modifications of the Tehuantepec contract were of little value so long as the civil war continued to rage.

Leaders in both Veracruz and Washington became concerned during the summer of 1859 with growing European support for the conservative regime. The

French minister de Gabriac had never disguised his partiality for the government in Mexico City. After recognition of Juárez by the United States, his efforts, frequently seconded by the British minister, became more open. De Gabriac forwarded to Paris a long petition addressed to the French emperor by sixty-five leading conservatives. The petitioners saw recognition as a disguise for direct Yankee intervention in the civil war. They called upon the emperor, the recognized champion of justice and civilization, to rescue Mexico from the anarchy and communism being spread by the United States.[33]

A gradual improvement in relations between the conservatives and Spain, capped by the signature of the Mon-Almonte Treaty in September 1859, was seen by the liberals as a preliminary to Anglo-French-Spanish agreement to intervene in favor of the Miramón government, which had replaced the Zuloaga regime in January of that year. In their view, Miramón's agreement to compensate Spain for the recent outrages against Spaniards and to resume payments under the Spanish convention of 1853 would provide a pretext for Spanish intervention at liberal-held Gulf ports to force payments which could not otherwise be made by the Miramón government.[34] Miramón demonstrated his financial insolvency in October when he gave $15 million in obligations to secure $600,000 in immediate credit. This was the infamous Jecker loan which would serve in 1861–62 as the pretext for French intervention.[35]

The financial distress of the Miramón government was not reflected in a corresponding improvement in the position of the liberals. The spring and summer brought an unrelieved string of defeats, beginning with the battle of Tacubaya in April. Military disasters and the failure to secure timely foreign monetary assistance added to the pessimism and dissension within liberal ranks. The cabinet rejected Miguel Lerdo's arrangements for ten thousand Yankee mercenaries in such a way as to cast doubts on his patriotism. This rejection, the earlier undercutting of his efforts to raise a loan, and the refusal to give him authority to negotiate a treaty in Washington caused him to refuse to rejoin the cabinet in November unless it would agree to a treaty with the United States. The defection of the strongman of the northeast, Santiago Vidaurri, in September was also a serious blow to the liberals. Vidaurri, whose persistent demand for complete freedom from federal controls had long been a sore point with liberal leaders and whose forces and prestige had not recovered from being soundly defeated by the conservatives at San Luis Potosí, now professed to fear a filibustering invasion from Texas and retired from the battle zone, taking most of the armed forces of the northeast with him.[36]

Mata felt that Mexico's prestige had fallen so low that many years of stable government would be necessary before private investors would support either government loans or development projects. Since the defeat of the liberals would mean the extinction of Mexican nationality, he was prepared for any sacrifice, even the sale of territory. Feeling that Mexico's survival hung in the balance, he saw concern for national honor and sovereignty as inadequate reason to reject foreign mercenaries or the grant to the United States of discretionary authority to protect the Tehuantepec transits. If the Yankee auxiliaries subscribed to the political ideas upon which the Veracruz government was based he questioned whether they could be considered aliens.[37] He preferred that discretionary power to intervene be included in a treaty involving a broad association of democracies, but if this were not possible, then it must be given in some other form.

All treaties, Mata argued, involve giving up some independence in return for a gain in another area. If the Tehuantepec and northern transits could be arranged, Mexico would gain more economically and socially than it would lose politically. The transits could be developed only under United States protection. With their development Mexico

> will experience a transformation that will change its way of life. The communications routes will serve as inexhaustible springs of wealth for the country; their construction and maintenance will employ thousands of men who today moan in misery or turn to robbery; they will enhance the value of our agricultural and mineral products, increasing their consumption and facilitating their export; they will give an immense value to lands that today lack value; they will guarantee the life and property of inhabitants of frontier states exposed today to the depredations and bloody knife of the savage; and they will contribute powerfully to maintaining the nationality of the country, tying together the interests of its inhabitants who are in such a state of isolation today from one another and from the center that they consider each other foreigners.[38]

Mata's desire to grant to the United States the unilateral right to protect lives and property in Mexico also reflected his belief that Buchanan was moving toward a tougher policy which would soon bring Yankee military forces into Mexico anyway. Naval units were being sent to Mexican ports on both coasts; in Washington more menacing instructions were drafted for McLane. The outrages committed against United States citizens and their property by the Miramón government in retaliation for the recognition of Juárez had created a situation where "the patient endurance which this Government and our citizens have displayed . . . has reached a limit beyond which it cannot be expected to continue. It is quite time that the proper remedy for these wrongs should be applied either by Mexican authorities themselves or else by the forces of the United States."[39] Apparently only Buchanan's view that congressional approval was necessary for the employment of armed forces prevented him from taking decisive action.

In his third annual message Buchanan again sought the necessary congressional approval for the employment of force in Mexico. Almost a fourth of the message was devoted to a review of conditions which, in Buchanan's view, justified a declaration of war. Noting that the liberal government wanted to pursue a policy of justice toward United States nationals but could not exercise effective power, he labeled Mexico a "wreck upon the ocean, drifting about as she is impelled by different factions." As a good neighbor, he asserted, the United States had a responsibility to intervene to prevent Mexico from destroying herself. With reasoning which foreshadowed the later Roosevelt Corollary, Buchanan noted that commercial and humanitarian considerations demanded the intervention of some outside power, and since its policy prohibited European intervention the United States must assume the responsibility.

Buchanan made clear his sympathy for the liberals and his belief that the conservative "bandits" in Mexico City were responsible for the deplorable conditions which had existed for several years. He recommended several means of punishing the conservative forces. If Congress would authorize him to use armed forces against them, he was confident that the Juárez government would agree to allow these forces to pass through its lines to reach the enemy. He also suggested that Congress might wish to have units of the regular army or of sympathetic volunteers placed at the disposal of Juárez. The latter suggestion may have been an attempt to gain congressional endorsement for mercenary forces such as those contracted for by Lerdo. Buchanan repeated his requests for authority to establish military control over Sonora and Chihuahua and to use naval forces in protecting the security of all transisthmian transportation routes. He made a special plea to use the navy in protecting his countrymen's lives and property in the ports of Mexico.[40]

Buchanan did not know that five days before his message went to Congress McLane had signed two treaties that would go far toward committing the United States to the kind of intervention he requested. McLane and Lerdo, after several conferences between themselves and with Buchanan, had returned to Veracruz in November. Upon his arrival, McLane found de la Fuente still unwilling to accept the terms demanded by Buchanan. The decision of Lerdo to remain aloof from the government until the cabinet agreed to a treaty with the United States resulted in the resignation of de la Fuente and the return of Ocampo to the Foreign Ministry. Ocampo reassumed responsibility for foreign affairs on 1 December, and only 14 days were required to complete the process of negotiating, drafting, and signing two agreements which together compromised conflicting Mexican and United States positions on all issues except the cession of Baja California.

The terms of the "Treaty of Transits and Commerce" and the "Convention . . . to Enforce Treaty Stipulations and to Maintain Order and Security in the Territories of Each of the Two Republics" were sufficiently ample and flexible to give the United States the desired transits and discretional authority without involving her in an entangling alliance, while providing Mexico with the long-sought financial resources and protective shadow of the United States. Archives in neither country reveal much about those last two weeks of negotiations. McLane's despatch forwarding the treaties to Washington contains contradictory statements: the treaties were based on the project suggested by Ocampo in July, and most of the key points were dictated by McLane; McLane adhered closely to his instructions, and he exercised great discretion in agreeing to the terms.[41]

The ambiguity of McLane's statements and other facets of the situation suggest that during the visit of McLane and Lerdo to the United States agreement was reached between them and Buchanan as to the general outline of an agreement based on Ocampo's proposals of the previous July. Lerdo, upon his return to

Veracruz, pressured Juárez into accepting the agreement. The subsequent negotiations between Ocampo and McLane consisted of each side attempting to improve its position by finding weak points in the other's stance or in the general understanding achieved in Washington. The character of McLane's covering despatch seems to support this interpretation; he passed over many key features of the treaties with little or no comment, suggesting that these were in accord with a previous general understanding, while making lengthy arguments in support of others, suggesting that these were points not covered or upon which he had been forced to retreat.

The treaty on transits and commerce was the longer and more complex of the two agreements.[42] The first five articles dealt with Tehuantepec transits. A perpetual right of way across the isthmus by any and all existing or future roads was confirmed to the United States and her citizens. Mexico bound herself to open ports of deposit on each side of the isthmus, to allow duty free use of port and transit facilities by all countries, and to insure that foreigners were not charged more for use of these facilities than Mexicans. United States mails would be allowed to use the transit without restriction. Both powers agreed to protect the security and neutrality of the route.

The discretionary power of the United States to protect the isthmus route was carefully worded; Mexico was recognized as having the first obligation to provide protection and only when she failed to do so would any right devolve upon the United States. The normal procedure for using United States forces in the area was defined as being in response to a request from or with the consent of the Mexican government, its minister at Washington, or "competent legally appointed local [Tehuantepec] authorities." Only "in the exceptional case . . . of unforeseen or imminent danger to the lives or property of citizens of the United States" could protection be extended without prior Mexican approval, and then only for the purpose of protecting lives and property in the transit area. When United States forces were used they would be withdrawn as soon as the necessity for their presence ceased, with Mexico having the right to determine when this had occurred. The United States had gained the highly prized discretionary power, but a more restricted power would be hard to imagine.

Not only were the discretionary powers less than desired, but the Tehuantepec agreement failed to place any restriction on the profits of the transit company. McLane pushed, in the final stages of negotiations, to limit the company to 15 percent profit but reported that Ocampo was adamant in his opposition to such a restriction, arguing that Mexico must never do anything to discourage foreign investment. McLane cited earlier Ocampo arguments on this point indicating that since the most secure investments elsewhere in Mexico paid 3–5 percent monthly interest, a 15 percent annual limit on Tehuantepec transit projects would insure the failure of the company.

The sixth and seventh articles gave the United States perpetual rights to two transit routes across the northern frontier on the same terms as Tehuantepec. The routes were defined as running from Matamoros or Camargo to Mazatlán, via

Monterrey, Saltillo, and Durango, and from Guaymas via Magdalena and Hermo-sillo to Rancho de Nogales or other suitable point on the frontier near 110° west longitude. The United States received the right to transport troops and military supplies by the Tehuantepec and Guaymas routes, and the companies operating these routes were required to transport United States and Mexican troops and supplies at half fares. There was an implied right of the United States to protect the northern routes on the same terms as Tehuantepec. Probably to placate liberal leaders from the northern frontier region, a provision was included specifically reserving Mexican sovereignty over the northern transits—no such reservation was made for Tehuantepec.

Two points desired by the United States were not included: the right to transport troops and military supplies over the Mazatlán route was specifically denied, and there was no indication that contracts to operate these routes required Washing-ton's approval or that contracts for railroad construction would carry generous land grants. The latter omissions must have caused strong protest since they had been consistently promised as enticements from the first mention of the northern transits by Comonfort in September 1857. McLane went to great lengths to justify the northern transits in his covering despatch. His pains to prove their value were probably meant to counterbalance the lack of controls over railroad contracts and the absence of land grants, of which he took no note.

Article 8 encompassed an expanded version of Forsyth's reciprocity treaty in 1857. But it involved a very unique form of reciprocity: the United States Congress would determine for both countries which articles would be admitted free of duty and what the duty would be on other items. Reciprocity, thus defined, would apply on the common frontier and also along the three transit routes. McLane's efforts to justify reciprocity indicate that it was not a part of the earlier understanding and was included at the insistence of the Mexicans. Like Forsyth earlier, McLane stressed how reciprocity would help settle and develop the Southwest while benefiting the commercial interests of all sections of the United States. The provision allowing the United States Congress to determine the extent of reciprocity appears to have been a Mexican concession to Yankee sensitivities on the matter.

The remaining articles of the treaty dealt with religious freedom, exemption from forced loans, compensation, and ratification. The amity and commerce treaty of 1831 was modified so as to give greater private and public religious freedom to United States nationals in Mexico. Yankees residing in Mexico were specifically exempted from all forced loans. A sum of $4 million was to be paid to Mexico "in consideration of the foregoing stipulations and in compensation for the revenue surrendered by Mexico on the goods and merchandise transported free of duty" through its territory.

Care was taken to avoid mentioning compensation for commercial privileges or transit routes. The negotiators doubtless recalled that Washington had condemned the purchase of commercial privileges in connection with the Montes-Forsyth treaties and that when Forsyth had recommended acceptance of Comonfort's offer to sell transit rights across northern Mexico Buchanan had informed him that "the importance to Mexico of a railroad across her Northern territory, ought to induce her to adopt the most liberal measures in order to secure the necessary protection and capital for its construction. It is hardly to be expected that the United States will pay . . . for the privilege of conferring on that country this great and important benefit."[43] Although Buchanan had reluctantly agreed to separate the territorial from the transit and other considerations, he would not agree to pay for transit rights and the like unless a territorial treaty was also signed. This refusal to recognize compensation for the transit routes probably prompted Mexico to delete all references to land grants or United States control over the railroad contracts.

The convention to enforce treaty stipulations compromised Buchanan's desire for unrestricted authority to use military force to protect United States interests with Ocampo's proposed alliance. The key passage of the convention provided that

> if any of the stipulations of existing Treaties between Mexico and the United States are violated, or the safety and security of the citizens of either Republic are endangered, within the territory of the other, and the legitimate and acknowledged government thereof may be unable, from any cause, to enforce such stipulations or to provide for such safety and security, it shall be obligatory on that government to seek the aid of the other in maintaining their due execution as well as order and security in the territory of that Republic where such violation and disorder occur.

The negotiators had skillfully combined divergent and conflicting objectives in such a fashion as to give each side something more than its minimal demands. Mexico could seek her neighbor's aid against both domestic and foreign threats, since either could endanger United States lives and property or violate treaty provisions. While the United Sates was not obligated to supply the aid, it was assuming enough responsibility to bring Mexico under its protective shadow, to enhance the status of its liberal government and to increase investors' confidence in its future. This responsibility for maintaining order in Mexico would seriously weaken the ability of the United States to press damage claims, a goal of Ocampo's earlier alliance proposal.

Flexibility and authority were the attractive features of the agreement for Buchanan. It would permit him to employ military force in Mexico independent of special congressional authority and without entangling alliances. The discretionary nature of the authority would allow great flexibility in determining which requests for aid effectively served national interests. Finally, the Monroe Doctrine would be strengthened and its unilateral character preserved.

The Juárez cabinet expected great results from the treaties. On 19 December Ocampo informed Mata of them and directed him to promote their early approval by the United States Senate. Ocampo extolled them as a victory for Mexico. Justice and right would now replace force as the standard of conduct in Mexico's domestic and foreign affairs. The treaties would establish for all time the principle that only those governments based on constitutional order were to be recognized in

Mexico. The mutuality of the convention, allowing either party to intervene in the other to protect order and the sanctity of treaties, was seen by Ocampo as the first step in the building of a new international order, an association of democracies for mutual protection. Without loss of territory or damage to national honor Mexico had secured these great abstract goals plus a compensation which would settle the troublesome United States claims and would give the liberal government the strength to reorganize its finances and crush the conservative rebels. Ocampo had no fear that the treaties would not be ratified by the United States. Mata was supplied with authority to exchange ratified copies and instructed to prevent delays in the ratification process.[44]

Although Ocampo abandoned the Foreign Ministry again on 22 January 1860,[45] his successors continued to push for early ratification of the treaties. Mata informed Veracruz that Congress acted only in response to party, press, friends, or money, and since Buchanan lacked the party strength to insure Senate approval of the treaties and House appropriation of the necessary funds, only money could bring the desired action.[46] Despite its strained financial position, the Veracruz government responded by issuing Mata unlimited authority to draw on Hacienda for the funds to secure favorable press coverage and whatever else might be necessary to insure ratification. When it became obvious that changes would be necessary if the treaties were to have a chance of Senate approval, Mata was given authority to ratify any changes that did not involve additional concessions to the United States or add to the burdens of Mexico. He was also empowered to extend for an additional six months the period during which ratification could take place. By June, Mata had lost hope and advised Veracruz to drop the treaties but was told to continue his efforts without moderation.[47]

How much money Mata may have used in his efforts to insure ratification and the recipients and purposes for which it was spent cannot be determined. He reported in general terms about securing friends in the press and Congress without giving names or specifying their cost. He had the two articles which he had published in New York during June 1858 reprinted in pamphlet form under the title *Mexico: Its Present Government and Its Political Parties.* According to Mata, the emphasis in this pamphlet was on the democratic and constitutional principles of the Veracruz government and on liberal Mexico as an open and fertile field for United States capital and technology. He hired Edward E. Dunbar, a correspondent for the *New York Times,* as publicist. Even after the defeat of the treaties was accepted by Mexico the services of Dunbar were retained, and his publication of the promotional journal *Mexican Papers* during late 1860 and early 1861 was subsidized in the amount of five thousand dollars.[48]

Not all Mexicans were pleased with the McLane-Ocampo Treaties and the prospects they held for a Yankee protectorate over Mexico. The Miramón government naturally denounced them and branded as traitors all who supported them.[49] The conservative press, particularly that of Mexico City, mounted an attack upon the treaties and the ''American lackies'' who signed them.[50] Even among liberals some questioned the wisdom of the policy they embodied. One liberal newspaper was quoted as saying, "Doesn't Sr Juárez know that the liberal party prefers to fall anew under the double despotism of the military and the clergy before committing itself to a foreign yoke?"[51] José C. Valadés, the best and most recent biographer of Ocampo, maintains that liberal opposition to the treaties resulted from party animosities or a lack of understanding, since the treaties represented a clear victory for Mexico and for their architect, Melchor Ocampo.[52]

McLane anticipated equally great results from the treaties. He felt that once the treaties were ratified he could "easily dictate terms to the Miramón government, obtain redress, and pacify this country." He had information indicating that Miramón would not continue the fight once Juárez had secured both money and official United States backing. In late January 1860 McLane recommended the adoption of the policy contained in the treaties even before they were ratified. "Let us take the constitutional government firmly by the hand," he wrote, "and we will in a twelve-month drive out of Mexico every anti-American element and pave the way for the acquisition of Cuba."[53] Like the Mexican liberals, McLane professed to be unable to see how the Senate could reject treaties which offered so many advantages.

Despite the hopes of McLane and the liberals for quick and easy ratification the treaties had rough going from the beginning. They arrived in Washington on 27 December and Buchanan immediately expressed keen disappointment at the absence of a territorial cession. Hoping that a territorial transfer could be arranged later with a stronger liberal government, Buchanan submitted the treaties to the Senate.[54] In February, McLane returned to Washington to use his influence with the Senate. After the treaties had been considered in several secret sessions, the complete texts were leaked and appeared in the *National Intelligencer* on 18 February 1860.[55] In March a treaty of commerce and friendship with Nicaragua which contained the same discretionary authority for United States protection of transit routes was rejected on the grounds that this would involve the United States in Nicaraguan domestic affairs. Even though Buchanan and Cass claimed not to be discouraged, Mata felt that the chances of approval had dimmed.

As consideration of the treaties continued, Mata found opposition to the reciprocity provision both in the Senate and the White House. Buchanan first suggested that the provision should be limited to goods crossing the frontier for ten years. Later Mata reported that the Republican opposition, led by Senator J. T. Simmons of Rhode Island, opposed the reciprocity provision unless amended. Conferences with Simmons revealed that the Republicans demanded four changes: first, to limit reciprocity to ten years; second, to make two separate and expanded lists of duty-free goods, one for each country; third, to extend reciprocity to all ports of each country; and fourth, to make clear that Mexico was granting reciprocity in return for compensation. A conference with Buchanan revealed that only the ten-year limit was acceptable to him. Mata left Buchanan and the Republicans to work out their differences, indicating that changes of this nature would be acceptable to Mexico. He hoped the treaty would be approved with the ten-year limit since this would allow Mexico to terminate reciprocity or to charge again for it.[56]

Mata was unaware that Simmons's amendments were designed to insure the defeat of the treaty. Expanding the free list and the area of its application, even for export-poor Mexico, was not likely to win votes in protectionist Republican circles. The amendment to tie compensation clearly to commercial privileges ran counter to Buchanan's views on commercial policy and nullified McLane's efforts to avoid this problem. When the treaty came to a vote on 31 May, however, it was defeated by sectional and party politics rather than the terms of the treaty and the proposed amendments. The Democrats voted down the amendments, and the unamended treaty was overwhelmed along party and sectional lines—eighteen Democratic votes in favor, fourteen of these southerners, and twenty-seven in opposition, twenty-one Republicans and six Democrats (twenty-three opposition votes from northerners).[57]

An incident off Veracruz in early March involving the United States navy must have had an adverse impact on the Senate's consideration of the treaties. Miramón, seeking to destroy the Juárez government before United States aid could be made available, attacked Veracruz again in late February. Miramón had purchased two warships at Havana to supplement his land attack. McLane, aware of the impending double-prong attack, requested approval to use United States forces to thwart it.[58] Instructions had not been sent nor had the attack occurred when McLane returned to Washington in January. The situation was simplified for Charles Elgee, the chargé, however, by a liberal decree of 24 February declaring the Miramón vessels pirates.[59] Elgee arranged conferences between the senior United States naval officer and the Veracruz authorities, and on 6 March United States vessels cooperated with those of the Veracruz government in capturing the "pirate" ships at Antón Lizardo, a few miles south of Veracruz.

When he learned of the action Buchanan endorsed it. "This government is clear and decided in its conviction," Washington later informed McLane, "that the capture . . . was proper and fully justified by the circumstances." Protests from the Spanish and Miramón governments were rejected. The prizes were carried to New Orleans where an admiralty court ruled, many months later, that their capture had been illegal. In the meantime Miramón's attack had been disrupted.[60] Many senators were probably convinced that the McLane-Ocampo Treaties would encourage more of such incidents.

Despite the continuation of Mexican hopes that the Senate would reverse itself, the negative vote of May proved decisive. In June the Senate agreed to reconsider the treaties, but only after the fall elections. Mata, hoping that the elections would return a comfortable Democratic margin, advised that the time for ratification be extended again.[61] In retrospect this recommendation suggests that despite his admiration for and long study and observation of the Yankee political system, Mata had failed to grasp the significance of the direction in which United States politics had been moving for years, that the sectional crisis had sapped the strength of those national institutions which had served to hold sectional passions in check. The old Whig party had collapsed under the strain, the Democratic party was breaking up into sectional bodies, and a vigorous new vehicle of sectional interest, the Republican party, was casting a giant shadow across the national scene. Despite these ominous signs an October meeting of the Juárez cabinet took up and debated another extension of the time for ratification. Only de la Fuente, who had opposed the signing of the treaties originally, was opposed to the extension. After listening to the arguments Juárez sided with de la Fuente and decided not to keep the treaties alive.[62]

This decision probably did not represent any change in attitude toward the policy contained in the treaties but rather was a reluctant realization that Senate approval was unattainable and a growing hope that conservative power was at last fading. The failure of Miramón's spring offensive against Veracruz had marked the beginning of improved military prospects for the liberals. In Washington Matías Romero, Mata's replacement, was reporting by September that the Republicans would win the elections and that they would reject anything recommended by Buchanan, including the treaties.[63]

The failure of the McLane-Ocampo Treaties did not mean that the liberals received no benefit from them. Although Mexico never received the $4 million specified in the treaties, the prospects of receiving such a sum enhanced the credit status of the Veracruz regime in the money markets. Even before the agreements were signed, Edward L. Plumb, holder of mining concessions in southern Mexico, was in Veracruz as an agent for a New York banking house to arrange for a loan and for the handling of money to be received under the treaties.[64]

How much credit, if any, Plumb may have made available is not known, but the credit picture improved rapidly. In early February Mata was authorized to negotiate a $500,000 loan in New York in anticipation of the ratification of the treaties. He was instructed to check first with Duncan, Sherman, and Company, who had indicated a desire to handle such a loan, but to take his time and arrange the loan on best possible terms for Mexico.[65] By this time Plumb was back in New York where he undertook to arrange the loan for Mata, but Mata reported that he could not get to New York to close the loan because of the need to work for treaty ratification and because he lacked the fifty-dollar fare. Mata found the time and money, however, for a few weeks later he had the arrangements completed for a loan with Duncan, Sherman and Company but had delayed signature in hopes of driving the interest rate down when he received word that his authority to contract for loans had been withdrawn.[66] Veracruz withdrew his power because it found that loans were available from agents in Veracruz on the same terms as in New York and with less delay. Although Mata felt that his position had been damaged by having to reject the loan at the last moment, he soon found that even more favorable offers were forthcoming, including one in which the bankers would undertake to guarantee the ratification of the treaties.[67] Details of actual loans are not available, but it is obvious that Mexico's credit rating enjoyed a rare upsurge.

In addition to improving Mexico's access to credit and sustaining liberal hopes, the treaties caused dissension among the European powers represented in Mexico and may have forestalled a French effort to secure accord for intervention. The French minister, de Gabriac, saw in them proof of his worst fears, that the United States policy was aimed at denying European powers access to markets in the Western Hemisphere. This policy, first clearly delineated in the Montes-Forsyth Treaties, was at the heart of the McLane-Ocampo Treaties. Repeating earlier arguments about the vital importance of Mexico's markets and precious metal production to the French economy, de Gabriac insisted that France must take the lead in establishing a common policy to block the plans of the ambitious Yankees.

The British were unwilling, however, to follow the French lead. Instead of adopting a hostile attitude toward the United States, the British minister, George Mathew, sought to enlist McLane's assistance in working out an armistice and compromise settlement of the Mexican civil war. Even worse, in de Gabriac's view, Mathew was becoming increasingly sympathetic toward the liberals. London was unwilling to act on any intervention proposal without first inviting United States participation and unwilling to approach Washington until the fate of the McLane-Ocampo Treaties had been determined. The latter occasioned a delay of some six months, after which the British were still reluctant to act without Washington's agreement. France, unwilling to act alone or with only the support of Spain, had to postpone for the moment her plans for intervention.[68] This respite may have been disastrous for Mexico in the long run. De Gabriac was replaced by the more capable Alphonse Dubois de Saligny, and France adopted a more cautious but independent policy which was to culminate in intervention in 1862.[69]

The opportunity offered by the availability of credit and by the neutralization of the European threat was used by the liberals during 1860 to bring the civil war to a successful conclusion. The constitutional armies under the command of Jesús González Ortega captured Mexico City on Christmas Day 1860 and the Juárez government moved up from Veracruz in early January 1861.

On the eve of final victory, however, Miguel Lerdo sought a compromise settlement using Gabor Naphegyi as intermediary. Lerdo's motives for this action are not clear. Being primarily concerned with economic development, Lerdo was pessimistic about the benefits to be gained from decisive military victory and had consistently sought a compromise solution that would stop the destruction.[70] In early November 1860 Lerdo may have still doubted the validity of optimistic military reports or he may have believed that the wiser policy was to allow the weakened conservatives to avoid defeat by cooperating in a program of national reconstruction and development.

Naphegyi, who had extensive business interest in Veracruz, Puebla, and Mexico City, served as the contact between Lerdo and the conservative leaders. The conservatives wanted Lerdo to come to Mexico City to work out a settlement. Lerdo indicated that any settlement would have to safeguard the constitution and the Reforma, and when the conservatives accepted this as a basis for discussion

Lerdo placed the matter before Juárez. Juárez rejected the proposal, indicating that the time had passed in which the conservatives could negotiate a settlement and that any attempt now would only be divisive for the liberals.[71]

The entry of Juárez into Mexico City on 11 January 1861 marked the formal end of the civil war which for three years had consumed almost all Mexico's energies, had diverted the liberals from their program of reform and development, and had caused immeasurable damages to those elements upon which economic development depended. The return of domestic peace to Mexico coincided with other developments which marked a sharp break in Mexican–United States relations. The Republican electoral victory of November 1860 touched off an internal crisis which would consume all the energies and attention of the United States for the next five years. This crisis was accompanied by and contributed to new crises in Mexico where the French, seizing the opportunity afforded by Yankee preoccupation elsewhere, used the decision of the victorious but bankrupt Juárez government to suspend payments on the national debt as a pretext to mount an intervention designed to establish a French-dominated monarchy in Mexico. As the simultaneous crises developed all meaningful economic relations between Mexico and the United States were suspended, although tenuous political relations were maintained by the Juárez government with Washington until the crises had passed.[72]

Throughout Mexico's civil war the policy pursued by the Yankees, whom the liberals considered as their natural allies, had worked to the detriment of both the liberals and their country. At almost any point between January 1858 and late 1860 a generous United States policy toward the Juárez government would have served to shorten the civil war. The liberals, seeking a protected status as a positive end in itself and as a means of gaining access to United States credit, gave Washington many opportunities to adopt a generous policy. Forsyth, Churchwell, and McLane were or became convinced of the wisdom of giving moral and material support to liberal government in Mexico. They were supported in this view by a number of private United States citizens with economic interests in Mexico, most notably Butterfield, who worked incessantly as a propagandist. The effort by the Juárez government, led by the *puros* Mata, Ocampo, and Miguel Lerdo, to secure United States aid through a protectorate arrangement, now labeled an alliance, and the granting of economic concessions followed the pattern established during the Comonfort administration. It won the support of official and private Yankees in Mexico but did little to alter the policy adopted by Buchanan in 1857.

The efforts of those seeking to put Mexican–United States relations on a new and more intimate basis failed because of the United States's adherence to traditional goals and attitudes toward Mexican affairs. Buchanan, seeking to leave an impressive territorial acquisition as a monument to his administration, refused to abandon his attempts to acquire vast portions of northwest Mexico. In view of recent history, he refused to believe that Mexicans could refuse to see the expediency of raising money through the sale of land. Forsyth recognized Zuloaga rather than Juárez because he believed the former more tractable on the territorial question. After breaking relations with the conservatives, Buchanan delayed recognition of the liberals for months, during which he threatened to seize portions of Mexico by force, as a means of convincing the liberals that only the sale of territory would secure United States recognition.

In the pressure-filled diplomatic negotiating and maneuvering that accompanied and followed recognition, the liberals, led by Ocampo, achieved what advantage there was to be had. They secured recognition by appearing to give in to Buchanan's demands for territory, but then proved to be very adept at finding ways to sidestep the question and to divert attention elsewhere. Their efforts bore fruit when Buchanan agreed to postpone territorial transfers until the Juárez government had been strengthened by aid given in return for commercial privileges. The resulting McLane-Ocampo Treaties were a clear victory for the Mexicans; they forced the United States to pay for agreements which the liberals had long been anxious to make, agreements which would establish closer economic ties between the two countries and would secure Yankee capital and technology for Mexican development. In the convention to enforce treaty obligations the liberals also acquired in disguise the long-sought protected status. Only the deteriorating congressional position of Buchanan's party and the growing sectional crisis in the United States prevented the ratification of the treaties and some effort at realization of the policy contained in them. As it was, the liberals were able to use the prospects of United States aid and protection to bring the civil war to a close. But the Buchanan policy of denying official credit to the liberal government had contributed to the prolongation of the civil war and to the creation of conditions under which private Yankee investors were unwilling to risk their capital on projects in Mexico.

Matías Romero, Mexican minister to the United States, in speaking to a New York audience in 1864, lamented the loss of this opportunity to draw the two republics closer together. Pointing to Mexico's great natural resources, Romero noted that "Mexico . . . is the most appropriate field for the enterprises of a commercial nation. Sagacious England perceived it some years ago and . . . has secured a greater part of the commerce of Mexico than other foreign nations." France, he said, was now intervening in an attempt to control that wealth. The United States should have secured a dominant position in the Mexican economy years earlier.

> The United States are better situated than any other to avail themselves of the immense wealth of Mexico. Being a nation next to our own, they have facilities for carrying on the frontier and coastwise commerce, and, being inferior to no other people in riches, activity, intelligence, and enterprising spirit, are called by nature to develop the great resources of Mexico.
>
> We are desposed [*sic*] to concede to them all the commercial advantages not inconsistent with our independence and soviergnty. When this shall have been done, the United States will derive all the advantages which they might obtain from annexation of Mexico, without suffering any of the inconveniences which such a step would produce. When we shall have arrived at that situation, our common political

and civil interests will give us a common policy, entirely continental and American, which no European nation will misunderstand with impunity.[73]

Romero felt that the United States had failed to act on this opportunity during the 1850s only because slavery interests had dictated a policy of territorial expansion. Romero's assessment of the situation and his view of the appropriate form for Mexican–United States relations bear a striking similarity to views expressed during the previous decade. Forsyth, McLane, Butterfield, Churchwell, Miguel Lerdo, Ocampo, Comonfort, Mata, and apparently even Juárez would have agreed with Romero's words.

Epilogue

While conclusions have already been drawn in each of the preceding chapters, a review and recasting of some of these in more general terms seems worthwhile. The most striking impression growing out of this study is the degree to which the Mexican liberals, despite their numerous political problems, were devoted, in both thought and action, to a program of economic development. The liberals, both *moderados* and *puros,* shared a deeply felt need to shed the colonial heritage, to enjoy the social, political, and economic benefits of a modernized economy, and to develop the resources of Mexico. In deed and word, Miguel Lerdo was most frequently in the forefront of this movement, but his goals, if not his methods, were shared by other leading figures, from the moderate Comonfort to radicals such as Zarco, Ocampo, and Juárez.

Mexican liberals also displayed an almost equally universal admiration for the political, economic, and social institutions (except slavery) of the United States and a desire to draw tighter the bonds between the two countries. They saw various advantages as obtainable from such a relationship: capital and technology for development, political security for a liberal regime against domestic and European enemies, and the creation of a hemispheric alliance for the protection and promotion of democracy and republicanism. To most liberals these benefits could best be secured by establishing Mexico as an economic protectorate of the United States.

Such a relationship was seriously considered by the liberals on three distinct occasions. Only on the first of these, August–September 1855, was it rejected, and then only because the moment was inopportune in terms of domestic politics. On the other two occasions, 1857 and 1859, liberal governments under the prodding of *puros* signed and actively supported treaties embodying the protectorate arrangement. Both the *moderado* Comonfort and the *puro* Juárez governments publicly endorsed treaties which, while avoiding mention of 'protectorate', provided in fact for such an arrangement. In neither case was there any significant public outcry against the treaties.

Reasonable, intelligent United States diplomacy could have secured a protectorate over Mexico at almost any time after the victory of the Ayutla Revolution in 1855. A relationship of that kind would have opened the Mexican resources and economy to unrestricted United States exploitation and development. What it might have meant to the future of the two countries is a fertile field for speculation. If the arrangement had been achieved early, before the constitution was published in February 1857, the Mexican civil war might have been avoided and with it most of the conditions which contributed to the subsequent French intervention. Had effective United States aid been extended to the liberals during 1858, the first year of the civil war, the liberals might have been able to shorten the civil war and minimize its destructive consequences and again have avoided many of the conditions which contributed to the French intervention.

On the United States side it seems reasonable to assume that adequate presidential leadership could have secured congressional approval of treaties giving the United States economic control over Mexico at any time prior to December 1859, when sectionalism and the weakened Democratic position in the 36th Congress rendered presidential leadership ineffective. What effect such an arrangement might have had on the developing sectional struggle is more difficult to assess. If the Mexican moves had been made in such a way as to strengthen, or appear to strengthen, the proslavery South, a final crisis might have been provoked at an earlier date over different questions and under very different conditions.

If, on the other hand, the policy of economic expansion in Mexico had been cast in terms of bringing national rather than sectional benefits it seems reasonable that the challenge of developing the real or imagined resources of Mexico, commercial and mineral, might have diverted attention sufficiently from sectionalism to have at least delayed the final crisis and the Civil War for years or possibly decades. Had the sectional crisis in the United States been moderated or indefinitely postponed it is unlikely that the French would have been willing to assume the risks involved in a unilateral intervention in Mexico. If the United States had achieved domination of Mexico, the French would have had to rationalize any subsequent intervention on ideological grounds (in behalf of conservatism and monarchy) rather than economic and commercial. As the British foresaw, United States dominance in Mexico would probably have enhanced European trade and investment prospects rather than damaged them.

The most difficult question to answer in this exercise of imagination is the long-term impact of Yankee domination on Mexican independence and nationalism. United States economic penetration and control of Mexico might have served, as Forsyth and de Gabriac prophesied, only as a preliminary period of Americanization prior to peaceful annexation. It takes no more active imagination, however, to see the special arrangement between Mexico and the United States as Ocampo envisioned it, as a first step toward the creation of hemispheric solidarity based upon an association of republican and more or less democratic states operating under a multilateral version of the Monroe Doctrine. It is equally plausible, however, to see a United States economic protectorate as the beginning of a long and superficially placid period of economic development for Mexico as a colony of her powerful neighbor and to see the relationship terminated by a violent and destructive war of national liberation.

Something akin to this took place during the *porfiriato,* 1876–1911, when by more casual and indirect methods United States interests gained a much smaller degree of dominance over the Mexican economy than had been envisioned by the *puros* and their Yankee friends in the 1850s. Many observers (including the great Mexican muralist Diego Rivera, who made this a theme of his mural on the revolution) see the violent upheaval which began in 1910 as a nationalistic struggle against foreign economic domination. Had a more formal and systematic economic protectorate been established in the 1850s, it might well have so submerged Mexican nationalism that the Mexican Revolution would have been delayed for several decades and transformed into a true war of national liberation against the foreign power holding economic sway. How such a struggle would have fitted into the global politics of the mid-twentieth century is sufficiently frightening to cure one of giving unbound freedom to the play of historical imagination.

But the special relationship was not established and credit, or blame, for this failure must be sought primarily in the United States, not Mexico. Much of the responsibility rests with Buchanan, who demonstrated time and again his lack of understanding of and sympathy for commercial and economic objectives. His vision of hemispheric policy was restricted by a blind faith in territorial manifest destiny. Lacking in imagination and decisiveness as a leader and seeing the presidency largely in passive terms, he was unable to divert national attention from the divisive questions of sectionalism and slavery. His appeals to the expansionist traditions were opposed by his own diplomatic agents and unheeded by Congress.

Buchanan may have been no more unrealistic, however, than were the advocates of a policy of economic expansion. As Mata and Benjamin discovered, the United States did not have a national capital structure capable of financing the types of development projects envisioned by Forsyth, Butterfield, and the Mexican liberals. In the absence of an adequate capital market the only alternative would have been governmental financing, and the most effective presidential leadership would have had little chance of carrying through such a policy in the face of mid-nineteenth-century attitudes about the proper role of government.

The French intervention and the United States civil war interrupted but did not destroy the pattern of relationships and attitudes which developed in Mexican–United States relations during the Reforma. Failure to make significant strides toward realizing their development goals did not lessen the Mexican liberal's faith in progress or his admiration of the United States as a model. During the restored republic positivism would give this belief in the inevitability of progress a pseudointellectual base, and the long *profiriato* would realize many of the developmental dreams of Miguel Lerdo, Prieto, Zarco, Mata, and the Reforma *puros*. Forsyth, Butterfield, Mata, and Miguel Lerdo had pointed the direction and pioneered the trail that would be followed by the next generation. Many of those who would lead the way down that trail, such as Edward Lee Plumb and Matías Romero, had served their apprenticeships during the Reforma.

Notes

Abbreviations

AGN	Archivo General de la Nación, Mexico City.
AHINAH	Archivo Histórico del Instituto Nacional de Antropología e Historia, Mexico City. This archive contains two collections of letters to Melchor Ocampo forming *legajos* 8-2 and 8-4 of "Papeles sueltos." Citations to these letters identify sender, recipient, date, *legajo,* and document number, e.g., Mata to Ocampo, 10 Sept. 1859, 8-4-197.
AMR	Archivo Matías Romero, Banco de México, Mexico City, divided into "cartas recibidas" (CR) and "cartas dirijidas" (CD).
ASRE	Archivo de la Secretaría de Relaciones Exteriores, Mexico City.
BP/PHS	Buchanan Papers, Pennsylvania Historical Society, Philadelphia.
GC/UT	Garcia Collection, University of Texas, Austin.
	CP, GC/UT-Comonfort Papers
	GFP, GC/UT-Gómez Farías Papers
JM	Juárez Manuscripts, Biblioteca Nacional, Mexico City.
MRE	Minister of Foreign Relations (Mexico).
NA	National Archives, Washington.
	NA/CD/T–Consular Despatches (Tampico).
	NA/CD/VC–Consular Despatches (Veracruz).
	NA/DD–Diplomatic Despatches (Mexico).
	NA/DI–Diplomatic Instructions (Mexico).
	NA/DN/M–Diplomatic Notes from Mexico.
	NA/DN/TM–Diplomatic Notes to Mexico.
	NA/DPR–Diplomatic Post Records (Mexico).
	NA/DPR/FM–Notes to Legation from Mexican government.
	NA/RBO–Report of Bureau Officers.
	NA/SM–Special Missions.
PRO	Public Records Office, London.

Introduction

1. Charles A. Hale, *Mexican Liberalism in the Age of Mora, 1821–1853* (New Haven: Yale University Press, 1968), pp. 1–9.

2. The best demonstration of liberal continuity is Jesús Reyes Heroles, *El liberalismo mexicano,* 3 vols. (Mexico City: Universidad Nacional Autónoma de México, Facultad de Derecho, 1957–61).

3. The best guides are Robert A. Potash's dated but still valuable "Historiography of Mexico since 1821," *Hispanic American Historical Review* 40 (1960): 383–424; and the bibliographic works of El Colegio de México, "Veinticinco años de investigación histórica en México," *Historia mexicana* 15 (1965–66): 155–445; and the annual *Bibliografía histórica mexicana* (Mexico City: El Colegio de México, 1967–).

4. The best economic treatments of the Reforma are Luis González et al., *La economía mexicana en la época de Juárez* (Mexico City: Secretaría de Industria y Comercio, 1972); Francisco López Cámara, *La estructura económica y social de México en la época de la reforma* (Mexico City: Siglo Veintiuno Editores, 1967); and Manuel Loza Macías, *El pensamiento económico y la constitución de 1857* (Mexico City: Editorial Jus, 1959). Richard A. Johnson, *The Mexican Revolution of Ayutla, 1854–1855* (Rock Island, Ill.: Augustana College Library, 1939) has excellent insights on the social and economic problems of the pre-Reforma setting. For a treatment of the liberal drive for material progress see Donathon C. Olliff, "Mexico's Mid-Nineteenth-Century Drive for Material Development," *SECOLAS Annals* 8 (1977): 19–29.

5. Walter V. Scholes, *Mexican Politics during the Juárez Regime, 1855–1872* (Columbia: University of Missouri Press, 1957). An application of the laissez-faire thesis to the intervention period is Thomas David Schoonover, *Dollars over Dominion: The Triumph of Liberalism in Mexican–United States Relations, 1861–1867* (Baton Rouge: Louisiana State University Press, 1978).

6. Schoonover, *Dollars over Dominion,* is a notable exception to this generalization, as is David M. Pletcher, *Rails, Mines, and Progress: Seven American Promoters in Mexico, 1867–1911* (Ithaca: Cornell University Press, 1958).

7. Olliff, "Material Development."

8. A good overview of Mexico's colonial economy is Charles C. Cumberland, *Mexico: The Struggle for Modernity* (New York: Oxford University Press, 1968), pp. 84–112. For the mining revival see David A. Brading, *Miners and Merchants in Bourbon Mexico, 1763–1810* (Cambridge: Cambridge University Press, 1971).

9. Eduardo Arcila Farías, *Reformas económicas del siglo xviii en Nueva España*, 2 vols. (Mexico City: SepSetentas, 1974), 2:89–112.

10. Cumberland, *Mexico,* pp. 149–55, summarizes the resulting problems.

11. Robert W. Randall, *Real del Monte, a British Mining Venture in Mexico* (Austin: University of Texas Press, 1972); and Newton Ray Gilmore, "Henry George Ward, British Publicist for Mexican Mines," *Pacific Historical Review* 32 (1963): 35–47.

12. Among the most informative accounts are Henry George Ward, *Mexico in 1827*, 2 vols. (London: H. Colburn, 1828); Joel R. Poinsett, *Notes on Mexico Made in the Autumn of 1822* (Philadelphia: H. C. Carey & I. Lea, 1824); and Frances E. Calderón de la Barca, *Life in Mexico,* ed. Howard T. Fisher and Marion H. Fisher (New York: Doubleday & Co., 1966).

13. Charles A. Hale, "The War with the United States and the Crisis in Mexican Thought," *The Americas* 14 (1957): 153–73; and Hale, *Age of Mora,* pp. 11–38.

14. The standard biography of Alamán is José C. Valadés, *Alamán, estadista e historiador* (Mexico City: Robredo, 1938).

15. C. Alan Hutchinson, "Valentín Gómez Farías: A Biographical Study," Ph.D. diss., University of Texas, 1948.

16. The studies of Santa Anna are legion; two of the more worthwhile are José Fuentes Mares, *Santa Anna: Aurora y ocaso de un comediante,* 3rd ed. (Mexico City: Editorial Jus, 1967); and Wilfrid Hardy Callcott, *Santa Anna: The Story of an Enigma Who Once Was Mexico* (Norman: University of Oklahoma Press, 1936).

The standard treatment of the political and military aspects of the Ayutla revolution is Johnson, *Revolution of Ayutla;* and the best overall treatment of this period is the too-brief Scholes, *Mexican Politics.*

17. Godoy still awaits a biographer. For the other leading *puros* see Carmen Blázquez,

Miguel Lerdo de Tejada: Un liberal veracruzano en la política nacional (Mexico City: El Colegio de México, 1978); Harry Bernstein, *Matías Romero, 1837–1898* (Mexico City: Fondo de Cultura Económica, 1973); Raymond C. Wheat, *Francisco Zarco: El portavoz liberal de la reforma* (Mexico City: Editorial Porrúa, 1957); José C. Valadés, *Don Melchor Ocampo, reformador de México* (Mexico City: Editorial Patria, 1954); Ralph Roeder, *Juárez and His Mexico*, 2 vols. (New York: Viking Press, 1947); Rafael Murillo Vidal, *José María Mata: Padre de la constitución de 1857* (Mexico City: Secretaría de Educación Pública, 1966); and Daniel Moreno, *Los hombres de la reforma*, 2nd ed. (Mexico City: B. Costa-Amic, 1970).

18. The best analyses of manifest destiny are Frederick Merk, *Manifest Destiny and Mission in American History: A Reinterpretation* (New York: Alfred A. Knopf, 1970); and Albert K. Weinberg, *Manifest Destiny: A Study of Nationalist Expansionism in American History* (Baltimore: Johns Hopkins Press, 1935).

Chapter 1

1. The passing of an older generation of liberal leaders is noted by Charles A. Hale, "The War with the United States and the Crisis in Mexican Thought," *The Americas* 14 (1957): 161.

2. Charles A. Hale, *Mexican Liberalism in the Age of Mora, 1821–1853* (New Haven: Yale University Press, 1968); Jesús Reyes Heroles, *El liberalismo mexicano*, 3 vols. (Mexico City: Universidad Nacional Autónoma de México, Facultad de Derecho, 1957–61); and David A. Brading, "Creole Nationalism and Mexican Liberalism," *Journal of Interamerican Studies and World Affairs* 15 (1973): 139–90, all explore these ties.

3. Brading, "Creole Nationalism," pp. 145–53.

4. Hale, "War and Crisis," pp. 153–73, deals with the impact of the war; the Díaz period is covered in Daniel Cosío Villegas, ed., *Historia moderna de México*, 8 vols. (Mexico City: Editorial Hermes, 1955–65).

5. Brading, "Creole Nationalism," pp. 144–50.

6. Rosaura Hernández Rodríguez, *Ignacio Comonfort: Trayectoria política. Documentos* (Mexico City: Universidad Nacional Autónoma de México, Instituto de Investigaciones Históricas, 1967), pp. 65–66.

7. Hale, "War and Crisis," pp. 153–73, explores the resulting crisis.

8. James Fred Rippy, *Joel R. Poinsett, Versatile American* (Durham: Duke University Press, 1935), pp. 121–28.

9. 21 Nov. 1846, cited in Reyes Heroles, *Liberalismo*, 2:376.

10. José C. Valadés, *Don Melchor Ocampo, reformador de México* (Mexico City: Editorial Patria, 1954), pp. 176–84; and Melchor Ocampo, *Obras completas de Melchor Ocampo* (Mexico City: F. Vazquez, 1901), vol. 2, *Escritos políticos*, prologue by Angél Pola, pp. 263–76. For the *Plan de Jarauta* see *Diccionario Porrúa de historia, biografía, y geografía de México*, 3rd ed., 2 vols. (Mexico City: Editorial Porrúa, 1970), 1:1112.

11. Hale, *Age of Mora*, pp. 207–14.

12. Dennis E. Berge, "A Mexican Dilemma: The Mexico City Ayuntamiento and the Question of Loyalty, 1846–1848," *Hispanic American Historical Review* 50 (1970): 229–56; Alejandro Villaseñor y Villaseñor, *Antón Lizardo. El tratado de MacLane-Ocampo. El brindis del desierto* (Mexico City: Editorial Jus, 1962), pp. 171–297; and Luis G. Zorilla, *Historia de las relaciones entre México y los Estados Unidos de América, 1800–1958*, 2 vols. (Mexico City: Editorial Porrúa, 1966), 1:209.

13. Rafael Murillo Vidal, *José María Mata: Padre de la constitución de 1857* (Mexico City: Secretaría de Educación Pública, 1966), pp. 3–5.

14. Zorilla, *México y los Estados Unidos,* 1:239–51.

15. Reyes Heroles, *Liberalismo,* 2:388–91.

16. Brading, "Creole Nationalism," p. 143; and Hale, "War and Crisis," pp. 153–73.

17. *Consideraciones sobre la situación política y social de la República mexicana en el año 1847* (Mexico City: Valdes y Redondas, 1848).

18. Reyes Heroles, *Liberalismo,* 2: 379–87, 391; and Jorge Gurria Lacroix, *Las ideas monárquicas de don Lucas Alamán* (Mexico City: Instituto de Historia, 1951), pp. 51–60.

19. *Consideraciones,* especially pp. 52–56.

20. Reyes Heroles, *Liberalismo,* 2:388–90; and *Diccionario Porrúa,* 1:870–72.

21. Miguel Ramos Arizpe, *Memoria sobre el estado de las provincias internas de oriente* (Mexico City: Universidad Nacional Autónoma de México, 1932), p. 83; and José María Luis Mora, *Méjico y sus revoluciones,* 3 vols. (Mexico City: Porrúa, 1950), 1: 45–47.

22. Brading, "Creole Nationalism," p. 150.

23. Letter, 18 Apr. 1853, in *El Heraldo* (Mexico City), 9 Sept. 1855.

24. *Diccionario Porrúa,* 1:1174, refers to Lerdo as the liberal representative in Santa Anna's government.

25. An interesting contemporary attempt to understand the significance of the confusing train of events which surrounded the decision to recall Santa Anna to power and the procedures followed in informing him and escorting him back from exile is found in reports and diary of the French minister to Mexico, André Levasseur, in Lilia Díaz, ed., *Versión francesa de México: Informes diplomáticos,* 4 vols. (Mexico City: El Colegio de México, 1963–67), 1:1–31. For Miguel Lerdo's role in the recall see Frank A. Knapp, *The Life of Sebastián Lerdo de Tejada, 1823–1889: A Study in Influence and Obscurity* (Austin: University of Texas Press, 1951; reprint ed., New York: Greenwood Press, 1968), pp. 47–48; and Jan Bazant, *A Concise History of Mexico from Hidalgo to Cárdenas, 1805–1940* (Cambridge: Cambridge University Press, 1977), pp. 68–69.

26. All Mexico City newspapers carried accounts of the bitter 1861 election struggle. Especially useful were those of *El Heraldo, El Siglo XIX,* and *El Monitor Republicano.*

27. M. Lerdo to Santa Anna, 18 Apr. 1853, in *El Heraldo* (Mexico City), 9 Sept. 1855.

28. "El Ministerio de Fomento," *El Heraldo* (Mexico City), 13 Oct. 1855, p. 2. For the evolution of Alamán's ideas on economic development see Hale, *Age of Mora,* pp. 249–80. For Alamán's involvement with the Banco de Avío see Robert A. Potash, *El banco de avío de México: El fomento de la industria, 1821–1846* (Mexico City: Fondo de Cultura Económica, 1959).

29. For discussion of liberal dedication to colonization see Hale, *Age of Mora;* and Brading, "Creole Nationalism."

30. A point made by both Hale, *Age of Mora,* pp. 246–47; and Brading, "Creole Nationalism," p. 175.

31. Dano to Paris, 4 Jan. 1854, in Díaz, *Versión francesa,* 1:88–93.

32. *El Heraldo* (Mexico City), 31 Mar. 1856, p. 3, and 25 June 1856, p. 2.

33. An excellent summary of transportation and its impact on the Mexican economy is found in John T. Pickett's special consular report, 22 Mar. 1854, NA/CD/VC.

34. M. Lerdo to Santa Anna, 18 Apr. 1853, in *El Heraldo* (Mexico City), 9 Sept. 1855.

35. 20 Feb. 1851, and 22 Oct. 1849.

36. 11 Dec. 1854.

37. Charles Allen Smart, *Viva Juárez! A Biography* (Philadelphia: J. B. Lippincott Co., 1963), p. 93; and Ocampo, *Obras*, 2:65–68.

38. Manuel Dublán and José María Lozano, comps., *Legislación mexicana o colección completa de las disposiciones legislativas expedidas desde la independencia de la República,* official ed., 45 vols. (Mexico City: Imprenta del Comercio de Dublán y Chávez, 1876–1910), 7: 79–80, 469–71.

39. *El Heraldo* (Mexico City), 24 July 1855.

40. Dublán and Lozano, *Legislación,* 7: 336–41, 245–56.

41. Ernesto de la Torre Villar, "La capital y sus primeros medios de transporte: Prehistoria de los tranvías," *Historia mexicana* 9 (1959–60): 231.

42. See *El Siglo XIX* (Mexico City) and *El Heraldo* (Mexico City) for Aug.–Oct. 1855.

43. Ernesto de la Torre Villar, "El ferrocarril de Tacubaya," *Historia mexicana* 9 (1959–60): 377–78.

44. *El Siglo XIX* (Mexico City), 7 July 1857.

45. Letter, 30 Sept. 1857, to *El Heraldo* (Mexico City), 6 Oct. 1857.

46. Frank A. Knapp, "Precursors of American Investment in Mexican Railroads," *Pacific Historical Review* 21 (1952): 44–45.

47. Miguel Lerdo de Tejada, *El comercio esterior de México desde la conquista hasta hoy* (Mexico City: Rafael, 1853), especially pp. 28–31; M. Lerdo to Santa Anna, 18 Apr. 1853, in *El Heraldo* (Mexico City), 9 Sept. 1855; and M. Lerdo to Juan Alvarez, 7 Dec. 1855, in *El Heraldo* (Mexico City), 28 and 29 Dec. 1855.

48. See various editorials on smuggling, especially that of 6 Oct. 1857. *El Siglo XIX* (Mexico City) also carried numerous editorials linking high tariffs and smuggling.

49. *El Heraldo* (Mexico City), 3 Dec. 1857.

50. Especially that of 28 Oct. 1855.

51. Francisco Zarco, *Historia del congreso extraordinario constituyente [1856–1857]* (Mexico City: El Colegio de México, 1956), pp. 919–22.

52. M. Lerdo to Santa Anna, 18 Apr. 1853, in *El Heraldo* (Mexico City), 9 Sept. 1855.

53. Quoted in Jesús Silva Herzog, *El pensamiento económica, social, y política de México, 1810–1964* (Mexico City: Instituto de Investigaciones Económicas, 1967), p. 241.

54. Various references to sewing machines and washing machines are found in Comonfort's accounting of his expenditures in the United States during an 1854 trip, CP, GC/UT. There are several letters between Ocampo and Mata on sewing machines in Ocampo Papers, AHINAH.

55. For example, Mata sent Ocampo and Juárez samples of interoceanic telegraph cable, Mata to Ocampo, 10 Sept. 1858, 8-4-107, AHINAH.

56. Walter V. Scholes, *Mexican Politics during the Juárez Regime, 1855–1872* (Columbia, University of Missouri Press, 1957), pp. 1–2.

57. Silva Herzog, *Pensamiento*, pp. 234, 245.

58. *El Siglo XIX* (Mexico City), 20 Feb. 1851.

59. Letter in *El Heraldo* (Mexico City), 6 Oct. 1857.

60. Used for semiexclusive categories by Hale, *Age of Mora*, p. 249.

61. 1 Mar. 1854.

62. *El Siglo XIX* (Mexico City), 6 Sept. 1850, and 20 Feb. 1851.

63. 28 Oct. 1855.

64. See M. Lerdo to Alvarez, 7 Dec. 1855, in *El Heraldo* (Mexico City), 28 and 29 Dec. 1855; and *El Siglo XIX* (Mexico City), 28 Oct. 1855.

65. James Buchanan, *Mr. Buchanan's Administration on the Eve of the Rebellion* (New York: D. Appleton & Co., 1866), pp. 268–70.

66. The "All Mexico" movement is the subject of John Douglas Pitts Fuller, *The Movement for the Acquisition of All Mexico, 1846–1848* (Baltimore: Johns Hopkins Press, 1936), and is best summarized in Frederick Merk, *Manifest Destiny and Mission in American History: A Reinterpretation* (New York: Alfred A. Knopf, 1970), pp. 107–201.

67. *Public Ledger* (Philadelphia), 25 Jan. 1848, quoted in Merk, *Manifest Destiny*, pp. 124–25.

68. James D. Richardson, comp., *A Compilation of the Messages and Papers of the Presidents, 1789–1897*, 10 vols. (Washington: Government Printing Office, 1896–99), 4: 545–46.

69. Letter in *Union* (Washington), 24 Dec. 1847, quoted in Merk, *Manifest Destiny*, pp. 119–20.

70. Merk, *Manifest Destiny*, p. 209.

71. Quoted in Richard W. Van Alstyne, *The Rising American Empire* (New York: Oxford University Press, 1960), p. 152.

72. Richardson, *Messages and Papers*, 5: 198, 435–36.

73. Merk, *Manifest Destiny*, pp. 202–27.

74. The most complete treatment of this treaty is Paul Neff Garber, *The Gadsden Treaty* (Philadelphia: University of Pennsylvania Press, 1923).

75. Diplomatic efforts to secure this route are summarized in James Fred Rippy, "Diplomacy of the United States and Mexico regarding the Isthmus of Tehuantepec, 1848–1860," *Mississippi Valley Historical Review* 6 (1919-20): 503–31; and Edward B. Glick, *Straddling the Isthmus of Tehuantepec* (Gainesville: University of Florida Press, 1959).

76. Merk, *Manifest Destiny*, pp. 128–31.

77. William Watson Davis, "Ante-Bellum Southern Commercial Conventions," *Transactions of the Alabama Historical Society, 1904* 5(1906): 153–202.

78. Davis, "Commercial Conventions," p. 187.

79. See particularly Gadsden's comments on this topic as reported by French Minister Jean Alexis de Gabriac to Paris, 1 Feb. 1855, in Díaz, *Versión francesa*, 1:163–65.

80. Carlos Butterfield, *United States and Mexican Mail Steamship Line: Statistics on Mexico* (New York: J. A. H. Hasbrouck & Co., 1860), pp. 86, 87–89, 44–45.

81. Based on surveys of spotty listings of foreigners arriving at Mexican ports contained in "Movimiento marítimo", AGN; and of only slightly more complete listings of passports issued by the American consulates in Mexico City and Veracruz, NA/CD/MC and VC.

Chapter 2

1. From the diary of the French minister, André Levasseur, in Lilia Díaz, ed., *Versión francesa de México: Informes diplomáticos*, 4 vols. (Mexico City: El Colegio de México, 1963–67), 1:11.

2. The Ceballos tariff schedule was published in *El Heraldo* (Mexico City), 4 Sept. 1855.

3. M. Lerdo to Santa Anna, 18 Apr. 1853, in *El Heraldo* (Mexico City), 9 Sept. 1855.

4. See Francisco Zarco, *Historia del congreso extraordinario constituyente [1856–1857]* (Mexico City: El Colegio de México, 1956), pp. 420–22.

5. Special consular report, John T. Pickett, 25 June 1854, NA/CD/VC.

6. Dano to Paris, 5 Mar. 1854, in Díaz, *Versión francesa,* 1:102–5.

7. Benito Juárez, *Documentos, discursos, y correspondencia,* ed. Jorge L. Tamayo, 12 vols. (Mexico City: Secretaría de Patrimonio Nacional, 1964–68), 2:13–14.

8. Juárez, *Documentos,* 2:15–21.

9. Plans of Ayutla and Acapulco are in Juárez, *Documentos,* 2:13–21. The expansion of presidential power is noted in Edmundo O'Gorman, "Procedentes y sentido de la revolución de Ayutla," *Seis estudios históricos de tema mexicano* (Jalapa: Universidad Veracruzana, 1960), pp. 99–144.

10. Decree published in *El Heraldo* (Mexico City), 2 Sept. 1855.

11. Dano to Paris, 1 Apr. 1854, in Díaz, *Versión francesa,* 1:105–7.

12. *El Heraldo* (Mexico City), 2 Sept. 1855; and decree of 5 Sept. 1855, in *El Heraldo* (Mexico City), 18 Sept. 1855.

13. Rosaura Hernández Rodríguez, *Ignacio Comonfort: Trayectoria política. Documentos* (Mexico City: Universidad Nacional Autónoma de México, Instituto de Investigaciones Históricas, 1967), pp. 126–35.

14. Instructions signed by Alvarez at La Providencia, Guerrero, 17 May 1854, certified by American Consul Charles L. Denman, Acapulco, 23 May 1854, in folder 17, CP, GC/UT. Because the same symbol ($) was used for the currencies of both countries, it is frequently impossible to determine whether sums cited in documents refer to dollars or pesos. The question is of little import, however, since the peso and the dollar were of equal value during the period under study, and no attempt will be made here to distinguish between the two.

15. Notarized and corrected copy of power of attorney, Alvarez to Comonfort, 17 May 1854, folder 17, CP, GC/UT.

16. Comonfort's New York loan contracts are in folder 17, CP, GC/UT. For conflicting accounts of Comonfort's fund-raising trip, see [Anselmo de la Portilla], *Historia de la revolución de México contra la dictadura del general Santa-Anna, 1853–1855* (Mexico City: Imprenta Vicente García Torres, 1856; reprint ed., Puebla: Editorial José M. Cajica, Jr., 1972), pp. 179–84; and Niceto de Zamacois, *Historia de México, desde sus tiempos mas remotos hasta nuestros días,* 22 vols. (Barcelona: J. F. Parres y Comp., 1876–1902), 13:817–18.

17. Vol. 3, pp. 905–11, NA/RBO.

18. George P. Hammond, ed., *The Larkin Papers,* 10 vols. (Berkeley: University of California Press, 1951–64), has numerous documents dealing with Ajuria and Temple. Fragmentary accounts of Temple's activities are found in Robert Glass Cleland, *The Cattle on a Thousand Hills: Southern California, 1850–1880,* 2nd ed. (Alhambra, Calif.: C. F. Braun & Co., 1951; facsimile reprint ed., San Marino, Calif.: Huntington Library, 1975); Lynn Bowman, *Los Angeles: Epic of a City* (Berkeley: Howell-North Books, 1974); William W. Robinson, *Los Angeles: A Profile* (Norman: University of Oklahoma Press, 1968); *Los Angeles, A Guide to the City and Its Environs,* 2nd ed. (New York: Hastings House, 1951); Benjamin Ignatius Hayes, *Pioneer Notes from the Diaries of Judge Benjamin Hayes, 1849–1875* (New York: Arno Press, 1976); and Theodore H. Hittell, *History of California,* 4 vols. (San Francisco: H. J. Stone & Co., 1898).

19. *Diccionario Porrúa de historia, biografía, y geografía de México,* 3rd ed., 2 vols. (Mexico City: Editorial Porrúa, 1970), 1: 479–80; [Portilla], *Historia de la revolución,* pp. 179–84; Luis G. Zorilla, *Historia de las relaciones entre México y los Estados Unidos de*

América, 1800–1958, 2 vols. (Mexico City: Editorial Porrúa, 1966), 1:253; and Richard A. Johnson, *The Mexican Revolution of Ayutla, 1854–1855* (Rock Island, Ill.: Augustana College Library, 1939), p. 82n.

20. Power of attorney, Temple to Ajuria, Mexico City, 23 Mar. 1854, in John Temple, "Memoria justificativa de los hechos que forman los reclamos de Mr. John Temple contra el Gob[iern]o de México," pp. 143–60, GC/UT. The other principal sources of documents relating to the loan are José Antonio de Mendizábal, *Exposición que José Antonio de Mendizábal, albacea de Don Juan Temple, dirige al gobierno mexicano pidiéndole el cumplimiento del contrato de 28 de Junio de 1856* (Mexico City: F. Díaz de León y Santiago White, 1868); and the claim file of John Temple, Claims against Mexico under the Convention of 1868, Records of Boundary and Claims Commissions and Arbitrations, Record Group 76, NA (hereinafter cited as Temple Claim, NA).

21. Copies of the Temple loan contract are found in Temple Claim, NA; and Temple, "Memoria justificativa," GC/UT. Since subsequent Mexican accounting procedures treated the $60,000 as a distinct and complete transaction (see accounting statement, folder 17, CP, GC/UT), most Mexican writers appear unaware of the other portion of the loan. So was the present writer: see Donathon C. Olliff, "The Economics of Mexican-United States Relations during the Reforma, 1854–1861" (Ph.D. diss., University of Florida, 1974).

22. No full copy of the Temple contract with Degollado agents is available. An extracted version is in memorial by Pedro Arriago on behalf of John Temple, 29 Mar. 1856, in Temple Claim, NA.

23. Order, 11 Dec. 1854, folder 17, CP, GC/UT.

24. Order, 19 Oct. 1855, document no. 8, Temple Claim, NA.

25. Rafael Murillo Vidal, *José María Mata: Padre de la constitución de 1857* (Mexico City: Secretaría de Educación Pública, 1966), pp. 10–11.

26. Mata to Ocampo, 8-1-4 through 8-1-54, AHINAH.

27. José C. Valadés, *Don Melchor Ocampo, reformador de México* (Mexico City: Editorial Patria, 1954), pp. 286–90.

28. Murillo, *Mata*, pp. 10–11.

29. Juárez, *Documentos*, 2:11; and *Diccionario Porrúa*, 2:1942–43.

30. For contracts with both Comonfort and Juárez governments, see Mata to Ocampo, 28 Aug. 1858, 8-4-105, AHINAH.

31. *Diccionario Porrúa*, 2:1942–43.

32. Juárez, *Documentos*, 2:8.

33. Levasseur to Paris, 28 and 30 Apr. and 4 and 31 May 1853, in Díaz, *Versión francesa*, 1: 40, 43–45, 49–50.

34. Zorilla, *México y los Estados Unidos*, 1:342–43.

35. Levasseur to Paris, 31 May 1853, in Díaz, *Versión francesa*, 1:48–49.

36. Alberto María Carreño, *La diplomacia extraordinaria entre México y Estados Unidos, 1789–1947*, 2nd ed., 2 vols. (Mexico City: Editorial Jus, 1961), 2:82–84.

37. Díaz, *Versión francesa*, vol. 1, especially pp. 50–169; and Rufus Kay Wyllys, *The French in Sonora (1850–1854)* (Berkeley: University of California Press, 1932).

38. James D. Richardson, comp., *A Compilation of the Messages and Papers of the Presidents, 1789–1897*, 10 vols. (Washington: Government Printing Office, 1896–99), 5: 198–99.

39. Roy Franklin Nichols, *Franklin Pierce: Young Hickory of the Granite Hills* (Philadelphia: University of Pennsylvania Press, 1931), p. 220.

40. Nichols, *Franklin Pierce,* pp. 266–68.

41. Paul Neff Garber, *The Gadsden Treaty,* (Philadelphia: University of Pennsylvania Press, 1923), pp. 12–14, 22–23, 58–61, 66–67, 80–82.

42. Nichols, *Franklin Pierce,* pp. 218–23.

43. Spotty treatments of the Cazneaus are Walter Prescott Webb, ed., *The Handbook of Texas,* 2 vols. (Austin: Texas State Historical Association, 1952), 1:318 and 2:122; Edward S. Wallace, *Destiny and Glory* (New York: Coward & McCann, 1957), pp. 245–75; William H. Goetzmann, *When the Eagle Screamed: The Romantic Horizon in American Diplomacy, 1800–1860* (New York: John Wiley & Sons, 1966), pp. 69–71; and Frederick Merk, *Manifest Destiny and Mission in American History: A Reinterpretation* (New York: Alfred A. Knopf, 1970), pp. 132–34.

44. Garber, *Gadsden Treaty,* pp. 69–74.

45. Marcy to Gadsden, 15 July 1853, NA/DI.

46. Memorandum of instructions to Christopher L. Ward, 2 Oct. 1853, NA/SM.

47. Garber, *Gadsden Treaty,* pp. 90–97, covers events surrounding Ward's special mission.

48. Gadsden to Manuel Díez de Bonilla, 9 Sept. 1853; Gadsden to Marcy, 18 Sept. 1853; Gadsden to Díez de Bonilla, 29 Nov. 1853; and Gadsden to Marcy, 5 Dec. 1853, NA/DD.

49. Walker's career is subject of William Z. Carr, *The World and William Walker* (New York: Harper & Row, 1963); Mexican reactions are in 6-2-10, ASRE; the French view is in Díaz, *Versión francesa,* 1: 79–83, 102–5.

50. Gadsden to Marcy, 18 Nov. 1853, NA/DD.

51. Richardson, *Messages and Papers,* 5:271–72.

52. Carreño, *Diplomacia extraordinaria,* 2:82–84, reproduces the terms of the proposed alliance.

53. L-E-1096, pp. 91ff., ASRE.

54. Garber, *Gadsden Treaty,* pp. 99–100.

55. Antonio López de Santa Anna, *Manifesto del presidente de la República a la nación* (Mexico City: Cumplido, 1855).

56. Gadsden to Díez de Bonilla, NA/DD.

57. "Notes of Diplomatic Conference for the Adjustment of Various Issues between the United States and Mexico," Dec. 1853, NA/DD.

58. Treaty terms summarized in Garber, *Gadsden Treaty,* pp. 103–4; the ratification battle, pp. 109–31; and the Charleston Commercial Convention in William Watson Davis, "Ante-Bellum Southern Commercial Conventions," *Transactions of the Alabama Historical Society, 1904* 5 (1906): 180–92.

59. The ratified treaty is given in Hunter Miller, ed., *Treaties and Other International Acts of the United States of America,* 8 vols. (Washington: Government Printing Office, 1930–48), 6:300–1.

60. Marcy to Gadsden, 11 May 1854, NA/DI; and Gadsden to Marcy, 21 May and 9 June 1854, NA/DD.

61. Dano to Paris, 4 Jan. 1854, in Díaz, *Versión francesa,* 1:88–93; and Garber, *Gadsden Treaty,* pp. 137–38.

62. Díaz, *Versión francesa,* 1:50–113, especially 83–86 and 94–97.

63. Garber, *Gadsden Treaty,* pp. 137–38. The British foreign office felt that Doyle had overreacted since they believed that the Clayton-Bulwer Treaty protected British Tehuantepec interests.

64. Levasseur to Paris, 31 May 1853; and Dano to Paris, 4 Jan. and 5 Mar. 1854, in Díaz, *Versión francesa,* 1: 47, 88–93, 102–3.

65. Ralph Roeder, *Juárez and His Mexico,* 2 vols. (New York: Viking Press, 1947), 1:109.

66. *El Heraldo* (Mexico City), 13 Aug. 1855.

67. Gadsden to Marcy, 1 Aug., 2 and 19 Sept., 18 Dec. 1854, 5 and 19 Feb., 18 May 1855, NA/DD.

68. Almonte to Marcy, 19 Oct. 1854, NA/DN/M.

69. Gadsden to Díez de Bonilla, 27 Jan. 1855, enclosed with Gadsden to Marcy, 5 Feb. 1855, NA/DD; Gadsden to Marcy, 17 Apr. 1855, NA/DD; and Almonte to Marcy, 14 May 1855, and 20 June 1855, NA/DN/M.

70. See especially Gadsden to Marcy, unofficial, 11 July 1855; an undated despatch received 31 Aug. 1855; 25 Nov. 1855; and 4 Oct. 1856, NA/DD.

71. Gadsden to Marcy, 5 Sept. 1854, NA/DD; and Garber, *Gadsden Treaty,* p. 169.

72. Robles Pezuela to MRE, IV/333(73:72)/750, ASRE.

73. Pickett to Marcy, 25 June 1854, NA/CD/VC.

74. *El Heraldo* (Mexico City), 4 Sept. 1855; and *Leyes, decretos, y ordenes que forman el derecho internacional mexicano o que se relacionan con el mismo* (Mexico City: Filomeno Mata, 1879), p. 656; Manuel Dublán and José María Lozano, *Legislación mexicana o colección completa de las disposiciones legislativas expedidas desde la independencia de la República,* official ed., 45 vols. (Mexico City: Imprenta del Comercio de Dublán y Chávez, 1876–1910), 7: 29–31; Pickett to Marcy, 21 Feb. 1854, NA/CD/VC; and Dano to Paris, 5 Mar. 1854, in Díaz, *Versión francesa,* 1:103.

75. Pickett to Marcy, 22 Mar. 1854, NA/CD/VC; Chase to Marcy, 31 Dec. 1854, NA/CD/T; and *El Heraldo* (Mexico City), 5 Sept. 1854.

76. Miscellaneous Letters, Department of State, NA. See especially letter from Lobach and Schepelera, 22 Mar. 1854.

77. *Daily Picayune* (New Orleans), 2 May 1854; *Mobile Register,* 20 June 1854; and Davis, "Commercial Conventions," pp. 199–203.

78. Report by de Gabriac, 31 Dec. 1854, in Díaz, *Versión francesa,* 1:158–59.

79. 9-H-I-6, ASRE. Some of the documents are also given in Carreño, *Diplomacia extraordinaria,* 2:98–107.

80. De Gabriac's despatches of Jan.–Mar. 1855, and Philippe Martinet to Paris, 15 Jan. 1854, in Díaz, *Versión francesa,* 1: 93–94, 159–69.

81. Díez de Bonilla to de Gabriac, 2 Mar. 1855, in Díaz, *Versión francesa,* 1:169–75.

82. In Díaz, *Versión francesa,* 1:175–93.

83. Gadsden to Marcy, despatches of July–Aug. 1855, especially unofficial despatch, 11 July 1855, NA/DD; and *El Heraldo* (Mexico City), 10 Aug. 1855.

84. De Gabriac to Paris, 11 July 1855, in Díaz, *Versión francesa,* 1:191.

85. *Diccionario Porrúa,* 1:376; and Roeder, *Juárez and His Mexico,* 1:116–17.

86. De Gabriac to Paris, 25 Aug. 1855, in Díaz, *Versión francesa,* 1:195.

87. *El Heraldo* (Mexico City), 10 Sept. 1855; and *El Monitor Republicano* (Mexico City), 13 Sept. 1855.

88. De Gabriac to Paris, 25 Aug. and 5 Sept. 1855, in Díaz, *Versión francesa,* 1: 195–200.

89. 4041, folder 58, GFP, GC/UT.

90. De Gabriac to Paris, 12 Oct. 1855, in Díaz, *Versión francesa,* 1:209–11; and *El Heraldo* (Mexico City), 17 Oct. 1855.

91. *El Heraldo* (Mexico City), 17 Oct. 1855; Gadsden to Marcy, 19 Oct. 1855, NA/DD; and de Gabriac to Paris, 12 and 19 Oct. 1855, in Díaz, *Versión francesa,* 1:209–13.

92. Carreño, *Diplomacia extraordinaria,* 2:84–86; José Ramón Pacheco, Mexican minister, Paris, to French foreign minister, 24 Oct. 1853; and Díez de Bonilla to de Gabriac, 2 Mar. 1855, in Díaz, *Versión francesa,* 1: 68–77, 169–75.

93. *El Heraldo* (Mexico City), 22 and 27 Sept. 1855.

94. *El Siglo XIX* (Mexico City), 28 Sept. 1855.

95. *El Heraldo* (Mexico City), 25 and 30 Sept. 1855.

96. Letter, 19 Sept. 1855, and undated draft in the hand of Gómez Farías, 4041, folder 58, GFP, GC/UT.

97. Alvarez to Gómez Farías, 25 Sept. 1855, 4047, folder 58, GFP, GC/UT.

98. Francisco Landero y Cos to Gómez Farías, 10 Sept. 1855, 4018, folder 58, GFP, GC/UT.

99. Pickett to Marcy, 4 Mar. 1855; signed receipt; and Pickett to Marcy, 4 Aug. 1855, NA/CD/VC.

100. "Applications and Recommendations for Public Office, Franklin Pierce and James Buchanan," NA; and Pickett to Buchanan, 4 Nov. 1857, BP/PHS.

101. De Gabriac to Paris, 13 and 19 Sept. 1855, in Díaz, *Versión francesa,* 1:201–5.

102. Gadsden to Marcy, 19 Oct. and 25 Nov. 1855, NA/DD.

103. *Diccionario Porrúa,* 1:873–74.

104. Hernández Rodríguez, *Comonfort,* pp. 58–59; and Santa Anna, *Manifesto.*

105. Garber, *Gadsden Treaty,* pp. 155–57, 171–73.

106. Almonte to Marcy, 3 Nov. 1855, NA/DN/M.

107. Gadsden to Marcy, 5 Dec. 1855, NA/DD.

108. See various despatches from Gadsden during 1856, especially that of 4 Oct., NA/DD.

109. Gadsden to Díez de Bonilla, exp. L-E-1932; Gadsden to Miguel María Arrioja, 16 Nov. 1855; and de Gabriac to Arrioja, 19 Nov. 1855, H/110(73:0)"857-58"/1, ASRE.

110. Gadsden to Marcy, 16 May 1856, NA/DD; and Marcy to Robles Pezuela, 24 June 1856, NA/DN/TM. See also Eugene Keith Chamberlin, "Baja California after Walker: The Zerman Enterprise," *Hispanic American Historical Review* 34 (1954): 175–89.

111. Robles Pezuela to MRE, 3 May 1856, exp. IV/333(73:72)/750, ASRE.

112. Marcy to Gadsden, NA/DI.

113. *El Siglo XIX* (Mexico City) and *El Heraldo* (Mexico City) for the last five months of 1855.

114. Zarco, *Congreso constituyente.* See Dublán and Lozano, *Legislación,* 7: 254–56, 336–41 for two such grants.

115. *El Heraldo* (Mexico City) issued frequent progress reports on these projects during 1855. See especially 24 July 1855.

116. Gadsden to Marcy, 4 Aug. 1856, NA/DD.

117. The principal source of information on Butterfield's early career is William Henry Shaw, *General Carlos Butterfield and His Labors in Behalf of International Prosperity on the American Continent* (Berryville, Va.: n.p., n.d.).

118. Carlos Butterfield, *United States and Mexican Mail Steamship Line: Statistics on Mexico* (New York: J. A. H. Hasbrouck & Co., 1860), pp. 7–9; and Gadsden to Marcy, 4 Aug. 1856, NA/DD.

119. *El Heraldo* (Mexico City), 10 Sept. 1856.

120. *El Heraldo* (Mexico City) apparently collected a number of Gadsden's candid

assessments of Mexicans but refrained from publishing these until after his departure, 18 and 21 Nov. 1856.

Chapter 3

1. Richard A. Johnson, *The Mexican Revolution of Ayutla, 1854–1855* (Rock Island, Ill.: Augustana College Library, 1939), pp. 101–9.

2. Wilfrid Hardy Callcott, *Church and State in Mexico, 1822–1857* (Durham: Duke University Press, 1926; reprint ed., New York: Octagon Press, 1965), pp. 238–41, 248–56, 267–68.

3. Miguel Lerdo de Tejada, *El comercio esterior de México desde la conquista hasta hoy* (Mexico City: Rafael, 1853), pp. 58–63; Carlos Butterfield, *United States and Mexican Mail Steamship Line: Statistics on Mexico* (New York: J. A. H. Hasbrouck & Co., 1860), appendix, p. 20; and Forsyth to Marcy, 2 Feb. 1857, NA/DD.

4. De Gabriac to Paris, 1 Feb. 1856, in Lilia Díaz, ed., *Versión francesa de México: Informes diplomáticos,* 4 vols. (Mexico City: El Colegio de México, 1963–67), 1: 250–51.

5. Congressional consideration of the question with supporting documents is found in Francisco Zarco, *Historia del congreso extraordinario constituyente [1856–1857]* (Mexico City: El Colegio de México, 1956), pp. 1296–342. Comments by French diplomats about Barron's smuggling activities and the Mexican attempt to expel him are scattered throughout the first volume of Díaz, *Versión francesa.* The question is treated briefly in Ralph Roeder, *Juárez and His Mexico,* 2 vols. (New York: Viking Press, 1947), 1:140; and Callcott, *Church and State,* p. 243.

6. Callcott, *Church and State,* pp. 245–46; and de Gabriac to Paris, 12 Oct. 1856 and 31 Mar. 1857, in Díaz, *Versión francesa,* 1: 345–47, 408–12. Accounts of anti-Spanish incidents are also found in the Mexico City press for the period, especially in *El Heraldo.*

7. Zarco, *Congreso constituyente,* pp. 801–8.

8. De Gabriac's despatches to Paris, beginning with 29 Dec. 1855; Tomás Murphy to French Foreign Ministry, 31 Mar. 1856; and unsigned and undated endorsement to a "Project for the Regeneration of Mexico" presented in Paris by A. de Radepont, 4 Oct. 1856; and the project, in Díaz, *Versión francesa,* 1: 242–381, 261–64, 328–42.

9. Butterfield, *Steamship Line,* p. 71; and Francisco López Cámara, *La estructura económica y social de México en la época de la reforma* (Mexico City: Siglo Veintiuno Editores, 1967), pp. 171–72.

10. Zarco, *Congreso constituyente,* pp. 1296–342.

11. The economic thought of the congress is analyzed by Manuel Loza Macías, *El pensamiento económico y la constitución de 1857* (Mexico City: Editorial Jus, 1959). References to the United States are to be found throughout Zarco, *Congreso constituyente;* the coincidence of dates is on p. 456, the travel documents and registration of foreigners on pp. 703–4.

12. Zarco, *Congreso constituyente,* pp. 1359, 1348–49, and 699–794.

13. Loza Macías, *Pensamiento económico,* pp. 234–35.

14. Commented on by John S. Cripps, secretary of legation, to Marcy, 5 June 1856, NA/DD.

15. For a copy of Ley Lerdo see Zarco, *Congreso constituyente,* pp. 423–27.

16. México, Ministerio de hacienda, *Memoria presentada al exmo. Sr. presidente sustituto de la República por el C. Miguel Lerdo de Tejada, dando cuenta de la marcha que han seguido los negocios de la hacienda pública, en el tiempo que tuvo a su cargo la*

secretaría de este ramo (Mexico City: Imprenta de Vicente García Torres, 1857), pp. 7–8.

17. The best treatment of the sale of church property is Jan Bazant, *Alienation of Church Wealth in Mexico: Social and Economic Aspects of the Liberal Revolution, 1856–1875*, ed. and trans. Michael P. Costeloe (Cambridge: Cambridge University Press, 1971).

18. Mexico, Hacienda, *Memoria* (1857), pp. 266–86; and Bazant, *Church Wealth*, p. 233.

19. *Diccionario Porrúa de historia, biografía, y geografía de México*, 3rd ed., 2 vols. (Mexico City: Editorial Porrúa, 1970) 1:875; and Zarco, *Congreso constituyente*, especially p. 34.

20. *El Heraldo* (Mexico City), 1–3 and 19 Feb. 1856.

21. Pickett to Marcy, 21 Feb. and 21 Mar. 1856, NA/CD/VC.

22. *El Heraldo* (Mexico City), 30 Nov. 1855.

23. Manuel Dublán and José María Lozano, comps. *Legislación mexicana o colección completa de las disposiciones legislativas expedidas desde la independencia de la República*, official ed., 45 vols. (Mexico City: Imprenta del Comercio de Dublán y Chávez, 1896–1910), 8:95.

24. *El Siglo XIX* (Mexico City), 5 Mar. 1856.

25. *El Heraldo* (Mexico City), 10 Sept. 1856, referred to him as an "Americano" and the French minister reported that Naphegyi was associated with New York banking interests, in Díaz, *Versión francesa*, 1: 439. His lack of United States citizenship resulted in the dismissal of his claim for damages. See Claim File of Gabor Naphegyi, Claims against Mexico under the Convention of 1868, Records of Boundary and Claims Commissions and Arbitrations, Record Group 76, NA. There are inconsistencies in the spelling of the name; Napheghy, Naphegy, Naphegyi, and Nafegyi are the variations most frequently encountered.

26. *El Heraldo* (Mexico City), 19 and 25 June 1856.

27. Dublán and Lozano, *Legislación*, 8:219–23. Ramsey had also translated the liberal *Apuntes para la historia de la guerra entre México y los Estados Unidos* (Mexico City: Tipografía de Manuel Payno, hijo, 1848) and published it as *The Other Side; or, Notes for the History of the War between Mexico and the United States* (New York: J. Wiley, 1850).

28. Dublán and Lozano, *Legislación*, 8:225–26; "Cartas de seguridad," tomo 150, legajo 30, AGN; Benito Juárez, *Documentos, discursos, y correspondencia*, ed. Jorge L. Tamayo, 12 vols. (Mexico City: Secretaría de Patrimonio Nacional, 1964–68), 3:174–75; and H/352(72:73)19, ASRE.

29. México, Ministerio de fomento, colonización, industria, y comercio, *Memoria de la secretaría de estado y del despacho de fomento, colonización, industria y comercio de la República mexicana, escrita por el ministro del ramo, C. Manuel Siliceo, para dar cuenta con ella al soberano congreso constitucional* (Mexico City: Imprenta de Vicente García Torres, 1857), p. 21.

30. *El Heraldo* (Mexico City), 30 Dec. 1855, 9 Feb. 1856; and Dublán and Lozano, *Legislación*, 8:95–97.

31. Rosaura Hernández Rodríguez, *Ignacio Comonfort: Trayectoria política. Documentos* (Mexico City: Universidad Nacional Autónoma de México, Instituto de Investigaciones Históricas, 1967), p. 58. While it is impossible to verify the exact amount of the total $300,000 loan that was made available beyond the initial $60,000, it is possible that the total reached at least $200,000. See Hernández Rodríguez, *Comonfort*, p. 50; and folder 15, CP, GC/UT.

32. Mexico, Hacienda, *Memoria* (1857), p. 6; *El Heraldo* (Mexico City), 24 Sept. 1856, reported the loan as $180,000; Temple made no mention of this loan in his "Memoria justificativa," GC/UT.

33. Temple, "Memoria justificativa," pp. 9–12, GC/UT. This lease underwent many changes over the next few years and later became the subject of claims against Mexico.

34. De Gabriac to Paris, 10 Dec. 1856, in Díaz, *Versión francesa*, 1:376–79.

35. Alvin Duckett, *John Forsyth, Political Tactician* (Athens: University of Georgia Press, 1962); and Eugene I. McCormac, "John Forsyth," in *The American Secretaries of State and Their Diplomacy,* ed. Samuel Flagg Bemis, vol. 8 (New York: Pageant Book Co., 1958) deal with the senior Forsyth; the Cincinnati convention was covered by *New York Daily Times,* 3–7 June 1856.

36. Thomas M. Owen, *History of Alabama and Dictionary of Alabama Biography,* 4 vols. (Chicago: S. J. Clarke Publishing Co., 1921), 3:598; petition, 22 Apr. 1854, "Applications and Recommendations for Public Office, Franklin Pierce and James Buchanan," NA; Robles Pezuela to Marcy, 9 May 1856, NA/DN/M; and Francis B. Heitman, ed., *Historical Register and Dictionary of the United States Army, from Its Organization, September 29, 1789, to March 2, 1903,* 2 vols. (Washington: Government Printing Office, 1903), 2:52.

37. Marcy to Forsyth, 4 Aug. 1856, NA/DI.

38. Robles Pezuela to MRE, 22 July 1856, H/323(73:73)/109, ASRE.

39. Marcy to Forsyth, 16 Aug. 1856, NA/DI.

40. H/350(72:73)1, ASRE.

41. Marcy to Forsyth, 3 Mar. 1857, NA/DI; Forsyth to Marcy, 2 and 10 Feb. 1857; and Forsyth to Cass, 18 Feb. 1858, NA/DD.

42. See Forsyth's editorials in the *Mobile Register,* especially that of 30 Sept. 1856, and in *DeBow's Commercial Review of the South and West* (New Orleans), especially that in 17(1854), pp. 363–78.

43. M. Lerdo, *El comercio.* Forsyth submitted Lerdo's figures to Washington as the results of his own study of Mexico's foreign trade, Forsyth to Marcy, 2 Feb. 1857, NA/DD.

44. Forsyth to Marcy, 8 Nov. 1856, NA/DD, and an enclosed letter from Forsyth to Pierce. While the letter is not filed with the despatch nor can it be located in the Pierce papers, its contents were summarized in a later despatch, Forsyth to Cass, 4 Apr. 1857, NA/DD.

45. David M. Pletcher, "Prospecting Expeditions across Central Mexico, 1856–57," *Pacific Historical Review* 21 (1952): 43–46; Dublán and Lozano, *Legislación,* 7: 332-334; Frank A. Knapp, "Precursors of American Investment in Mexican Railroads," *Pacific Historical Review* 21 (1952): 43–46; and *El Heraldo* (Mexico City), 29 Dec. 1856.

46. Butterfield, *Steamship Line,* pp. 65, 159.

47. Forsyth to Marcy, 8 Nov. 1856, NA/DD.

48. José Fuentes Mares, *Juárez y los Estados Unidos,* 5th ed. (Mexico City: Editorial Jus, 1972), p. 58.

49. For excerpts from this speech and a discussion of its significance see the last pages of chapter 6.

50. Forsyth to Marcy, 8 Nov. 1856, and enclosed letter to Pierce, NA/DD.

51. [México, Secretaría de relaciones exteriores], *Funcionarios de la secretaría de relaciones desde el año de 1821 a 1940* (Mexico City: n.p., 1940), p. 83.

52. Pletcher, "Prospecting Expeditions," pp. 24–25.

53. Forsyth to Marcy, 8, 14, 15, and 19 Nov. 1856, NA/DD.

54. Antonio de la Fuente to Gadsden, 22 Oct. 1856, vol. 12, NA/DPR/FM.

55. Forsyth to M. Lerdo, 19 Nov. and 2 Dec. 1856, enclosed with Forsyth to Marcy, 1 Jan. 1857, NA/DD; and M. Lerdo to Forsyth, 1 Dec. 1856, in vol. 12, NA/DPR/FM.

56. Memorandum of interview, enclosed with Forsyth to Marcy, 19 Dec. 1856, NA/DD. No copy of this memorandum or reference to the meeting was found in the archives of the Mexican foreign ministry.

57. Forsyth to Marcy, 19 Dec. 1856, NA/DD.

58. Fuentes Mares, *Juárez,* p. 59; de Gabriac to Paris, Nov.-Dec. 1856, in Díaz, *Versión francesa,* 1:359–81; and Forsyth's despatches Nov.–Dec. 1856, NA/DD.

59. Forsyth to Marcy, 8 Nov. 1856, NA/DD; Fuentes Mares, *Juárez,* pp. 55–58; and de Gabriac to Paris, 11 Nov. 1856, in Díaz, *Versión francesa,* 1:363–65.

60. *El Heraldo* (Mexico City), 21 and 25 Dec. 1856; Mata to Ocampo, 25 Dec. 1856 and 4 Jan. 1857, 8-4-70 and 71, AHINAH; and Forsyth to Marcy, 1 and 15 Jan. 1857, NA/DD.

61. Ezequiel Montes to Forsyth, 8 Jan. 1857, vol. 12, NA/DPR/FM; Forsyth to Marcy, 2 Feb. 1857, NA/DD; and folio 272, III/350(72:73)/1, ASRE.

62. Forsyth to Marcy, 30 Jan. and 2 and 10 Feb. 1857, NA/DD; and copies of agreements enclosed with Forsyth to Marcy, 10 Feb. 1857, NA/DD.

63. "Bases p[ar]a un arreglo definitivo entre México y los Estados Unidos," 22 Jan. 1857, p. 62, folio 272, III/350(72:73)/1, ASRE.

64. Exchange of notes, Forsyth and Montes, 24 and 25 Jan. 1857, and related working papers, pp. 32, 56–58, and 65–68, folio 272, III/350(72:73)/1, ASRE.

65. Pickett to Marcy, 22 Mar. 1854, NA/CD/VC.

66. *El Heraldo* (Mexico City), 15 Feb. 1856; *El Siglo XIX* (Mexico City), 13 Feb. 1856; and *El Heraldo* (Mexico City), 17–19 July 1856, containing references to endorsements by other newspapers in Mexico City and New Orleans.

67. Butterfield, *Steamship Line,* pp. 8–9.

68. *El Heraldo* (Mexico City), 30 Sept. 1856, reproducing and endorsing the article from *Mexican Estraordinary* (Mexico City).

69. For details of the postal-treaty negotiations see exchanges of notes, Forsyth and Montes, 24 and 25 Jan. and 1, 2, and 3 Feb. 1857, and related working papers, pp. 3, 5–7, 11–23, 56–58, 63–68, and 181–95, folio 272, III/350(72:73)/1, ASRE; and Forsyth to Marcy, 2 Feb. 1857, NA/DD.

70. *El Heraldo* (Mexico City), 5 and 8 Feb. 1857; *Mexican Estraordinary* (Mexico City), 5 Feb. 1857; and *Trait d'Union* (Mexico City), 6 Feb. 1857.

71. Claims convention, enclosed with Forsyth to Marcy, 10 Feb. 1857, NA/DD; and pp. 65–68 and 91–93, folio 272, III/350(72:73)/1, ASRE.

72. Forsyth to Marcy, 2 and 10 Feb. 1857, NA/DD.

73. Forsyth to Cass, 4 Apr. 1857, and 18 Feb. 1858, NA/DD.

74. *El Heraldo* (Mexico City), 16 Nov. 1856, and 28 Jan. and 8 Feb. 1857; *El Siglo XIX* (Mexico City), 12 Feb. 1857; *Trait d'Union* (Mexico City), 8 Feb. 1857; and *El Estandarte Nacional* (Mexico City), 7 Feb. 1857.

75. Editorials in this vein were carried by *El Heraldo* (Mexico City), 15 and 21 Feb. 1857; *El Siglo XIX* (Mexico City), 13 Feb. and 5 Mar. 1857; and *El Estandarte Nacional* (Mexico City), 4 Mar. 1857.

76. *El Heraldo* (Mexico City), 29 Mar. and 12 Apr. 1857.

77. De Gabriac to Paris, 22 Feb. 1857, in Díaz, *Versión francesa,* 1:404–5.

78. Juárez to Matías Romero, 4 Apr. 1857, AMR/CR.

79. Manifesto published in *El Siglo XIX* (Mexico City), 16 Mar. 1857, and *El Heraldo* (Mexico City), 18–19 Mar. 1857.

80. Montes to Robles, 10 and 11 Feb. 1857, pp. 146–47 and 149, folio 272, III/350(72:73)/1, ASRE; and William Henry Shaw, *General Carlos Butterfield and His Labors in Behalf of Prosperity on the American Continent* (Berryville, Va.: n.p., n.d.), p. 3.

81. James D. Richardson, comp., *A Compilation of the Messages and Papers of the Presidents, 1789–1897,* 10 vols. (Washington: Government Printing Office, 1896–99), 5: 414.

82. Robles to MRE, 15, 19, and 20 Feb. and 11 Mar. 1857, pp. 132–34, 136–39, 198–99, and 240–42, folio 272, III/350(72:73)/1, ASRE.

83. Montes to Robles, 10 Feb. and 20 Mar. 1857, pp. 146–47 and 200, folio 272, III/350(72:73)/1, ASRE.

84. Pletcher, "Prospecting Expeditions," p. 31; and Shaw, *Butterfield,* pp. 3–4.

85. 16 and 17 Feb. 1857.

86. Robles to MRE, 1 Mar. 1857, pp. 237–40, folio 272, III/350(72:73)/1, ASRE.

87. Marcy to Forsyth, 3 Mar. 1857, NA/DI.

88. Robles to MRE, 11 and 16 Mar. 1857, pp. 33–34 and 241–48, folio 272, III/350(72:73)/1, ASRE.

89. Cass to Forsyth, 11 Mar. 1857, NA/DI.

90. Robles to MRE, 19 Mar. 1857, pp. 203–4, folio 272, III/350(72:73)/1, ASRE.

91. Cass to Forsyth, 17 Nov. 1857, NA/DI.

92. Lettson to London, 15 Feb. 1857, PRO, Foreign Office, 97/275.

93. De Gabriac to Paris, 1 and 26 July, 29 Aug., and 1 Sept. 1857, in Díaz, *Versión francesa,* 1: 303–5, 311–13, and 318–23.

94. De Gabriac to Paris, 1 Sept. 1856, endorsing A. de Radepont's "Project for the Regeneration of Mexico," in Díaz, *Versión francesa,* 1: 323, 328–42.

95. De Gabriac to Paris, 26 Oct. and 1, 11, and 19 Nov. 1856, in Díaz, *Versión francesa,* 1: 352–54, 359–61, 363–67.

96. De Gabriac to Paris, 30 Jan. 1857, in Díaz, *Versión francesa,* 1:384–86.

97. De Gabriac to Paris, 12 and 22 Feb. 1857, in Díaz, *Versión francesa,* 1: 396–98, 404–5.

98. MRE to Mexican ministers, Paris and London, 3 Mar. 1857, pp. 220–25, folio 272, III/350(72:73)/1, ASRE.

99. Clarendon to Lettson, 3 Apr. 1857, and Whitehead, Foreign Bondholders Association, to Clarendon, 20 Apr. 1857, PRO, Foreign Office, 97/275.

100. De Gabriac to Paris, 12 Feb. 1857, in Díaz, *Versión francesa,* 1:396–98.

101. Pickett to Marcy, 22 Mar. 1854, NA/CD/VC.

102. De Gabriac to Paris, 26 Mar. 1857, in Díaz, *Versión francesa,* 1:407–8.

Chapter 4

1. A brief but adequate summary of the Mexican political scene during 1857 is Walter V. Scholes, *Mexican Politics during the Juárez Regime, 1855–1872* (Columbia: University of Missouri Press, 1957), pp. 12–24.

2. Philip Shriver Klein, *President James Buchanan: A Biography* (University Park: Pennsylvania State University Press, 1962), pp. 183–92, 194–205, 211–20, 222, 230–33, 238–41; and Rushmore G. Horton, *The Life and Public Service of James Buchanan, Late*

Minister to England and Formally Minister to Russia, Senator and Representative in Congress, and Secretary of State; Including the Most Important of His State Papers, authorized ed. (New York: Derby & Jackson, 1856).

3. Roy Franklin Nichols, *The Disruption of American Democracy* (New York: Macmillan Co., 1948), pp. 4–8, 57, 67; Robert Douthat Meade, *Judah P. Benjamin, Confederate Statesman* (New York: Oxford University Press, 1943), pp. 105–7, 111–13; Louis Martin Sears, *John Slidell* (Durham: Duke University Press, 1925), especially pp. 122–24; and Klein, *Buchanan,* pp. 252–55.

4. James D. Richardson, comp., *A Compilation of the Messages and Papers of the Presidents, 1789–1897,* 10 vols. (Washington: Government Printing Office, 1896–99), 5: 435–36, 469.

5. Klein, *Buchanan,* pp. 276, 279.

6. Cass to Forsyth, NA/DI.

7. Details in Meade, *Benjamin,* pp. 121–23, suggest that stocks, bonds, and commissions could produce some $160,000 for Benjamin from the venture.

8. Cass to Forsyth, 17 July 1857, NA/DI; Forsyth to Cass, 24 Nov. 1857, NA/DD; and de Gabriac to Paris, 27 Nov. 1857, in Lilia Díaz, ed., *Versión francesa de México: Informes diplomáticos,* 4 vols. (Mexico City: El Colegio de México, 1963–67), 1:368–74.

9. Forsyth to Cass, 4 Apr. 1857, NA/DD.

10. Forsyth to Montes, 3 Apr. 1857, pp. 227–36, folio 272, III/(72:73)/1, ASRE.

11. Forsyth to Cass, unofficial, 10 Apr. 1857, and subsequence despatches, NA/DD.

12. Forsyth to Cass, 15 Sept. and 24 Nov. 1857, NA/DD.

13. S. Lerdo to Robles, 1 Sept. 1857, pp. 540–41, H/110(73:0)"857-858"/1, ASRE.

14. The complicated course of action pursued by Forsyth in dealing both with the Mexican government and with the Tehuantepec negotiators is reconstructed from his despatches to Cass during Sept., Oct., and Nov. 1857, NA/DD (especially useful for their contents and enclosures are those of 15, 26, and 29 Sept. and 24 Nov.); S. Lerdo to Robles, 1 Sept. 1857, and other foreign ministry documents of the period, pp. 244–48 and 540–41, H/110(73:0)"857-858"/1, ASRE.

15. Benjamin and La Sere to Buchanan, 19 Sept. 1857, copy enclosed with Cass to Forsyth, 20 Oct. 1857, NA/DI.

16. Annulling decree, 3 Sept. 1857, in Manuel Dublán and José María Lozano, comps., *Legislación mexicana o colección completa de las disposiciones legislativas expedidas desde la independencia de la República,* official ed., 45 vols. (Mexico City: Imprenta del Comercio de Dublán y Chávez, 1876–1910), 8:567.

17. The contract is in Dublán and Lozano, *Legislación,* 8:567–71; and Benito Juárez, *Documentos, discursos, y correspondencia,* ed. Jorge L. Tamayo, 12 vols. (Mexico City: Secretaría de Patrimonio Nacional, 1964–68), 3: 382–87.

18. Charges were contained in Forsyth to Cass, 15 Sept. and 24 Nov. 1857, NA/DD; and in Benjamin and La Sere to Buchanan, 19 Sept. 1857, enclosed with Cass to Forsyth, 20 Oct. 1857, NA/DI. Forsyth's initial defense was contained in his despatch of 15 Sept. 1857; his rebuttal to Benjamin's charges in that of 24 Nov. 1857, NA/DD.

19. Cass to Forsyth, 17 Nov. 1857, NA/DI.

20. Forsyth's revised plan was first outlined in despatches of 26 and 29 Sept. 1857, NA/DI. It was further elaborated and refined in the several despatches submitted during October and November 1857, NA/DD.

21. Cass to Forsyth, 17 Nov. 1857, NA/DI.

22. Forsyth to Cass, 18 Nov. 1857, NA/DD.

23. José Fuentes Mares, *Juárez y los Estados Unidos,* 5th ed. (Mexico City: Editorial Jus, 1972), pp. 70–72; and Ralph Roeder, *Juárez and His Mexico,* 2 vols. (New York: Viking Press, 1947), 1:144–48.

24. Forsyth to Cass, 17 Oct. and 18 Nov. 1857, NA/DD.

25. For Forsyth's specific maneuvers see de Gabriac to Paris, 22 Nov. 1857, in Díaz, *Versión francesa,* 1:438–39.

26. Forsyth to Cass, 18 Nov. 1857, NA/DD.

27. De Gabriac to Paris, 22 Nov. 1857, in Díaz, *Versión francesa,* 1:438–39.

28. Forsyth to Cass, 18 Nov. and 17 Dec. 1857, and 14 Jan. 1858, NA/DD.

29. Roeder, *Juárez,* 1:147; and de Gabriac to Paris, 18 Dec. 1857, in Díaz, *Versión francesa,* 1:442–47.

30. Events described in Walker Fearn, secretary of legation, to Cass, 1 Jan. 1858, NA/DD; Roeder, *Juárez,* 1:148–53; Fuentes Mares, *Juárez,* pp. 73–74; de Gabriac to Paris, 28 Dec. 1857, in Díaz, *Versión francesa,* 1:447–48; and Forsyth to Cass, 14 Jan. 1858, NA/DD.

31. Description of events based on the several United States despatches, 14–29 Jan. 1858, NA/DD; and French despatches, 28 Dec. 1857–10 Feb. 1858, in Díaz, *Versión francesa,* 1:447–59. Preparations for Comonfort's flight in French despatch, 22 Nov. 1857, in Díaz, *Versión francesa,* 1:438–39.

32. De Gabriac to Paris, 22 Nov. 1857, 5 and 12 Jan. 1858, in Díaz, *Versión francesa,* 1: 438–39, 451–56; passenger lists, Veracruz, in "Movimiento marítimo," tomo 38, legajo 10, AGN; H/653"857"/1, ASRE; Carlos Butterfield, *United States and Mexican Mail Steamship Line: Statistics on Mexico* (New York: J. A. H. Hasbrouck & Co., 1860), pp. 9–10; Manuel Silicio, minister of Fomento, to Forsyth, 5 Jan. 1858, in NA/DPR/FM; vol. 3, NA/RBO; Mata to Ocampo, 15 Aug. 1859, 8-4-134, AHINAH; and Luis G. Cuevas, foreign minister of conservative government, to Robles, 17 Feb. 1858, p. 592, H/110(73:0)"857-858"/1, ASRE.

33. Forsyth to Cass, 14 Jan. 1858, NA/DD.

34. Charles Allen Smart, *Viva Juárez! A Biography* (New York: J. B. Lippincott Co., 1963), pp. 168–70.

35. *Diccionario Porrúa de historia, biografía, y geografía de México,* 3rd ed., 2 vols. (Mexico City: Editorial Porrúa, 1970), 1:875.

36. Forsyth to Cass, 29 Jan. 1858, NA/DD.

37. *El Heraldo* (Mexico City), 23 Jan. 1858, carried a complete listing of the Juárez cabinet.

38. Forsyth to Cass, 30 Jan. 1858, NA/DD.

39. Forsyth to Ocampo, 30 Jan. 1858, pp. 31–32, H/110(73:0)"858-859"/1, ASRE.

40. Ocampo to Forsyth, 26 Jan. 1858, p. 4, H/110(73:0)"858-859"/1, ASRE; and Ocampo to Forsyth, 30 Jan. 1858, in NA/DPR/FM.

41. 1 Feb. 1858, in NA/DPR/FM.

42. 2 Feb. 1858, in NA/DPR/FM.

43. NA/DPR/FM.

44. James Buchanan, *Mr. Buchanan's Administration on the Eve of the Rebellion* (New York: D. Appleton & Co., 1866), pp. 268–69; and Stuart A. MacCorkle, *American Policy of Recognition towards Mexico* (Baltimore: Johns Hopkins Press, 1933), p. 48.

45. Fuentes Mares, *Juárez,* pp. 74–76.

46. Ocampo to Robles, 10 Feb. 1858, pp. 28–29, H/110(73:0)"858-859"/1, ASRE; and Robles to Cuevas, 6 Mar. 1858, in *Colección de documentos inéditos o muy raros relativos*

a la reforma en México, 2 vols. (Mexico City: Instituto Nacional de Antropología y Historia, 1957–58), 1:89–91.

47. Mata to Ocampo, 30 Mar., 20 Apr., 5 and 20 May 1858, 8-4-95, 96, 97, and 98, AHINAH; and Mata to MRE, 20 and 21 Aug. 1858, pp. 65–68 and 70, H/100(73:0)"858-859"/1, ASRE.

48. The "Jane McManus Cazneau Papers" at the University of Texas, Austin, contains a brief unattributed biographical sketch which states that Jane boasted of a distant and ill-defined kinship with Buchanan.

49. Cazneau to Buchanan, 6 June 1858, BP/PHS.

50. Mata to Ocampo, 21 Aug. 1858, 8-4-105, AHINAH.

51. Mata to MRE, 20 Aug. 1858, pp. 65–68, H/100(73:0)"858-59"/1, ASRE.

52. Mata to Juárez, 2 July 1858, *legajo* 1, doc. 32, JM.

53. Forsyth to Cass, 30 Jan., 13 Feb., and 1 Mar. 1858, NA/DD.

54. Forsyth to Cass, 18 Mar. 1858, NA/DD; and Forsyth to Cuevas, 22 Mar. 1858, enclosed with Forsyth to Cass, 2 Apr. 1858, NA/DD.

55. Cuevas to Forsyth, 5 Apr. 1858, enclosed with Forsyth to Cass, 16 Apr. 1858, NA/DD.

56. Forsyth to Cuevas, 8 Apr. 1858, enclosed with Forsyth to Cass, 16 Apr. 1858, NA/DD.

57. Forsyth to Cass, unofficial, 15 Apr. 1858, NA/DD.

58. Forsyth to Cass, 18 May 1858, with enclosed copies of tax decrees of 15 May 1858, and 1 and 17 June 1858, NA/DD.

59. Forsyth to Black, 22 May 1858, copy enclosed with Forsyth to Cass, 1 June 1858, NA/DD.

60. Forsyth to Cass, 17 June 1858, NA/DD; and de Gabriac to Paris, 16 June 1858, in Díaz, *Versión francesa,* 2:22–23.

61. Forsyth to Cuevas, 22 and 27 May 1858, and Cuevas to Forsyth, 25 May 1858, enclosed with Forsyth to Cass, 1 June 1858, NA/DD.

62. Copies in NA/DPR/FM.

63. Forsyth to Cass, 17 June 1858, NA/DD. No record of this conference could be found in Mexican archives, and material on Forsyth's relations with the conservative government is extremely spotty.

64. Cuevas to Robles, 4 June 1858, pp. 621–23, H/110(73:0)"857-858"/1, ASRE.

65. Forsyth to Cass, 17 June 1858, NA/DD.

66. Cass to Forsyth, 23 June and 15 July 1858, NA/DI.

67. The details of the Migel case as presented in this and the following paragraphs are synthesized from Forsyth to Cass, 17, 19, and 25 June 1858, NA/DD; de Gabriac to Paris, 16 and 19 June 1858, in Díaz, *Versión francesa,* 2:22–25; Migel to Cass, 22 July 1858, pp. 21–22, H/110(73:0)"858-63"/1, ASRE; and Cuevas to Robles, 18 June 1858, pp. 834–37, H/110(73:0)"857-858"/1, ASRE.

68. Cass to Forsyth, 15 July 1858, NA/DI.

69. Joaquín María de Castillo y Lanzas, conservative MRE, to Mexican minister, Paris, 31 Aug. 1858, H/323(73:72)/109, ASRE; and Cass, undated endorsement to Robles of letter, Migel to Cass, 22 July 1858, pp. 21–22, H/110(73:0)"858-63"/1, ASRE.

70. Forsyth to Cass, 1 July, 1 and 31 Aug. 1858, NA/DD; Castillo y Lanzas to Robles, 18 Dec. 1858, p. 815, H/110(73:0)"857-858"/1, ASRE; and Castillo y Lanzas to Mexican minister, Paris, 31 Aug. 1858, H/323(73:72)/109, ASRE.

71. MRE to Mata, 19 June 1858, pp. 40–43, H/110(73:0)"858-59"/1, ASRE; and Mata

to Ocampo, 13 and 14 Jul., 19 Aug., and 26 Sept. 1858, 8-4-101, 102, 104, and 108, AHINAH.

Chapter 5

1. Forsyth to Cass, 1 Mar. and 3 Apr. 1858, NA/DD.

2. José C. Valadés, *Don Melchor Ocampo, reformador de México* (Mexico City: Editorial Patria, 1954), pp. 341–42; and R. B. J. Twyman, consul, to Cass, 5 May 1858, NA/CD/VC.

3. Carlos Butterfield, *United States and Mexican Mail Steamship Line: Statistics on Mexico* (New York: J. A. H. Hasbrouck & Co., 1860), pp. 9–10, 64–66, 79–94, 108–9.

4. Mata to Ocampo, 21 Aug. 1858, 8-4-105, AHINAH.

5. James D. Richardson, comp., *A Compilation of the Messages and Papers of the Presidents, 1789–1897*, 10 vols. (Washington, Government Printing Office, 1896–99), 5: 435–36, 444–48, 466–69.

6. Samuel Houston, *The Writings of Sam Houston, 1813–1863*, ed. Amelia W. Williams and Eugene C. Barker, 8 vols. (Austin: University of Texas Press, 1938–43), 7: 33–34; *Congressional Globe*, 35th Cong., 1st Sess., pp. 735–36; and Robles to Manuel G. Zamora, governor of Veracruz, 21 Feb. 1858, in *Colección de documentos inéditos o muy raros relativos a la reforma en México*, 2 vols. (Mexico City: Instituto Nacional de Antropología y Historia, 1957–58), 1:91–93.

7. Houston, *Writings*, 7:85–86; and Robles to MRE, 21 Apr. 1858, 6-2-14, ASRE.

8. *New York Times*, 18 June 1858; Llerena Friend, *Sam Houston, the Great Designer* (Austin: University of Texas Press, 1954), p. 299; and Houston, *Writings*, 7: 183–85, 343–67.

9. Richardson, *Messages and Papers*, 5:512–14.

10. *Colección de documentos relativos a la reforma*, 1:123–40.

11. Mata to MRE, 20 Aug. 1858, pp. 65–68, H/100(73:0)"858-59"/1, ASRE; Mata to Ocampo, 10, 17, and 26 Sept. and 2 Oct. 1858, 8-4-106, 107, 108, and 109, AHINAH; and Cass to Robles, 3 Aug. 1858, p. 23, H/110(73:0)"858-63"/1, ASRE.

12. Forsyth to Buchanan, 7 Feb., 14 and 20 Mar. 1859, BP/PHS; and Richardson, *Messages and Papers*, 5:513.

13. Butterfield to Plumb, 12 July 1861, 4-2-5624, ASRE.

14. Mata to Ocampo, 22 and 24 Dec. 1858, 8-4-112 and 113, AHINAH.

15. *Diccionario Porrúa de historia, biografía, y geografía de México*, 3rd ed., 2 vols. (Mexico City: Editorial Porrúa, 1970), 1:875; and de Gabriac to Paris, 29 Dec. 1858, in Lilia Díaz, ed., *Versión francesa de México: Informes diplomáticos*, 4 vols. (Mexico City: El Colegio de México, 1963–67), 2:50–52.

16. Alfred C. Ramsey to Buchanan, 19 and 21 Jan. 1859, BP/PHS.

17. 3 Sept. 1858, filed in NA/CD/VC.

18. Twyman to Cass, 21 Dec. 1858, NA/CD/VC.

19. Forsyth to Cass, 25 June, 1 July, and 1 and 31 Aug. 1858, NA/DD.

20. De Gabriac to Paris, 1 Aug. 1858, and Jean Jacques Pelissier, French ambassador at London, to Paris, 27 Sept. 1858, in Díaz, *Versión francesa*, 2: 34–36, 44–45.

21. Cass to Churchwell, 27 Dec. 1858, NA/SM.

22. Benito Juárez, *Documentos, discursos, y correspondencia*, ed. Jorge L. Tamayo, 12 vols. (Mexico City: Secretaría de Patrimonio Nacional, 1964–68), 3:467–73.

23. 21 Jan. 1859, NA/CD/VC.

24. McLane to Cass, 7 Jan. 1860, NA/DD, requested Twyman's removal for chronic alcoholism and general incompetence.

25. 21 Jan. 1859, NA/CD/VC.

26. Churchwell to Cass, 8 Feb. 1859, NA/SM.

27. José Fuentes Mares, *Miramón, el hombre,* 2nd ed. (Mexico City: Contrapuntos, 1975), pp. 38–43, has an interesting inside look at these maneuverings based on the papers of Concha Lombardo de Miramón, wife of Miguel Miramón.

28. Churchwell to Cass, 8 Feb. 1859, NA/SM.

29. Churchwell to Buchanan, 22 Feb. 1859, BP/PHS.

30. Paul Murray, *Tres norteamericanos y su participación en el desarrollo del tratado McLane-Ocampo, 1856–1860* (Guadalajara: Imprenta Gráfica, 1946), pp. 28–30; and José Fuentes Mares, *Juárez y los Estados Unidos,* 5th ed. (Mexico City: Editorial Jus, 1972), pp. 106–7.

31. Forsyth to Cass, from Mobile, 22 Nov. 1858, NA/DD; and protest of MRE, 14 Apr. 1859, pp. 5–7, L-E-1317, ASRE.

32. Churchwell to Cass, 21 Feb. 1859, NA/SM.

33. Churchwell to Buchanan, 22 Feb. 1859, BP/PHS.

34. MRE to Mata, 21 Feb. 1859, p. 75, H/110(73:0)"858-59"/1, ASRE; Mata to Ocampo, 19 Feb. 1859, 8-4-114, AHINAH; and Mata to Juárez, 2 July 1858, JM.

35. MRE to Mata, 21 Feb. 1859, p. 75, H/110(73:0)"858-59"/1, ASRE; and Mata to Ocampo, 8 Mar. 1859, 8-4-115 and 116, AHINAH.

36. *Senate Journal,* 35th Cong., 2nd Sess., p. 343; and Richardson, *Messages and Papers,* 5:538–40.

37. Mata to Ocampo, 8 Mar. 1859, 8-4-116, AHINAH.

38. Cass to McLane, 7 Mar. 1859, NA/DI.

39. Mata to Ocampo, 8 and 31 Mar. 1859, 8-4-116 and 117, AHINAH.

40. Cass to McLane, 7 Mar. 1859, NA/DI; and McLane to Cass, 7 Apr. 1859, enclosing notes between McLane and Ocampo, NA/DD.

41. Robles to MRE, 21 June 1858, in *Colección de documentos relativos a la reforma,* pp. 123–40; and Manuel Dublán and José María Lozano, comps., *Legislación mexicana o colección completa de las disposiciones legislativas expedidas desde la independencia de la República,* official ed., 45 vols. (Mexico City: Imprenta del Comercio de Dublán y Chávez, 1876–1910), 8:666–67.

42. Mata to MRE, 3 Feb. 1859, H/651.1(72:73)"859"/, ASRE; and Mata to Ocampo, 19 Feb. 1859, 8-4-114, AHINAH; and M. Lerdo, Fomento, to MRE, 1 Apr. 1859, H/651.1(72:73)"859"/, ASRE.

43. Circular, 6 Apr. 1859, in vol. 12, NA/DPR.

44. Protest of MRE, 14 Apr. 1859, pp. 5–7, L-E-1317, ASRE; and McLane to MRE, 26 Apr. 1859, and circular, 28 Apr. 1859, in vol. 12, NA/DPR.

45. Loan authority from Guillermo Prieto, Hacienda, 2 Mar. 1858, and Ocampo to Mata, 3 Mar. 1858, pp. 10–14, H/110(73:0)"858-59"/1, ASRE.

46. Letter of authority from M. Lerdo, 7 Apr. 1859, p. 46, H/110(73:0)"858-59"/1, ASRE.

Chapter 6

1. MRE to Mata, p. 204, H/110(73:0)"858-59"/1, ASRE.

2. Robert M. McLane, *Reminiscences, 1827–1897* (privately printed, 1903), pp. 143–44.

3. Summaries of the missing despatches, numbers 2–5, are contained in vol. 13, NA/RBO.

4. McLane to Cass, 21 Apr. 1859, NA/DD.

5. Vol. 13, NA/RBO.

6. Cass to McLane, 24 May and 30 July 1859, NA/DI.

7. Negotiation details were reconstructed from four archival sources: McLane's despatches with enclosures, diplomatic post records (Mexico), and reports of bureau officers, vol. 13, all in NA; and H/110(73:0)"858-59"/1, ASRE.

8. Mata to Ocampo, 19 and 23 May 1859, 8-4-121 and 122, AHINAH.

9. Notes between McLane and Ocampo relating to the Tacubaya incident and the alliance proposal are scattered among McLane's despatches, NA/DD; the diplomatic post records (Mexico), NA/DPR; and H/110(73:0)"858-59"/1, ASRE. Ralph Roeder, *Juárez and His Mexico,* 2 vols. (New York: Viking Press, 1947), 1:196–202, has the most dispassionate account of the Tacubaya incident.

10. Vol. 13, NA/DPR.

11. Instructions to McLane from late June on consistently held that an alliance was unacceptable. The most direct rejections were Cass to McLane, 19 July and 4 Nov. 1859, NA/DI.

12. McLane to Cass, 25 June 1859, NA/DD.

13. Mata to Juárez, 2 July 1858, *legajo* 1, doc. 32, JM; Ocampo to Mata, 7 and 23 Apr. 1859, H/110(73:0)"858-59"/1, ASRE; and Mata to Ocampo, 19 Feb. and 6 May 1859, 8-4-114 and 120, AHINAH.

14. H/110(73:0)"858-59"/1, ASRE; and NA/DPR.

15. McLane to Cass, 21 Apr. and 25 June 1859, NA/DD.

16. Cass to McLane, 24 May 1859, NA/DI.

17. Ocampo to McLane, 9 July 1859, NA/DPR/FM.

18. William Henry Shaw, *General Carlos Butterfield and His Labors in Behalf of International Prosperity on the American Continent* (Berryville, Va.: n.p., n.d.), p. 4; and Butterfield to Plumb, 21 July 1861, 4-2-5624, ASRE.

19. P. 46, H/110(73:0)"858-59"/1, ASRE; and Mata to Ocampo, 14 Apr., 6, 19, and 23 May, and 3 June 1859, 8-4-118, 120, 121, 122, and 123, AHINAH.

20. Roeder, *Juárez,* 1:202–9.

21. Manifesto, 7 July 1859, reproduced in Melchor Ocampo, *Obras completas de Melchor Ocampo* (Mexico City: F. Vazquez, 1901), vol. 2, *Escrítos politicos,* prologue by Angél Pola, pp. 113–42.

22. Decree enclosed with McLane to Cass, 12 July 1859, NA/DD.

23. McLane to Cass, 12 July 1859, NA/DD.

24. Ocampo reviewed the issuance of this decree in a pamphlet published in 1861 and reprinted in Ocampo, *Obras,* pp. 151–204.

25. Mata to Ocampo, 14 Apr. and 15 and 19 Sept. 1859, 8-4-118, 139, and 140, AHINAH.

26. McLane to Cass, 6 June and 10 July 1859, NA/DD; and Cass to McLane, 30 July 1859, NA/DI.

27. [México. Secretária de Relaciones exteriores], *Funcionarios de la secretaría de relaciones desde el año de 1821 a 1940* (Mexico City: n.p., 1940), p. 73.

28. McLane to Cass, 27, 28, and 31 Aug. 1859, NA/DD.

29. John Temple, "Memoria justificativa de los hechos que forman los reclamos de Mr.

John Temple contra el Gob[iern]o de México,'' pp. 12–19, GC/UT; and Black to McLane, 14 Apr. 1859, NA/DPR.

30. Numerous such petitions were enclosed with the consular despatches from Veracruz and Tampico during 1858–59.

31. Cass to McLane, 4 Nov. 1859, NA/DI.

32. Mata to Ocampo, 6 May and 19 Sept. 1859, 8-4-120 and 140, AHINAH.

33. Letter, 27 Apr. 1859, in Lilia Díaz, *Versión francesa de México: Informes diplomaticos,* 4 vols. (Mexico City: El Colegio de México, 1963–67), 2:79–82.

34. Alejandro Villaseñor y Villaseñor, *Antón Lizardo. El tratado de MacLane-Ocampo. El brindis del desierto* (Mexico City: Editorial Jus, 1962), pp. 116–17; José Fuentes Mares, *Juárez y los Estados Unidos,* 5th ed. (Mexico City, Editorial Jus, 1972), p. 137; and de Gabriac to Paris, 27 Nov. 1859, in Díaz, *Versión francesa,* 2:119–21. Details of the negotiations and resulting treaty are in México, Secretaría de relaciones exteriores, *Archivo histórico diplomático mexicano,* 42 vols. (Mexico City: Secretaría de relaciones exteriores, 1924–38; reprint ed., Mexico City: Editorial Porrúa, 1971), vol. 13, *El tratado Mon-Almonte.*

35. Manuel Payno, *México y sus cuestiones financieras con Inglaterra, la España, y la Francia* (Mexico City: Cumplido, 1862), pp. 254–76.

36. Walter V. Scholes, *Mexican Politics during the Juárez Regime, 1855–1872* (Columbia: University of Missouri Press, 1957), p. 35n; McLane to Cass, 7 Dec. 1859, NA/DD; Roeder, *Juárez,* 1:211; Fuentes Mares, *Juárez,* p. 137; and Ivie E. Cadenhead, Jr., *Benito Juárez* (New York: Twayne Publishers, 1973), pp. 53–56.

37. Mata to Ocampo, 19 Sept. 1859, 8-4-140, AHINAH.

38. Mata to MRE, 4 Nov. 1859, pp. 235–42, H/110(73:0)''858-59''/1, ASRE.

39. Cass to McLane, 21 Nov. 1859, NA/DI.

40. James D. Richardson, comp., *A Compilation of the Messages and Papers of the Presidents, 1789–1897,* 10 vols. (Washington: Government Printing Office, 1896–99), 5: 563–70.

41. McLane to Cass, 21 Nov. and 7 and 15 Dec. 1859, NA/DD.

42. Copies of both are in ''unperfected treaties'' file, NA.

43. Cass to Forsyth, 17 Nov. 1857, NA/DI.

44. Ocampo to Mata, 19 Dec. 1859, pp. 252–54, H/110(73:0)''858-59''/1, ASRE.

45. [México. Relaciones exteriores], *Funcionarios,* p. 78.

46. Mata to MRE, 6 Jan. 1860, pp. 256–59, H/110(73:0)''858-59''/1, ASRE.

47. MRE to Mata, 28 Jan., 5, 9, and 15 May, and 15 June 1860, pp. 260, 325, 327, 330, and 336, H/110(73:0)''858-59''/1, ASRE.

48. Expediente 10, H/110(73:0)''858-59''/1, ASRE, contains numerous papers relating to Dunbar's activities.

49. Protest, 17 Dec. 1859, enclosed with McLane to Cass, 22 Dec. 1859, NA/DD.

50. Villaseñor, *Antón Lizardo,* p. 215.

51. Scholes, *Mexican Politics,* pp. 36–37.

52. José C. Valadés, *Don Melchor Ocampo, Reformador de México* (Mexico City: Editorial Patria, 1954), pp. 362–63.

53. McLane to Cass, 22 Dec. 1859 and 21 Jan. 1860, NA/DD.

54. Cass to McLane, 7 Jan. 1860, NA/DI.

55. James Morton Callahan, *American Foreign Policy in Mexican Relations* (New York: Macmillan Company, 1932), p. 271.

56. Mata to MRE, 16 Mar., 17 Apr., and 9 May 1860, pp. 303 and 305–23, H/110(73:0)"858-59"/1, ASRE.

57. Callahan, *American Foreign Policy*, p. 271; and Mata to MRE, 1 June 1860, pp. 335–37, H/110(73:0)"858-59"/1, ASRE.

58. McLane to Cass, 21 Jan. 1860, NA/DD.

59. Elgee to Cass, 6 Mar. 1860, NA/DD.

60. Cass to McLane, 28 Apr. 1860, NA/DI. No objective study has been made of this incident: the best, but unobjective, is Fuentes Mares, *Juárez*, pp. 172–80; the most detailed study, but very biased, is Villaseñor, *Antón Lizardo*, pp. 11–58.

61. Mata to MRE, 27 June 1860, p. 343, H/110(73:0)"858-59"/1, ASRE.

62. Scholes, *Mexican Politics*, p. 37.

63. Romero to MRE, 5 Sept. 1860, in Benito Juárez, *Documentos, discursos, y correspondencia*, ed. Jorge L. Tamayo, 12 vols. (Mexico City: Secretaría de Patrimonio Nacional, 1964–68), 3:11–13.

64. Frank A. Knapp, "Precursors of American Investment in Mexican Railroads," *Pacific Historical Review* 21 (1952): 50.

65. MRE to Mata, 3 Feb. 1860, I/131/1873, ASRE.

66. Mata to Ocampo, 29 Feb. 1860, 8-2-10, AHINAH; and Mata to MRE, 2 Mar. 1860, I/131/1873, ASRE.

67. M. Lerdo, Hacienda, to MRE, 2 Feb. 1860, MRE to Mata, 2 Feb. 1860, and Mata to MRE, 2 Mar. 1860, I/131/1873, ASRE.

68. Despatches from de Gabriac to Paris on the McLane-Ocampo treaties, the need for intervention, de Gabriac's efforts to secure support among the diplomatic corps, and Mathew's efforts as a mediator, together with notes between Paris and London on Mexican developments, are in Díaz, *Versión francesa*, 2:123–63. Letters exchanged among Mathew, U.S. Consul John Black, and the United States legation at Veracruz are enclosed with despatches from the legation, Dec. 1859–June 1860, NA/DD.

69. The change in French policy is outlined in instructions to Saligny, 30 May 1860, and Saligny's memorandum on Mexican affairs, 7 June 1860, in Díaz, *Versión francesa*, 2:164–76.

70. M. Lerdo's earlier peace efforts are summarized in Scholes, *Mexican Politics*, pp. 38–39.

71. M. Lerdo to Juárez, 4 Nov. 1860, and Juárez to M. Lerdo, 8 Nov. 1860, in Juárez, *Documentos*, 3: 31–32, 38.

72. Thomas David Schoonover, *Dollars over Dominion: The Triumph of Liberalism in Mexican–United States Relations, 1861–1867* (Baton Rouge: Louisiana State University Press, 1978), is an excellent study of these relations.

73. *Proceedings of a Meeting of Citizens of New-York, to Express Sympathy and Respect for the Mexican Republican Exiles, Held at Cooper Institute, July 19, 1865, with an Appendix Containing the Speeches of the Hon. Matias Romero, Envoy Extraordinary and Minister Plenipotentiary of the Mexican Republic in the United States, at Two Banquets Previously Given in New-York* (New York: John A. Gray & Green, 1865), appendix, pp. 49–57. A more polished version of this speech is given in Matías Romero, *Mexico and the United States: A Study of Subjects Affecting Their Political, Commercial, and Social Relations Made with a View to Their Promotion* (New York: G. P. Putnam's Sons, 1898), pp. 383–87.

Bibliography

Because this book is based firmly on archival and other forms of primary source material and makes use of secondary materials only to flesh out the pictures that emerged from the primary sources, I believe that the reader will benefit most by having my comments on sources limited to those materials that formed the core of research for this work and out of which emerged its basic thesis. The following bibliography is thus divided into two parts: the first will identify and comment only on the primary materials and the few secondary works that were essential sources for this study; the second will list in traditional bibliographic fashion all the many sources cited in this work.

Major archival collections crucial to this study are located in Mexico City, Austin (Texas), and Washington. Existing works dealing with Mexican–United States relations during the Reforma, or any other period for that matter, have utilized the archival materials of Mexico City only infrequently, those of the García Collection of the University of Texas more frequently, and Washington's National Archives too often. Both specialized and more general studies published in both countries have often relied on the latter for practically all their primary documentation.

This excessive dependence on United States documentation has been made more acute by the fact that most of the research has been limited to the so-called diplomatic correspondence, consisting of diplomatic despatches from United States ministers to Mexico and diplomatic instructions from Washington to those agents. This type of material is easy to use: despatches and instructions for the nineteenth century are arranged chronologically by country and are widely available on microfilm. Equally accessible but less frequently consulted are the consular communications between Washington and the several consular posts in Mexico. Consular despatches, while not totally lacking in political reporting, are valuable more for their coverage of commercial and economic developments and for information they contain on the activities of United States citizens in the area. While the quality of consular reporting varies, reflecting the interests and abilities of the particular consul involved, the despatches of John Black at Mexico City, John T. Pickett at Veracruz, and Franklin Chase at Tampico during the 1850s demonstrate high levels of both interest and ability and are frequently more informative on existing conditions than are their diplomatic counterparts.

In addition to consular and diplomatic communications, the "General Records of the Department of State" in the National Archives also include the less accessible, hence less used, but equally valuable "Reports of Bureau Officers." These are summaries of information from both diplomatic and consular despatches that was deemed worthy of being brought to the attention of the secretary of state and the president. They are thus a gauge of what was considered important in Washington. On occasion these summaries are also the only means to determine the content of despatches missing from the chronological files.

Two large collections of archival material related to the functions of the Department of State have so far escaped detailed scrutiny by researchers. The "Records of Foreign Service Posts of the Department of State" contain the files maintained by the United States legation in Mexico. These files give the researcher a more detailed picture of the activities of the minister and the nuances of his relations with his hosts. They also clearly demonstrate that on occasion the facts reported to Washington by the minister differed in significant ways from the same facts as reflected in the legation's files. The "Records of Boundary and Claims Commissions and Arbitrations" contain the numerous and often well-documented files of claims lodged against Mexico by United States citizens under the 1868 claims convention. While many of the claimants clearly exaggerated the extent of the damages they had suffered, their claim files contain a wealth of valuable economic information and shed considerable light on the role of United States entrepreneurs and on their relationships with various Mexican governments and individual officials. The claim files of Carlos Butterfield, John Temple, and Gabor Naphegyi are particularly informative for the Reforma period.

A valuable but little-used National Archives collection is the "Applications and Recommendations for Public Office" for the presidential administrations of the period. From these records one can identify the individuals and groups with sufficient interest in Mexico and adequate political leverage to attempt to influence the selection of consular and diplomatic agents to fill posts there.

The García Collection of the University of Texas (Austin) contains the papers of many Mexican leaders of the period. Some of these collections, such as those of Santos Degollado, Jesús González Ortega, Manuel Doblado, Antonio de la Fuente, and Mariano Riva Palacio, while not represented in the source citations of this book, were still helpful in understanding the atmosphere in which the Reforma occurred and in identifying many of the friendships which would have an important impact on Reforma activity. Two collections were specifically relevant and are frequently cited in this study: the papers of Vicente Gómez Farías, the liberal elder statesman of the period, and those of Ignacio Comonfort, Ayutla rebel and president, 1855–58. The García Collection also has the only known copy of John Temple's unpublished "Memoria justificativa," consisting of several hundred valuable documents relating to Temple's leasing and operation of the Mexico City mint. While some of these documents are available in other archival sources, many are unique to this *memoria*.

The most useful public archives of Mexico City for this study are the Archivo de la Secretaría de Relaciones Exteriores and the Archivo Histórico del Instituto Nacional de Antropología e Historia. The former, the foreign ministry archive, is somewhat more difficult to use, partly because its material is arranged into subject-matter categories the rationale for which is not always clear. As a result of overlapping subject categories or perhaps confusion on the part of those doing the original filing, documents relating to the same subject are too often scattered among several subject files. Despite any difficulty in locating material, the documents in this archive are absolutely essential to full and objective treatment of Mexican–United States relations. They represent the necessary view from the other side on issues and developments. They also frequently reinforce the impression gained from the diplomatic post records of the National Archives: United States ministers were not averse to reporting what they wished Washington to know rather than what had really transpired. By comparing the official records of both countries the researcher is able to see a much broader and more interesting picture than either source would have revealed alone. For example, one sees that Mexican officials were often able to lead United States ministers carefully toward predetermined positions by assuming stances hostile to those positions. The ministers then reported to Washington on their successes in overcoming the ignorant opposition of inept Mexican officials.

The Archivo Histórico del Instituto Nacional de Antropología e Historia houses two valuable collections of Melchor Ocampo's letters, mostly from his friend, political ally, and eventual son-in-law, José María Mata. In addition to revealing the deep and trusting personal tie between these two leaders, the letters are filled with candid expressions of opinion on numerous affairs of state. For example, while Mata was minister at Washington he would routinely dispatch two communications on the same day, an official report to the ministry and a letter to Ocampo, who frequently was also the foreign minister. In the official letter he would report on developments in a formal fashion; in the private note he would give the facts behind these developments and his personal opinion on them.

Mexican newspapers are also indispensable sources of information, both for the task of tracing specific developments and for understanding prevailing attitudes. Mexico City's Hemeroteca Nacional has a fine collection of newspapers for the Reforma period, but overcrowded reading rooms and traffic noises make it a difficult place for the researcher to work. Fortunately, most of its runs of major newspapers, such as *El Siglo XIX, El Monitor Republicano,* and *El Heraldo,* have been microfilmed and are available in United States libraries. The value of microfilm in preserving historical source material is illustrated in the case of *El Heraldo.* The originals of this valuable newspaper, essential to understanding *puro* attitudes, have disappeared from the shelves of the Hemeroteca since they were filmed some three decades ago.

Several published collections of documents merit mention. The availability of United States diplomatic material in microform should obviate the need for the serious scholar to consult William R. Manning's multivolume *Diplomatic Correspondence of the United States: Inter-American Affairs, 1831–1860,* but a word of caution is in order. Manning, a career employee of the Department of State, allowed his departmental and national loyalties to influence his editing of Reforma-era documents to the extent that passages most embarrassing for the United States are deleted without explanation or comment. A similar collection of diplomatic documentation, which appears to have received more objective editing, is Lilia Díaz's four-volume *Versión francesa de México,* covering the period 1853–67. This extremely useful collection provides the scholar with a third perspective from which to view Mexican–United States relations. Indispensable for research into nineteenth-century Mexican economic developments is the monumental *Legislación mexicana o colección completa de las disposiciones legislativas . . . de la República,* compiled by Manuel Dublán and José María Lozano, which contains, in addition to the many laws passed by Congress, the numerous grants, concessions, and contracts made to both national and foreign entrepreneurs. Also of great use are the first three volumes of Juárez's *Documentos, discursos, y correspondencia,* ably edited by Jorge L. Tamayo. Although most of the documents contained therein are readily available in archives, Tamayo has brought them together in a convenient form and has provided informative introductions to each section of documents. The most serious weakness of the collection is the editor's decision to use Manning's work, commented on above, as his source for United States diplomatic documents.

Memorias of governmental ministries are an excellent source of information. Unfortunately, few of these were issued during the Reforma. Of the two issued during the period under study, for *Fomento* by Manuel Siliceo and for *Hacienda* by Miguel Lerdo, the latter is the more valuable for its treatment of the economic problems and policies of the Comonfort government. In a category by itself is the documentary history of the constitutional congress published in 1857 by Francisco Zarco, a newspaper editor and member of congress. The reissue of this work in 1956 by the Colegio de México under the title *Historia del congreso extraordinario constituyente [1856–1857]* not only made it available again but increased its usefulness by correcting errors in the original edition, adding explanatory material, and providing essential indexing.

The activities of United States entrepreneurs resulted in the publication of valuable special-purpose documentary collections. Carlos Butterfield, in his quest for congressional subsidies for his proposed Gulf steamship venture, provides useful documents and statistics in *United States and Mexican Mail Steamship Line.* José Antonio de Mendizábal, long-time agent for the Temple interests in Mexico and executor of the Temple estate, performed a similar task with his *Exposición que . . . dirige al gobierno mexicano.*

Most of the secondary works dealing with this period, as noted in the Introduction, have little to say on the subject at hand. A notable exception in general works is Charles Cumberland's *Mexico: The Struggle for Modernity,* which remains the best interpretative treatment of the socioeconomic developments of the mid-nineteenth century. Most surveys of Mexican–United States relations pass through the Reforma with, at best, only brief mention of the McLane-Ocampo treaties. Two works which do give some detailed attention to the events described in this study suffer from other weaknesses. James Morton Callahan's *American Foreign Policy in Mexican Relations* is outdated, is written in a stiff and inelegant style, and is based almost exclusively on United States documentation—yet it is still the most detailed account of the diplomatic relations of the Reforma. Luis G. Zorrilla's *Historia de las relaciones entre México y los Estados Unidos* is the best overall treatment of the period and is the only work to make extensive use of the archival material of both countries, but as with most surveys it does not probe beyond the surface facts.

Of the more specialized works, Charles Hale's *Mexican Liberalism in the Age of Mora* is a significant exploration of the political and economic attitudes which characterized the decades preceding the Reforma. For the broader sweep of liberal development, Jesús Reyes Heroles's *El liberalismo mexicano* reflects the prevailing orthodoxy. Walter V. Scholes's *Mexican Politics during the Juárez Regime* is a brief but insightful treatment of the liberal fortunes during the intervention and the restored republic as well as the Reforma.

Biographic studies constitute a final category of works which warrant comment. Generally works in English are very weak. None of the United States participants have been treated biographically, and of the several Mexicans who have been the subjects of English-language biographies only those of Juárez by Roeder and Smart approach acceptable levels. Biographical studies in Spanish are more plentiful, if not always of better quality than those in English. Of particular note are the studies of Lucas Alamán and Melchor Ocampo by José C. Valadés. The biographical works of José Fuentes Mares are also excellent examples of historical scholarship despite the author's tendency to overstock his writing with statements designed to be shocking, ironic, and iconoclastic. His biographic studies of Santa Anna and Miramón contain perceptive interpretations based on solid documentation. The best of Fuentes Mares's biographical works are his tetralogy *Juárez y los Estados Unidos, Juárez y el imperio, Juárez y la intervención, and Juárez y la república* (Mexico City: Editorial Jus, 1960–65). While they were published separately, the four volumes collectively constitute a unified study of Juárez as Mexican leader. Only the first volume in the series deals specifically with the Reforma, yet the entire series is valuable for understanding the character, attitudes, and methods of Juárez. The most serious deficiency in them is the author's tendency to rely too heavily on United States documentation, in both archival and published form.

Carmen Blázquez's biographical study of Miguel Lerdo de Tejada became available only after the manuscript for this book had been completed and accepted for publication. A quick perusal of the work reveals that while it contains some heretofore unknown details, it does not materially alter the picture that had emerged from a study of original sources. It suffers from several weaknesses. Too often the work degenerates into a chronology without integrating the events into the larger picture; the work is too heavily dependent on published documentary collections, especially Manning's via Tamayo's Juárez collection; and most seriously, the author appears to feel compelled to bow to orthodoxy in her evaluation of her subject. Although she frequently expresses admiration for Miguel Lerdo, Blázquez gives us a picture of him as the black sheep of the Reforma *puros* for his espousal of a United States protectorate over Mexico. As the present work clearly demonstrates, the desire to have Mexico become a protectorate of the United States was common among all varieties of liberals, from the moderate middle-of-the-road Comonfort to the extreme *puros* such as Juárez, Mata, Ocampo, and Romero. This attitude reflected not a lack of patriotism, but a desperation born out of a keen sense of the need for material development, an almost mystical belief in the transforming powers of capital and technology, and a pessimism produced by three decades of government by chaos in Mexico. While Miguel Lerdo may have been more openly spurred by partisan politics and personal political ambition than some of his colleagues, the desire for progress and material development which he and most liberals saw as attainable only through the intervention of exterior forces was also the product of an outlook that put societal welfare above the narrower demands of nationalism.

The following bibliography contains the sources cited in this work or mentioned in the author's comments.

Archives and Manuscripts

Archivo de la Secretaría de Relaciones Exteriores. Mexico City.
Archivo General de la Nación. Mexico City:
  Ramos: Cartas de seguridad
            Fomento
            Gobernación
            Movimiento marítimo
Archivo Matías Romero, Banco de México. Mexico City.
Comonfort Papers, García Collection. University of Texas, Austin.
Gómez Farías Papers, García Collection. University of Texas, Austin.
Hutchinson, C. Alan. "Valentín Gómez Farías: A Biographical Study." Ph.D. dissertation, University of Texas, 1948.
Jane McManus Cazneau Papers. Archives, University of Texas, Austin.
Juárez Manuscripts. Biblioteca Nacional, Mexico City.
National Archives, Washington:
  Applications and Recommendations for Public Office.
  General Records of the Department of State.
  Records of Boundary and Claims Commissions and Arbitrations.
  Records of the Foreign Service Posts of the Department of State.
Ocampo Manuscripts. Archivo Histórico del Instituto Nacional de Antropología e Historia, Mexico City.
Olliff, Donathon C. "The Economics of Mexican–United States Relations during the Reforma, 1854–1861." Ph.D. dissertation, University of Florida, 1974.
Public Record Office. London:
  Foreign Office.

Temple, John. "Memoria justificativa de los hechos que forman los reclamos de Mr. John Temple contra el Gob[iern]o de México," García Collection. University of Texas, Austin.

Newspapers

Daily Picayune (New Orleans).
DeBow's Commercial Review of the South and West (New Orleans).
El Estandarte Nacional (Mexico City).
El Heraldo (Mexico City).
Mexican Estraordinary (Mexico City).
The Mobile Register.
El Monitor Republicano (Mexico City).
New York Herald.
New York Times.
El Siglo XIX (Mexico City).
Trait d'Union (Mexico City).

Published Works

Apuntes para la historia de la guerra entre México y los Estados Unidos. Mexico City: Tipografía de Manuel Payno, hijo, 1848.

Arcila Farías, Eduardo. *Reformas económicas del siglo xviii en Nueva España.* 2 vols. Mexico City: SepSetentas, 1974.

Bazant, Jan. *A Concise History of Mexico from Hidalgo to Cárdenas, 1805–1940.* Cambridge: Cambridge University Press, 1977.

————. *Alienation of Church Wealth in Mexico: Social and Economic Aspects of the Liberal Revolution, 1856–1875.* Edited and translated by Michael P. Costeloe. Cambridge: Cambridge University Press, 1971.

Berge, Dennis E. "A Mexican Dilemma: The Mexico City Ayuntamiento and the Question of Loyalty, 1846–1848." *Hispanic American Historical Review* 50 (1970):229–56.

Bernstein, Harry. *Matías Romero, 1837–1898.* Mexico City: Fondo de Cultura Económica, 1973.

Bibliografía histórica mexicana. Mexico City: El Colegio de México, 1967–.

Blázquez, Carmen. *Miguel Lerdo de Tejada: Un liberal veracruzano en la política nacional.* Mexico City: El Colegio de México, 1978.

Bowman, Lynn. *Los Angeles: Epic of a City.* Berkeley: Howell-North Books, 1974.

Brading, David A. "Creole Nationalism and Mexican Liberalism." *Journal of Interamerican Studies and World Affairs* 15 (1973):139–90.

————. *Miners and Merchants in Bourbon Mexico, 1763–1810.* Cambridge: Cambridge University Press, 1971.

Buchanan, James. *Mr. Buchanan's Administration on the Eve of the Rebellion.* New York: D. Appleton & Co., 1866.

Butterfield, Carlos. *United States and Mexican Mail Steamship Line: Statistics on Mexico.* New York: J. A. H. Hasbrouck & Co., 1860.

Cadenhead, Ivie E., Jr. *Benito Juárez.* New York: Twayne Publishers, 1973.

Calderón de la Barca, Frances E. *Life in Mexico.* Edited by Howard T. Fisher and Marion H. Fisher, New York: Doubleday & Co., 1966.

Callahan, James Morton. *American Foreign Policy in Mexican Relations*. New York: Macmillan Co., 1932.

Callcott, Wilfrid Hardy. *Church and State in Mexico, 1822–1857*. Durham: Duke University Press, 1926. Reprint. New York: Octagon Press, 1965.

————. *Santa Anna: The Story of an Enigma Who Once Was Mexico*. Norman: University of Oklahoma Press, 1936.

Carr, William Z. *The World and William Walker*. New York: Harper & Row, 1963.

Carreño, Alberto María. *La diplomacia extraordinaria entre México y Estados Unidos, 1789–1947*. 2nd ed. 2 vols. Mexico City: Editorial Jus, 1961.

Chamberlin, Eugene Keith. "Baja California after Walker: The Zerman Enterprise." *Hispanic American Historical Review* 34 (1954):175–89.

Cleland, Robert Glass. *The Cattle of a Thousand Hills: Southern California, 1850–1880*. 2nd ed. Alhambra, Calif.: C. F. Braun & Co., 1951. Facsimile reprint. San Marino, Calif.: Huntington Library, 1975.

Colección de documentos inéditos o muy raros relativos a la reforma en México; Obtenidos en su mayor parte de los Archivos de las Secretarías de Relaciones Exteriores y Defensa Nacional, y otros depósitos documentales de la ciudad de México y de fuera de ella. 2 vols. Mexico City: Instituto Nacional de Antropología y Historia, 1957–58.

[El Colegio de México]. "Veinticinco años de investigación histórica de México." *Historia mexicana* 15 (1965–66):155–445.

Consideraciones sobre la situación política y social de la República mexicana en el año 1847. Mexico City: Valdes y Redondas, 1848.

Cosío Villegas, Daniel, ed. *Historia moderna de México*. 8 vols. Mexico City: Editorial Hermes, 1955–65.

Cumberland, Charles C. *Mexico: The Struggle for Modernity*. New York: Oxford University Press, 1968.

Davis, William Watson. "Ante-Bellum Southern Commercial Conventions." *Transactions of the Alabama Historical Society, 1904* 5 (1906):153–202.

Díaz, Lilia, ed. *Versión francesa de México: Informes diplomáticos*. 4 vols. Mexico City: El Colegio de México, 1963–67.

Diccionario Porrúa de historia, biografía, y geografía de México. 3rd ed. 2 vols. Mexico City: Editorial Porrúa, 1970.

Dublán, Manuel, and Lozano, José María, comps. *Legislación mexicana o colección completa de las disposiciones legislativas expedidas desde la independencia de la República*. Official ed. 45 vols. Mexico City: Imprenta del Comercio de Dublán y Chávez, 1876–1910.

Duckett, Alvin. *John Forsyth, Political Tactician*. Athens: University of Georgia Press, 1962.

Friend, Llerena. *Sam Houston, the Great Designer*. Austin: University of Texas Press, 1954.

Fuentes Mares, José. *Juárez y los Estados Unidos*. 5th ed. Mexico City: Editorial Jus, 1972.

————. *Miramón, el hombre*. 2nd ed. Mexico City: Contrapuntos, 1975.

————. *Santa Anna: Aurora y ocaso de un comediante*. 3rd ed. Mexico City: Editorial Jus, 1967.

Fuller, John Douglas Pitts. *The Movement for the Acquisition of All Mexico, 1846–1848*. Baltimore: Johns Hopkins Press, 1936.

Garber, Paul Neff. *The Gadsden Treaty*. Philadelphia: University of Pennsylvania Press, 1923.

Gilmore, Newton Ray. "Henry George Ward, British Publicist for Mexican Mines." *Pacific Historical Review* 32 (1963):35–47.

Glick, Edward B. *Straddling the Isthmus of Tehuantepec*. Gainesville: University of Florida Press, 1959.

Goetzmann, William H. *When the Eagle Screamed: The Romantic Horizon in American Diplomacy, 1800–1860*. New York: John Wiley & Sons, 1966.

González, Luis; Florescano, Enrique; Lanzagorta, Maria del Rosario; Bazant, Jan; Flores Caballero, Romero; and Herrera Canales, Inéz. *La economía mexicana en la época de Juárez*. Mexico City: Secretaría de Industria y Comercio, 1972.

Gurria Lacroix, Jorge. *Las ideas monárquicas de don Lucas Alamán*. Mexico City: Instituto de Historia, 1951.

Hale, Charles A. *Mexican Liberalism in the Age of Mora, 1821–1853*. New Haven: Yale University Press, 1968.

————. "The War with the United States and the Crisis in Mexican Thought." *The Americas* 14 (1957):153–73.

Hammond, George P., ed. *The Larkin Papers*. 10 vols. Berkeley: University of California Press, 1951–64.

Hayes, Benjamin Ignatius. *Pioneer Notes from the Diaries of Judge Benjamin Hayes, 1849–1875*. New York: Arno Press, 1976.

Heitman, Francis B., ed. *Historical Register and Dictionary of the United States Army, from Its Organization, September 29, 1789, to March 2, 1903*. 2 vols. Washington: Government Printing Office, 1903.

Hernández Rodríguez, Rosaura. *Ignacio Comonfort: Trayectoria política. Documentos*. Mexico City: Universidad Nacional Autónoma de México, Instituto de Investigaciones Históricas, 1967.

Hittell, Theodore H. *History of California*. 4 vols. San Francisco: H. J. Stone & Co., 1898.

Horton, Rushmore G. *The Life and Public Service of James Buchanan, Late Minister to England and Formally Minister to Russia, Senator and Representative in Congress, and Secretary of State; Including the Most Important of His State Papers*. Authorized ed. New York: Derby & Jackson, 1856.

Houston, Samuel. *The Writings of Sam Houston, 1813–1863*. Edited by Amelia W. Williams and Eugene C. Barker. 8 vols. Austin: University of Texas Press, 1938–43.

Johnson, Richard A. *The Mexican Revolution of Ayutla, 1854–1855*. Rock Island, Ill.: Augustana College Library, 1939.

Juárez, Benito. *Documentos, discursos, y correspondencia*. Edited by Jorge L. Tamayo. 12 vols. Mexico City: Secretaría de Patrimonio Nacional, 1964–68.

Klein, Philip Shriver. *President James Buchanan: A Biography*. University Park: Pennsylvania State University Press, 1962.

Knapp, Frank A. "Precursors of American Investment in Mexican Railroads." *Pacific Historical Review* 21 (1952):43–64.

————. *The Life of Sebastián Lerdo de Tejada, 1823–1889: A Study in Influence and Obscurity*. Austin: University of Texas Press, 1951. Reprint. New York: Greenwood Press, 1968.

Lerdo de Tejada, Miguel. *El comercio esterior de México desde la conquista hasta hoy*. Mexico City: Rafael, 1853.

Leyes, decretos, y ordenes que forman el derecho internacional mexicano o que se relacionan con el mismo. Mexico City: Filomeno Mata, 1879.

López Cámara, Francisco. *La estructura económica y social de México en la época de la reforma.* Mexico City: Siglo Veintiuno Editores, 1967.

Los Angeles, a Guide to the City and Its Environs. 2nd ed. New York: Hastings House, 1951.

Loza Macías, Manuel. *El pensamiento económico y la constitución de 1857.* Mexico City: Editorial Jus, 1959.

MacCorkle, Stuart A. *American Policy of Recognition towards Mexico.* Baltimore: Johns Hopkins Press, 1933.

McCormac, Eugene I. ''John Forsyth.'' In *The American Secretaries of State and Their Diplomacy,* edited by Samuel Flagg Bemis, vol. 8. New York: Pageant Book Co., 1958.

McLane, Robert M. *Reminiscences, 1827–1897.* Privately printed, 1903.

Manning, William R., ed. *Diplomatic Correspondence of the United States: Inter-American Affairs, 1831–1860.* 12 vols. Washington: Carnegie Endowment for International Peace, 1932–39.

Meade, Robert Douthat. *Judah P. Benjamin, Confederate Statesman.* New York: Oxford University Press, 1943.

Mendizábal, José Antonio de. *Exposición que José Antonio de Mendizábal, albacea de Don Juan Temple, dirige al gobierno mexicano pidiéndole el cumplimiento del contrato de 28 de Junio de 1856.* Mexico City: F. Díaz de León y Santiago White, 1868.

Merk, Frederick. *Manifest Destiny and Mission in American History: A Reinterpretation.* New York: Alfred A. Knopf, 1970.

México. Ministerio de fomento, colonización, industria, y comercio. *Memoria de la secretaría de estado y del despacho de fomento, colonización, industria, y comercio de la República mexicana, escrita por el ministro del ramo, C. Manuel Siliceo, para dar cuenta con ella al soberano congreso constitucional.* Mexico City: Imprenta de Vicente García Torres, 1857.

México. Ministerio de hacienda. *Memoria presentada al exmo. Sr. presidente sustituto de la República por el C. Miguel Lerdo de Tejada, dando cuenta de la marcha que han seguido los negocios de la hacienda pública, en el tiempo que tuvo a su cargo la secretaría de este ramo.* Mexico City: Imprenta de Vicente García Torres, 1857.

México. Secretaría de relaciones exteriores. *Archivo histórico diplomático mexicano.* 42 vols. Mexico City: Secretaría de relaciones exteriores, 1924–38. Reprint. Mexico City: Editorial Porrúa, 1971.

[_____]. *Funcionarios de la secretaría de relaciones desde el año de 1821 a 1940.* Mexico City: n.p., 1940.

Miller, Hunter, ed. *Treaties and Other International Acts of the United States of America.* 8 vols. Washington: Government Printing Office, 1930–48.

Mora, José María Luis. *Méjico y sus revoluciones.* 3 vols. Mexico City: Porrúa, 1950.

Moreno, Daniel. *Los hombres de la reforma.* 2nd ed. Mexico City: B. Costa-Amic, 1970.

Murillo Vidal, Rafael. *José María Mata: Padre de la constitución de 1857.* Mexico City: Secretaría de Educación Pública, 1966.

Murray, Paul. *Tres norteamericanos y su participación en el desarrollo del tratado McLane-Ocampo, 1856–1860.* Guadalajara: Imprenta Gráfica, 1946.

Nichols, Roy Franklin. *Franklin Pierce: Young Hickory of the Granite Hills.* Philadelphia: University of Pennsylvania Press, 1931.

_____. *The Disruption of American Democracy.* New York: Macmillan Co., 1948.

Ocampo, Melchor. *Obras completas de Melchor Ocampo.* Mexico City: F. Vazquez, 1901. Vol. 2, *Escritos políticos,* prologue by Angél Pola.

O'Gorman, Edmundo. "Procedentes y sentido de la revolución de Ayutla." In *Seis estudios históricos de tema mexicano.* Jalapa: Universidad Veracruzana, 1960.

Olliff, Donathon C. "Mexico's Mid-Nineteenth-Century Drive for Material Development." *SECOLAS Annals* 8 (1977):19–29.

Owen, Thomas M. *History of Alabama and Dictionary of Alabama Biography.* 4 vols. Chicago: S. J. Clarke Publishing Co., 1921.

Payno, Manuel. *México y sus cuestiones financieras con Inglaterra, la España y la Francia.* Mexico City: Cumplido, 1862.

Pletcher, David M. "Prospecting Expeditions across Central Mexico, 1856–57." *Pacific Historical Review* 21 (1952):21–42.

————. *Rails, Mines, and Progress: Seven American Promoters in Mexico, 1867–1911.* Ithaca: Cornell University Press, 1958.

Poinsett, Joel R. *Notes on Mexico Made in the Autumn of 1822.* Philadelphia: H. C. Carey & I. Lea, 1824.

[Portilla, Anselmo de la]. *Historia de la revolución de México contra la dictadura del general Santa-Anna, 1853–1855.* Mexico City: Imprenta Vicente García Torres, 1856. Reprint. Puebla: Editorial José M. Cajica, Jr., 1972.

Potash, Robert A. *El banco de avío de México: El fomento de la industria, 1821–1846.* Mexico City: Fondo de Cultura Económica, 1959.

————. "Historiography of Mexico since 1821." *Hispanic American Historical Review* 40 (1960):383–424.

Proceedings of a Meeting of Citizens of New-York, to Express Sympathy and Respect for the Mexican Republican Exiles, Held at Cooper Institute, July 19, 1865, with an Appendix Containing the Speeches of the Hon. Matias Romero, Envoy Extraordinary and Minister Plenipotentiary of the Mexican Republic in the United States, at Two Banquets Previously Given in New-York. New York: John A. Gray & Green, 1865.

Ramos Arizpe, Miguel. *Memoria sobre el estado de las provincias internas de oriente.* Mexico City: Universidad Nacional Autónoma de México, 1932.

Ramsey, Albert C., ed. and trans. *The Other Side; or, Notes for the History of the War between Mexico and the United States.* New York: J. Wiley, 1850.

Randall, Robert W. *Real del Monte, a British Mining Venture in Mexico.* Austin: University of Texas Press, 1972.

Reyes Heroles, Jesús. *El liberalismo mexicano.* 3 vols. Mexico City: Universidad Nacional Autónoma de México, Facultad de Derecho, 1957–61.

Richardson, James D., comp. *A Compilation of the Messages and Papers of the Presidents, 1789–1897.* 10 vols. Washington: Government Printing Office, 1896–99.

Rippy, James Fred. "Diplomacy of the United States and Mexico regarding the Isthmus of Tehuantepec, 1848–1860." *Mississippi Valley Historical Review* 6 (1919-20):503–31.

————. *Joel R. Poinsett, Versatile American.* Durham: Duke University Press, 1935.

Robinson, William W. *Los Angeles: A Profile.* Norman: University of Oklahoma Press, 1968.

Roeder, Ralph. *Juárez and His Mexico.* 2 vols. New York: Viking Press, 1947.

Romero, Matías. *Mexico and the United States: A Study of Subjects Affecting Their Political, Commercial, and Social Relations Made with a View to Their Promotion.* New York: G. P. Putnam's Sons, 1898.

Santa Anna, Antonio López de. *Manifesto del presidente de la República a la nación.* Mexico City: Cumplido, 1855.

Scholes, Walter V. *Mexican Politics during the Juárez Regime, 1855–1872.* Columbia: University of Missouri Press, 1957.

Schoonover, Thomas David. *Dollars over Dominion: The Triumph of Liberalism in Mexican–United States Relations, 1861–1867.* Baton Rouge: Louisiana State University Press, 1978.

Sears, Louis Martin. *John Slidell.* Durham: Duke University Press, 1925.

Shaw, William Henry. *General Carlos Butterfield and His Labors in Behalf of International Prosperity on the American Continent.* Berryville, Va.: n.p., n.d.

Silva Herzog, Jesús. *El pensamiento económica, social, y política de México, 1810–1964.* Mexico City: Instituto de Investigaciones Económicas, 1967.

Smart, Charles Allen. *Viva Juárez! A Biography.* Philadelphia: J. B. Lippincott Co., 1963.

Torre Villar, Ernesto de la. "El ferrocarril de Tacubaya." *Historia mexicana* 9 (1959–60):377–92.

———. "La capital y sus primeros medios de transporte: Prehistoria de las tranvías." *Historia mexicana* 9 (1959–60):215–48.

Valadés, José C. *Alamán, estadista e historiador.* Mexico City: Robredo, 1938.

———. *Don Melchor Ocampo, reformador de México.* Mexico City: Editorial Patria, 1954.

Van Alstyne, Richard W. *The Rising American Empire.* New York: Oxford University Press, 1960.

Villaseñor y Villaseñor, Alejandro. *Antón Lizardo. El tratado de MacLane-Ocampo. El brindis del desierto.* Mexico City: Editorial Jus, 1962.

Wallace, Edward S. *Destiny and Glory.* New York: Coward & McCann, 1957.

Ward, Henry George. *Mexico in 1827.* 2 vols. London: H. Colburn, 1828.

Webb, Walter Prescott, ed. *The Handbook of Texas.* 2 vols. Austin: Texas State Historical Association, 1952.

Weinberg, Albert K. *Manifest Destiny: A Study of Nationalist Expansionism in American History.* Baltimore: Johns Hopkins Press, 1935.

Wheat, Raymond C. *Francisco Zarco: El portavoz liberal de la reforma.* Mexico City: Editorial Porrúa, 1957.

Wyllys, Rufus Kay. *The French in Sonora (1850–1854).* Berkeley: University of California Press, 1932.

Zamacois, Niceto de. *Historia de México, desde sus tiempos más remotos hasta nuestros días.* 22 vols. Barcelona: J. F. Parres y Comp., 1876–1902.

Zarco, Francisco. *Historia del congreso extraordinario constituyente [1856–1857].* Mexico City: El Colegio de México, 1956.

Zorilla, Luis G. *Historia de las relaciones entre México y los Estados Unidos de América, 1800–1958.* 2 vols. Mexico City: Editorial Porrúa, 1966.

Index

Acapulco: Ceballos tariff in, 31–32; role in Ayutla Revolution, 32–34, 44, 64; arms shipped to, 33; trade activity of Ajuria and Temple in, 34; railroad concession for, 63–64; loans repaid with customs revenues of, 64; Juárez cabinet stops at, 112

Acapulco, Plan of, 31, 61

Admiralty court (U.S.), 147

Advisory commissions, 64

Agrarian democracy, 14

Agriculture (Mexico): conditions at independence, 2; impact of transportation cost on, 18; advisory commission created for, 64; Butterfield's views on, 113

Ajuria, Gregoria de: role in loans to Ayutla rebels, 33–34; background of, 34; loan to Comonfort government, 64–65; owner of newspaper *El Estandarte Nacional*, 65; gives assistance to Comonfort, 95, 97

Alabama, 65, 113

Alamán, Lucas: political role of, 3; supports monarchy, 3, 13; role in Santa Anna government, 5, 15; death of, 5; economic views of, 15–16; attitude toward United States, 36–38; requests French aid, 37–38

Alcabalas, 21–22, 61

Alliance, Anglo-French: French seek against United States, 46–47, 59, 149

Alliance, United States-Mexico: rumored, 49; Forsyth proposes, 68–69; Twyman advocates, 119; desired by Juárez government, 126; Ocampo proposes, 129, 131–32; equivalent of protectorate, 132; U.S. reaction to proposal, 132–33; impact on Monroe Doctrine, 132–33; loans endanger, 137; military necessity for, 138; in McLane-Ocampo Treaties, 144

All Mexico movement, 25–26, 29, 39

Almonte, Juan N., 37, 139

Alvarez, Juan: role in Ayutla Revolution, 10, 31–32, 44; military background of, 11; *puros* dominate government of, 11, 58; as interim president, 30, 48, 51; economic views of, 31–32; U.S. recognition of, 48–49, 99; reaction to protectorate idea, 49–50; appoints pro-U.S. cabinet, 52; replaced by Comonfort, 52–53;

Zerman as agent of, 53; conservatives oppose, 57; role in anti-Spanish outbreaks, 59; Fomento Ministry under, 62

"Americanization" of Mexico: Forsyth on, 69, 70–71, 91; in Montes-Forsyth Treaties, 76; Houston on, 114

"Americanization" of Sonora, 133

Amerindian heritage, 17

Anarchy, 139

Annexation (of Mexican territory by United States): protectorate as alternative to, 7, 69, 70–71; U.S. sentiment for, 25–27; Santa Anna on, 42; pro-U.S. sentiment in northwest Mexico, 43; economic domination as alternative to, 68; De Gabriac's view of, 80; as goal of Montes-Forsyth Treaties, 90; Houston opposes, 114. *See also* Territorial expansion; Territory, sale of

Annexation, Canadian, 114

Antiforeignism in the United States, 18

Anti-Spanish outbreaks, 58–59, 71

Anti-United States sentiment, 69

Antón Lizardo, 63–64, 147

Antón Lizardo incident, 147

Appleton, John, 86

Archives, Mexican Foreign Ministry, 65–66, 72

Arias, Juan de Dios, 61

Arista, Mariano, 13–14, 30

Arizona, 122, 125, 133

Arms: Comonfort secures, 33; Butterfield's role in securing, 54, 135; impact of U.S. recognition on purchase of, 100; Zuloaga government seeks, 118; Mata's role in securing, 129

Army (Mexico): during Herrera administration, 12; recruitment policy of, 18; in Plan of Ayutla, 31; Santa Anna dismisses officers of, 37; Butterfield serves in, 54; liberals need to control, 68; Santa Anna subverts, 95; doubts on ability of, 104–5; conservatives receive support of, 111

Army (U.S.), 141

Arriaga, Ponciano, 11–12, 14, 35

Arrioja, Manuel, 35

Asylum: Miguel Lerdo receives in U.S. legation, 68, 109, 121

Augusta, Georgia, 65
Austria, 135
Ayuntamiento (Mexico City), 12
Ayutla, Plan of: proclaimed, 10, 14; provisions of, 31; amended by Plan of Acapulco, 31; economic content of, 31–32; relation to Gadsden Treaty, 44; conservatives endorse, 48; mandates constitutional congress, 60
Ayutla rebels: U.S. support for, 48, 52; Butterfield supplies arms to, 54; divisions among, 58; loans to, 64
Ayutla Revolution: centennial of, 1; new liberal leadership, 10; United States role in, 10; fails to defeat conservatives, 30; sets pattern for U.S.-Mexican relations, 30; forms government, 30; economic features of, 30–32; seeks U.S. aid, 32–35; impact on Gadsden Treaty ratification, 43; impact of Gadsden Treaty on, 44; Gadsden recommends support of, 44–45; economic development during, 53–54; fails to unite country, 57

Baja California: filibustering expeditions in, 38–39, 41–42, 46, 53; United States desires to purchase, 41, 87, 111–12, 127; in proposed boundary treaty, 103; pearl fisheries at, 107; in Churchwell protocol, 122; Mata's position on sale of, 122–23, 131; Ocampo rejects sale of, 124; McLane's instructions on, 124; Buchanan's determination to purchase, 127; Ocampo's strategy to avoid sale of, 129–32; McLane believes Juárez will sell, 130; lack of agreement on, 134; willingness of liberals to sell, 135; Miguel Lerdo's effort to save, 136; excluded from McLane-Ocampo Treaties, 141
Balance-of-power in Western Hemisphere, 37–38, 47
Banco de Avío (development bank), 16, 49
Barron, Eustaquio: ordered expelled from Mexico, 58, 60
Belgium, 23
Benjamin, Judah P., 28; considered for ministership, 65; role in Buchanan's nomination and election, 86; role in Louisiana Tehuantepec Company, 86–93, 138; influences Buchanan's Mexican policy, 87–88; brings instructions to Forsyth, 88; dispute with Forsyth, 89–93; Forsyth introduces to Comonfort, 90; diary of, 92; Forsyth's charges against, 92–93; Buchanan seeks to counter charges of favoritism to, 134; fails to raise capital for Louisiana Tehuantepec Company,

138. *See also* Louisiana Tehuantepec Company
Black, John: U.S. consul, 105, 138
Black Sea: Gulf of Mexico compared to, 47
Boundary (Mexico-United States): difficulty in defining, 12, 39–40, 122; Gadsden's view of natural boundary, 39; in Treaty of Guadalupe Hidalgo, 40; Gadsden's instructions on, 40; Santa Anna's willingness to negotiate on, 41; in Gadsden Treaty, 41–43; Forsyth's instructions on, 87–88. *See also* Territorial expansion; Territory, sale of
Brading, David A., 14
Brazos Santiago, Texas, 133
Brownsville, Texas, 35
Buchanan, James: role in failure of plans for protectorate, 8; role in failure of Montes-Forsyth and McLane-Ocampo Treaties, 8; lack of appreciation of economic factors, 8; expansionist policy of, 8, 26, 113, 150–52; erroneously gives Juárez military rank, 25; suggests protectorate over Mexico, 26; Forsyth opposes policies of, 76, 88–90; Robles frightened by election of, 78; retention of Forsyth, 79, 94; rejects Montes-Forsyth Treaties, 79–80; views of, 85; influences policy of Franklin Pierce, 85; public career of, 85; nomination and election of, 85–86; campaign biography of, 86; influence of sectionalism and slavery on Mexican policy of, 86; inaugural address, 86; defines two methods of expansion, 86, 113–14; condemns filibustering, 86, 114; instructions to Forsyth, 87–88; Forsyth proposes protectorate to, 91; Benjamin and Forsyth appeal to, 92–93; chastizes Forsyth, 93–94; restates Mexican policy, 94, 110, 113, 124, 127; on recognition of Zuloaga government, 99; reaction to Juárez government's request for recognition, 100; relations with Jane Cazneau, 100–1; Mata's interview with, 101; recommends publicity to reverse U.S. policy, 101; promises to recall Forsyth, 102; requests Mata remain in Washington, 102, 108; changes attitude toward Juárez government, 108–9; reviews Mexican policy, 108–11; proposes military protectorate, 111, 115, 141; pressures Juárez government to sell territory, 111–12; reaffirms policy of territorial expansion and control of Tehuantepec transits, 113, 124, 127; sees purchase or migration of Yankees as means of achieving goals, 113–14; requests congressional authority to use force, 114–15, 123, 140–41; reports

to Congress on Mexican relations, 115, 140–41; view of presidential power, 115; Houston's influence on, 115; pro-liberal pressures on, 116; delays recognition, 116, 123–24; expects conservative offers on Sonora and Chihuahua, 116–17; seeks highest bid for recognition, 116–18; treatment of Forsyth, 116; requests Butterfield's views, 116; factors forcing recognition of Juárez government, 117–23; appoints Churchwell as special agent, 118; Churchwell reports to, 122; reaction to Miramón's attack on Veracruz, 124; view of frontier transits, 127, 143–44; changes negotiating stance, 129; position on Tehuantepec transits, 130; seeks to break negotiating impasse, 131; reaction to alliance proposal, 132–33; McLane attempts to change policy of, 133–34; attempts to counter favoritism charge, 134; role in Miguel Lerdo loan mission, 136–37; Mata believes is preparing for intervention, 140; conference with Miguel Lerdo and McLane, 141; reaction to McLane-Ocampo Treaties, 144, 146; Mata's report on weakness of, 145; endorses action of U.S. Navy at Antón Lizardo, 147; assessment of policy of, 150–52; impact on Mexico of policies of, 150–51

Buchanan administration: Mexican policy of, 26, 79, 84–88, 90–94; expansion policy of, 26; commercial policy of, 79; retention of Forsyth, 79, 94; explains position on Montes-Forsyth Treaties, 79–80; Forsyth's opposition to policy of, 88–90; failure of Mexican policy of, 90–94; Forsyth seeks support for protectorate scheme from, 104; maintains relations with Zuloaga minister in Washington, 109; loses recognition contest to Juárez government, 127

Butterfield, Carlos: supports U.S. protectorates in Latin America, 8, 113; deals in arms, 33, 135; background of, 54; role in negotiating postal treaty, 54–55; efforts to establish mail-steamer service, 54–55, 67, 112–13; acquires property under Ley Lerdo, 62; influence on Forsyth, 67; supports U.S. economic domination of Mexico, 67; view of Montes-Forsyth Treaties, 73; origin of interest in steamer service, 74; as Mexican agent in ratification of Montes-Forsyth, 78; aid to Comonfort, 97; as agent for Juárez government, 109, 112–13, 134–35; seeks congressional support for steamer service, 112–23; advocates U.S. economic domination of Mexico, 113; Buchanan

requests views of, 116; role in Mata's presentation of credentials, 134; supports Mexican liberals, 150–52

Cabinet crisis, 71–72
Calderón de la Barca, Angel, 38
California: gold rush, 27, 33–34; desire for railroad to, 27; Comonfort seeks loans in, 33; Temple's activities in, 33–34; Ajuria's wealth gained in, 34; Santa Anna prohibits use of coinage from, 37; filibustering activity in, 41, 43–44, 53; Plumb from, 66; freight rates to Arizona, 133
Camargo, 142–43
Canada, 54, 63, 66, 114
Canals, 24
Capital: Louisiana Tehuantepec Company seeks, 138
Capital, foreign: Mexicans seek from United States, 8, 54; liberals lift restraints from, 54; role of Fomento Ministry in attracting, 62; liberal press endorses measures to attract, 63; reform manifesto seeks to attract, 136; Mata convinced of unavailability of, 137; Mata publicizes Mexico as fertile field for, 145
Capital, Spanish: loss of, 2
Capitalism: role in Reforma, 2
Carrera, Martín, 48, 57
Cartas de seguridad (identity documents), 61
Carvajal, José María, 35
Cass, Lewis: rejects Montes-Forsyth Treaties, 79–80; appointed secretary of state, 86; Benjamin charged with belittling, 92; reaction to Forsyth's stance, 107; orders Forsyth to withdraw legation, 109; requests that Migel be allowed to return to Mexico, 109; interview with Mata, 116; reaction to alliance proposal, 132–33
Caste war (Yucatán), 3, 12
Catholicism: Gadsden's view of, 44
Caudillo politics, 3
Cazneau, Jane McManus: background of, 40; also known as Jane Storms, 40; uses pen name of Cora Montgomery, 40; secret mission to Mexico, 40; interest in Santo Domingo, 40; influence on Pierce, 40, 100; kinship with Buchanan, 100; Mata enlists services of, 100–1; performs public relations tasks for Mata, 101–2, 113; speculator in Spanish America, 113; services rewarded, 125; impact of Mexican civil war on concessions of, 138
Cazneau, William L.: husband of Jane McManus, 40; aids Mexican liberal cause, 113;

speculator in Spanish America, 113; receives
wagon road concession, 125; impact of Mex-
ican civil war on concessions of, 138
Ceballos, Juan, 30, 33, 35. *See also* Tariffs,
Ceballos
Celaya, battle of, 103, 112
Central America: de Gabriac wants to protect
from the United States, 80; negotiations for
British withdrawal from, 85; area for U.S.
expansion, 85; Buchanan on acquisition of,
86; Houston proposes protectorate over, 114;
Buchanan requests authority to use force in,
114
Cerro Gordo, battle of, 12
Charleston, 43
Chase, Franklin: U.S. consul, 46
Chihuahua (state): boundary problem, 40;
United States desires to purchase, 41, 87,
103, 141; Buchanan proposes military protectorate over, 114, 141; Twyman opposes
military protectorate over, 119; Churchwell
on wealth of, 122; U.S. Congress rejects
military protectorate over, 123
Church: impact of Ley Lerdo on, 62; Forsyth on
need to control, 68; constitution (1857) on,
94; as principal supporter of Zuloaga government, 102; Forsyth uses in attempting to force
a sale of territory, 102; supports conservatives
in civil war, 102, 111
Church property: in rumored protectorate
treaties, 49, 51; under Ley Lerdo, 58, 62;
threatened by liberal movement, 102; Mata
authorized to mortgage, 109, 126; liberal estimates of value of, 121; nationalization
planned, 122; nationalization of, 135–37;
Ocampo modifies nationalization decree,
136–37
Churchwell, William M.: special mission of,
118–23; visits various Mexican cities, 118,
138; attitude toward Miramón and Zuloaga,
119, recommends recognition of Juárez government, 119–20; on military prospects of
Juárez government, 120; on Miramón's elevation to presidency, 120; veracity of, 121–22;
reports to Buchanan, 122; advocates economic protectorate, 123; Juárez's choice for
U.S. minister, 123; as loan agent for Juárez
government, 134–35; impact of his mission
on position of Temple's mint, 138; supports
Mexican liberals, 150–52
Churchwell mission, 118–23; objectives of, 118;
Twyman's reaction to, 118–19; Forsyth's
possible connection with, 121–22

Churchwell protocol: basis for recognition of
Juárez government, 122; similarity to Montes-
Forsyth Treaties, 122; role in final recognition
agreement, 124; Juárez government resists
terms of, 124–25; McLane aid Juárez govern-
ment in avoiding terms of, 130
Cincinnati, Democratic convention, 53, 65
Citizenship, Mexican, 54, 61
Civil corporations, under Ley Lerdo, 62
Civil war *(Guerra de la Reforma)*, 5, 10; pro-
duces generation of liberal military leaders,
11; begins in Mexico City, 96; commercial
impact of, 109; Buchanan and Forsyth seek to
use to force sale of territory, 110; damages
U.S. interests, 111, 137; description of, 111;
Mata comments on impact of, 138; Miguel
Lerdo seeks compromise end to, 149–50;
McLane-Ocampo Treaties contribute to end-
ing, 149; impact of U.S. policy on, 150–51
Claims convention: Mexico-Spain, 58–59
Claims convention, Mexico-United States. *See*
Montes-Forsyth Treaties, claims convention
Claims (Mexican), 41, 75–76
Claims (U.S.): Gadsden's instructions on, 40;
in Gadsden Treaty, 43; Forsyth's instructions
on, 65, 87; in Pierce's report to Congress, 78;
territorial expansion linked to, 87; Cuevas re-
fuses to negotiate on, 103; Forsyth's proposal
on, 103–4; U.S. public aroused over, 111;
Buchanan estimates size of, 115; Churchwell
protocol on, 122; Mata's instructions on, 126;
amount reduced, 137; McLane-Ocampo
Treaties restricts ability to press, 144
Clayton-Bulwer Treaty, 85
Clergy: constitutional congress considers, 60
Coahuila, 41, 115
Coal: concession, 67
Coastal regions: controlled by liberals, 111
Coastal trade: in Montes-Forsyth Treaties, 75
Cocoa: export potential of, 113
Coffee: export potential of, 113
Coinage, 37
Colombia: Santa Anna return from, 14–15
Colonization, law, 18; advisory commission for,
64; in reform manifesto, 135–36. *See also*
Immigration
Colorado River, 39, 42
Commerce (Mexico): importance of railroads
to, 20; impact of smuggling on, 21; liberal
views on, 21–22; conditions of, 45–46; im-
pact of civil war on, 138
Commercial conventions (southern), 27–28, 43,
46

Commercial expansion (U.S.): Pierce endorses, 39; Gadsden's instructions on, 40–41; de Gabriac fears, 80; in 1856 Democratic party platform, 85–86; Forsyth advocates, 91; Buchanan's view of, 93. *See also* Protectorate

Commercial policy (U.S.): under rumored protectorate treaties, 49; Forsyth's views on, 66, 69; of Buchanan administration, 79

Commercial relations, 65, 72, 122

Communism: United States charged with spreading, 139

Comonfort, Ignacio: *puros* dominate government of, 11; military background of, 11; purchases a sewing machine, 22; prohibits collection of *alcabalas*, 32; influence on goals of Ayutla Revolution, 32; mercantile connections, 32–34; loan mission to United States, 32–35; secures arms, 33; loan contract with Temple, 33–35; protectorate treaties renounced in name of, 49; acknowledges U.S. aid to Ayutla rebels, 52; becomes interim president, 52–53; attitude toward U.S. domination, 52–53; appoints Siliceo as minister of Fomento, 62; comments on importance of Temple and Ajuria loans, 64; Forsyth's view of, 67; efforts to displace as president, 68, 69–71; accepts Miguel Lerdo's resignation, 71; letter to Pierce, 79; suspends constitution, 85, 96; meets representatives of competing Tehuantepec transit groups, 90; rejects treaties proposed by Forsyth, 90; offers railroad transits on frontier to United States, 91; refuses to negotiate away advantages contracted with Louisiana Tehuantepec Company, 92; indicates willingness to sell territory, 94; manipulates congressional elections, 94; lack of liberal support, 94–95; attitude toward constitution, 94–95; aided by Ajuria, 95, 97; plays upon U.S. fear of Europe, 95–96; attempts coup d'etat, 96–97; arrests Juárez, 96; dismisses Congress, 96; seeks monetary aid from France and United States, 96; releases Juárez and recognizes him as constitutional president, 96–97; delays creation of Zuloaga government, 97; exile of, 97; liberals feel deceived by, 100

Comonfort administration: dominated by *puros*, 11; Gadsden cools toward, 52–53; requests recall of Gadsden, 53; leases Mexico City mint to Temple, 64–65; favors newspaper of Ajuria, 65; Miguel Lerdo provokes cabinet crisis in, 71; desire for closer ties with United States, 72, 77–78, 84–85, 150–52; reaction to

Montes-Forsyth Treaties, 77–78; internal struggle between *puros* and *moderados*, 84; opposes sale of territory, 88; negotiations with Louisiana Tehuantepec Company, 90–92; position deteriorates, 94–95; Forsyth attempts to bolster, 95–96; fall of, 96–97; seeks U.S. protectorate, 150–52

Congress (Mexico): reviews Fomento activity, 53, 62; investigates de Gabriac-Zarco incident, 59; considers order expelling Barron, 60; elections for, 94; Comonfort dismisses, 96; McLane believes will reject sale of territory, 130. *See also* Constitutional congress

Congress (U.S.): considers proposed steamer service, 28, 67; considers military protectorate proposal, 111, 115–16, 123; power over reciprocity in McLane-Ocampo Treaties, 143; Mata authorized to use money to secure approval of McLane-Ocampo Treaties by, 145

Conservative government: Forsyth recognizes, 85; refuses to cede territory, 85; Buchanan describes grounds for war against, 115; Robles attempts to seize control of, 117; Buchanan expects to close land deal with, 117; European support for, 123, 138–39; improved relations with Spain, 139; Buchanan recommends punishment of, 141. *See also* Miramón government; Zuloaga government

Conservative press, 145

Conservatives (Mexico): support monarchy, 3, 59; desire foreign protection, 4, 13, 59, 68, 139; assume power, 5; attitude toward United States, 7, 36–38, 50, 139; refuse support to Herrera administration, 13; reaction to Gadsden Treaty, 36; turn against Santa Anna, 44; endorse Plan of Ayutla, 48; Gadsden charges with seeking U.S. protectorate, 50; revolts against liberal governments, 57–58, 64; possible alliance with European powers, 68; British and French support for, 71; opposition to constitution (1857), 84–85, 94; oppose sale of territory, 85; role in Comonfort's coup d'etat, 96; popular support for, 111; Forsyth labels tools of de Gabriac, 117; petition French emperor for aid, 139; charge United States with spreading anarchy and communism, 139; seek compromise end to civil war, 149–50

Consideraciones sobre la situación política y social de la República mexicana en el año 1847, 13

Constitution (1857): Mata's role in, 5; provisions of, 60–61; issuance and implementation of, 84–85, 94; opposition to, 84–85, 94; Forsyth encourages suspension of, 85; Comonfort suspends, 85, 96; fails to protect church, 94; elevates Juárez and Lerdo laws to constitutional precepts, 94; local government support for, 96; Buchanan demands English translation of, 100; Forsyth predicts death of, 112

Constitutional congress, 58, 60–63

Consuls (U.S.): Denman, 33; Pickett, 45–46; 51, 63, 81–82; Chase, 46; Black, 105, 138; exequators suspended, 138

Convention . . . to Enforce Treaty Stipulations and to Maintain Order and Security in the Territories of Each of the Two Republics. *See* McLane-Ocampo Treaties

Córdova, 118

Core region, 111

Cotton, 59, 72, 74

Court of St. James, 85

Cozumel, 138

Crimean War, 46

Cripps, John S., 48

Cuba, 36, 40, 54, 101; Gadsden desires acquisition of, 27–28; Spain fears U.S. threat to, 38; Pierce policy toward, 39; France fears U.S. acquisition, 47, 80; invasion threatened from, 58–59; Buchanan's views on, 85; 1856 Democratic party platform on, 85–86; Spanish plan to safeguard, 95–96; Butterfield compares to Mexico, 112–13; McLane sees McLane-Ocampo Treaties as facilitating acquisition of, 146

Cuernavaca, 48, 54, 99

Cuevas, Luis: foreign minister in Zuloaga government, 103; relations with Forsyth, 103–8; refuses to negotiate boundary change, 103; Forsyth characterizes, 104; orders expulsion of Migel, 107–8; lectures Forsyth on international law and diplomatic practice, 108

Customs rebates: as method of repaying loan, 72, 73–74

Customs revenues (Mexico), 58, 60, 74, 109, 122

Customs revenues (U.S.), 76

Dano, Alphonse, 18, 30–31, 43–44

Davis, Jefferson, 39

DeBow's Commercial Review, 26, 27

Debts, foreign (Mexico): British control of, 58, 70; impact on Reforma governments, 60; Forsyth sees as threat to liberal Mexico, 68; under Montes-Forsyth Treaties, 72; in Churchwell protocol, 122; British and French joint fleets demonstrate to press for payment, 123; nationalization of church property as means of paying off, 135–36

Degollado, Santos: Military experience, 11; loan from Temple, 35; expels Barron, 58, 60; defeat at Tacubaya, 131, 135; calls for nationalization of church property, 135

Democratic administrations: expansion policies of, 26

Democratic convention (1856), 53, 65, 85–86

Democratic party: internal divisions of, 40; Pierce seeks to heal rifts in, 40; Cincinnati convention of, 53, 65, 85–86; 1856 platform, 85–86; impact of sectionalism on, 147–48

Denman, Charles L.: U.S. consul, 33

Development Ministry. *See* Fomento Ministry

Díaz administration: similarity of Reforma programs to those of, 64

Díaz, Porfirio, 5, 10

Diccionario Porrúa, 34

Díez de Bonilla, Manuel: role in negotiating Gadsden Treaty, 42–43; reacts to changes in Gadsden Treaty, 43; requests recall of Gadsden, 45; seeks French protection, 47, seeks U.S. support, 47

Diplomatic Corps, 48, 105

Doblado, Manuel: military experience of, 11; opposes peace settlement with United States, 11–12; shifts from *puro* to *moderado* ranks, 12; Comonfort contacts, 97; as governor of Guanajuato, 97, 98–99; seeks U.S. recognition of Juárez government, 98–99

Don Simplicio (Mexico City), 13

Doyle, Percy W., 42, 43–44

Dunbar, Edward E., 145

Duncan, Sherman and Company, 148

Durango (state), 5, 41, 59, 142–43

East Asia, 27; Pierce's policy toward, 39

Eastern question, 47

Ecclesiastical corporations, under Ley Lerdo, 62

Economic conditions (Mexico): colonial period and independence, 2; impact of political instability on, 3; under Santa Anna, 30–31, 45–46; during Ayutla Revolution, 53

Economic development: liberals emphasize, 10; Zarco warns against overemphasis on, 24–25; debated in constitutional congress, 61; U.S. protectorate as means of achieving, 69; recognition as stimulant for, 126; reform manifesto on, 136; Mata's views on, 140

Economic imperialism: Forsyth's views consonant with, 82–83

Economic problems: role in Reforma, 1–2
Economic progress: importance in liberal thought, 14
Economic protectorate. *See* Protectorate (U.S.)
Economic theory: Mexican liberal attitudes towards, 23
Elections: for Mexican Congress, 94
Elections, U.S. (1860), 147–48, 150
Electoral law (Mexico): changes in, 94
Elgee, Charles, 147
Elite. *See* Upper class
El Paso: boundary problems, 40, 122
Employment: Miguel Lerdo on lack of opportunity for, 16; impact of Ley Lerdo on, 62
England: as industrial model, 23
English Bondholders' Association: reaction to Montes-Forsyth Treaties, 80–81; support Houston's protectorate proposal, 114
English Convention (debt), 72, 122
Englishmen: numbers in Mexico, 93
Entrepreneurs: liberals seek from abroad, 6–7, 135
Esparza, Marcos, 13–14
Estandarte Nacional, El (Mexico City), newspaper owned by Ajuria: 34, 65, 97; given favored treatment by Comonfort, 65, 97
Europe: Mexican conservatives desire protection of, 4; Mexican liberals seek protection from, 6–7; Santa Anna seeks mercenaries in, 42; Gadsden on influence of, 44; de Gabriac fears U.S. power over, 47
Executive agreement: by McLane and Ocampo, 133
Exequators: withdrawn from U.S. consuls, 138
Expansionism (U.S.). *See* Territorial expansion (U.S.)
Exports (Mexico), 18, 58, 66

Falconnet, F. P.: British banker involved in Sloo's Tehuantepec transits grant, 87–88; Louisiana Tehuantepec Company responsible for debt to, 91, 92
Familial ties: importance of in Mexico, 14–15
Federal District (Mexico): Butterfield acquires property in, 62
Filibustering: during Herrera administration, 12; Walker's Baja California expedition, 38–39, 41–42, 46; French fear of, 38–39; Raousset's Sonora expedition, 39, 43–44; Pierce issues proclamation against, 42; agreement to suppress in Gadsden Treaty, 42–43; French attempts to prevent, 43–44; Zerman's Baja California expedition, 53, 70, 97; Buchanan

condemns, 86, 114; Houston's protectorate project designed to prevent, 114; Mata on, 123; Vidaurri fears, 139
Fiscal condition: Miguel Lerdo on, 69–70; of Zuloaga government, 102
Floods: in France, 59
Florida: role in control of Gulf of Mexico, 27–28
Fomento Ministry (Development Ministry): seeks U.S. capital, 8; Miguel Lerdo's role in, 15, 17, 62, 135; creation of, 16–17; railroad concessions of, 19–20, 63–64; precedent-establishing actions, 22–23; activities reviewed by Congress, 53; approves postal treaty, 55; Manuel Siliceo as minister, 62; congressional decision to retain, 62; Naphegyi as colonization and technology agent for, 63; on property rights for foreigners, 63; grants tramway concession, 63–64; Plumb secures grant from 67; given supervisory power over Louisiana Tehuantepec Company, 91
Force: Forsyth on use of, 104, 106; Buchanan requests congressional authority to use, 114, 115, 123; United States desires unilateral right to employ to protect Tehuantepec transits, 130–31
Forced loans: Forsyth charges tax measure constitutes, 105; Cass rules tax measure was not, 107; under McLane-Ocampo Treaties, 143
Foreign capital. *See* Capital, foreign
Foreign currency: Santa Anna prohibits use of, 37; recognized as legal tender, 63
Foreigners: admired by liberals, 25; as dealt with by constitution (1857), 61; Congress debates restrictions on, 61; property rights of, 62–63; role in Mexican development, 136
Foreign Ministry (Mexico): reaction to Walker expedition, 41; approves postal treaty, 55; foreigners to register with, 61, 63; archives of 65–66, 115; orders expulsion of Migel, 107; of Miramón government protests U.S. recognition of Juárez government, 126
Foreign models: liberal press on use of, 23
Foreign trade (Mexico): factors inhibiting, 2; postindependence position of, 3; Great Britian dominates, 58, 66; Miguel Lerdo's statistical study of, 66; Butterfield's desire to divert to United States, 67; effect of Montes-Forsyth Treaties on, 76
Forsyth, John: racial attitude of, 7, 69; supports U.S. protectorate over Mexico, 8, 70–71, 91, 104–5; background of, 65; appointed minister to Mexico, 65; instructions for mission, 65–

66; economic views of, 66; assumes ministerial duties, 66–67; early views of Comonfort, 67; economic protectorate project of, 67–68; establishes ties with Miguel Lerdo, 68–69; proposes U.S.-Mexican alliance, 68–69; ties with *puro* leaders, 69; view of Mexican resources, 69; on U.S. commercial interests in Mexico, 69; discusses protectorate with Miguel Lerdo, 69; on "Americanizing" Mexico, 69, 70–71, 91; role in Mexican cabinet crisis, 71; negotiates Montes-Forsyth Treaties, 72–76; on British domination of Mexico, 76; opposes Buchanan's territorial expansion policy, 76, 87, 88–89, 91; Robles pleased Buchanan to retain, 79; informed of rejection of Montes-Forsyth Treaties, 79–80; de Gabriac's attitude toward, 80; views consonant with economic imperialism, 82–83; encourages suspension of constitution (1857), 85; attempts to force Zuloaga government to sell territory, 85, 102–8; chooses between liberal and conservative government, 85, 97–99; recognizes conservative government, 85, 95–97; retention by Buchanan administration, 86–87, 94; instructions to, 87–88; attempts to change Buchanan's Mexican policy, 88, 91, 104; on Comonfort administration's opposition to sale of territory, 88; opposes Buchanan's Tehuantepec transits policy, 89; relations with Benjamin, 89–93; attempts to insure failure of Buchanan's Mexican policy, 89–90; introduces representatives of competing Tehuantepec transits groups to Comonfort, 90; presents draft treaties to Comonfort, 90; proposes protectorate as alternative to territorial expansion, 91; role in negotiations between Comonfort administration and Louisiana Tehuantepec Company, 90–92; dispute with Benjamin, 92–93; offers to resign, 93; chastized by Buchanan, 93–94; seeks to strengthen position of Comonfort administration, 95–97; calls for U.S. intervention, 96; recognizes Zuloaga government, 98–99; justifies failure to recognize Juárez government, 98–99; liberals feel betrayed by, 99–100; uses manifest destiny arguments for sale of territory, 102; Buchanan promises to recall, 102; analyzes fiscal position of Zuloaga government, 102; threatens use of force, 103, 106; adopts plan to force sale of territory or collapse of Zuloaga government, 103; describes members of Zuloaga government, 104; pursues protectorate contrary to instructions, 105; challenges Zuloaga

government on tax decree, 105–8; avoids trap set by Zuloaga government, 106–7; recall requested, 107; lectured by Cuevas, 108; breaks relations with Zuloaga government, 108; aids liberals in Mexico City, 109; remains in Mexico after breaking relations, 109; Cass orders withdrawal of mission of, 109; Buchanan blames for failure of Mexican policy, 110; predicts death of constitution (1857), 112; condemns Juárez government, 112; returns to United States, 116; demands to return as minister, 116; resigns, 116; Buchanan's treatment of, 116; explores recognition with Mata, 116; comments on Mexican conservatives, 117; departure from Mexico, 121; protection and promotion of Miguel Lerdo, 121; possible influence on Juárez government, 121; possible connection with Churchwell mission, 121–22; resignation forces Buchanan to act, 123; support for Mexican liberals, 150–52

Forsyth, John (the elder), 65

Forts: Buchanan proposes in Chihuahua and Sonora, 115

France: attitude toward U.S. protectorate over Mexico, 7; Mexican conservatives seek ties with, 13; Santa Anna administration requests aid of, 37–38; seeks to use commercial interests in Mexico against United States, 38; importance of trade relations with United States to, 38; reaction to filibustering activity, 38–39; encourages settlement of Frenchmen in frontier area, 38–39; develops rationale for intervention in Mexico, 39; reaction to Gadsden Treaty, 43–44; importance of Mexican trade to, 47, 149; hostility to Reforma, 57; relations with Reforma governments, 59; Forsyth sees Comonfort as tool of, 67; Forsyth sees as threat to liberals, 68; support for Mexican conservatives, 71, 111; as guardian of world order, 80; Comonfort claims support from, 95–96; Zuloaga government requests aid of, 117; joins British in fleet demonstration off Veracruz, 123, 125; war with Austria, 135; liberals fear intervention in civil war, 139; Romero on Mexican policy of, 151

Freedom of travel: in constitution (1857), 61

Free trade: relationship to smuggling, 21; Mexican liberal views on, 21–23; liberal press on, 21; Miguel Lerdo's views on, 21–22; factor in returning Santa Anna to power, 30; Alvarez decrees on, 31–32; role in Comonfort's rise to interim presidency, 32; Juárez impressed by in United States, 36; Forsyth desires along frontier, 73

Freight rates: impact of executive agreement on, 133

French emperor: arbitrator role in Montes-Forsyth Treaties, 73; Mexican conservatives petition, 139

French goods: price and quality, 80–81

French intervention, 10, 11, 39

Frenchmen: numbers in Mexico, 47, 93

French merchants, 105

Frontier: Gadsden threatens U.S. occupation, 46; U.S. press demands seizure of, 78; United States threatens seizure of, 85, 87; Buchanan proposes military protectorate over, 111, 115, 141; liberal control of, 111; executive agreement on, 133

Frontier conditions: U.S. responsibility for preventing Indian raids along, 41; Forsyth proposes using violence as pretext for seizure, 104; arouse U.S. public, 111; in Buchanan's justification of military protectorate, 115; in McLane's justification of recognition, 125

Frontier reciprocity: Forsyth's instructions on, 65–66; Forsyth's commitment to, 66, 91; treaty proposed by Forsyth, 103; Cuevas refuses to negotiate on, 103; Juárez government seeks to interest United States in, 133; in McLane-Ocampo Treaties, 143. *See also* Montes-Forsyth Treaties, frontier reciprocity; Reciprocity

Frontier transits: Comonfort proposes, 91; Forsyth supports, 91; Juárez government support for, 101, 120, 122–23, 133; in Churchwell protocol, 122; Mata on sale of, 122–23; concession to William L. Cazneau, 125; Buchanan's view of, 127, 143–44; Ocampo seeks to interest United States in, 131; in executive agreement, 133–34; Mata on importance of, 140; in McLane-Ocampo Treaties, 142–43; McLane justifies, 143; Buchanan refuses to pay for, 143–44. *See also* Reciprocity

Fuente, Juan Antonio de la: role in Ayutla Revolution and Reforma, 11; refuses to sign postal treaty, 55; attitude toward negotiations with United States, 137–38, 141; opposes extension of time for ratification of McLane-Ocampo Treaties, 148

Fuentes Mares, José: Mexican historian, 67, 99, 121

Fueros: restricted by Ley Juárez, 58

Gabriac, Jean Alexis de: French minister to Mexico, 39; fear of United States, 46–47, 59, 80–82, 149; on Gadsden's alcoholism 48; charges Gadsden with supporting pro-Alvarez *puros,* 48; attitude toward British, 52; denounces Zerman expedition, 53; seeks military government under Comonfort, 59; incident with Zarco, 59; seeks Anglo-French alliance, 149; support for Mexican conservatives, 71, 105, 117, 138–39; on Montes-Forsyth Treaties, 77, 80–82, 149; sees United States as threat to world civilization, 80; relations with Comonfort, 95–97; French merchants criticize for supporting conservative government tax measure, 105; replaced by Saligny, 149

Gadsden, James: racial views of, 7, 39, 82; expansionist views of, 27–28; anti-British attitude of, 27–28; opposition to All Mexico movement, 39; appointed minister, 39; instructions to, 40–41; attitude toward filibustering, 41–42, 53; negotiating techniques of, 41–42; attitude toward Mexican Catholicism, 44; attitude toward European influence, 44; support for Ayutla rebels, 44–45, 48, 52; post-treaty relations with Santa Anna administration, 44–48; recall requested, 45, 53; de Gabriac charges with alcoholism, 48; support for pro-Alvarez *puros,* 48; refuses to recognize government of Carrera, 48; insults diplomatic corps, 48; recognizes Alvarez government, 48–49, 99; reaction to protectorate treaties, 49–50; pro-liberal stance of, 52; cools toward Comonfort administration, 52–53; reaction to Zerman expedition, 53; role in railroad dedication, 54; attempts to appeal to Mexican people, 55; disdain for Mexicans, 55; ends ministership, 55; evaluation of effectiveness, 55–56, 60; influence on Plumb, 67; seeks release of Zerman prisoners, 70

Gadsden Treaty, 26–27; impact on Mexican domestic politics, 37; negotiation of, 41–42; terms of, 42–43; U.S. Senate approval, 42–43; ratification of, 43; Gadsden's reaction to ratified version, 43; Mexican reaction to, 43; European reaction to, 43–44; impact on Ayutla Revolution, 44; money due under, 52–53; Forsyth to expand U.S. rights under, 87–88; Louisiana Tehuantepec Company's contract weakens U.S. position under, 91; Mexico seeks to nullify U.S. rights under, 131

Garay grant: acquired by Hargous, 39–40; included in Louisiana Tehuantepec Company, 87

Gas lighting: projects for Veracruz and Mexico City, 63; impact of civil war on, 138

Georgia, 65

Germans: numbers in Mexico, 93; Mata arranges for settlement of, 138

Gila River: in Gadsden's instructions, 41

Godoy, José Antonio: role in Reforma, 5; founder and editor of *El Heraldo,* 14; supports Montes-Forsyth Treaties, 76–77

Goicuria, Domingo de: befriends Juárez, 36

Gómez Farías, Benito: seeks U.S. recognition, 98

Gómez Farías, Valentín: as liberal leader, 4; given military rank by *New York Times,* 25; on U.S. support of Ayutla rebels, 48; on protectorate treaties, 50; father of Benito Gómez Farías, 98

González, José Dionisio: railroad concession to, 64

González Ortega, Jesús: military experience of, 10; capture of Mexico City, 149

Government, role in economy. *See* Laissez-faire

Great Britain: rivalry with United States, 25–26; Gadsden's attitude toward, 27–28; U.S. steamer service as means of lessening influence of, 28; reaction to Santa Anna's request for aid, 38, 42; Mexico appeals for aid of, 42; reaction to Gadsden Treaty, 43–44; de Gabriac charges with supporting United States, 52, 149; policy toward Mexico, 58; relations with Reforma government, 58; Barron affair, 58; dominates Mexican foreign trade, 58, 66, 150–52; sympathy for U.S. expansionism, 59; Canadian frontier reciprocity treaty with, 66; influence over Comonfort, 67; control of Mexico's foreign debt, 68; threat of intervention by, 70; support for Mexican conservatives, 71; fleet at Veracruz, 71, 123, 125; Forsyth on domination of Mexico by, 76; Montes-Forsyth Treaties as means of weakening position of, 78; de Gabriac on possible war with Mexico, 80; Buchanan as minister to, 85; Comonfort claims support of, 95–96; Butterfield urges United States replace in dominating Mexican economy, 113; Zuloaga government requests aid of, 117; Churchwell reports on influence of, 122; joins French in fleet demonstration off Veracruz, 123, 125; refuses to protect U.S. interests, 138; liberals fear intervention by, 139; Romero on Mexican policy of, 150–52

Guadalajara: Comonfort's military headquarters, 32; telegraph lines to, 54

Guadalupe Hidalgo, Treaty of: 39; boundary according to, 40; United States released from claims under, 41; signed by government at Querétaro, 99

Guanajuato: independence movement in, 3; Juárez government formed at, 97, 98, 102, 112; Doblado suggests U.S. legation in, 98–99

Guanajuato (state): Doblado as governor of, 98

Guaymas: railroad concession, 19; Raousset's expedition to, 39; transit routes, 122, 133, 142–43

Guerrero: Ayutla Revolution in, 10, 14, 44; mining concession in, 67

Guerrero, Mexican naval vessel, 78

Guerrilla forces: in war against United States, 11–12

Gulf of California: Gadsden to secure port on, 41; Gadsden Treaty provisions on, 42; ports opened on, 63; transit connections with Texas, 91, 120; in proposed boundary treaty, 103; in Churchwell protocol, 122

Gulf of Mexico, 17–18, 47, 85–86

Hacienda Ministry (Treasury Ministry): approves postal treaty, 55; fiscal plight of, 60; Miguel Lerdo as minister of, 69, 71, 135; Ocampo as minister of, 136–37

Hale, Charles A., 1

Hammeken, George L.: Tacubaya tramway contract, 63–64, 138

Hargous, P. A.: secures Garay Tehuantepec grant, 39–40; instructions delivered to Gadsden by agent of, 41; treatment of interests in Gadsden Treaty, 42–43; involvement in Louisiana Tehuantepec Company, 87–89; failure of company of, 135

Heraldo, El (Mexico City): *puro* voice, 5; founded 14; Miguel Lerdo's letter reprinted in, 15; defends Miguel Lerdo's service in Santa Anna administration, 15; on immigration, 17–18, 19; free-trade views of, 21, 32; warns against foreign models, 23; denounces protectorate treaties, 49; supports Montes-Forsyth Treaties, 76–77

Hermosillo, 142–43

Herrera, José Joaquín: administration of, 12–13

Hitchcock and Company: arms sale, 33

Houston, Sam: introduces protectorate proposal, 114–15

Huerta, Epitacio: buries silver on U.S. legation grounds, 109

Iguala, Plan of, 2

Immigration: Mexican views on, 17–19; liberals modify views on, 17–18; racist support for, 17–18; liberals send agents to United States and Europe, 18; linked to railroad construction, 19; Frenchmen in frontier areas, 38–39; in protectorate treaties, 49; United States wishes to divert to Mexico, 51; considered by constitutional congress, 60–61; liberal press endorses, 63; Naphegyi as agent for, 63; special fares for, 74; effect of protectorate scheme on, 93; effect of alliance on, 119; in reform manifesto, 136; Mata arranges for German settlers, 138

Imports (Mexico): origin of, 58, 66

Independence, Mexican: economic consequences of, 2–3

India, 67

Indians, border raids: during Herrera administration, 12; U.S. responsibility for, 41; Montes-Forsyth on claims for 73; Forsyth uses to argue for sale of territory, 103

Indigo: potential export of, 113

Industrialization: Mexican desire for, 14, 23; impact of high transportation costs on, 18

International law: Forsyth cites, 105–6; Cuevas lectures Forsyth on, 108

Intervention, British: threat of, 70

Intervention, European: conservatives court, 68; Houston's protectorate to forestall, 114, U.S. alliance to protect Mexico from, 132; threat of, 135; Buchanan on, 140; McLane-Ocampo Treaties may have forestalled, 149

Intervention, French: relationship to Reforma, 1; Jecker loan pretext for, 139; basis of, 150

Intervention, United States: liberals' desire for, 67–68, 130–31; Forsyth calls for, 96; Buchanan desires unilateral right for, 130, 140–41; McLane threatens, 131–32; Mata on granting unilateral right for, 139–40; mutual right of in McLane-Forsyth Treaties, 144–45

Iron: concession for, 67

Isthmian transits: in 1856 Democratic party platform, 85–86

Jackson, Andrew, 65

Jalapa, 5, 14–15; Churchwell visits, 118

Jalisco: Degollado as governor of, 58, 60

Jarauta, Plan of, 12

Jecker loan, 139

Jewelry; Migel involved in, 107

Johnston, Joseph: accompanied McLane to Veracruz, 134–35

Juárez, año de, 1

Juárez, Benito: cult of adulation of, 1; role in Reforma, 5, 11; role in Ayutla Revolution, 10; road-building program of, 19; given military rank by Buchanan and *New York Times*, 25; exiled to New Orleans, 35–36; friendship with La Sere, 36, 123; in Alvarez cabinet, 52; supports Montes-Forsyth Treaties, 77; opposes sale of territory, 95; as chief justice and ex officio vice-president, 95; in Comonfort coup d'etat, 96–98; Comonfort recognizes as constitutional president, 96–98; escapes to Guanajuato, 97, 98; Forsyth warns against protectorate under, 104; sails with cabinet from Manzanillo to Veracruz, 112; Churchwell interviews, 120; Churchwell on age of, 121; seeks to have Churchwell appointed U.S. minister, 123; justifies basis of U.S. recognition, 125–26; on sale of Baja California, 130; on ratification of McLane-Ocampo Treaties, 148; rejects compromise end of civil war, 149–50; returns to Mexico City, 150

Juárez government: established at Guanajuato, 97, 98, 102, 112; importance of U.S. recognition to, 98–99; escapes from western Mexico, 100, 102; finds refuge in Veracruz, 102, 112; Forsyth hopes to recognize, 108–9; deterioration of position, 109; struggle for U.S. recognition, 111–28; attitude on boundary change, 111–12; foreign policy, 112; finds refuge in Veracruz, 112; Forsyth condemns, 112; factors forcing Buchanan to recognize, 117–23; Churchwell's mission to, 118–23; Churchwell recommends recognition of, 119–20; reportedly enticing Miramón to attack Veracruz, 120; popular support of, 120; Forsyth's possible influence on, 121; angered at delay in recognition, 124; resists Miramón's attack on Veracruz, 124–25; recognized by United States, 125; modifies Louisiana Tehuantepec Company contract, 125; Miramón government protests recognition of, 126; negotiating stance of, 129–32; seeks to interest United States in frontier reciprocity and transits, 133; fiscal plight of, 135; issues reform manifesto and nationalization decree, 135–36; unable to protect U.S. citizens and interests, 138; Viduarri abandons, 139; dissensions within, 139; Miguel Lerdo refuses to rejoin, 139; rejects United States mercenaries, 139; reaction to McLane-Ocampo Treaties, 143–45; decrees Miramón government ships as pirates, 147; refuses to extend ratification time for McLane-Ocampo Treaties, 148; improved military prospects of, 148; strengthened by McLane-Ocampo Treaties, 148–49; moves from Veracruz to Mexico City, 149; impact of U.S. policy on, 150–51; sought U.S. protectorate, 150–52

Juntas de mejoras materiales, 22

Junta directiva de caminos de hierro, 64

Junta revolucionaria: activities in the United States, 35

Kansas: slavery question in, 115–16

Kansas-Nebraska Act: exacerbates sectionalism, 85

Labor: availability in Mexico, 18

Laissez-faire: role in Reforma, 2; liberal views on, 22–23

Land titles: Gadsden Treaty provisions on, 42

La Paz, Baja California: Walker expedition to, 41; Zerman expedition to, 53; Migel involved in pearl fisheries at, 107

Lapegre (Louisiana bank president), 135

La Sere, Emile: editor of *The Louisiana Courier,* 36; friendship with Juárez, 36, 123; role in Louisiana Tehuantepec Company, 87–88, 90; meets Comonfort, 90; as loan agent for Juárez government, 109, 112, 127; propagandist for Juárez government, 112; mutual friend of Juárez and McLane, 123

Latin America: Butterfield advocates U.S. economic protectorate over, 8, 113; U.S. Congress interest in economic domination of, 28; Pierce's policy toward, 39; Democratic party platform on, 85–86

Legal tender: law recognizing foreign currency as, 63

Legation (U.S.): Miguel Lerdo receives asylum in, 68, 109, 121; liberals bury silver on grounds of, 109

Lerdo de Tejada, Miguel: role during Reforma, 5; role in Ayutla Revolution, 11; as *puro* leader, 11; pushed for reform during U.S. occupation, 12; labeled as traitor, 12, 15; cooperation with U.S. occupation forces, 12; participation in Santa Anna administration, 14–22; liberals approve participation in Santa Anna administration, 14; as delegate in Santa Anna escort, 14–15; familial ties with Santa Anna, 14–15; political role (1855–61), 15; similarity of views to those of Alamán, 15; letter to Santa Anna, 15–22; identifies economic factors bringing Santa Anna to power, 15–16; on role of government, 16; economic development plan, 16–21; on importance of railroads, 18–21, 22; free trade views, 21–22; role in creation of precedents by Fomento ministry, 22–23; laissez-faire views of, 22–23; Santa Anna ignores advice of, 30; de-

nounces protectorate treaties, 49; liberal press defends for serving under Santa Anna, 53; admiration for United States, 57; on Ley Lerdo, 62; publishes statistical study of Mexican foreign trade, 66; as originator of economic protectorate scheme, 67–68; efforts to replace Comonfort as president, 68, 69; close relations with Forsyth, 68, 69, 104, 121; given asylum in U.S. legation, 68, 109, 121; assists Plumb in securing concessions, 69; provokes cabinet crisis, 69–71; resigns from Comonfort cabinet, 71; de Gabriac's attitude toward, 80; Churchwell describes as pro-United States, 121; agrees to Churchwell protocol, 122; role in origin of alliance proposal, 132; seeks alternative to sale of territory, 135–37; role in nationalization of church property, 135–37; loan mission to United States, 136–37, 139; strained relations with Ocampo, 137; crisis resulting from failure of loan mission, 137; refused permission to negotiate treaty, 137; arranges for U.S. mercenaries, 139, 141; refuses to rejoin Juárez government, 139; returns to Veracruz, 141; role in negotiation of McLane-Ocampo Treaties, 141–42; seeks compromise end to civil war, 149–50; seeks U.S. protectorate, 150–52

Lerdo de Tejada, Sebastián: role in Ayutla Revolution and Reforma, 10–11; as foreign minister, 89–92; rejects Buchanan's Mexican policy, 90–92

Lettson, William Garrow: British chargé, 59, 71; reaction to Montes-Forsyth Treaties, 80–81

Levasseur, André: French minister, 27–28

Ley Juárez, 58; elevated to constitutional precept, 94

Ley Lerdo: attacking church property, 58; provisions of, 62; Miguel Lerdo's rationale for, 62; results of, 62; approved by Congress, 62; elevated to constitutional precept, 94; role in Comonfort's coup d'etat, 96; relationship to decree nationalizing church property, 136–37

Liberalism (Mexico): similarity of views to those of positivism, 24

Liberal party (Mexico): origins of, 3

Liberal press: reprints Miguel Lerdo's letter to Santa Anna, 15; defends Miguel Lerdo for serving under Santa Anna, 15, 53; on free trade, 21; reaction to protectorate treaties of 1855, 49–50; defends Fomento Ministry and Miguel Lerdo, 53; endorses measures to attract foreign immigrants and investments,

63; takes sides in cabinet crisis, 71; supports steamer service proposal, 74; reaction to McLane-Ocampo Treaties, 145–46

Liberals (Mexico): views of, 2–4; weaknesses of, 3–4; recognize need for foreign protector, 4; relationship of *puros* to, 4–5; overthrow Santa Anna, 5; view United States as model, 5–7; fear U.S. expansionism, 6; desire U.S. protectorate, 6–8, 13, 67–68, 82, 150–52; support Montes-Forsyth Treaties, 8, 77–80; fail to achieve desired relationship with United States, 8; emphasis on economic development, 10; attachment to United States, 10, 28–29, 100, 130–31, 150–52; emergence of new generation of, 10–11, 24–25, 28; impact of United States on, 11; cooperate with U.S. occupation forces, 12; reject Mexico's colonial past, 13; desire to regenerate Mexico, 13; Miguel Lerdo as spokesman for, 14; desire to industrialize, 14, 23; political principles of, 14; importance of economics to, 14; hope to convert Santa Anna, 15; views on immigration, 17–18; views on transportation, 18–21; support for railroads, 19–21; views on commerce, 21–22, views on free trade, 21–23; views on progress, 22; fascination with machines, 22; economic thought of, 22–23; admiration of foreigners, 25; exiled to United States, 35–36; reaction to Gadsden Treaty, 36; create government, 48–49; reaction to protectorate treaties, 49–50; Gadsden turns against government of, 52–53; attitude toward Santa Anna government, 53; favor U.S. capital, 54; lift restraints on foreign economic activity, 54; refuse compromise with conservatives, 57; views in constitutional congress, 60–63; failure of reform program of, 64; lack of economic nationalism, 68; Forsyth wishes to use, 69; factors promoting support of protectorate by, 82; lack of support for Comonfort, 94–95; reaction to U.S. recognition of Zuloaga government, 99–100; attitude toward Comonfort, 100; consider United States as "natural ally," 100; position in civil war (Mexico), 111; lack of popular support for, 111; reaction to military protectorate proposal, 117; fear French intervention, 117; Twyman on, 118; Churchwell supports, 120, 150–52; reaction to Mon-Almonte Treaty, 139; reaction to McLane-Ocampo Treaties, 146; win civil war (Mexico), 149; impact of U.S. policy on, 150–52; Yankee supporters of, 150–52

Loan bank. See *Banco de Avío*

Loans (Mexico): liberals seek from United States, 6–7, 32–35, 70, 111–12, 135–37; Comonfort's loan mission, 32–35; from Temple, 33–35; under protectorate treaties, 49; liberals' need for, 68; Miguel Lerdo proposes United States make, 70; Buchanan's rejection of, 93; sought by Comonfort administration, 95, 97; Mata seeks in New York, 100, 109, 122, 129, 148–49; Mata sees recognition as pre-condition for, 100; importance to Juárez government of U.S. loans, 111–12; Mata's authority for, 126–27; recognition the key to, 126–27; Mata's limited success in raising, 134–35; use of nationalized church property to secure, 135–37; Miguel Lerdo's loan mission, 136–37, 139; Mata on availability of, 137; impact of McLane-Ocampo Treaties on availability of, 148–49

Local government (Mexico): support for constitution (1857), 96

London, 8, 138

Los Angeles, 33–34

Louisiana Courier (New Orleans): La Sere edits, 36

Louisiana Tehuantepec Company: benefits from La Sere-Juárez friendship, 36; Benjamin's role in, 86; formation, 87; favored by Buchanan's Mexican policy, 87–89; frail nature of, 88; Benjamin and La Sere negotiate with Comonfort administration on behalf of, 90–92; made subservient to Fomento Ministry, 91; transit contract terms, 91–92; contract modified, 125; United States wishes to limit profits of, 134, 142; impact of Hargous bankruptcy on, 135; impact of civil war (Mexico) on, 138; attempts to raise capital in London, 138

Lower class. See Working class

MacCorkle, Stuart A.: on recognition, 99

Machines: liberal fascination with, 22

Machinists: trained by steamer service, 72–74

McLane-Ocampo Treaties, 8, 141–49; lack of archival materials on, 141; result from meeting of Buchanan, Miguel Lerdo, and McLane, 141–42; negotiation of, 141–44; transits and commerce provisions, 142–44; convention, 144; Buchanan's reaction to, 144; Juárez government reaction to, 144–45; Mexican opposition to, 145–46; text published in *National Intelligencer,* 146; proposed amendments to, 146–47; U.S. Senate consideration of, 146–

48; U.S. banker offers to guarantee ratification of, 148; Juárez government refuses to extend ratification time, 148; results of, 148–49; improve credit status of Juárez government, 148–49; cause dissension among European powers, 149

McLane, Robert M.: slave state origin, 7; supports U.S. protectorate, 8, 133; friendship with La Sere, 123; appointed minister, 123; instructions to, 123–24; arrives Veracruz, 124; works out compromise basis for recognition, 124–25; recognizes Juárez government, 125; commits United States to respect Mexican sovereignty and territorial integrity, 126; submits draft boundary and transits treaties, 130; reaction to "Tacubaya massacre," 131; reaction to alliance proposal, 132–33; signs executive agreement, 133; seeks to change Buchanan's Mexican policy, 133–34; warns of Lerdo's loan mission, 136; requests new instructions, 137; Temple appeals for protection of, 138; returns to United States for consultations, 138; view of military alliance, 138; new instructions for, 140; returns to Veracruz, 141; negotiates McLane-Ocampo Treaties, 141–44; pushes to limit profits of Louisiana Tehuantepec Company, 142; justifies frontier reciprocity and transits 143; view of McLane-Ocampo Treaties, 146; requests permission to use U.S. Navy against Miramón government ships, 147; supporter of Mexican liberals, 150–52

Magdalena (Sonora): on transit route, 142–43

Mails (U.S.): use of Tehuantepec transits, 142

Manifest destiny: goals served by protectorate, 7; interest in Mexico, 25–27; interest in Cuba and Caribbean, 26–27; influence on Pierce policy, 40; Gadsden uses arguments of, 41; Buchanan endorses, 86–87; Forsyth uses arguments of, 102–3

Manufacturing: Forsyth's view of, 66

Manzanillo: railroad concessions involving, 19; Alvarez tariff in, 32; Juárez cabinet sails from, 112

Marcy, William L.: instructions to Gadsden, 40–41; refuses to recall Gadsden, 45, 53; instructions to Forsyth, 65–67; role in failure of Montes-Forsyth, 79

Márquez, Leonardo: role in "Tacubaya massacre," 131

Maryland, 123

Masonic lodges: promoted by Poinsett, 11

Massachusetts, 28, 113

Mata, José María: role in Reforma, 5; recognizes lack of capital in United States, 8; appointed minister in Washington, 8, 100; role in Ayutla Revolution, 10; member of dominant *puro* group, 11; background of 12; exiled to New Orleans, 12, 35–36; admiration for United States, 12, 57; free-trade views, 21; purchases sewing machine, 22; secretary of *junta revolucionaria,* 35; instructions as minister, 100; relationship to Ocampo, 100; visits Washington, 100; seeks loans, 100, 109, 122, 129, 148–49; pessimism of, 100–1, 122–23, 139–40; enlists services of Jane Cazneau, 101–2; reaction to interview with Buchanan, 101; publishes pro-Juárez articles, 101–2; second conference with Buchanan, 102; interview with Cass, 116; competes with Robles for U.S. favor, 116; encourages U.S. recognition, 116–17; sees recognition as automatic, 123; returns to Veracruz for consultations, 123; helps prepare McLane for mission, 123–24; delay in recognizing undermines Churchwell protocol, 124; charges Buchanan with timidity, 124; recommends concession to Cazneaus, 125; stresses tie between credit and recognition, 126; loan authority of, 126–27, 148; recommends early agreement with United States, 131; presents credentials, 134; success in raising loans, 134–35, 148; role in failure of Miguel Lerdo's loan mission, 137; on impact of Mexican civil war on foreign investors, 138; arranges for German settlers, 138; supports use of mercenaries, 139–40; social and economic views of, 140; instructed to promote ratification of McLane-Ocampo Treaties, 144–45; hires Dunbar as publicist, 145; on congressional weakness of Buchanan, 145; publishes promotional pamphlet, 145; subsidizes *Mexican Papers,* 145; efforts to secure approval of McLane-Ocampo Treaties, 145–47; lack of understanding of U.S. politics, 147–48; impact of McLane-Ocampo Treaties on loan arrangements of, 148; Romero replaces as minister, 148; sought U.S. protectorate, 150–52

Matamoros: railroad concession to, 64; on transit route, 142–43

Material improvement: liberal attitude toward, 22

Material improvement committees, 22

Material improvement tariff, 64

Material progress: *puro* dedication to, 68

Mathew, George: British minister, 149

Maximilian's empire, 10, 11

Mazatlán: Ajuria and Temple trade with, 34; French consul at, 47; customs revenues to repay loan, 64; in Churchwell protocol, 122; executive agreement on transit route involving, 133; in McLane-Ocampo Treaties, 142–43

Mejía, José A.: Hammeken's father-in-law, 63

Mercenaries: Santa Anna seeks in Europe, 42; Zuloaga requests of France, 117; Miguel Lerdo hires in United States, 139, 141; Mata supports use of, 139–40; Buchanan supports sending to Mexico, 141

Mesilla valley: boundary dispute, 40

Mexican cession: Buchanan's role in highlighted, 86

Mexican Liberalism in the Age of Mora. 1821–1853 (Hale), 1

Mexican Papers: promotional journal, 145

Mexico: colonial period, 2; independence, 2–3; during 1840s, 3; internal conditions after war with United States, 13; United States lacks knowledge of, 25; U.S. desire to annex, 25–27; Benjamin's recommended policy toward, 28; France sees as buffer against United States, 39; compared to Ottoman Empire, 47; Gadsden on "democratizing," 52; debtor status of, 60; Butterfield's desire for economic protectorate status for, 67; Forsyth proposes alliance with, 68–69; Buchanan's policy toward, 84–88, 114–15; refuses to recognize sale of Sloo grant, 87; compared to Cuba in economic value to United States, 112–13; Buchanan requests authority to use force in, 114–15

Mexico City: *ayuntamiento* cooperates with U.S. occupation forces, 12; U.S. occupation, 13; railroad concessions involving, 19, 63–64; Santa Anna abandons, 30; gas lighting project for, 63; concession for tramway to Tacubaya, 63–64; Forsyth's arrival at, 67; Montes-Forsyth Treaties supported by press of, 76–77; recognition and control of, 98–99; archbishop pressures Zuloaga government to sell territory, 102; controlled by conservatives in civil war, 111; Churchwell visits, 118; Juárez government plans to attack, 120, 125; capture by army of González Ortega, 149; Juárez government moves to, 149–50

Mexico: Its Present Government and Its Political Parties: pamphlet by Mata, 145

Michoacán, 5; Ocampo as governor, 12; road building in, 19; Plumb secures concessions in, 67; bishop presses Zuloaga government to sell territory, 102

Migel, Salomon: expelled from Mexico for refusing to pay taxes, 107–8; requests permission to return to Mexico, 109

Military: political power role in Mexico, 10

Militia: Comonfort's service with, 11

Mining: during colonial period, 2; Mexico loses Spanish technology after independence, 2; English speculation in, 3; advisory commission created for, 64; Plumb's concessions for, 67; reform manifesto on, 136

Minnesota, 113

Mint: Temple's lease of Mexico City's, 64–65, 97; impact of Mexican civil war on, 138; Temple suspends operations, 138

Miramón government: United States breaks relations with, 124; protests U.S. recognition of Juárez government, 126; fiscal plight of, 139; makes Jecker loan, 139; reaction to McLane-Ocampo Treaties, 145; purchases warships, 147; protests U.S. naval action at Antón Lizardo, 147; weakens, 148

Miramón, Miguel: Churchwell labels usurper, 119; preparing siege of Veracruz, 120; becomes conservative president, 120; Buchanan frightened by attack on Veracruz by, 124; attack on Veracruz, 124–25, 147

Missouri: treaty article (1831) on, 133

Mobile: steamer service to, 28; Forsyth in, 65

Mobile Register: owned and edited by Forsyth, 65

Moderados: faction defined, 4, views of 4–5; relationship with *puros,* 5; in Herrera administration, 13; support Carrera as interim president, 57; Comonfort's elevation to presidency a victory for, 58

Molina del Rey, battle of, 55

Mon-Almonte Treaty, 139

Monarchy: conservative support for, 3, 13; French support in Mexico, 59, 80

Monitor Republicano, El (Mexico City): on use of guerilla forces, 11–12; analyzes Mexico's problems, 13; attention to economic matters, 14; supports immigration, 17; Gadsden denounces protectorate treaties in, 49–50

Monopolies: liberal views on 21–22; prohibited by constitution (1857), 61

Monroe Doctrine: Democratic party platform on, 85–86; impact of proposed alliance on, 132–33

Monterrey: railroad concession involving, 64;

Vidaurri *cacique* of, 84; on transit route, 142–43

Montes, Ezequiel: appointed foreign minister, 71–72; negotiates Montes-Forsyth Treaties, 72–76

Montes-Forsyth Treaties, 8, 66, 72–83, 91, 110, 122, 149; similarity to protectorate proposal, 72; terms of, 72–73; negotiation of, 72–76; Mexico City press support for, 76–77; Forsyth's arguments for, 76–77; Comonfort administration's justification of, 77–78; Mexican liberals support, 77–80; Robles instructed to work for, 78; Comonfort administration attempts to insure ratification of, 78–79; Pierce administration refuses to submit to Senate, 79; rejected by Buchanan, 79–80, 110; reaction of French merchants in Mexico to, 80–81; reaction of English bondholders to, 80–81; British and French reaction to, 80–82; reasons for failure of, 82–83; annexation as ultimate goal of, 91; similarity to Churchwell protocol, 122; compared to McLane-Ocampo Treaties, 149

Montes-Forsyth Treaties, claims convention, 73, 75–76

Montes-Forsyth Treaties, frontier reciprocity, 73, 75–76

Montes-Forsyth Treaties, General convention, 73

Montes-Forsyth Treaties, loan, 72–74

Montes-Forsyth Treaties, postal, 72–75

Montgomery: southern commercial convention at, 27

Montgomery, Cora: pen name of Jane Cazneau, 40

Mora, José María Luis: liberal leader, 3, 17, 18

Morelia, cathedral of: burial on U.S. legation grounds of silver from, 109

Morelos: anti-Spanish actions in, 59

Morelos, José María: Alvarez served under, 11

Mortmain, Ley Lerdo on, 62

Most-favored-nation clause; Forsyth cites in protesting tax measure, 105–6

Naphegyi, Gabor: background of, 62–63; acquires property under Ley Lerdo, 62; gas lighting projects of, 63; as Fomento agent, 63; assists Forsyth aid Comonfort, 95; impact of civil war (Mexico) on interests of, 138; involved in effort to end civil war (Mexico), 149–50

Napoleon III: Santa Anna seeks aid of, 37. *See also*, French emperor

National Archives (U.S.): records of, 130

National Intelligencer, 146

Nationalism: as factor in Mexican policy of United States, 119

Nationalization. *See* Church property

National market (Mexico): impact of transportation costs on, 18

Natural boundary: as proposed by Gadsden, 39; as proposed by Forsyth, 103

Navigation Act, Mexican (1854): issued, 30; repealed, 63

Navy (Mexico): surplus officers of, 74

Navy (U.S.): Forsyth on use of, 69; Buchanan requests authority to use, 114, 123, 141; *Saratoga* visits Mexican ports, 117; U.S. merchants request protection by, 138; presence increased along Mexican coast, 138, 140; action at Antón Lizardo, 147; admiralty court rules on action at Antón Lizardo, 147

New Mexico: boundary problems of, 40; treaty provisions on, 133

New Orleans: Mata sent as prisoner of war, 12; liberals visit, 23–24, 35–36; desire for railroad to California, 27; proposed steamer service from, 28, 72–74; liberal exiles active in, 35–36; trade with Veracruz, 46; Hammeken from, 63; railroad company organized in, 64; Forsyth and Plumb travel from, 66–67; Buchanan adopts policies favorable to, 86; Louisiana Tehuantepec Company in, 87–88; Juárez and cabinet stop at, 112; Juárez government financial agents in, 127; admiralty court in, 147

New York: Ceballos in, 33; Comonfort seeks loans in, 33–35; Mata seeks loans in, 100, 109, 122, 129, 148–49; bankers pressure Buchanan to recognize Juárez government, 116; Juárez government financial agents in, 127; freight rates to Arizona, 133

New York Herald: supports Montes-Forsyth Treaties, 78–79; publishes pro-Juárez articles, 101–2

New York Times: coverage of Mexico, 25; Dunbar correspondent for, 145

Nicaragua: Walker expedition to, 86, 114; Buchanan requests authority to use force in, 115; U.S. Senate rejects treaty with, 146

Nogales, Rancho de (Arizona): transit route to, 142–43

Nuevo Leon: United States desire to purchase, 41

Oaxaca, 5; Juárez as governor of, 19, 77

Ocampo, Melchor: role in Reforma, 5, 11; role in Ayutla Revolution, 11; opposes peace settlement with United States, 11–12; as governor of Michoacán, 12, 19; serves in Arista administration, 13–14; supporter of agrarian democracy, 14; charges Miguel Lerdo with betraying Reforma, 15; purchases sewing machine, 22; exiled to New Orleans, 35; role in *junta revolucionaria,* 35; in Alvarez cabinet, 52; as foreign minister in Juárez government, 98, 123–37; 141–45; attempts to secure U.S. recognition, 98–99, 100; relationship to Mata, 100, 123; Churchwell on, 121; role in Churchwell protocol, 122, 124; finds recognition compromise, 124; opposes sale of territory, 126, 129–32; originates alliance proposal, 132; signs executive agreement, 133; opposes limits on profits of Louisiana Tehuantepec Company, 139, 142; role in failure of Miguel Lerdo's loan mission, 136–37; strained relations with Miguel Lerdo, 137; negotiates McLane-Ocampo Treaties, 141–44; extolls McLane-Ocampo Treaties, 144–45; seeks U.S. protectorate, 150–52

Orizaba: Churchwell visits, 118

Osollo, Luis: chief of conservative army, 104

Ostend Manifesto: on Cuba, 35

Ottoman empire: Mexico likened to, 47

Otway, L. C.: British minister, 105; refuses to protect U.S. interests, 138; supports conservative government, 139

Pachuca: location of Real del Monte mine, 3

Packet service, Veracruz-New Orleans: subsidies for, 74

Panama: Juárez and cabinet visit, 112; Buchanan requests authority to use force in, 115

Partido Revolucionario Institutional (PRI), 1

Patronage: Buchanan's rule on, 86

Payno, Manuel: on value of railroads, 20

Pearl fisheries; at La Paz, Baja California, 107

Perote: Churchwell visits, 118

Pickett, John T.: U.S. consul, 45–46, 51, 63, 81–82

Pierce, Franklin: responds to Young America movement, 26; advocates territorial expansion, 26, 39; endorses commercial expansion, 39; military experience in Mexico, 40; friendship with Jane Cazneau, 40; issues antifilibustering proclamation, 42; reaction to Gadsden Treaty, 42–43; Mexican policy of, 65; appoints Forsyth minister to Mexico, 65; on claims against Mexico, 78; reaction to Montes-Forsyth Treaties, 79; Buchanan's influence on, 85

Pierce administration: expansion policy of, 26;

Mexican policy of, 39–41; instructions to Gadsden, 40–41; refuses to submit Montes-Forsyth Treaties to Senate, 79

Pinal, L.: free-trade advocate, 21

Plan of Acapulco. *See* Acapulco, Plan of

Plan of Ayutla. *See* Ayutla, Plan of

Plan of Iguala (1821), 2

Plan of Jarauta, 12

Plan of Tacubaya, 96

Plumb, Edward Lee: arrives in Mexico, 66–67; secures Fomento concessions, 67, 69; seeks approval of Montes-Forsyth Treaties, 78; as loan agent, 148

Poinsett, Joel: ministership to Mexico, 11

Polk, James K.: seeks alternative to annexation, 26; Buchanan as secretary of state under, 85

Porfiriato: U.S. economic interests in, 2

Portilla, Anselmo de la: historian cited, 34

Positivism: compared to liberalism of 1850s, 24

Postal treaty (1856): negotiation of, 54–55

Postal treaty: Forsyth's instruction on, 65; Butterfield's support for, 67; Miguel Lerdo's support for, 70; Forsyth proposes to Washington, 91; Cuevas refuses to negotiate on, 103. *See also* Montes-Forsyth Treaties, postal

Post Office Ministry (Mexico): approves 1856 Postal Treaty, 55

Post Office (U.S.): subsidizes packet service, 74; grants mail contract, 125

Presidential power (Mexico): in Plan of Ayutla, 31; in Plan of Acapulco, 31; in constitution (1857), 61

Presidential power (U.S.): Buchanan's interpretation of, 115, 138, 140; McLane warned of limits of, 138

PRI (Partido Revolucionario Institucional), 1

Prieto, Guillermo: opposes peace settlement with United States, 11–12; serves in Arista administration, 14; views on free trade, 21; views on laissez-faire, 22; quoted on progress, 22; in Alvarez cabinet, 52

Princeton: Forsyth graduate of, 65

Profits: United States desires to limit in Tehuantepec transits, 134, 142

Progress: railroads symbol of, 19–21; liberal views on, 22; reform manifesto on, 136

Pronunciamientos: in favor of *religión y fueros,* 68; by Zuloaga at Tacubaya, 96

Propaganda: favorable to Juárez government, 112, 116

Property: rights of foreigners, 61, 63

Protection: of U.S. citizens, 131, 138. *See also* names of individual citizens

Protectorate: political sensitivities to use of term

in Mexico, 7–8, 77; recognition of need for, 13

Protectorate (European); conservatives desire, 4; Gadsden works to prevent, 44–45

Protectorate (U.S.): liberal desire for, 4, 24–25, 57, 117, 130–31, 150–52; *puro* desire for, 6–7, 67–68, 123; as alternative to annexation, 7, 68, 69, 70–71; United States support for, 7–8, 82, 114–15; suggested by Buchanan during war, 26; move to establish after fall of Santa Anna, 49–51; treaties for (1855), 50–51; as proposed to Robles, 50–51; possible U.S. involvement in proposal for, 51, 117; factors promoting liberal support for, 57; Forsyth's plan for, 67–68; Butterfield supports, 67; intimidation by naval forces as alternative to, 69; Miguel Lerdo and Forsyth discuss, 69; proposed to Comonfort cabinet, 69–71; Miguel Lerdo's proposal compared to Montes-Forsyth Treaties on, 72; conditions conducive to, 82; Montes-Forsyth Treaties contained economic basis for, 82–83; Forsyth argues for a policy of, 91, 93, 104, 105; Jane Cazneau's claims compared to, 101; Forsyth pursues against orders, 105; Forsyth claims support for, 106; Juárez government's need for, 112; Houston's proposal for, 114–15; Churchwell endorses, 120–23; Mata on, 123; degree provided for by McLane-Ocampo Treaties, 144

Protectorate (U.S.-military): Buchanan requests congressional authority for, 111, 115, 141; U.S. Congress refuses authorization for, 111, 123; Buchanan presses Juárez government to sell territory by threatening, 111–12; liberals react to proposal for, 117; Twyman warns against, 119

Prussia: Santa Anna requests military aid of, 37–38

Puebla: railroad concessions involving, 19, 63–64; conservative revolts in 58, 64; Naphegyi acquires property in, 62

Puros: faction within liberal ranks, 4–5; views of, 4–8, 22, 60–61, 67–68; political role during Reforma, 5, 11, 58; seek U.S. protectorate, 6–7, 67–68, 150–52; support Montes-Forsyth Treaties, 8; reason for failure of their economic policy, 8; oppose peace settlement with United States, 11–12; support Plan of Jarauta, 12; cooperate with U.S. occupation forces, 12; serve in Arista administration, 13–14; attitude toward progress, 22; Gadsden charged with supporting, 48;

conservatives try to keep from power, 57; role in constitutional congress, 58, 60–61; views as expressed in constitutional congress, 60–61; view of Fomento Ministry, 62; Forsyth on, 67; Forsyth's ties with, 69; support effort to replace Comonfort with Miguel Lerdo, 69, 71; rally to support of Miguel Lerdo, 71; alienated by Comonfort, 94; exclusion from Congress of, 94

Querétaro: location of Mexican government during U.S. occupation of Mexico City, 13; Doblado suggests locating U.S. legation at, 98–99

Racism: as a factor in opposition to U.S. annexation of Mexican territory, 7–8, 82, 119; as basis for support for immigration to Mexico, 17–18; liberals retreat from, 18; in Forsyth's views, 69, 82; as factor in U.S. Mexican policy, 119

Railroads: Miguel Lerdo's views on, 18–21; concessions for, 19, 20, 63–64, 91, 120, 143; immigration stimulated by construction of, 19; as test of Ayutla Revolution, 19–20; liberal support for, 19–21, 91, 120; as symbols of progress, 19–21; inauguration of line to Villa Guadalupe, 20, 54; Payno on value of, 20; Miguel Lerdo suggests subsidies for, 20–21; restored republic's emphasis on, 21; Miguel Lerdo recommends government build and operate, 22; effect of laissez-faire policy on construction of, 22–23; in Tehuantepec Isthmus, 27, 86; advisory commission for, 64; Plumb's interest in, 67; Louisiana interests in, 86; Comonfort offers concessions for, 91; Buchanan's view of concession for, 93; Churchwell reports on, 120, 122; concessions under McLane-Ocampo Treaties, 143

Railroads, U.S. transcontinental: 39–41

Ramírez, Ignacio: views of, 21, 22

Ramsey, Albert C.: acquires railroad concession, 63–64

Raousset de Boulbon, Gaston: expedition to Sonora, 39; impact on French Mexican policy of filibustering of, 43–44

Real del Monte: English investment in, 3; railroad concession involving, 19

Recall: Gadsden's, 45, 47, 53, 60; Forsyth's, 107

Reciprocity: Gadsden's attempts to negotiate on, 54; basis of opposition to McLane-Ocampo Treaties, 146–47. *See also* Frontier reciprocity

Recognition (U.S.): of Carrera government, 48; of Alvarez government, 48, 99; basis for in Mexico, 98–99; Buchanan on conditions for, 100; Mata relates to loans, 100, 126; Juárez government's desire for, 101, 108, 111–12, 122–23; conservative government inherits that of Comonfort, 111; considered by U.S. cabinet, 116, 123–24; Buchanan seeks highest bidder for, 116–18; factors forcing Buchanan to grant to Juárez government, 117–23; Churchwell to make recommendations on, 118; Twyman's views on, 118–19; Churchwell's recommendations on, 119–20; Churchwell protocol as basis for, 122; Mata advises sacrifices to obtain, 122–23; Buchanan delays, 123–24; McLane's instructions on, 123–24; compromise basis for, 124; of Juárez government, 125; McLane justifies, 125–26; Juárez justifies, 125–26; Miramón government protests, 126; Juárez government's expectations from, 126–27, 129, 135; Juárez government wins contest over, 127; fails to bring sufficient loans, 135; impact on European support of conservative government, 139

Reexport trade (U.S.): impact of Montes-Forsyth Treaties on, 76

Reforma: defined, 1, 5; historical treatment of, 1–2; objectives of, 2, 10; provokes civil war, 10; United States role in, 10; civilian domination of government during, 11; reappearance of liberal pro-protectorate sentiment during, 24; U.S. citizens attracted by, 28; conservatives threaten program of, 57–58

Reform manifesto (7 July 1859), 135–36

Reform program: impact of civil war on, 112; Churchwell reports on, 122

Regeneration: liberal plans for, 13–14

Reibaud, Francisco: proposes steamer service, 74

Religión y fueros: revolts in the name of, 68

Religious freedom: considered by constitutional congress, 60; in McLane-Ocampo Treaties, 143

Republican party (U.S.): impact of sectionalism on, 148

Republicans: role in rejection of McLane-Ocampo Treaties, 146–47

Restored republic (1867–76): emphasis on railroads during, 21

Richthofen, Baron von: Prussian minister, 37–38

Rio Grande: railroad concessions involving, 19;

91; running boundary from, 39; entry ports opened along, 63; in proposed boundary treaty, 103; in Churchwell protocol, 122

Río Yaqui: in proposed boundary treaty, 103

Robles Pezuela, Manuel: New York agent for Ayutla rebels, 50–51; role in bringing protectorate treaties to Mexico, 50–51, 117; political opportunism of, 51, 100, 117; requests Gadsden's recall, 53; on Forsyth's appointment, 65; instructions on Montes-Forsyth Treaties, 78; frightened by Buchanan's election, 78; on Forsyth's retention, 79; supports Zuloaga government, 100; Buchanan administration maintains relations with, 108; competes with Mata, 116; as agent for Buchanan, 116–17, 123; attempts coup against conservative government, 117; Churchwell on actions of, 120

Romero, Matías: role in Reforma, 5; chides United States, 68, 151–52; dedication to material progress of, 68; replaces Mata as minister, 148; laments U.S. economic failure in Mexico, 151–52

Roosevelt corollary: de Gabriac foresees version of, 52; Buchanan foreshadows, 140–41

Rosa, Luis de la: death of, 55, 74

Rothschild: Hammeken agent for, 63

Russia: Gadsden's sympathy for, 46; possible U.S. alliance with, 46–47

Sacrificios: island off Veracruz, 124

"Sage of Wheatland," Buchanan's epithet, 86

Saligny, Alphonse Dubois de: French minister, 149

Saltillo: transit route involving, 142–43

San Dimas, Durango: anti-Spanish actions at, 59

San Francisco: Comonfort seeks loans in, 33; filibustering activity in, 41, 43–44, 53; freight rates to Arizona from, 133

San Luis Potosí: Vidaurri's defeat at, 139

Santa Anna, administration of: fall of, 5, 19, 30, 47–48; Miguel Lerdo serves in, 15; colonization law of, 18; progress of railroads during, 19; navigation act of, 30; freedom of trade under, 30–31; adverse economic impact of, 30–31; exiles leading liberals, 35–36; pro-European policies of, 36–38; hostility toward United States of, 36–38; appoints Almonte minister to United States, 37; Gadsden's post-treaty relations with, 44–48; French abandon support of, 47; seeks U.S. support, 47; liberals seek to destroy all traces of, 53; Gadsden denounces Zerman expedition to, 53

Santa Anna, Antonio López de: returns from Colombian exile, 5, 14–15; collapse of the government of, 5, 10, 19, 30, 47–48; familial ties
with Miguel Lerdo, 14–15; background of,
14–15; returned to power by conservatives,
14–15; Miguel Lerdo's conditions for serving
under, 14–22; liberals hope to convert, 15;
ignores economic advice of Miguel Lerdo, 30;
anti-U.S. attitude of, 36–38; dismisses army
officers, 37; requests Prussian aid, 37–38;
willing to negotiate boundary change,
41; seeks mercenaries, 42; requests British
aid, 42; reaction to Walker expedition,
42; assessment of Gadsden Treaty, 42; proposes alliance with Spain, 42; precipitates
Ayutla Revolution, 44; seeks to halt debt payments to British, 44; flees into exile, 47–48;
blames United States for downfall, 52; dedi-
cates railroad, 54; Butterfield serves as aide
to, 54; Plumb has as partner the son-in-law of,
67; Forsyth on sale of territory by, 88; policy
of Comonfort contrasted with that of, 90;
Spain rumored aiding, 95–96; rumored return
of, 103
Santa Anna de Tamaulipas. *See* Tampico
Santacilia, Pedro: befriends Juárez, 36
Santa Teresa: paper factory owned by Ajuria, 34
Saratoga, U.S. naval ship, 117, 119
Savannah, U.S. naval ship, 124
Science: liberal attitude toward, 22
Sectionalism (U.S.): southern attitudes on, 27;
reflected in consideration of Gadsden Treaty,
43; Forsyth views on, 66; impact of Montes-
Forsyth Treaties on, 76; role in 1856 election,
85; Forsyth relates protectorate to, 93; Hous-
ton's proposal to counter, 114; impact of
McLane-Ocampo Treaties on, 143; role in rejection of McLane-Ocampo Treaties, 147; impact on 1860 elections, 147–48
Senate (U.S.): debates Gadsden Treaty, 42–43;
failure to submit Montes-Forsyth Treaties to,
79–80; rejects military protectorate proposal,
11, 123; rejects treaty with Nicaragua, 146;
considers McLane-Ocampo Treaties, 146–48
Separation of church and state: reform manifesto
calls for, 136
Sewing machines: leading liberals purchase, 22
Siglo XIX, El (Mexico City): edited by Zarco, 5;
analyzes Mexico's problems, 13; attention to
economic matters, 14; reprints Miguel Lerdo's letter to Santa Anna, 15; defends Miguel
Lerdo's service under Santa Anna, 15; sup-

ports immigration, 17; on transportation de-
velopment, 18–19; on need for subsidies, 22;
warns against foreign models, 23; role in de
Gabriac-Zarco incident, 59
Siliceo, Manuel: opposes peace settlement with
United States, 11–12; switches from *puro* to
moderado position, 12; as *Fomento* minister,
62
Simmons, J. T.: Rhode Island senator, 146–47
Skilled labor: scarcity of, 18
Slavery: impact on U.S. policy, 26, 86; Houston
on, 114; Romero on, 152
Slave states: Houston hopes to see created, 114
Slidell, John: role in election of Buchanan, 86
Sloo, A. G.: acquires Tehuantepec transit grant,
40; included in Louisiana Tehuantepec Company, 87; sends agent to Mexico, 88; Buchanan against interests of, 89
Sloo Grant: complicates U.S. policy, 39–40;
under Gadsden Treaty, 43; influence on Pickett's appointment, 51; sale to Hargous, 87;
annulled, 91–92
Smuggling: during Herrera administration, 12;
related to free trade, 21; Barron case, 58, 60
Sonora: Raousset's expedition to, 39; U.S. desire to purchase, 41, 87, 111–12, 124, 130;
entry ports opened in, 63; in proposed boundary treaty, 103; Forsyth proposes seizing,
104; proposed military protectorate over, 111,
115, 123, 141; Twyman warns against protectorate over, 119; Churchwell reports on,
122; wagon-road concession in, 125; dispute
over public lands in, 125
Soulé, Pierre: as Sloo agent, 90; as loan agent,
135
South America: de Gabriac on, 80
South (U.S.): desires commercial expansion,
27–28
Spain: conservatives seek ties with, 13; Santa
Anna requests aid of, 38, 42; Santa Anna
proposes alliance with, 42; hostility to Reforma, 57; threatens Mexico, 58–59; attacks
on citizens and property of, 58–59, 71; breaks
relations, 59; role in Mexico's foreign debt,
68; possible war with Mexico, 80; plan to
repossess Spanish America, 95–96; Zuloaga
government requests aid of, 117; liberals fear
intervention by, 139; protests U.S. naval action, 147
Spaniards: numbers in Mexico, 93
Spanish heritage: liberal rejection of, 17
Speculators: prey on debt-ridden Reforma governments, 60

Steamer service: supported in U.S. Congress, 28, 113; Veracruz-New Orleans, 46, 72–74, 112–13; Butterfield works to establish, 54–55, 67, 112–13; in 1856 postal treaty, 55; in Montes-Forsyth Treaties, 72–73; press support for, 74; Forsyth proposes, 91; subsidy proposal dies in U.S. Congress, 113

Stewart, William G: builder of telegraph lines, 54, 138

Storms, Jane. *See* Cazneau, Jane M.

Subsidies: for railroads, 20–21, 64; for steamer service, 54–55, 73–74, 112–13. *See also* Laissez-faire

Sugar: potential for in Mexico, 113

Survey team: executive agreement provides for, 133; Johnston appointed to, 135

Tacubaya: tramline to, 19–20, 63–64, 138; *pronunciamiento* at, 96; battle of, 131, 135, 139; "massacre of," 131

Tamaulipas: U.S. desire to purchase, 41; border disorders in, 115

Tampico: railroad concessions involving, 19; U.S. commercial interests at, 46, 117, 138; Migel ordered expelled through, 107; U.S. naval protection requested for, 117, 138

Tariffs (Mexico): liberal views on, 21, 31–32, 52; Ceballos, 30–32; increased by Santa Anna administration, 30–31; Alvarez uses as war measure, 32; under protectorate treaties, 49; de Gabriac sees reductions as detrimental to Eruope, 52; as a factor in British policy, 58; new schedule issued, 63; for material improvements, 64; advisory commission created for, 64; Forsyth instructed to work to lower, 65; under McLane-Ocampo Treaties, 143

Taxes: impact of Ley Lerdo on, 62; Forsyth challenges Zuloaga government on basis of, 105–8; Forsyth protests, 105–6; Cass rules on, 107

Technology: attitude of liberals toward, 22, 135–36, 145; Naphegyi as Fomento agent for, 63; reform manifesto seeks to attract, 135–36; Mata seeks, 145

Tehuantepec Isthmus: transit rights across, 27; entry ports opened in, 63, 142–43; Buchanan requests authority to use force in, 115. *See also,* Tehuantepec transits

Tehuantepec transits: U.S. policy on, 39–40, 65, 87–88, 90–91, 113–14; conflicting grants covering, 39–40; Gadsden's instructions on, 40–41; under Gadsden Treaty, 42–43; Forsyth's instructions on 65, 87–88; Benjamin's

involvement in, 65, 86–88, 91–92; basis for opposition to Montes-Forsyth Treaties, 79; railroad interests in, 86; political importance of, 87–88; Louisiana Tehuantepec Company's interest in, 87–88, 91–92; Forsyth opposes Buchanan's policy on, 89; Forsyth presents draft treaty on, 90–91; Forsyth on speculators in, 92–93; Jane Cazneau on, 101; Forsyth's proposal on, 103–4; Cuevas refuses to negotiate on, 103; Buchanan's desire to control, 113–14, 130; in Churchwell protocol, 122; McLane's instructions on, 124, 127; as factor in recognition, 125; Juárez government's position on, 129–31; negotiations on, 130–31; Mata's position on, 131, 140; alliance proposal originates out of, 132; U.S. protection of, 134, 142; in McLane-Ocampo Treaties, 142–43

Telegraph: Stewart's work on, 54, 138

Temple, John: background of, 33–34; loan contracts with Ayutla rebels, 33–35; loans to liberals, 64–65; leases Mexico City mint, 64–65; Ajuria as mint agent for, 97; impact of civil war on interests of, 138

Tennessee: Churchwell from, 118

Tepic, Jalisco: expulsion of British consul from, 58, 60

Territorial expansion (U.S.): feared by liberals, 6–7; racial opposition to, 7–8, 82; advocated by *DeBow's Commercial Review*, 26; under Gadsden Treaty, 26, 42–43; Pierce endorses, 39; Democratic party interest in, 40; Gadsden's instructions on, 40–41; French fear of, 46–47; British attitude toward, 59; Forsyth opposes Buchanan's policy of, 76, 82, 88–89, 91, 108–9; Robles fears, 78; basis of Buchanan's Mexican policy, 78, 84–87, 110, 113–14, 150–52; as a factor in Buchanan's nomination, 85; Buchanan endorses two methods of, 86, 113–14; linked to claims settlement, 87; Forsyth argues for indirect methods of, 91; Forsyth's recommendations on, 97; role in recognition of Zuloaga government, 98–99; Buchanan's policy endangered by commercial propaganda, 116; McLane's instructions on, 124, 127; McLane opposes Buchanan's policy of, 133–34; Miguel Lerdo's loan mission endangers Buchanan's policy of, 137; basis of U.S. recognition policy, 150–52. *See also,* Territory, sale of

Territorial integrity (Mexican): guaranteed by protectorate treaties, 49; McLane commits United States to respect, 126

Territory, sale of: under Santa Anna, 44, 47, 88; Forsyth believes conservatives will agree to, 85; opposition of Juárez to, 95, 120, 126, 129–31; Forsyth requests increase in price for, 95, 102; Forsyth on methods for, 97; role in recognition of Zuloaga government, 98–99; Jane Cazneau on, 101; Forsyth to force Zuloaga government to agree to, 102–8; Cuevas refuses, 103; attempts to use civil war to force, 110; threat of military protectorate used to press liberal government on, 111–12; Buchanan expects from conservative government, 117; Churchwell reports on prospects for, 120; in Churchwell protocol, 122; McLane's instructions on, 124; Ocampo develops strategy to avoid, 126, 129–32; Miramón government charges U.S. recognition policy based on, 126; McLane presents proposal for, 130; McLane reports prospects for, 130; Miguel Lerdo seeks alternative to, 135–37; separate negotiations for, 137. *See also* Territorial expansion (U.S.)

Texas: liberals impressed by economic growth of, 24; Jane Cazneau's activities in, 40; Buchanan's reference to, 86; support for steamer service in, 113; Houston as gubernatorial candidate in, 114; Churchwell reports on transits rights to, 120; Vidaurri fears filibusterers from, 139

Tobacco: Mexican market for, 54; export potential of, 113

Toombs, Robert: Georgia senator, 28

Trade: prohibitions by Santa Anna, 30–31; disrupted by revolts, 58; reform manifesto seeks to promote, 135

Trait d'Union (Mexico City): reports protectorate treaties, 49

Tramline: to Villa Guadalupe, 19; Hammeken's Tacubaya concession, 63–64, 138

Transits: Buchanan's views on, 93; in Churchwell protocol, 122; Washington agrees to negotiate separately on, 137; Mata on importance of, 140; U.S. power to protect, 143. *See also* Frontier transits; Tehuantepec transits

Transportation (Mexico): at independence, 2; lack of facilities for, 18; liberals' attitude toward, 18–21; foreign visitors on, 18; Zarco on, 18–19; Miguel Lerdo on, 18–21

Transportation (U.S.): model for liberals, 24; role of Tehuantepec Isthmus in, 27, 29

Travel: constitution (1857) guarantees freedom of, 61

Treasury Ministry (Mexico). *See* Hacienda Ministry

Treasury (U.S.): Mata seeks credit from, 137

Treaties: Mata's view on, 140

Treaties, protectorate: rumors of, 49–51

Treaty, commercial (Great Britain-Mexico): cited by Forsyth, 105

Treaty of Amity and Commerce (1831): Gadsden seeks to replace, 54; Mexico agrees to renegotiate, 73; Forsyth cites, 105–6; executive agreement under, 133; amended by McLane-Ocampo Treaties, 143

Treaty of Guadalupe Hidalgo, 39, 99

Trist, Nicholas: peace terms arranged by, 26

Tucson, Arizona: transit route to, 133

Turner, captain of *Saratoga,* 119

Twyman, R. B. J.: U.S. consul, 118–19

United States: liberals desire protection of, 4, 13, 24, 57, 59; as model for liberal reformers, 5–8, 10, 14, 23–24, 60–61; fears European intervention in Mexico, 7; role in world capital market, 8; role in Ayutla Revolution and Reforma, 10; war with Mexico, 11–13; *puros* oppose peace settlement with, 11–12; refuses military aid to Herrera administration, 12–13; occupation of Mexico City, 13; Mexico seeks closer economic ties with, 24, 72; liberals seek protectorate by, 24, 150–52; lack of interest in and knowledge of Mexico, 25, 60; liberals' attitude toward, 25–28, 150–52; as source of aid to Ayutla rebels, 32–35, 48, 52; Santa Anna requests French aid against, 37–38; Spain fears threat to Cuba by, 38; importance to France of trade with, 38; France wishes to use Mexico against, 39; compared to Russia, 47; possible official involvement in 1855 protectorate proposal, 51; as ''model republic'' in constitutional congress, 60–61; Forsyth proposes alliance with Mexico, 68–69; de Gabriac's views of, 80–81, 149; breaks relations with conservative government, 85; importance to Juárez of recognition by, 98–99; liberals feel their ''natural ally'' is, 100; Butterfield argues for domination over Mexican economy, 113; Zuloaga government seeks understanding with, 117–18; Britain refuses to protect interests of, 138; Mata desires to grant unilateral right of intervention to, 139–40; military rights under McLane-Ocampo Treaties, 143; impact of Mexican civil war on Mexican policy of, 150–51; Romero on Mexican policy of, 150–52

United States citizens: Forsyth uses against Zuloaga government, 105–8

Upper class: Miguel Lerdo's view of, 16; acquire property under Ley Lerdo, 62; support conservatives, 111

Vacant lands: Mexico needs to fill up, 17
Valadés, José M.: cited on McLane-Ocampo Treaties, 146
Van Buren, Martin: the elder Forsyth as secretary of state under, 65
Vanilla: export potential of, 113
Veracruz, 5, 46; railroad concessions involving, 19, 64; U.S. consul at, 45, 63, 81–82, 118–19; steamer service to New Orleans from, 46, 72–74, 112–13; Butterfield as *alcalde* of, 54; gas lighting project for, 63; British fleet visit to, 71, 123; Comonfort departs into exile from, 97; Juárez government finds refuge in, 102, 111–12; U.S. merchants petition for naval presence at, 117, 138; Churchwell visits, 118–22; Miramón's attacks on, 120, 123–24, 147; Mata returns for consultation to, 123; joint British and French fleet demonstration off, 123; McLane and Miguel Lerdo return to, 141–42; loans available in, 148; Juárez government leaves, 149
Vermont: senator favors steamer service, 113
Vidaurri, Santiago, 84, 139
Villa Guadalupe: railroad concession involving, 19

Wagon roads: Zarco calls for, 18–19; William Cazneau's concession for, 125, 138
Walker, William: filibustering expeditions of, 38–39, 41, 86, 114; Mexican reaction to expeditions of, 41–42; Gadsden's reaction to expedition of, 41–42, 46; Buchanan condemns Nicaraguan expedition of, 86, 114
War, Austro-French, 135
War: Buchanan on conditions justifying with Mexico, 140–41
War: de Gabriac believes United States wishes to provoke between Mexico and European powers, 80
War, Mexico-United States: 1, 3, 25, 27; impact on Mexican liberals, 10–13; Santa Anna dismisses all officers who surrendered during, 37; impact on Buchanan's expansionist views, 85
Ward, Christopher L.: diplomatic courier, 41
West Indies: Gadsden wishes to force British out of, 27–28
Wheat: French concern for control of areas producing, 47
Whig party (U.S.): impact of sectionalism on, 148

Whigs: support Buchanan's election, 86
Wilson, Henry: senator supporting steamer service, 28
Working class: Miguel Lerdo on, 16; Ley Lerdo's impact on, 62; support conservatives, 111
World capital market, 8, 137

Yorkino masonic lodges, 11
"Young America" sentiment, 25
Yucatán: caste war in, 3, 12; Gadsden desires acquisition of, 27–28; land grants made in, 101

Zarco, Francisco: role in Reforma, 5, 11; role in Ayutla Revolution, 11; defines regeneration task, 13; supports transportation development, 18–19; on free trade, 21; on laissez-faire, 22; cites United States as transportation model, 24; warns against overemphasis on economic development, 24–25; involved in incident with French minister, de Gabriac, 59
Zavala, Lorenzo de: as liberal leader, 3, 17
Zenteno, Estevan: railroad concession of, 64
Zerman, Jean Napoleon: filibustering expedition of, 53; seeks protection as U.S. citizen, 70; aids Comonfort, 97; as loan agent for Juárez government, 109, 112; as propaganda agent for Juárez government, 112
Zerman expedition: to Baja California, 53; prisoners used in protectorate consideration, 70–72; Forsyth demands better treatment for prisoners of, 70; charges dropped against prisoners of, 97
Zocalo: tramline connection with Tacubaya, 19–20, 63–64
Zuloaga, Félix: revolts in favor of Comonfort dictatorship, 96; signals Forsyth to present boundary proposal, 103; Forsyth characterizes, 104: indicates willingness to sell territory, 106–7: requests French mercenaries, 117; Churchwell on, 118–19
Zuloaga government: created, 97; liberals warn U.S. against recognizing, 98–99; Forsyth recognizes, 98–99; Forsyth analyzes fiscal plight of, 102; Forsyth attempts to force to sell territory, 102–8; Forsyth describes members of, 104; Forsyth encourages revolts against, 104–5; Forsyth challenges tax decree of, 105–8; requests recall of Forsyth, 107; Forsyth breaks relations with, 108; requests aid of European powers, 117; seeks understanding with United States, 117–18; impact on Temple's mint operation, 138